MW01032147

Monthly Payment Amortization Tables for Small Loans

JULIAN MERITZ

FIRST EDITION

Copyright

Terms of Use and Disclaimer

Contact Info

Web   MeritzPress.com
Facebook MeritzPress
Twitter   @MeritzPress

How To Get Your Bonus Gift

Thank you for buying our book! We worked hard to create it, and we hope you'll find it a valuable tool that will serve you well.

This small book was created to be a practical tool for anyone who needs to deal with loan payments, and prefers to do it the old fashioned way. It's inexpensive, it doesn't need batteries, cannot be hacked, and there's no screen to break. It will last a lifetime or more - you won't need to replace it every year.

Please **submit a positive honest review to book's Amazon page**. More positive reviews mean more eyes on the book's Amazon page and hopefully more readers. Which in turn keeps us in business and preserves book's low price.

After your review to Amazon is submitted, jump to our web site at MeritzPress.com to **request your bonus gift***. Click the contact form, and tell us that you wrote a nice review, and we will reply with a pdf bonus content* that didn't make it to this book.

If you are on Facebook, Twitter, Instagram, or any other social media, and like our book, please tell your friends too. Especially if you think they may find it useful. And follow us to stay in touch.

Finally, if the book didn't work for you, please tell us what we should change or improve. Your feedback makes the next edition and other books better and more useful.

* Standard disclaimer applies - offer is valid for limited time only, and quantities are limited.

Register for Updates and Corrections

Please make a quick trip to MeritzPress.com and register your book. Why? We're not perfect, and we make mistakes. When we do, we admit it, and do our best to correct them. If you are registered, you'll be the first to know. If an updated edition is out, you'll be first to know too.

If you find an error, please report it at the same place. Thank you!

Bulk Orders

If you'd like to order 5 or more copies of this book, we would like to offer you a discount. Please contact us at MeritzPress.com

More from MERITZ PRESS

Look for other books and publications by Meritz Press at MeritzPress.com

About MERITZ PRESS

We are a fresh ultra-efficient operation looking to publish books that are unique in one or more ways. We create and build on the back of our parent company's 25 years of experience in publishing, advertising, and design world, as well as in web and software development area. Taking advantage of that expertise mixture allows for faster production of better and less expensive publications.

Sponsor or Advertise in This Book

This type of reference book is relatively expensive to produce and offers only a very small profit potential in return ... when everything works out. But it can also be an excellent vehicle for a company or business, who would like promote their name or product. Sponsorship bylines and display ads are just two of many options.

If you think your company or product is a good match with what this book offers, please contact us at MeritzPress.com and let's talk.

Customized Books for Your Business

We can produce and deliver a customized version of this book exactly to your specifications. **Car, motorcycle, boat, RV dealerships, credit unions, small banks, financial advisors, schools and universities, attorneys, insurance** ... the list goes on. It's a unique promotional item to give out to your customers, who will actually use it! The books stay with their owners for a very long time, and your business promotional benefits are obvious.

The front and back cover can be replaced with your artwork, and the intro pages updated with your language. The content pages typically remain as they are now, but some flexibility is there too.

Very low minimum quantities, quick delivery times, and prices that make it worthwhile for business of any size. Contact us at MeritzPress.com, and let's talk.

How To Use This Book?

Monthly Payment Amortization Tables for Small Loans! Sounds like a title for the bestseller list, doesn't it? Well, maybe not quite, but the book does exactly what it spells out to do. Combined with very low cost, the fact it IS a book and not a computer or phone application without need for power and battery and updates and charging and security and skills and ... we think it is simply a good old fashioned value, a tool anyone needs and can use.

It does one thing and it does it exactly as you might expect. You need to know your monthly loan payment? Look up the page that has your **loan amount (1)** at the top, or an amount closest to it, find your **interest rate (2)** row and column with **number of years (3)** the loan is going to last for, and your **monthly payment (4)** is where the row and column intersect. If your loan amount, interest rate, or term is not exact, the monthly payment will be off, but usually close enough to give you an idea. No clicking, no typing, no turning on and off, it's printed right in front of you.

Look at the numbers next to your payment and start contemplating what would the loan look like with a few less years. Or better interest rate. Flip a page and see what the payment could look like if you borrow more. Or less! It's simple, and intuitive. It lets you focus on your deal without distractions.

The book is a small 5 x 8 paperback format, it fits to any briefcase, purse, and even some pockets. Take it to the car, motorcycle, RV, or boat dealer with you, to your bank or credit union, and use it to quickly find the right numbers, remove confusion and complexity in negotitations. If you work at a dealership or financial institution, if you are an insurance or legal professional, you will often find it helpful. It will save your and your clients' time, add transparency to the deal and trust to your reputation.

It is just a tool to help you along the way, you yourself are responsible for the decisions you make. But you already knew that!

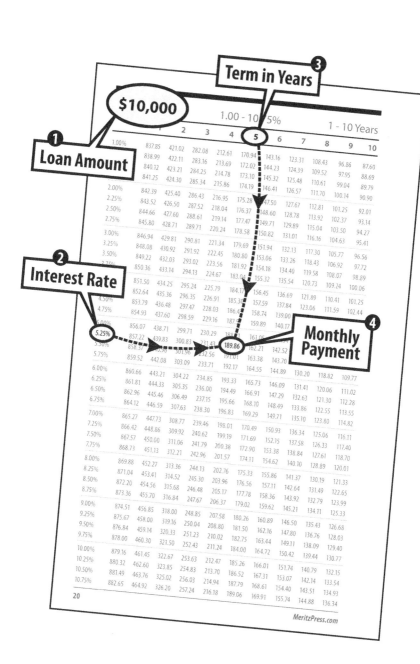

Term in Years

$10,000   1.00 – 10.75%   1 – 10 Years

Loan Amount **Interest Rate** **Monthly Payment**

	1	2	3	4	5	6	7	8	9	10
1.00%	837.85	421.02	282.08	212.61	170.94	143.16	123.31	108.43	96.86	87.60
	838.99	422.11	283.16	213.69	172.02	144.23	124.39	109.52	97.95	88.69
	840.12	423.21	284.25	214.78	173.10	145.32	125.48	110.61	99.04	89.79
	841.25	424.30	285.34	215.86	174.19	146.41	126.57	111.70	100.14	90.90
2.00%	842.39	425.40	286.43	216.95	175.28	147.50	127.67	112.81	101.25	92.01
2.25%	843.52	426.50	287.52	218.04	176.37	148.60	128.78	113.92	102.37	93.14
2.50%	844.66	427.60	288.61	219.14	177.47	149.71	129.89	115.04	103.50	94.27
2.75%	845.80	428.71	289.71	220.24	178.58	150.82	131.01	116.16	104.63	95.41
3.00%	846.94	429.81	290.81	221.34	179.69	151.94	132.13	117.30	105.77	96.56
3.25%	848.08	430.92	291.92	222.45	180.80	153.06	133.26	118.43	106.92	97.72
3.50%	849.22	432.03	293.02	223.56	181.92	154.18	134.40	119.58	108.07	98.89
3.75%	850.36	433.14	294.13	224.67	183.04	155.32	135.54	120.73	109.24	100.06
4.00%	851.50	434.25	295.24	225.79	184.17	156.45	136.69	121.89	110.41	101.25
4.25%	852.64	435.36	296.35	226.91	185.30	157.59	137.84	123.06	111.59	102.44
4.50%	853.79	436.48	297.47	228.03	186.45	158.74	139.00			
4.75%	854.93	437.60	298.59	229.16	187.60	159.89	140.17			
5.00%	856.07	438.71	299.71	230.29	188.73	161.06				
5.25%	857.22	439.83	300.83	231.43	189.86	162.21	142.52			
5.50%	858.37		301.96	232.56	191.01	163.38	143.70			
5.75%	859.52	442.08	303.09	233.71	192.17	164.55	144.89	130.20	118.82	109.77
6.00%	860.66	443.21	304.22	234.85	193.33	165.73	146.09	131.41	120.06	111.02
6.25%	861.81	444.33	305.35	236.00	194.49	166.91	147.29	132.63	121.30	112.28
6.50%	862.96	445.46	306.49	237.15	195.66	168.10	148.49	133.86	122.55	113.55
6.75%	864.12	446.59	307.63	238.30	196.83	169.29	149.71	135.10	123.80	114.82
7.00%	865.27	447.73	308.77	239.46	198.01	170.49	150.93	136.34	125.06	116.11
7.25%	866.42	448.86	309.92	240.62	199.19	171.69	152.15	137.58	126.33	117.40
7.50%	867.57	450.00	311.06	241.79	200.38	172.90	153.38	138.84	127.61	118.70
7.75%	868.73	451.13	312.21	242.96	201.57	174.11	154.62	140.10	128.89	120.01
8.00%	869.88	452.27	313.36	244.13	202.76	175.33	155.86	141.37	130.19	121.33
8.25%	871.04	453.41	314.52	245.30	203.96	176.56	157.11	142.64	131.49	122.65
8.50%	872.20	454.56	315.68	246.48	205.17	177.78	158.36	143.92	132.79	123.99
8.75%	873.36	455.70	316.84	247.67	206.37	179.02	159.62	145.21	134.11	125.33
9.00%	874.51	456.85	318.00	248.85	207.58	180.26	160.89	146.50	135.43	126.68
9.25%	875.67	458.00	319.16	250.04	208.80	181.50	162.16	147.80	136.76	128.03
9.50%	876.84	459.14	320.33	251.23	210.02	182.75	163.44	149.11	138.09	129.40
9.75%	878.00	460.30	321.50	252.43	211.24	184.00	164.72	150.42	139.44	130.77
10.00%	879.16	461.45	322.67	253.63	212.47	185.26	166.01	151.74	140.79	132.15
10.25%	880.32	462.60	323.85	254.83	213.70	186.52	167.31	153.07	142.14	133.54
10.50%	881.49	463.76	325.02	256.03	214.94	187.79	168.61	154.40	143.51	134.93
10.75%	882.65	464.92	326.20	257.24	216.18	189.06	169.91	155.74	144.88	136.34

$1,000 1.00 - 10.75% 1 - 10 Years

	1	2	3	4	5	6	7	8	9	10
1.00%	83.79	42.10	28.21	21.26	17.09	14.32	12.33	10.84	9.69	8.76
1.25%	83.90	42.21	28.32	21.37	17.20	14.42	12.44	10.95	9.79	8.87
1.50%	84.01	42.32	28.42	21.48	17.31	14.53	12.55	11.06	9.90	8.98
1.75%	84.13	42.43	28.53	21.59	17.42	14.64	12.66	11.17	10.01	9.09
2.00%	84.24	42.54	28.64	21.70	17.53	14.75	12.77	11.28	10.13	9.20
2.25%	84.35	42.65	28.75	21.80	17.64	14.86	12.88	11.39	10.24	9.31
2.50%	84.47	42.76	28.86	21.91	17.75	14.97	12.99	11.50	10.35	9.43
2.75%	84.58	42.87	28.97	22.02	17.86	15.08	13.10	11.62	10.46	9.54
3.00%	84.69	42.98	29.08	22.13	17.97	15.19	13.21	11.73	10.58	9.66
3.25%	84.81	43.09	29.19	22.24	18.08	15.31	13.33	11.84	10.69	9.77
3.50%	84.92	43.20	29.30	22.36	18.19	15.42	13.44	11.96	10.81	9.89
3.75%	85.04	43.31	29.41	22.47	18.30	15.53	13.55	12.07	10.92	10.01
4.00%	85.15	43.42	29.52	22.58	18.42	15.65	13.67	12.19	11.04	10.12
4.25%	85.26	43.54	29.64	22.69	18.53	15.76	13.78	12.31	11.16	10.24
4.50%	85.38	43.65	29.75	22.80	18.64	15.87	13.90	12.42	11.28	10.36
4.75%	85.49	43.76	29.86	22.92	18.76	15.99	14.02	12.54	11.40	10.48
5.00%	85.61	43.87	29.97	23.03	18.87	16.10	14.13	12.66	11.52	10.61
5.25%	85.72	43.98	30.08	23.14	18.99	16.22	14.25	12.78	11.64	10.73
5.50%	85.84	44.10	30.20	23.26	19.10	16.34	14.37	12.90	11.76	10.85
5.75%	85.95	44.21	30.31	23.37	19.22	16.46	14.49	13.02	11.88	10.98
6.00%	86.07	44.32	30.42	23.49	19.33	16.57	14.61	13.14	12.01	11.10
6.25%	86.18	44.43	30.54	23.60	19.45	16.69	14.73	13.26	12.13	11.23
6.50%	86.30	44.55	30.65	23.71	19.57	16.81	14.85	13.39	12.25	11.35
6.75%	86.41	44.66	30.76	23.83	19.68	16.93	14.97	13.51	12.38	11.48
7.00%	86.53	44.77	30.88	23.95	19.80	17.05	15.09	13.63	12.51	11.61
7.25%	86.64	44.89	30.99	24.06	19.92	17.17	15.22	13.76	12.63	11.74
7.50%	86.76	45.00	31.11	24.18	20.04	17.29	15.34	13.88	12.76	11.87
7.75%	86.87	45.11	31.22	24.30	20.16	17.41	15.46	14.01	12.89	12.00
8.00%	86.99	45.23	31.34	24.41	20.28	17.53	15.59	14.14	13.02	12.13
8.25%	87.10	45.34	31.45	24.53	20.40	17.66	15.71	14.26	13.15	12.27
8.50%	87.22	45.46	31.57	24.65	20.52	17.78	15.84	14.39	13.28	12.40
8.75%	87.34	45.57	31.68	24.77	20.64	17.90	15.96	14.52	13.41	12.53
9.00%	87.45	45.68	31.80	24.89	20.76	18.03	16.09	14.65	13.54	12.67
9.25%	87.57	45.80	31.92	25.00	20.88	18.15	16.22	14.78	13.68	12.80
9.50%	87.68	45.91	32.03	25.12	21.00	18.27	16.34	14.91	13.81	12.94
9.75%	87.80	46.03	32.15	25.24	21.12	18.40	16.47	15.04	13.94	13.08
10.00%	87.92	46.14	32.27	25.36	21.25	18.53	16.60	15.17	14.08	13.22
10.25%	88.03	46.26	32.38	25.48	21.37	18.65	16.73	15.31	14.21	13.35
10.50%	88.15	46.38	32.50	25.60	21.49	18.78	16.86	15.44	14.35	13.49
10.75%	88.27	46.49	32.62	25.72	21.62	18.91	16.99	15.57	14.49	13.63

	1	2	3	4	5	6	7	8	9	10
11.00%	88.38	46.61	32.74	25.85	21.74	19.03	17.12	15.71	14.63	13.78
11.25%	88.50	46.72	32.86	25.97	21.87	19.16	17.25	15.84	14.76	13.92
11.50%	88.62	46.84	32.98	26.09	21.99	19.29	17.39	15.98	14.90	14.06
11.75%	88.73	46.96	33.10	26.21	22.12	19.42	17.52	16.12	15.04	14.20
12.00%	88.85	47.07	33.21	26.33	22.24	19.55	17.65	16.25	15.18	14.35
12.25%	88.97	47.19	33.33	26.46	22.37	19.68	17.79	16.39	15.33	14.49
12.50%	89.08	47.31	33.45	26.58	22.50	19.81	17.92	16.53	15.47	14.64
12.75%	89.20	47.42	33.57	26.70	22.63	19.94	18.06	16.67	15.61	14.78
13.00%	89.32	47.54	33.69	26.83	22.75	20.07	18.19	16.81	15.75	14.93
13.25%	89.43	47.66	33.81	26.95	22.88	20.21	18.33	16.95	15.90	15.08
13.50%	89.55	47.78	33.94	27.08	23.01	20.34	18.46	17.09	16.04	15.23
13.75%	89.67	47.89	34.06	27.20	23.14	20.47	18.60	17.23	16.19	15.38
14.00%	89.79	48.01	34.18	27.33	23.27	20.61	18.74	17.37	16.33	15.53
14.25%	89.90	48.13	34.30	27.45	23.40	20.74	18.88	17.51	16.48	15.68
14.50%	90.02	48.25	34.42	27.58	23.53	20.87	19.02	17.66	16.63	15.83
14.75%	90.14	48.37	34.54	27.70	23.66	21.01	19.16	17.80	16.78	15.98
15.00%	90.26	48.49	34.67	27.83	23.79	21.15	19.30	17.95	16.92	16.13
15.25%	90.38	48.61	34.79	27.96	23.92	21.28	19.44	18.09	17.07	16.29
15.50%	90.49	48.72	34.91	28.08	24.05	21.42	19.58	18.24	17.22	16.44
15.75%	90.61	48.84	35.03	28.21	24.19	21.55	19.72	18.38	17.37	16.60
16.00%	90.73	48.96	35.16	28.34	24.32	21.69	19.86	18.53	17.53	16.75
16.25%	90.85	49.08	35.28	28.47	24.45	21.83	20.00	18.68	17.68	16.91
16.50%	90.97	49.20	35.40	28.60	24.58	21.97	20.15	18.82	17.83	17.06
16.75%	91.09	49.32	35.53	28.73	24.72	22.11	20.29	18.97	17.98	17.22
17.00%	91.20	49.44	35.65	28.86	24.85	22.25	20.44	19.12	18.14	17.38
17.25%	91.32	49.56	35.78	28.98	24.99	22.39	20.58	19.27	18.29	17.54
17.50%	91.44	49.68	35.90	29.11	25.12	22.53	20.73	19.42	18.45	17.70
17.75%	91.56	49.80	36.03	29.24	25.26	22.67	20.87	19.57	18.60	17.86
18.00%	91.68	49.92	36.15	29.37	25.39	22.81	21.02	19.72	18.76	18.02
18.25%	91.80	50.04	36.28	29.51	25.53	22.95	21.16	19.88	18.91	18.18
18.50%	91.92	50.17	36.40	29.64	25.67	23.09	21.31	20.03	19.07	18.34
18.75%	92.04	50.29	36.53	29.77	25.80	23.23	21.46	20.18	19.23	18.50
19.00%	92.16	50.41	36.66	29.90	25.94	23.38	21.61	20.33	19.39	18.67
19.25%	92.28	50.53	36.78	30.03	26.08	23.52	21.76	20.49	19.55	18.83
19.50%	92.40	50.65	36.91	30.16	26.22	23.66	21.91	20.64	19.71	19.00
19.75%	92.51	50.77	37.04	30.30	26.35	23.81	22.06	20.80	19.87	19.16
20.00%	92.63	50.90	37.16	30.43	26.49	23.95	22.21	20.95	20.03	19.33
20.25%	92.75	51.02	37.29	30.56	26.63	24.10	22.36	21.11	20.19	19.49
20.50%	92.87	51.14	37.42	30.70	26.77	24.24	22.51	21.27	20.35	19.66
20.75%	92.99	51.26	37.55	30.83	26.91	24.39	22.66	21.42	20.51	19.83

	1	2	3	4	5	6	7	8	9	10
1.00%	167.57	84.20	56.42	42.52	34.19	28.63	24.66	21.69	19.37	17.52
1.25%	167.80	84.42	56.63	42.74	34.40	28.85	24.88	21.90	19.59	17.74
1.50%	168.02	84.64	56.85	42.96	34.62	29.06	25.10	22.12	19.81	17.96
1.75%	168.25	84.86	57.07	43.17	34.84	29.28	25.31	22.34	20.03	18.18
2.00%	168.48	85.08	57.29	43.39	35.06	29.50	25.53	22.56	20.25	18.40
2.25%	168.70	85.30	57.50	43.61	35.27	29.72	25.76	22.78	20.47	18.63
2.50%	168.93	85.52	57.72	43.83	35.49	29.94	25.98	23.01	20.70	18.85
2.75%	169.16	85.74	57.94	44.05	35.72	30.16	26.20	23.23	20.93	19.08
3.00%	169.39	85.96	58.16	44.27	35.94	30.39	26.43	23.46	21.15	19.31
3.25%	169.62	86.18	58.38	44.49	36.16	30.61	26.65	23.69	21.38	19.54
3.50%	169.84	86.41	58.60	44.71	36.38	30.84	26.88	23.92	21.61	19.78
3.75%	170.07	86.63	58.83	44.93	36.61	31.06	27.11	24.15	21.85	20.01
4.00%	170.30	86.85	59.05	45.16	36.83	31.29	27.34	24.38	22.08	20.25
4.25%	170.53	87.07	59.27	45.38	37.06	31.52	27.57	24.61	22.32	20.49
4.50%	170.76	87.30	59.49	45.61	37.29	31.75	27.80	24.85	22.56	20.73
4.75%	170.99	87.52	59.72	45.83	37.51	31.98	28.03	25.08	22.79	20.97
5.00%	171.21	87.74	59.94	46.06	37.74	32.21	28.27	25.32	23.03	21.21
5.25%	171.44	87.97	60.17	46.29	37.97	32.44	28.50	25.56	23.28	21.46
5.50%	171.67	88.19	60.39	46.51	38.20	32.68	28.74	25.80	23.52	21.71
5.75%	171.90	88.42	60.62	46.74	38.43	32.91	28.98	26.04	23.76	21.95
6.00%	172.13	88.64	60.84	46.97	38.67	33.15	29.22	26.28	24.01	22.20
6.25%	172.36	88.87	61.07	47.20	38.90	33.38	29.46	26.53	24.26	22.46
6.50%	172.59	89.09	61.30	47.43	39.13	33.62	29.70	26.77	24.51	22.71
6.75%	172.82	89.32	61.53	47.66	39.37	33.86	29.94	27.02	24.76	22.96
7.00%	173.05	89.55	61.75	47.89	39.60	34.10	30.19	27.27	25.01	23.22
7.25%	173.28	89.77	61.98	48.12	39.84	34.34	30.43	27.52	25.27	23.48
7.50%	173.51	90.00	62.21	48.36	40.08	34.58	30.68	27.77	25.52	23.74
7.75%	173.75	90.23	62.44	48.59	40.31	34.82	30.92	28.02	25.78	24.00
8.00%	173.98	90.45	62.67	48.83	40.55	35.07	31.17	28.27	26.04	24.27
8.25%	174.21	90.68	62.90	49.06	40.79	35.31	31.42	28.53	26.30	24.53
8.50%	174.44	90.91	63.14	49.30	41.03	35.56	31.67	28.78	26.56	24.80
8.75%	174.67	91.14	63.37	49.53	41.27	35.80	31.92	29.04	26.82	25.07
9.00%	174.90	91.37	63.60	49.77	41.52	36.05	32.18	29.30	27.09	25.34
9.25%	175.13	91.60	63.83	50.01	41.76	36.30	32.43	29.56	27.35	25.61
9.50%	175.37	91.83	64.07	50.25	42.00	36.55	32.69	29.82	27.62	25.88
9.75%	175.60	92.06	64.30	50.49	42.25	36.80	32.94	30.08	27.89	26.15
10.00%	175.83	92.29	64.53	50.73	42.49	37.05	33.20	30.35	28.16	26.43
10.25%	176.06	92.52	64.77	50.97	42.74	37.30	33.46	30.61	28.43	26.71
10.50%	176.30	92.75	65.00	51.21	42.99	37.56	33.72	30.88	28.70	26.99
10.75%	176.53	92.98	65.24	51.45	43.24	37.81	33.98	31.15	28.98	27.27

	1	2	3	4	5	6	7	8	9	10
11.00%	176.76	93.22	65.48	51.69	43.48	38.07	34.24	31.42	29.25	27.55
11.25%	177.00	93.45	65.71	51.93	43.73	38.32	34.51	31.69	29.53	27.83
11.50%	177.23	93.68	65.95	52.18	43.99	38.58	34.77	31.96	29.81	28.12
11.75%	177.46	93.91	66.19	52.42	44.24	38.84	35.04	32.23	30.09	28.41
12.00%	177.70	94.15	66.43	52.67	44.49	39.10	35.31	32.51	30.37	28.69
12.25%	177.93	94.38	66.67	52.91	44.74	39.36	35.57	32.78	30.65	28.98
12.50%	178.17	94.61	66.91	53.16	45.00	39.62	35.84	33.06	30.94	29.28
12.75%	178.40	94.85	67.15	53.41	45.25	39.88	36.11	33.34	31.22	29.57
13.00%	178.63	95.08	67.39	53.65	45.51	40.15	36.38	33.61	31.51	29.86
13.25%	178.87	95.32	67.63	53.90	45.76	40.41	36.66	33.89	31.80	30.16
13.50%	179.10	95.55	67.87	54.15	46.02	40.68	36.93	34.18	32.08	30.45
13.75%	179.34	95.79	68.11	54.40	46.28	40.94	37.20	34.46	32.38	30.75
14.00%	179.57	96.03	68.36	54.65	46.54	41.21	37.48	34.74	32.67	31.05
14.25%	179.81	96.26	68.60	54.90	46.80	41.48	37.76	35.03	32.96	31.35
14.50%	180.05	96.50	68.84	55.16	47.06	41.75	38.03	35.31	33.26	31.66
14.75%	180.28	96.74	69.09	55.41	47.32	42.02	38.31	35.60	33.55	31.96
15.00%	180.52	96.97	69.33	55.66	47.58	42.29	38.59	35.89	33.85	32.27
15.25%	180.75	97.21	69.58	55.92	47.84	42.56	38.87	36.18	34.15	32.57
15.50%	180.99	97.45	69.82	56.17	48.11	42.83	39.16	36.47	34.45	32.88
15.75%	181.23	97.69	70.07	56.42	48.37	43.11	39.44	36.76	34.75	33.19
16.00%	181.46	97.93	70.31	56.68	48.64	43.38	39.72	37.06	35.05	33.50
16.25%	181.70	98.17	70.56	56.94	48.90	43.66	40.01	37.35	35.35	33.81
16.50%	181.94	98.40	70.81	57.19	49.17	43.94	40.30	37.65	35.66	34.13
16.75%	182.17	98.64	71.06	57.45	49.44	44.21	40.58	37.94	35.97	34.44
17.00%	182.41	98.88	71.31	57.71	49.71	44.49	40.87	38.24	36.27	34.76
17.25%	182.65	99.12	71.55	57.97	49.97	44.77	41.16	38.54	36.58	35.08
17.50%	182.88	99.37	71.80	58.23	50.24	45.05	41.45	38.84	36.89	35.40
17.75%	183.12	99.61	72.05	58.49	50.52	45.33	41.74	39.14	37.20	35.72
18.00%	183.36	99.85	72.30	58.75	50.79	45.62	42.04	39.45	37.51	36.04
18.25%	183.60	100.09	72.56	59.01	51.06	45.90	42.33	39.75	37.83	36.36
18.50%	183.84	100.33	72.81	59.27	51.33	46.18	42.62	40.05	38.14	36.68
18.75%	184.07	100.57	73.06	59.54	51.61	46.47	42.92	40.36	38.46	37.01
19.00%	184.31	100.82	73.31	59.80	51.88	46.75	43.22	40.67	38.77	37.33
19.25%	184.55	101.06	73.57	60.06	52.16	47.04	43.51	40.98	39.09	37.66
19.50%	184.79	101.30	73.82	60.33	52.43	47.33	43.81	41.28	39.41	37.99
19.75%	185.03	101.55	74.07	60.59	52.71	47.62	44.11	41.60	39.73	38.32
20.00%	185.27	101.79	74.33	60.86	52.99	47.91	44.41	41.91	40.05	38.65
20.25%	185.51	102.04	74.58	61.13	53.27	48.20	44.71	42.22	40.38	38.98
20.50%	185.75	102.28	74.84	61.39	53.55	48.49	45.02	42.53	40.70	39.32
20.75%	185.99	102.53	75.09	61.66	53.83	48.78	45.32	42.85	41.02	39.65

$3,000   1.00 - 10.75%   1 - 10 Years

	1	2	3	4	5	6	7	8	9	10
1.00%	251.36	126.31	84.62	63.78	51.28	42.95	36.99	32.53	29.06	26.28
1.25%	251.70	126.63	84.95	64.11	51.60	43.27	37.32	32.85	29.38	26.61
1.50%	252.04	126.96	85.27	64.43	51.93	43.60	37.64	33.18	29.71	26.94
1.75%	252.38	127.29	85.60	64.76	52.26	43.92	37.97	33.51	30.04	27.27
2.00%	252.72	127.62	85.93	65.09	52.58	44.25	38.30	33.84	30.38	27.60
2.25%	253.06	127.95	86.26	65.41	52.91	44.58	38.63	34.18	30.71	27.94
2.50%	253.40	128.28	86.58	65.74	53.24	44.91	38.97	34.51	31.05	28.28
2.75%	253.74	128.61	86.91	66.07	53.57	45.25	39.30	34.85	31.39	28.62
3.00%	254.08	128.94	87.24	66.40	53.91	45.58	39.64	35.19	31.73	28.97
3.25%	254.42	129.28	87.57	66.73	54.24	45.92	39.98	35.53	32.08	29.32
3.50%	254.76	129.61	87.91	67.07	54.58	46.26	40.32	35.87	32.42	29.67
3.75%	255.11	129.94	88.24	67.40	54.91	46.59	40.66	36.22	32.77	30.02
4.00%	255.45	130.27	88.57	67.74	55.25	46.94	41.01	36.57	33.12	30.37
4.25%	255.79	130.61	88.91	68.07	55.59	47.28	41.35	36.92	33.48	30.73
4.50%	256.14	130.94	89.24	68.41	55.93	47.62	41.70	37.27	33.83	31.09
4.75%	256.48	131.28	89.58	68.75	56.27	47.97	42.05	37.62	34.19	31.45
5.00%	256.82	131.61	89.91	69.09	56.61	48.31	42.40	37.98	34.55	31.82
5.25%	257.17	131.95	90.25	69.43	56.96	48.66	42.76	38.34	34.91	32.19
5.50%	257.51	132.29	90.59	69.77	57.30	49.01	43.11	38.70	35.28	32.56
5.75%	257.85	132.62	90.93	70.11	57.65	49.37	43.47	39.06	35.65	32.93
6.00%	258.20	132.96	91.27	70.46	58.00	49.72	43.83	39.42	36.02	33.31
6.25%	258.54	133.30	91.61	70.80	58.35	50.07	44.19	39.79	36.39	33.68
6.50%	258.89	133.64	91.95	71.14	58.70	50.43	44.55	40.16	36.76	34.06
6.75%	259.23	133.98	92.29	71.49	59.05	50.79	44.91	40.53	37.14	34.45
7.00%	259.58	134.32	92.63	71.84	59.40	51.15	45.28	40.90	37.52	34.83
7.25%	259.93	134.66	92.97	72.19	59.76	51.51	45.65	41.28	37.90	35.22
7.50%	260.27	135.00	93.32	72.54	60.11	51.87	46.01	41.65	38.28	35.61
7.75%	260.62	135.34	93.66	72.89	60.47	52.23	46.39	42.03	38.67	36.00
8.00%	260.97	135.68	94.01	73.24	60.83	52.60	46.76	42.41	39.06	36.40
8.25%	261.31	136.02	94.36	73.59	61.19	52.97	47.13	42.79	39.45	36.80
8.50%	261.66	136.37	94.70	73.94	61.55	53.34	47.51	43.18	39.84	37.20
8.75%	262.01	136.71	95.05	74.30	61.91	53.71	47.89	43.56	40.23	37.60
9.00%	262.35	137.05	95.40	74.66	62.28	54.08	48.27	43.95	40.63	38.00
9.25%	262.70	137.40	95.75	75.01	62.64	54.45	48.65	44.34	41.03	38.41
9.50%	263.05	137.74	96.10	75.37	63.01	54.82	49.03	44.73	41.43	38.82
9.75%	263.40	138.09	96.45	75.73	63.37	55.20	49.42	45.13	41.83	39.23
10.00%	263.75	138.43	96.80	76.09	63.74	55.58	49.80	45.52	42.24	39.65
10.25%	264.10	138.78	97.15	76.45	64.11	55.96	50.19	45.92	42.64	40.06
10.50%	264.45	139.13	97.51	76.81	64.48	56.34	50.58	46.32	43.05	40.48
10.75%	264.80	139.48	97.86	77.17	64.85	56.72	50.97	46.72	43.46	40.90

$3,000

11.00 - 20.75%

1 - 10 Years

	1	2	3	4	5	6	7	8	9	10
11.00%	265.14	139.82	98.22	77.54	65.23	57.10	51.37	47.13	43.88	41.33
11.25%	265.49	140.17	98.57	77.90	65.60	57.49	51.76	47.53	44.29	41.75
11.50%	265.85	140.52	98.93	78.27	65.98	57.87	52.16	47.94	44.71	42.18
11.75%	266.20	140.87	99.29	78.63	66.35	58.26	52.56	48.35	45.13	42.61
12.00%	266.55	141.22	99.64	79.00	66.73	58.65	52.96	48.76	45.55	43.04
12.25%	266.90	141.57	100.00	79.37	67.11	59.04	53.36	49.17	45.98	43.48
12.50%	267.25	141.92	100.36	79.74	67.49	59.43	53.76	49.59	46.40	43.91
12.75%	267.60	142.27	100.72	80.11	67.88	59.83	54.17	50.00	46.83	44.35
13.00%	267.95	142.63	101.08	80.48	68.26	60.22	54.58	50.42	47.26	44.79
13.25%	268.30	142.98	101.44	80.86	68.64	60.62	54.98	50.84	47.69	45.24
13.50%	268.66	143.33	101.81	81.23	69.03	61.02	55.39	51.26	48.13	45.68
13.75%	269.01	143.68	102.17	81.60	69.42	61.42	55.81	51.69	48.56	46.13
14.00%	269.36	144.04	102.53	81.98	69.80	61.82	56.22	52.11	49.00	46.58
14.25%	269.71	144.39	102.90	82.36	70.19	62.22	56.64	52.54	49.44	47.03
14.50%	270.07	144.75	103.26	82.73	70.58	62.62	57.05	52.97	49.88	47.49
14.75%	270.42	145.10	103.63	83.11	70.98	63.03	57.47	53.40	50.33	47.94
15.00%	270.77	145.46	104.00	83.49	71.37	63.44	57.89	53.84	50.77	48.40
15.25%	271.13	145.82	104.36	83.87	71.76	63.84	58.31	54.27	51.22	48.86
15.50%	271.48	146.17	104.73	84.25	72.16	64.25	58.74	54.71	51.67	49.32
15.75%	271.84	146.53	105.10	84.64	72.56	64.66	59.16	55.15	52.12	49.79
16.00%	272.19	146.89	105.47	85.02	72.95	65.08	59.59	55.59	52.58	50.25
16.25%	272.55	147.25	105.84	85.41	73.35	65.49	60.01	56.03	53.03	50.72
16.50%	272.90	147.61	106.21	85.79	73.75	65.90	60.44	56.47	53.49	51.19
16.75%	273.26	147.97	106.59	86.18	74.16	66.32	60.87	56.92	53.95	51.67
17.00%	273.61	148.33	106.96	86.57	74.56	66.74	61.31	57.36	54.41	52.14
17.25%	273.97	148.69	107.33	86.95	74.96	67.16	61.74	57.81	54.87	52.62
17.50%	274.33	149.05	107.71	87.34	75.37	67.58	62.18	58.26	55.34	53.09
17.75%	274.68	149.41	108.08	87.73	75.77	68.00	62.61	58.72	55.80	53.57
18.00%	275.04	149.77	108.46	88.12	76.18	68.42	63.05	59.17	56.27	54.06
18.25%	275.40	150.13	108.83	88.52	76.59	68.85	63.49	59.63	56.74	54.54
18.50%	275.75	150.50	109.21	88.91	77.00	69.27	63.94	60.08	57.21	55.02
18.75%	276.11	150.86	109.59	89.31	77.41	69.70	64.38	60.54	57.69	55.51
19.00%	276.47	151.23	109.97	89.70	77.82	70.13	64.82	61.00	58.16	56.00
19.25%	276.83	151.59	110.35	90.10	78.23	70.56	65.27	61.46	58.64	56.49
19.50%	277.19	151.96	110.73	90.49	78.65	70.99	65.72	61.93	59.12	56.99
19.75%	277.54	152.32	111.11	90.89	79.06	71.42	66.17	62.39	59.60	57.48
20.00%	277.90	152.69	111.49	91.29	79.48	71.86	66.62	62.86	60.08	57.98
20.25%	278.26	153.05	111.87	91.69	79.90	72.29	67.07	63.33	60.56	58.47
20.50%	278.62	153.42	112.26	92.09	80.32	72.73	67.52	63.80	61.05	58.97
20.75%	278.98	153.79	112.64	92.49	80.74	73.17	67.98	64.27	61.54	59.48

	1	2	3	4	5	6	7	8	9	10
1.00%	335.14	168.41	112.83	85.05	68.37	57.26	49.32	43.37	38.74	35.04
1.25%	335.59	168.85	113.27	85.48	68.81	57.69	49.76	43.81	39.18	35.48
1.50%	336.05	169.28	113.70	85.91	69.24	58.13	50.19	44.24	39.62	35.92
1.75%	336.50	169.72	114.13	86.34	69.67	58.56	50.63	44.68	40.06	36.36
2.00%	336.96	170.16	114.57	86.78	70.11	59.00	51.07	45.12	40.50	36.81
2.25%	337.41	170.60	115.01	87.22	70.55	59.44	51.51	45.57	40.95	37.25
2.50%	337.86	171.04	115.45	87.66	70.99	59.88	51.96	46.02	41.40	37.71
2.75%	338.32	171.48	115.88	88.10	71.43	60.33	52.40	46.47	41.85	38.16
3.00%	338.77	171.92	116.32	88.54	71.87	60.77	52.85	46.92	42.31	38.62
3.25%	339.23	172.37	116.77	88.98	72.32	61.22	53.31	47.37	42.77	39.09
3.50%	339.69	172.81	117.21	89.42	72.77	61.67	53.76	47.83	43.23	39.55
3.75%	340.14	173.25	117.65	89.87	73.22	62.13	54.22	48.29	43.70	40.02
4.00%	340.60	173.70	118.10	90.32	73.67	62.58	54.68	48.76	44.16	40.50
4.25%	341.06	174.15	118.54	90.76	74.12	63.04	55.14	49.22	44.64	40.98
4.50%	341.51	174.59	118.99	91.21	74.57	63.50	55.60	49.69	45.11	41.46
4.75%	341.97	175.04	119.44	91.66	75.03	63.96	56.07	50.16	45.59	41.94
5.00%	342.43	175.49	119.88	92.12	75.48	64.42	56.54	50.64	46.07	42.43
5.25%	342.89	175.93	120.33	92.57	75.94	64.88	57.01	51.12	46.55	42.92
5.50%	343.35	176.38	120.78	93.03	76.40	65.35	57.48	51.60	47.04	43.41
5.75%	343.81	176.83	121.24	93.48	76.87	65.82	57.96	52.08	47.53	43.91
6.00%	344.27	177.28	121.69	93.94	77.33	66.29	58.43	52.57	48.02	44.41
6.25%	344.73	177.73	122.14	94.40	77.80	66.76	58.91	53.05	48.52	44.91
6.50%	345.19	178.19	122.60	94.86	78.26	67.24	59.40	53.54	49.02	45.42
6.75%	345.65	178.64	123.05	95.32	78.73	67.72	59.88	54.04	49.52	45.93
7.00%	346.11	179.09	123.51	95.78	79.20	68.20	60.37	54.53	50.03	46.44
7.25%	346.57	179.54	123.97	96.25	79.68	68.68	60.86	55.03	50.53	46.96
7.50%	347.03	180.00	124.42	96.72	80.15	69.16	61.35	55.54	51.04	47.48
7.75%	347.49	180.45	124.88	97.18	80.63	69.65	61.85	56.04	51.56	48.00
8.00%	347.95	180.91	125.35	97.65	81.11	70.13	62.34	56.55	52.07	48.53
8.25%	348.42	181.37	125.81	98.12	81.59	70.62	62.84	57.06	52.59	49.06
8.50%	348.88	181.82	126.27	98.59	82.07	71.11	63.35	57.57	53.12	49.59
8.75%	349.34	182.28	126.73	99.07	82.55	71.61	63.85	58.08	53.64	50.13
9.00%	349.81	182.74	127.20	99.54	83.03	72.10	64.36	58.60	54.17	50.67
9.25%	350.27	183.20	127.66	100.02	83.52	72.60	64.86	59.12	54.70	51.21
9.50%	350.73	183.66	128.13	100.49	84.01	73.10	65.38	59.64	55.24	51.76
9.75%	351.20	184.12	128.60	100.97	84.50	73.60	65.89	60.17	55.77	52.31
10.00%	351.66	184.58	129.07	101.45	84.99	74.10	66.40	60.70	56.31	52.86
10.25%	352.13	185.04	129.54	101.93	85.48	74.61	66.92	61.23	56.86	53.42
10.50%	352.59	185.50	130.01	102.41	85.98	75.12	67.44	61.76	57.40	53.97
10.75%	353.06	185.97	130.48	102.90	86.47	75.63	67.97	62.30	57.95	54.54

	1	2	3	4	5	6	7	8	9	10
11.00%	353.53	186.43	130.95	103.38	86.97	76.14	68.49	62.83	58.50	55.10
11.25%	353.99	186.90	131.43	103.87	87.47	76.65	69.02	63.37	59.06	55.67
11.50%	354.46	187.36	131.90	104.36	87.97	77.16	69.55	63.92	59.61	56.24
11.75%	354.93	187.83	132.38	104.85	88.47	77.68	70.08	64.46	60.17	56.81
12.00%	355.40	188.29	132.86	105.34	88.98	78.20	70.61	65.01	60.74	57.39
12.25%	355.86	188.76	133.34	105.83	89.48	78.72	71.15	65.56	61.30	57.97
12.50%	356.33	189.23	133.81	106.32	89.99	79.24	71.68	66.12	61.87	58.55
12.75%	356.80	189.70	134.29	106.81	90.50	79.77	72.23	66.67	62.44	59.14
13.00%	357.27	190.17	134.78	107.31	91.01	80.30	72.77	67.23	63.01	59.72
13.25%	357.74	190.64	135.26	107.81	91.53	80.83	73.31	67.79	63.59	60.32
13.50%	358.21	191.11	135.74	108.31	92.04	81.36	73.86	68.35	64.17	60.91
13.75%	358.68	191.58	136.23	108.80	92.56	81.89	74.41	68.92	64.75	61.51
14.00%	359.15	192.05	136.71	109.31	93.07	82.42	74.96	69.49	65.33	62.11
14.25%	359.62	192.52	137.20	109.81	93.59	82.96	75.51	70.06	65.92	62.71
14.50%	360.09	193.00	137.68	110.31	94.11	83.50	76.07	70.63	66.51	63.31
14.75%	360.56	193.47	138.17	110.82	94.64	84.04	76.63	71.20	67.10	63.92
15.00%	361.03	193.95	138.66	111.32	95.16	84.58	77.19	71.78	67.70	64.53
15.25%	361.51	194.42	139.15	111.83	95.69	85.12	77.75	72.36	68.29	65.15
15.50%	361.98	194.90	139.64	112.34	96.21	85.67	78.31	72.94	68.89	65.76
15.75%	362.45	195.37	140.13	112.85	96.74	86.22	78.88	73.53	69.50	66.38
16.00%	362.92	195.85	140.63	113.36	97.27	86.77	79.45	74.12	70.10	67.01
16.25%	363.40	196.33	141.12	113.87	97.80	87.32	80.02	74.70	70.71	67.63
16.50%	363.87	196.81	141.62	114.39	98.34	87.87	80.59	75.30	71.32	68.26
16.75%	364.34	197.29	142.11	114.90	98.87	88.43	81.17	75.89	71.93	68.89
17.00%	364.82	197.77	142.61	115.42	99.41	88.98	81.74	76.49	72.54	69.52
17.25%	365.29	198.25	143.11	115.94	99.95	89.54	82.32	77.08	73.16	70.15
17.50%	365.77	198.73	143.61	116.46	100.49	90.10	82.90	77.68	73.78	70.79
17.75%	366.24	199.21	144.11	116.98	101.03	90.67	83.49	78.29	74.40	71.43
18.00%	366.72	199.70	144.61	117.50	101.57	91.23	84.07	78.89	75.03	72.07
18.25%	367.20	200.18	145.11	118.02	102.12	91.80	84.66	79.50	75.65	72.72
18.50%	367.67	200.66	145.61	118.55	102.66	92.37	85.25	80.11	76.28	73.37
18.75%	368.15	201.15	146.12	119.07	103.21	92.94	85.84	80.72	76.91	74.02
19.00%	368.63	201.63	146.62	119.60	103.76	93.51	86.43	81.34	77.55	74.67
19.25%	369.10	202.12	147.13	120.13	104.31	94.08	87.03	81.95	78.18	75.32
19.50%	369.58	202.61	147.64	120.66	104.87	94.66	87.62	82.57	78.82	75.98
19.75%	370.06	203.10	148.15	121.19	105.42	95.23	88.22	83.19	79.46	76.64
20.00%	370.54	203.58	148.65	121.72	105.98	95.81	88.82	83.81	80.11	77.30
20.25%	371.02	204.07	149.16	122.25	106.53	96.39	89.43	84.44	80.75	77.97
20.50%	371.50	204.56	149.68	122.79	107.09	96.97	90.03	85.06	81.40	78.63
20.75%	371.98	205.05	150.19	123.33	107.65	97.56	90.64	85.69	82.05	79.30

$5,000   1.00 - 10.75%   1 - 10 Years

	1	2	3	4	5	6	7	8	9	10
1.00%	418.93	210.51	141.04	106.31	85.47	71.58	61.66	54.22	48.43	43.80
1.25%	419.49	211.06	141.58	106.85	86.01	72.12	62.20	54.76	48.97	44.35
1.50%	420.06	211.60	142.12	107.39	86.55	72.66	62.74	55.30	49.52	44.90
1.75%	420.63	212.15	142.67	107.93	87.09	73.20	63.29	55.85	50.07	45.45
2.00%	421.19	212.70	143.21	108.48	87.64	73.75	63.84	56.40	50.63	46.01
2.25%	421.76	213.25	143.76	109.02	88.19	74.30	64.39	56.96	51.19	46.57
2.50%	422.33	213.80	144.31	109.57	88.74	74.86	64.95	57.52	51.75	47.13
2.75%	422.90	214.35	144.86	110.12	89.29	75.41	65.50	58.08	52.31	47.71
3.00%	423.47	214.91	145.41	110.67	89.84	75.97	66.07	58.65	52.88	48.28
3.25%	424.04	215.46	145.96	111.22	90.40	76.53	66.63	59.22	53.46	48.86
3.50%	424.61	216.01	146.51	111.78	90.96	77.09	67.20	59.79	54.04	49.44
3.75%	425.18	216.57	147.06	112.34	91.52	77.66	67.77	60.37	54.62	50.03
4.00%	425.75	217.12	147.62	112.90	92.08	78.23	68.34	60.95	55.20	50.62
4.25%	426.32	217.68	148.18	113.46	92.65	78.80	68.92	61.53	55.79	51.22
4.50%	426.89	218.24	148.73	114.02	93.22	79.37	69.50	62.12	56.39	51.82
4.75%	427.46	218.80	149.29	114.58	93.78	79.95	70.08	62.71	56.99	52.42
5.00%	428.04	219.36	149.85	115.15	94.36	80.52	70.67	63.30	57.59	53.03
5.25%	428.61	219.92	150.42	115.71	94.93	81.11	71.26	63.90	58.19	53.65
5.50%	429.18	220.48	150.98	116.28	95.51	81.69	71.85	64.50	58.80	54.26
5.75%	429.76	221.04	151.54	116.85	96.08	82.28	72.45	65.10	59.41	54.88
6.00%	430.33	221.60	152.11	117.43	96.66	82.86	73.04	65.71	60.03	55.51
6.25%	430.91	222.17	152.68	118.00	97.25	83.46	73.64	66.32	60.65	56.14
6.50%	431.48	222.73	153.25	118.57	97.83	84.05	74.25	66.93	61.27	56.77
6.75%	432.06	223.30	153.81	119.15	98.42	84.65	74.85	67.55	61.90	57.41
7.00%	432.63	223.86	154.39	119.73	99.01	85.25	75.46	68.17	62.53	58.05
7.25%	433.21	224.43	154.96	120.31	99.60	85.85	76.08	68.79	63.17	58.70
7.50%	433.79	225.00	155.53	120.89	100.19	86.45	76.69	69.42	63.81	59.35
7.75%	434.36	225.57	156.11	121.48	100.78	87.06	77.31	70.05	64.45	60.01
8.00%	434.94	226.14	156.68	122.06	101.38	87.67	77.93	70.68	65.09	60.66
8.25%	435.52	226.71	157.26	122.65	101.98	88.28	78.56	71.32	65.74	61.33
8.50%	436.10	227.28	157.84	123.24	102.58	88.89	79.18	71.96	66.40	61.99
8.75%	436.68	227.85	158.42	123.83	103.19	89.51	79.81	72.60	67.05	62.66
9.00%	437.26	228.42	159.00	124.43	103.79	90.13	80.45	73.25	67.71	63.34
9.25%	437.84	229.00	159.58	125.02	104.40	90.75	81.08	73.90	68.38	64.02
9.50%	438.42	229.57	160.16	125.62	105.01	91.37	81.72	74.55	69.05	64.70
9.75%	439.00	230.15	160.75	126.21	105.62	92.00	82.36	75.21	69.72	65.39
10.00%	439.58	230.72	161.34	126.81	106.24	92.63	83.01	75.87	70.39	66.08
10.25%	440.16	231.30	161.92	127.41	106.85	93.26	83.65	76.53	71.07	66.77
10.50%	440.74	231.88	162.51	128.02	107.47	93.89	84.30	77.20	71.75	67.47
10.75%	441.33	232.46	163.10	128.62	108.09	94.53	84.96	77.87	72.44	68.17

	1	2	3	4	5	6	7	8	9	10
11.00%	441.91	233.04	163.69	129.23	108.71	95.17	85.61	78.54	73.13	68.88
11.25%	442.49	233.62	164.29	129.84	109.34	95.81	86.27	79.22	73.82	69.58
11.50%	443.08	234.20	164.88	130.45	109.96	96.46	86.93	79.90	74.52	70.30
11.75%	443.66	234.78	165.48	131.06	110.59	97.10	87.60	80.58	75.22	71.01
12.00%	444.24	235.37	166.07	131.67	111.22	97.75	88.26	81.26	75.92	71.74
12.25%	444.83	235.95	166.67	132.28	111.85	98.40	88.93	81.95	76.63	72.46
12.50%	445.41	236.54	167.27	132.90	112.49	99.06	89.61	82.64	77.34	73.19
12.75%	446.00	237.12	167.87	133.52	113.13	99.71	90.28	83.34	78.05	73.92
13.00%	446.59	237.71	168.47	134.14	113.77	100.37	90.96	84.04	78.77	74.66
13.25%	447.17	238.30	169.07	134.76	114.41	101.03	91.64	84.74	79.49	75.39
13.50%	447.76	238.89	169.68	135.38	115.05	101.69	92.32	85.44	80.21	76.14
13.75%	448.35	239.47	170.28	136.01	115.69	102.36	93.01	86.15	80.94	76.88
14.00%	448.94	240.06	170.89	136.63	116.34	103.03	93.70	86.86	81.67	77.63
14.25%	449.52	240.66	171.50	137.26	116.99	103.70	94.39	87.57	82.40	78.39
14.50%	450.11	241.25	172.10	137.89	117.64	104.37	95.09	88.29	83.14	79.14
14.75%	450.70	241.84	172.72	138.52	118.29	105.05	95.78	89.01	83.88	79.90
15.00%	451.29	242.43	173.33	139.15	118.95	105.73	96.48	89.73	84.62	80.67
15.25%	451.88	243.03	173.94	139.79	119.61	106.41	97.19	90.45	85.37	81.43
15.50%	452.47	243.62	174.55	140.42	120.27	107.09	97.89	91.18	86.12	82.21
15.75%	453.06	244.22	175.17	141.06	120.93	107.77	98.60	91.91	86.87	82.98
16.00%	453.65	244.82	175.79	141.70	121.59	108.46	99.31	92.64	87.63	83.76
16.25%	454.25	245.41	176.40	142.34	122.26	109.15	100.02	93.38	88.39	84.54
16.50%	454.84	246.01	177.02	142.99	122.92	109.84	100.74	94.12	89.15	85.32
16.75%	455.43	246.61	177.64	143.63	123.59	110.53	101.46	94.86	89.91	86.11
17.00%	456.02	247.21	178.26	144.28	124.26	111.23	102.18	95.61	90.68	86.90
17.25%	456.62	247.81	178.89	144.92	124.94	111.93	102.90	96.36	91.45	87.69
17.50%	457.21	248.41	179.51	145.57	125.61	112.63	103.63	97.11	92.23	88.49
17.75%	457.81	249.02	180.14	146.22	126.29	113.33	104.36	97.86	93.00	89.29
18.00%	458.40	249.62	180.76	146.87	126.97	114.04	105.09	98.62	93.78	90.09
18.25%	459.00	250.22	181.39	147.53	127.65	114.75	105.82	99.38	94.57	90.90
18.50%	459.59	250.83	182.02	148.18	128.33	115.46	106.56	100.14	95.35	91.71
18.75%	460.19	251.44	182.65	148.84	129.02	116.17	107.30	100.90	96.14	92.52
19.00%	460.78	252.04	183.28	149.50	129.70	116.88	108.04	101.67	96.94	93.34
19.25%	461.38	252.65	183.91	150.16	130.39	117.60	108.78	102.44	97.73	94.15
19.50%	461.98	253.26	184.55	150.82	131.08	118.32	109.53	103.21	98.53	94.98
19.75%	462.57	253.87	185.18	151.49	131.77	119.04	110.28	103.99	99.33	95.80
20.00%	463.17	254.48	185.82	152.15	132.47	119.76	111.03	104.77	100.13	96.63
20.25%	463.77	255.09	186.46	152.82	133.17	120.49	111.78	105.55	100.94	97.46
20.50%	464.37	255.70	187.09	153.49	133.86	121.22	112.54	106.33	101.75	98.29
20.75%	464.97	256.31	187.73	154.16	134.56	121.95	113.30	107.12	102.56	99.13

	1	2	3	4	5	6	7	8	9	10
1.00%	502.71	252.61	169.25	127.57	102.56	85.89	73.99	65.06	58.12	52.56
1.25%	503.39	253.27	169.90	128.22	103.21	86.54	74.64	65.71	58.77	53.22
1.50%	504.07	253.92	170.55	128.87	103.86	87.19	75.29	66.36	59.42	53.87
1.75%	504.75	254.58	171.20	129.52	104.51	87.85	75.94	67.02	60.09	54.54
2.00%	505.43	255.24	171.86	130.17	105.17	88.50	76.60	67.69	60.75	55.21
2.25%	506.11	255.90	172.51	130.83	105.82	89.16	77.27	68.35	61.42	55.88
2.50%	506.80	256.56	173.17	131.48	106.48	89.83	77.93	69.02	62.10	56.56
2.75%	507.48	257.22	173.83	132.14	107.15	90.49	78.61	69.70	62.78	57.25
3.00%	508.16	257.89	174.49	132.81	107.81	91.16	79.28	70.38	63.46	57.94
3.25%	508.85	258.55	175.15	133.47	108.48	91.83	79.96	71.06	64.15	58.63
3.50%	509.53	259.22	175.81	134.14	109.15	92.51	80.64	71.75	64.84	59.33
3.75%	510.21	259.88	176.48	134.80	109.82	93.19	81.32	72.44	65.54	60.04
4.00%	510.90	260.55	177.14	135.47	110.50	93.87	82.01	73.14	66.25	60.75
4.25%	511.59	261.22	177.81	136.15	111.18	94.56	82.71	73.84	66.95	61.46
4.50%	512.27	261.89	178.48	136.82	111.86	95.24	83.40	74.54	67.67	62.18
4.75%	512.96	262.56	179.15	137.50	112.54	95.94	84.10	75.25	68.38	62.91
5.00%	513.64	263.23	179.83	138.18	113.23	96.63	84.80	75.96	69.10	63.64
5.25%	514.33	263.90	180.50	138.86	113.92	97.33	85.51	76.68	69.83	64.38
5.50%	515.02	264.57	181.18	139.54	114.61	98.03	86.22	77.40	70.56	65.12
5.75%	515.71	265.25	181.85	140.22	115.30	98.73	86.93	78.12	71.29	65.86
6.00%	516.40	265.92	182.53	140.91	116.00	99.44	87.65	78.85	72.03	66.61
6.25%	517.09	266.60	183.21	141.60	116.70	100.15	88.37	79.58	72.78	67.37
6.50%	517.78	267.28	183.89	142.29	117.40	100.86	89.10	80.32	73.53	68.13
6.75%	518.47	267.96	184.58	142.98	118.10	101.58	89.82	81.06	74.28	68.89
7.00%	519.16	268.64	185.26	143.68	118.81	102.29	90.56	81.80	75.04	69.67
7.25%	519.85	269.32	185.95	144.37	119.52	103.02	91.29	82.55	75.80	70.44
7.50%	520.54	270.00	186.64	145.07	120.23	103.74	92.03	83.30	76.57	71.22
7.75%	521.24	270.68	187.33	145.77	120.94	104.47	92.77	84.06	77.34	72.01
8.00%	521.93	271.36	188.02	146.48	121.66	105.20	93.52	84.82	78.11	72.80
8.25%	522.62	272.05	188.71	147.18	122.38	105.93	94.27	85.58	78.89	73.59
8.50%	523.32	272.73	189.41	147.89	123.10	106.67	95.02	86.35	79.68	74.39
8.75%	524.01	273.42	190.10	148.60	123.82	107.41	95.77	87.13	80.46	75.20
9.00%	524.71	274.11	190.80	149.31	124.55	108.15	96.53	87.90	81.26	76.01
9.25%	525.40	274.80	191.50	150.02	125.28	108.90	97.30	88.68	82.05	76.82
9.50%	526.10	275.49	192.20	150.74	126.01	109.65	98.06	89.47	82.86	77.64
9.75%	526.80	276.18	192.90	151.46	126.75	110.40	98.83	90.25	83.66	78.46
10.00%	527.50	276.87	193.60	152.18	127.48	111.16	99.61	91.04	84.47	79.29
10.25%	528.19	277.56	194.31	152.90	128.22	111.91	100.38	91.84	85.29	80.12
10.50%	528.89	278.26	195.01	153.62	128.96	112.67	101.16	92.64	86.11	80.96
10.75%	529.59	278.95	195.72	154.35	129.71	113.44	101.95	93.44	86.93	81.80

$6,000   11.00 - 20.75%   1 - 10 Years

	1	2	3	4	5	6	7	8	9	10
11.00%	530.29	279.65	196.43	155.07	130.45	114.20	102.73	94.25	87.76	82.65
11.25%	530.99	280.34	197.14	155.80	131.20	114.97	103.53	95.06	88.59	83.50
11.50%	531.69	281.04	197.86	156.53	131.96	115.75	104.32	95.88	89.42	84.36
11.75%	532.39	281.74	198.57	157.27	132.71	116.52	105.12	96.69	90.26	85.22
12.00%	533.09	282.44	199.29	158.00	133.47	117.30	105.92	97.52	91.11	86.08
12.25%	533.79	283.14	200.00	158.74	134.23	118.08	106.72	98.34	91.95	86.95
12.50%	534.50	283.84	200.72	159.48	134.99	118.87	107.53	99.17	92.81	87.83
12.75%	535.20	284.55	201.44	160.22	135.75	119.65	108.34	100.01	93.66	88.70
13.00%	535.90	285.25	202.16	160.96	136.52	120.44	109.15	100.84	94.52	89.59
13.25%	536.61	285.96	202.89	161.71	137.29	121.24	109.97	101.68	95.39	90.47
13.50%	537.31	286.66	203.61	162.46	138.06	122.03	110.79	102.53	96.25	91.36
13.75%	538.02	287.37	204.34	163.21	138.83	122.83	111.61	103.38	97.13	92.26
14.00%	538.72	288.08	205.07	163.96	139.61	123.63	112.44	104.23	98.00	93.16
14.25%	539.43	288.79	205.80	164.71	140.39	124.44	113.27	105.08	98.88	94.06
14.50%	540.14	289.50	206.53	165.47	141.17	125.25	114.10	105.94	99.77	94.97
14.75%	540.84	290.21	207.26	166.23	141.95	126.06	114.94	106.81	100.65	95.88
15.00%	541.55	290.92	207.99	166.98	142.74	126.87	115.78	107.67	101.55	96.80
15.25%	542.26	291.63	208.73	167.75	143.53	127.69	116.62	108.54	102.44	97.72
15.50%	542.97	292.35	209.46	168.51	144.32	128.50	117.47	109.42	103.34	98.65
15.75%	543.68	293.06	210.20	169.27	145.11	129.33	118.32	110.29	104.24	99.58
16.00%	544.39	293.78	210.94	170.04	145.91	130.15	119.17	111.17	105.15	100.51
16.25%	545.10	294.50	211.68	170.81	146.71	130.98	120.03	112.06	106.06	101.44
16.50%	545.81	295.21	212.43	171.58	147.51	131.81	120.89	112.94	106.98	102.39
16.75%	546.52	295.93	213.17	172.36	148.31	132.64	121.75	113.83	107.90	103.33
17.00%	547.23	296.65	213.92	173.13	149.12	133.48	122.61	114.73	108.82	104.28
17.25%	547.94	297.37	214.66	173.91	149.92	134.32	123.48	115.63	109.74	105.23
17.50%	548.65	298.10	215.41	174.69	150.73	135.16	124.35	116.53	110.67	106.19
17.75%	549.37	298.82	216.16	175.47	151.55	136.00	125.23	117.43	111.60	107.15
18.00%	550.08	299.54	216.91	176.25	152.36	136.85	126.11	118.34	112.54	108.11
18.25%	550.79	300.27	217.67	177.03	153.18	137.70	126.99	119.25	113.48	109.08
18.50%	551.51	301.00	218.42	177.82	154.00	138.55	127.87	120.16	114.42	110.05
18.75%	552.22	301.72	219.18	178.61	154.82	139.40	128.76	121.08	115.37	111.02
19.00%	552.94	302.45	219.94	179.40	155.64	140.26	129.65	122.00	116.32	112.00
19.25%	553.66	303.18	220.70	180.19	156.47	141.12	130.54	122.93	117.28	112.99
19.50%	554.37	303.91	221.46	180.99	157.30	141.98	131.44	123.85	118.23	113.97
19.75%	555.09	304.64	222.22	181.78	158.13	142.85	132.34	124.79	119.19	114.96
20.00%	555.81	305.37	222.98	182.58	158.96	143.72	133.24	125.72	120.16	115.95
20.25%	556.53	306.11	223.75	183.38	159.80	144.59	134.14	126.66	121.13	116.95
20.50%	557.24	306.84	224.51	184.18	160.64	145.46	135.05	127.60	122.10	117.95
20.75%	557.96	307.58	225.28	184.99	161.48	146.34	135.96	128.54	123.07	118.95

	1	2	3	4	5	6	7	8	9	10
1.00%	586.50	294.71	197.46	148.83	119.66	100.21	86.32	75.90	67.80	61.32
1.25%	587.29	295.48	198.21	149.59	120.41	100.96	87.08	76.66	68.56	62.09
1.50%	588.08	296.25	198.97	150.34	121.17	101.72	87.84	77.42	69.33	62.85
1.75%	588.88	297.01	199.73	151.10	121.93	102.49	88.60	78.19	70.10	63.63
2.00%	589.67	297.78	200.50	151.87	122.69	103.25	89.37	78.97	70.88	64.41
2.25%	590.47	298.55	201.26	152.63	123.46	104.02	90.15	79.74	71.66	65.20
2.50%	591.26	299.32	202.03	153.40	124.23	104.80	90.92	80.53	72.45	65.99
2.75%	592.06	300.10	202.80	154.17	125.00	105.57	91.71	81.31	73.24	66.79
3.00%	592.86	300.87	203.57	154.94	125.78	106.36	92.49	82.11	74.04	67.59
3.25%	593.65	301.64	204.34	155.71	126.56	107.14	93.28	82.90	74.84	68.40
3.50%	594.45	302.42	205.11	156.49	127.34	107.93	94.08	83.71	75.65	69.22
3.75%	595.25	303.20	205.89	157.27	128.13	108.72	94.88	84.51	76.47	70.04
4.00%	596.05	303.97	206.67	158.05	128.92	109.52	95.68	85.32	77.29	70.87
4.25%	596.85	304.75	207.45	158.84	129.71	110.32	96.49	86.14	78.11	71.71
4.50%	597.65	305.53	208.23	159.62	130.50	111.12	97.30	86.96	78.94	72.55
4.75%	598.45	306.32	209.01	160.41	131.30	111.92	98.12	87.79	79.78	73.39
5.00%	599.25	307.10	209.80	161.21	132.10	112.73	98.94	88.62	80.62	74.25
5.25%	600.05	307.88	210.58	162.00	132.90	113.55	99.76	89.45	81.47	75.10
5.50%	600.86	308.67	211.37	162.80	133.71	114.37	100.59	90.30	82.32	75.97
5.75%	601.66	309.46	212.16	163.59	134.52	115.19	101.42	91.14	83.18	76.84
6.00%	602.47	310.24	212.95	164.40	135.33	116.01	102.26	91.99	84.04	77.71
6.25%	603.27	311.03	213.75	165.20	136.14	116.84	103.10	92.84	84.91	78.60
6.50%	604.07	311.82	214.54	166.00	136.96	117.67	103.95	93.70	85.78	79.48
6.75%	604.88	312.62	215.34	166.81	137.78	118.50	104.80	94.57	86.66	80.38
7.00%	605.69	313.41	216.14	167.62	138.61	119.34	105.65	95.44	87.54	81.28
7.25%	606.49	314.20	216.94	168.44	139.44	120.19	106.51	96.31	88.43	82.18
7.50%	607.30	315.00	217.74	169.25	140.27	121.03	107.37	97.19	89.33	83.09
7.75%	608.11	315.79	218.55	170.07	141.10	121.88	108.23	98.07	90.23	84.01
8.00%	608.92	316.59	219.35	170.89	141.93	122.73	109.10	98.96	91.13	84.93
8.25%	609.73	317.39	220.16	171.71	142.77	123.59	109.98	99.85	92.04	85.86
8.50%	610.54	318.19	220.97	172.54	143.62	124.45	110.86	100.74	92.96	86.79
8.75%	611.35	318.99	221.78	173.37	144.46	125.31	111.74	101.65	93.88	87.73
9.00%	612.16	319.79	222.60	174.20	145.31	126.18	112.62	102.55	94.80	88.67
9.25%	612.97	320.60	223.41	175.03	146.16	127.05	113.51	103.46	95.73	89.62
9.50%	613.78	321.40	224.23	175.86	147.01	127.92	114.41	104.38	96.67	90.58
9.75%	614.60	322.21	225.05	176.70	147.87	128.80	115.31	105.30	97.61	91.54
10.00%	615.41	323.01	225.87	177.54	148.73	129.68	116.21	106.22	98.55	92.51
10.25%	616.23	323.82	226.69	178.38	149.59	130.57	117.11	107.15	99.50	93.48
10.50%	617.04	324.63	227.52	179.22	150.46	131.45	118.02	108.08	100.46	94.45
10.75%	617.86	325.44	228.34	180.07	151.33	132.34	118.94	109.02	101.42	95.44

	1	2	3	4	5	6	7	8	9	10
11.00%	618.67	326.25	229.17	180.92	152.20	133.24	119.86	109.96	102.38	96.43
11.25%	619.49	327.07	230.00	181.77	153.07	134.14	120.78	110.91	103.35	97.42
11.50%	620.31	327.88	230.83	182.62	153.95	135.04	121.71	111.86	104.33	98.42
11.75%	621.12	328.70	231.67	183.48	154.83	135.94	122.64	112.81	105.31	99.42
12.00%	621.94	329.51	232.50	184.34	155.71	136.85	123.57	113.77	106.29	100.43
12.25%	622.76	330.33	233.34	185.20	156.60	137.76	124.51	114.73	107.28	101.44
12.50%	623.58	331.15	234.18	186.06	157.49	138.68	125.45	115.70	108.27	102.46
12.75%	624.40	331.97	235.02	186.93	158.38	139.60	126.39	116.67	109.27	103.49
13.00%	625.22	332.79	235.86	187.79	159.27	140.52	127.34	117.65	110.28	104.52
13.25%	626.04	333.62	236.70	188.66	160.17	141.44	128.30	118.63	111.28	105.55
13.50%	626.86	334.44	237.55	189.53	161.07	142.37	129.25	119.62	112.30	106.59
13.75%	627.69	335.26	238.39	190.41	161.97	143.30	130.22	120.61	113.31	107.64
14.00%	628.51	336.09	239.24	191.29	162.88	144.24	131.18	121.60	114.34	108.69
14.25%	629.33	336.92	240.09	192.16	163.79	145.18	132.15	122.60	115.36	109.74
14.50%	630.16	337.75	240.95	193.05	164.70	146.12	133.12	123.60	116.39	110.80
14.75%	630.98	338.58	241.80	193.93	165.61	147.07	134.10	124.61	117.43	111.87
15.00%	631.81	339.41	242.66	194.82	166.53	148.02	135.08	125.62	118.47	112.93
15.25%	632.63	340.24	243.52	195.70	167.45	148.97	136.06	126.63	119.52	114.01
15.50%	633.46	341.07	244.37	196.59	168.37	149.92	137.05	127.65	120.56	115.09
15.75%	634.29	341.91	245.24	197.49	169.30	150.88	138.04	128.67	121.62	116.17
16.00%	635.12	342.74	246.10	198.38	170.23	151.84	139.03	129.70	122.68	117.26
16.25%	635.94	343.58	246.96	199.28	171.16	152.81	140.03	130.73	123.74	118.35
16.50%	636.77	344.42	247.83	200.18	172.09	153.78	141.04	131.77	124.81	119.45
16.75%	637.60	345.26	248.70	201.08	173.03	154.75	142.04	132.81	125.88	120.55
17.00%	638.43	346.10	249.57	201.99	173.97	155.72	143.05	133.85	126.95	121.66
17.25%	639.26	346.94	250.44	202.89	174.91	156.70	144.06	134.90	128.03	122.77
17.50%	640.10	347.78	251.31	203.80	175.86	157.68	145.08	135.95	129.12	123.89
17.75%	640.93	348.62	252.19	204.71	176.80	158.67	146.10	137.00	130.21	125.01
18.00%	641.76	349.47	253.07	205.62	177.75	159.65	147.12	138.06	131.30	126.13
18.25%	642.59	350.31	253.95	206.54	178.71	160.65	148.15	139.13	132.39	127.26
18.50%	643.43	351.16	254.83	207.46	179.66	161.64	149.18	140.19	133.50	128.39
18.75%	644.26	352.01	255.71	208.38	180.62	162.64	150.22	141.26	134.60	129.53
19.00%	645.10	352.86	256.59	209.30	181.58	163.64	151.26	142.34	135.71	130.67
19.25%	645.93	353.71	257.48	210.23	182.55	164.64	152.30	143.42	136.82	131.82
19.50%	646.77	354.56	258.37	211.15	183.52	165.65	153.34	144.50	137.94	132.97
19.75%	647.60	355.42	259.25	212.08	184.48	166.66	154.39	145.58	139.06	134.12
20.00%	648.44	356.27	260.15	213.01	185.46	167.67	155.44	146.67	140.19	135.28
20.25%	649.28	357.13	261.04	213.95	186.43	168.69	156.50	147.77	141.31	136.44
20.50%	650.12	357.98	261.93	214.88	187.41	169.70	157.56	148.86	142.45	137.61
20.75%	650.96	358.84	262.83	215.82	188.39	170.73	158.62	149.96	143.58	138.78

	1	2	3	4	5	6	7	8	9	10
1.00%	670.28	336.82	225.66	170.09	136.75	114.52	98.65	86.75	77.49	70.08
1.25%	671.19	337.69	226.53	170.95	137.61	115.39	99.52	87.61	78.36	70.95
1.50%	672.10	338.57	227.40	171.82	138.48	116.26	100.39	88.49	79.23	71.83
1.75%	673.00	339.44	228.27	172.69	139.35	117.13	101.26	89.36	80.11	72.72
2.00%	673.91	340.32	229.14	173.56	140.22	118.00	102.14	90.25	81.00	73.61
2.25%	674.82	341.20	230.01	174.44	141.10	118.88	103.02	91.14	81.90	74.51
2.50%	675.73	342.08	230.89	175.31	141.98	119.77	103.91	92.03	82.80	75.42
2.75%	676.64	342.97	231.77	176.19	142.86	120.66	104.81	92.93	83.70	76.33
3.00%	677.55	343.85	232.65	177.07	143.75	121.55	105.71	93.84	84.62	77.25
3.25%	678.46	344.74	233.53	177.96	144.64	122.45	106.61	94.75	85.53	78.18
3.50%	679.37	345.62	234.42	178.85	145.53	123.35	107.52	95.66	86.46	79.11
3.75%	680.29	346.51	235.30	179.74	146.43	124.25	108.43	96.59	87.39	80.05
4.00%	681.20	347.40	236.19	180.63	147.33	125.16	109.35	97.51	88.33	81.00
4.25%	682.11	348.29	237.08	181.53	148.24	126.07	110.27	98.45	89.27	81.95
4.50%	683.03	349.18	237.98	182.43	149.14	126.99	111.20	99.39	90.22	82.91
4.75%	683.94	350.08	238.87	183.33	150.06	127.91	112.13	100.33	91.18	83.88
5.00%	684.86	350.97	239.77	184.23	150.97	128.84	113.07	101.28	92.14	84.85
5.25%	685.78	351.87	240.67	185.14	151.89	129.77	114.01	102.23	93.11	85.83
5.50%	686.69	352.77	241.57	186.05	152.81	130.70	114.96	103.19	94.08	86.82
5.75%	687.61	353.66	242.47	186.96	153.73	131.64	115.91	104.16	95.06	87.82
6.00%	688.53	354.56	243.38	187.88	154.66	132.58	116.87	105.13	96.05	88.82
6.25%	689.45	355.47	244.28	188.80	155.59	133.53	117.83	106.11	97.04	89.82
6.50%	690.37	356.37	245.19	189.72	156.53	134.48	118.80	107.09	98.04	90.84
6.75%	691.29	357.27	246.10	190.64	157.47	135.43	119.77	108.08	99.04	91.86
7.00%	692.21	358.18	247.02	191.57	158.41	136.39	120.74	109.07	100.05	92.89
7.25%	693.14	359.09	247.93	192.50	159.35	137.35	121.72	110.07	101.07	93.92
7.50%	694.06	360.00	248.85	193.43	160.30	138.32	122.71	111.07	102.09	94.96
7.75%	694.98	360.91	249.77	194.37	161.26	139.29	123.70	112.08	103.12	96.01
8.00%	695.91	361.82	250.69	195.30	162.21	140.27	124.69	113.09	104.15	97.06
8.25%	696.83	362.73	251.61	196.24	163.17	141.24	125.69	114.11	105.19	98.12
8.50%	697.76	363.65	252.54	197.19	164.13	142.23	126.69	115.14	106.23	99.19
8.75%	698.68	364.56	253.47	198.13	165.10	143.21	127.70	116.17	107.29	100.26
9.00%	699.61	365.48	254.40	199.08	166.07	144.20	128.71	117.20	108.34	101.34
9.25%	700.54	366.40	255.33	200.03	167.04	145.20	129.73	118.24	109.41	102.43
9.50%	701.47	367.32	256.26	200.99	168.01	146.20	130.75	119.29	110.47	103.52
9.75%	702.40	368.24	257.20	201.94	168.99	147.20	131.78	120.34	111.55	104.62
10.00%	703.33	369.16	258.14	202.90	169.98	148.21	132.81	121.39	112.63	105.72
10.25%	704.26	370.08	259.08	203.86	170.96	149.22	133.85	122.45	113.72	106.83
10.50%	705.19	371.01	260.02	204.83	171.95	150.23	134.89	123.52	114.81	107.95
10.75%	706.12	371.93	260.96	205.79	172.94	151.25	135.93	124.59	115.90	109.07

$8,000   11.00 - 20.75%   1 - 10 Years

	1	2	3	4	5	6	7	8	9	10
11.00%	707.05	372.86	261.91	206.76	173.94	152.27	136.98	125.67	117.01	110.20
11.25%	707.99	373.79	262.86	207.74	174.94	153.30	138.03	126.75	118.12	111.34
11.50%	708.92	374.72	263.81	208.71	175.94	154.33	139.09	127.83	119.23	112.48
11.75%	709.86	375.65	264.76	209.69	176.95	155.36	140.15	128.93	120.35	113.62
12.00%	710.79	376.59	265.71	210.67	177.96	156.40	141.22	130.02	121.47	114.78
12.25%	711.73	377.52	266.67	211.65	178.97	157.44	142.29	131.12	122.60	115.94
12.50%	712.66	378.46	267.63	212.64	179.98	158.49	143.37	132.23	123.74	117.10
12.75%	713.60	379.40	268.59	213.63	181.00	159.54	144.45	133.34	124.88	118.27
13.00%	714.54	380.33	269.55	214.62	182.02	160.59	145.54	134.46	126.03	119.45
13.25%	715.48	381.27	270.52	215.61	183.05	161.65	146.63	135.58	127.18	120.63
13.50%	716.42	382.22	271.48	216.61	184.08	162.71	147.72	136.71	128.34	121.82
13.75%	717.36	383.16	272.45	217.61	185.11	163.78	148.82	137.84	129.50	123.01
14.00%	718.30	384.10	273.42	218.61	186.15	164.85	149.92	138.97	130.67	124.21
14.25%	719.24	385.05	274.39	219.62	187.18	165.92	151.03	140.11	131.84	125.42
14.50%	720.18	386.00	275.37	220.62	188.23	167.00	152.14	141.26	133.02	126.63
14.75%	721.12	386.94	276.34	221.63	189.27	168.08	153.25	142.41	134.21	127.85
15.00%	722.07	387.89	277.32	222.65	190.32	169.16	154.37	143.56	135.39	129.07
15.25%	723.01	388.84	278.30	223.66	191.37	170.25	155.50	144.72	136.59	130.30
15.50%	723.96	389.80	279.29	224.68	192.43	171.34	156.63	145.89	137.79	131.53
15.75%	724.90	390.75	280.27	225.70	193.48	172.44	157.76	147.06	138.99	132.77
16.00%	725.85	391.70	281.26	226.72	194.54	173.53	158.90	148.23	140.20	134.01
16.25%	726.79	392.66	282.24	227.75	195.61	174.64	160.04	149.41	141.42	135.26
16.50%	727.74	393.62	283.24	228.78	196.68	175.74	161.18	150.59	142.64	136.51
16.75%	728.69	394.58	284.23	229.81	197.75	176.85	162.33	151.78	143.86	137.77
17.00%	729.64	395.54	285.22	230.84	198.82	177.97	163.49	152.97	145.09	139.04
17.25%	730.59	396.50	286.22	231.88	199.90	179.09	164.64	154.17	146.32	140.31
17.50%	731.54	397.46	287.22	232.91	200.98	180.21	165.81	155.37	147.56	141.58
17.75%	732.49	398.43	288.22	233.96	202.06	181.33	166.97	156.58	148.81	142.86
18.00%	733.44	399.39	289.22	235.00	203.15	182.46	168.14	157.79	150.06	144.15
18.25%	734.39	400.36	290.22	236.05	204.24	183.59	169.32	159.00	151.31	145.44
18.50%	735.34	401.33	291.23	237.10	205.33	184.73	170.50	160.22	152.57	146.73
18.75%	736.30	402.30	292.24	238.15	206.43	185.87	171.68	161.44	153.83	148.03
19.00%	737.25	403.27	293.25	239.20	207.52	187.01	172.86	162.67	155.10	149.34
19.25%	738.21	404.24	294.26	240.26	208.63	188.16	174.05	163.90	156.37	150.65
19.50%	739.16	405.22	295.27	241.32	209.73	189.31	175.25	165.14	157.65	151.96
19.75%	740.12	406.19	296.29	242.38	210.84	190.47	176.45	166.38	158.93	153.28
20.00%	741.08	407.17	297.31	243.44	211.95	191.62	177.65	167.63	160.21	154.60
20.25%	742.03	408.14	298.33	244.51	213.07	192.78	178.86	168.87	161.50	155.93
20.50%	742.99	409.12	299.35	245.58	214.18	193.95	180.07	170.13	162.80	157.27
20.75%	743.95	410.10	300.37	246.65	215.30	195.12	181.28	171.39	164.10	158.60

	1	2	3	4	5	6	7	8	9	10
1.00%	754.07	378.92	253.87	191.35	153.84	128.84	110.98	97.59	87.17	78.84
1.25%	755.09	379.90	254.85	192.32	154.81	129.81	111.95	98.56	88.15	79.82
1.50%	756.11	380.89	255.82	193.30	155.79	130.79	112.93	99.55	89.14	80.81
1.75%	757.13	381.87	256.80	194.28	156.77	131.77	113.92	100.53	90.13	81.81
2.00%	758.15	382.86	257.78	195.26	157.75	132.75	114.91	101.53	91.13	82.81
2.25%	759.17	383.85	258.77	196.24	158.74	133.74	115.90	102.53	92.13	83.82
2.50%	760.20	384.84	259.75	197.23	159.73	134.74	116.90	103.53	93.15	84.84
2.75%	761.22	385.84	260.74	198.22	160.72	135.74	117.91	104.55	94.17	85.87
3.00%	762.24	386.83	261.73	199.21	161.72	136.74	118.92	105.57	95.19	86.90
3.25%	763.27	387.83	262.72	200.20	162.72	137.75	119.94	106.59	96.23	87.95
3.50%	764.29	388.82	263.72	201.20	163.73	138.77	120.96	107.62	97.27	89.00
3.75%	765.32	389.82	264.72	202.21	164.74	139.78	121.99	108.66	98.31	90.06
4.00%	766.35	390.82	265.72	203.21	165.75	140.81	123.02	109.70	99.37	91.12
4.25%	767.38	391.83	266.72	204.22	166.77	141.83	124.06	110.75	100.43	92.19
4.50%	768.41	392.83	267.72	205.23	167.79	142.87	125.10	111.81	101.50	93.27
4.75%	769.44	393.84	268.73	206.25	168.81	143.90	126.15	112.87	102.57	94.36
5.00%	770.47	394.84	269.74	207.26	169.84	144.94	127.21	113.94	103.66	95.46
5.25%	771.50	395.85	270.75	208.28	170.87	145.99	128.27	115.01	104.74	96.56
5.50%	772.53	396.86	271.76	209.31	171.91	147.04	129.33	116.09	105.84	97.67
5.75%	773.56	397.87	272.78	210.34	172.95	148.10	130.40	117.18	106.94	98.79
6.00%	774.60	398.89	273.80	211.37	174.00	149.16	131.48	118.27	108.05	99.92
6.25%	775.63	399.90	274.82	212.40	175.04	150.22	132.56	119.37	109.17	101.05
6.50%	776.67	400.92	275.84	213.43	176.10	151.29	133.64	120.48	110.29	102.19
6.75%	777.70	401.93	276.87	214.47	177.15	152.36	134.74	121.59	111.42	103.34
7.00%	778.74	402.95	277.89	215.52	178.21	153.44	135.83	122.70	112.56	104.50
7.25%	779.78	403.97	278.92	216.56	179.27	154.52	136.94	123.83	113.70	105.66
7.50%	780.82	405.00	279.96	217.61	180.34	155.61	138.04	124.95	114.85	106.83
7.75%	781.86	406.02	280.99	218.66	181.41	156.70	139.16	126.09	116.01	108.01
8.00%	782.90	407.05	282.03	219.72	182.49	157.80	140.28	127.23	117.17	109.19
8.25%	783.94	408.07	283.07	220.77	183.57	158.90	141.40	128.38	118.34	110.39
8.50%	784.98	409.10	284.11	221.83	184.65	160.01	142.53	129.53	119.51	111.59
8.75%	786.02	410.13	285.15	222.90	185.74	161.12	143.66	130.69	120.70	112.79
9.00%	787.06	411.16	286.20	223.97	186.83	162.23	144.80	131.85	121.89	114.01
9.25%	788.11	412.20	287.25	225.04	187.92	163.35	145.95	133.02	123.08	115.23
9.50%	789.15	413.23	288.30	226.11	189.02	164.47	147.10	134.20	124.28	116.46
9.75%	790.20	414.27	289.35	227.18	190.12	165.60	148.25	135.38	125.49	117.69
10.00%	791.24	415.30	290.40	228.26	191.22	166.73	149.41	136.57	126.71	118.94
10.25%	792.29	416.34	291.46	229.35	192.33	167.87	150.58	137.76	127.93	120.19
10.50%	793.34	417.38	292.52	230.43	193.45	169.01	151.75	138.96	129.16	121.44
10.75%	794.39	418.43	293.58	231.52	194.56	170.16	152.92	140.17	130.39	122.70

$9,000   11.00 - 20.75%   1 - 10 Years

	1	2	3	4	5	6	7	8	9	10
11.00%	795.43	419.47	294.65	232.61	195.68	171.31	154.10	141.38	131.63	123.98
11.25%	796.48	420.52	295.72	233.70	196.81	172.46	155.29	142.59	132.88	125.25
11.50%	797.54	421.56	296.78	234.80	197.93	173.62	156.48	143.81	134.13	126.54
11.75%	798.59	422.61	297.86	235.90	199.06	174.78	157.67	145.04	135.39	127.83
12.00%	799.64	423.66	298.93	237.00	200.20	175.95	158.87	146.28	136.66	129.12
12.25%	800.69	424.71	300.00	238.11	201.34	177.12	160.08	147.51	137.93	130.43
12.50%	801.75	425.77	301.08	239.22	202.48	178.30	161.29	148.76	139.21	131.74
12.75%	802.80	426.82	302.16	240.33	203.63	179.48	162.51	150.01	140.49	133.06
13.00%	803.86	427.88	303.25	241.45	204.78	180.67	163.73	151.27	141.78	134.38
13.25%	804.91	428.93	304.33	242.57	205.93	181.86	164.95	152.53	143.08	135.71
13.50%	805.97	429.99	305.42	243.69	207.09	183.05	166.18	153.79	144.38	137.05
13.75%	807.03	431.05	306.51	244.81	208.25	184.25	167.42	155.07	145.69	138.39
14.00%	808.08	432.12	307.60	245.94	209.41	185.45	168.66	156.34	147.00	139.74
14.25%	809.14	433.18	308.69	247.07	210.58	186.66	169.91	157.63	148.32	141.10
14.50%	810.20	434.24	309.79	248.20	211.75	187.87	171.16	158.92	149.65	142.46
14.75%	811.26	435.31	310.89	249.34	212.93	189.09	172.41	160.21	150.98	143.83
15.00%	812.32	436.38	311.99	250.48	214.11	190.31	173.67	161.51	152.32	145.20
15.25%	813.39	437.45	313.09	251.62	215.29	191.53	174.94	162.81	153.66	146.58
15.50%	814.45	438.52	314.20	252.76	216.48	192.76	176.21	164.12	155.01	147.97
15.75%	815.51	439.59	315.30	253.91	217.67	193.99	177.48	165.44	156.37	149.36
16.00%	816.58	440.67	316.41	255.06	218.86	195.23	178.76	166.76	157.73	150.76
16.25%	817.64	441.74	317.53	256.22	220.06	196.47	180.04	168.08	159.09	152.17
16.50%	818.71	442.82	318.64	257.37	221.26	197.71	181.33	169.42	160.47	153.58
16.75%	819.78	443.90	319.76	258.53	222.47	198.96	182.62	170.75	161.84	155.00
17.00%	820.84	444.98	320.87	259.70	223.67	200.22	183.92	172.09	163.23	156.42
17.25%	821.91	446.06	322.00	260.86	224.88	201.47	185.22	173.44	164.61	157.85
17.50%	822.98	447.15	323.12	262.03	226.10	202.73	186.53	174.79	166.01	159.28
17.75%	824.05	448.23	324.24	263.20	227.32	204.00	187.84	176.15	167.41	160.72
18.00%	825.12	449.32	325.37	264.37	228.54	205.27	189.16	177.51	168.81	162.17
18.25%	826.19	450.40	326.50	265.55	229.77	206.54	190.48	178.88	170.22	163.62
18.50%	827.26	451.49	327.63	266.73	231.00	207.82	191.81	180.25	171.64	165.07
18.75%	828.34	452.59	328.77	267.92	232.23	209.10	193.14	181.62	173.06	166.54
19.00%	829.41	453.68	329.90	269.10	233.46	210.39	194.47	183.00	174.48	168.01
19.25%	830.48	454.77	331.04	270.29	234.70	211.68	195.81	184.39	175.91	169.48
19.50%	831.56	455.87	332.18	271.48	235.95	212.97	197.16	185.78	177.35	170.96
19.75%	832.63	456.96	333.33	272.68	237.19	214.27	198.50	187.18	178.79	172.44
20.00%	833.71	458.06	334.47	273.87	238.44	215.58	199.86	188.58	180.24	173.93
20.25%	834.79	459.16	335.62	275.07	239.70	216.88	201.21	189.98	181.69	175.42
20.50%	835.87	460.26	336.77	276.28	240.96	218.19	202.57	191.39	183.15	176.92
20.75%	836.94	461.37	337.92	277.48	242.22	219.51	203.94	192.81	184.61	178.43

	1	2	3	4	5	6	7	8	9	10
1.00%	837.85	421.02	282.08	212.61	170.94	143.16	123.31	108.43	96.86	87.60
1.25%	838.99	422.11	283.16	213.69	172.02	144.23	124.39	109.52	97.95	88.69
1.50%	840.12	423.21	284.25	214.78	173.10	145.32	125.48	110.61	99.04	89.79
1.75%	841.25	424.30	285.34	215.86	174.19	146.41	126.57	111.70	100.14	90.90
2.00%	842.39	425.40	286.43	216.95	175.28	147.50	127.67	112.81	101.25	92.01
2.25%	843.52	426.50	287.52	218.04	176.37	148.60	128.78	113.92	102.37	93.14
2.50%	844.66	427.60	288.61	219.14	177.47	149.71	129.89	115.04	103.50	94.27
2.75%	845.80	428.71	289.71	220.24	178.58	150.82	131.01	116.16	104.63	95.41
3.00%	846.94	429.81	290.81	221.34	179.69	151.94	132.13	117.30	105.77	96.56
3.25%	848.08	430.92	291.92	222.45	180.80	153.06	133.26	118.43	106.92	97.72
3.50%	849.22	432.03	293.02	223.56	181.92	154.18	134.40	119.58	108.07	98.89
3.75%	850.36	433.14	294.13	224.67	183.04	155.32	135.54	120.73	109.24	100.06
4.00%	851.50	434.25	295.24	225.79	184.17	156.45	136.69	121.89	110.41	101.25
4.25%	852.64	435.36	296.35	226.91	185.30	157.59	137.84	123.06	111.59	102.44
4.50%	853.79	436.48	297.47	228.03	186.43	158.74	139.00	124.23	112.78	103.64
4.75%	854.93	437.60	298.59	229.16	187.57	159.89	140.17	125.41	113.97	104.85
5.00%	856.07	438.71	299.71	230.29	188.71	161.05	141.34	126.60	115.17	106.07
5.25%	857.22	439.83	300.83	231.43	189.86	162.21	142.52	127.79	116.38	107.29
5.50%	858.37	440.96	301.96	232.56	191.01	163.38	143.70	128.99	117.60	108.53
5.75%	859.52	442.08	303.09	233.71	192.17	164.55	144.89	130.20	118.82	109.77
6.00%	860.66	443.21	304.22	234.85	193.33	165.73	146.09	131.41	120.06	111.02
6.25%	861.81	444.33	305.35	236.00	194.49	166.91	147.29	132.63	121.30	112.28
6.50%	862.96	445.46	306.49	237.15	195.66	168.10	148.49	133.86	122.55	113.55
6.75%	864.12	446.59	307.63	238.30	196.83	169.29	149.71	135.10	123.80	114.82
7.00%	865.27	447.73	308.77	239.46	198.01	170.49	150.93	136.34	125.06	116.11
7.25%	866.42	448.86	309.92	240.62	199.19	171.69	152.15	137.58	126.33	117.40
7.50%	867.57	450.00	311.06	241.79	200.38	172.90	153.38	138.84	127.61	118.70
7.75%	868.73	451.13	312.21	242.96	201.57	174.11	154.62	140.10	128.89	120.01
8.00%	869.88	452.27	313.36	244.13	202.76	175.33	155.86	141.37	130.19	121.33
8.25%	871.04	453.41	314.52	245.30	203.96	176.56	157.11	142.64	131.49	122.65
8.50%	872.20	454.56	315.68	246.48	205.17	177.78	158.36	143.92	132.79	123.99
8.75%	873.36	455.70	316.84	247.67	206.37	179.02	159.62	145.21	134.11	125.33
9.00%	874.51	456.85	318.00	248.85	207.58	180.26	160.89	146.50	135.43	126.68
9.25%	875.67	458.00	319.16	250.04	208.80	181.50	162.16	147.80	136.76	128.03
9.50%	876.84	459.14	320.33	251.23	210.02	182.75	163.44	149.11	138.09	129.40
9.75%	878.00	460.30	321.50	252.43	211.24	184.00	164.72	150.42	139.44	130.77
10.00%	879.16	461.45	322.67	253.63	212.47	185.26	166.01	151.74	140.79	132.15
10.25%	880.32	462.60	323.85	254.83	213.70	186.52	167.31	153.07	142.14	133.54
10.50%	881.49	463.76	325.02	256.03	214.94	187.79	168.61	154.40	143.51	134.93
10.75%	882.65	464.92	326.20	257.24	216.18	189.06	169.91	155.74	144.88	136.34

$10,000   11.00 - 20.75%   1 - 10 Years

	1	2	3	4	5	6	7	8	9	10
11.00%	883.82	466.08	327.39	258.46	217.42	190.34	171.22	157.08	146.26	137.75
11.25%	884.98	467.24	328.57	259.67	218.67	191.62	172.54	158.44	147.64	139.17
11.50%	886.15	468.40	329.76	260.89	219.93	192.91	173.86	159.79	149.04	140.60
11.75%	887.32	469.57	330.95	262.11	221.18	194.20	175.19	161.16	150.44	142.03
12.00%	888.49	470.73	332.14	263.34	222.44	195.50	176.53	162.53	151.84	143.47
12.25%	889.66	471.90	333.34	264.57	223.71	196.80	177.87	163.91	153.26	144.92
12.50%	890.83	473.07	334.54	265.80	224.98	198.11	179.21	165.29	154.68	146.38
12.75%	892.00	474.24	335.74	267.04	226.25	199.42	180.56	166.68	156.10	147.84
13.00%	893.17	475.42	336.94	268.27	227.53	200.74	181.92	168.07	157.54	149.31
13.25%	894.35	476.59	338.14	269.52	228.81	202.06	183.28	169.47	158.98	150.79
13.50%	895.52	477.77	339.35	270.76	230.10	203.39	184.65	170.88	160.42	152.27
13.75%	896.70	478.95	340.56	272.01	231.39	204.72	186.02	172.30	161.88	153.77
14.00%	897.87	480.13	341.78	273.26	232.68	206.06	187.40	173.72	163.34	155.27
14.25%	899.05	481.31	342.99	274.52	233.98	207.40	188.78	175.14	164.80	156.77
14.50%	900.23	482.49	344.21	275.78	235.28	208.74	190.17	176.57	166.28	158.29
14.75%	901.40	483.68	345.43	277.04	236.59	210.09	191.57	178.01	167.76	159.81
15.00%	902.58	484.87	346.65	278.31	237.90	211.45	192.97	179.45	169.24	161.33
15.25%	903.76	486.06	347.88	279.58	239.21	212.81	194.37	180.90	170.74	162.87
15.50%	904.94	487.25	349.11	280.85	240.53	214.17	195.78	182.36	172.24	164.41
15.75%	906.13	488.44	350.34	282.12	241.85	215.54	197.20	183.82	173.74	165.96
16.00%	907.31	489.63	351.57	283.40	243.18	216.92	198.62	185.29	175.25	167.51
16.25%	908.49	490.83	352.81	284.68	244.51	218.30	200.05	186.76	176.77	169.07
16.50%	909.68	492.02	354.04	285.97	245.85	219.68	201.48	188.24	178.29	170.64
16.75%	910.86	493.22	355.28	287.26	247.18	221.07	202.92	189.72	179.83	172.22
17.00%	912.05	494.42	356.53	288.55	248.53	222.46	204.36	191.21	181.36	173.80
17.25%	913.23	495.62	357.77	289.85	249.87	223.86	205.81	192.71	182.90	175.39
17.50%	914.42	496.83	359.02	291.14	251.22	225.26	207.26	194.21	184.45	176.98
17.75%	915.61	498.03	360.27	292.45	252.58	226.67	208.72	195.72	186.01	178.58
18.00%	916.80	499.24	361.52	293.75	253.93	228.08	210.18	197.23	187.57	180.19
18.25%	917.99	500.45	362.78	295.06	255.30	229.49	211.65	198.75	189.14	181.80
18.50%	919.18	501.66	364.04	296.37	256.66	230.91	213.12	200.27	190.71	183.42
18.75%	920.37	502.87	365.30	297.68	258.03	232.34	214.60	201.80	192.29	185.04
19.00%	921.57	504.09	366.56	299.00	259.41	233.77	216.08	203.34	193.87	186.67
19.25%	922.76	505.30	367.83	300.32	260.78	235.20	217.57	204.88	195.46	188.31
19.50%	923.95	506.52	369.09	301.65	262.16	236.64	219.06	206.42	197.06	189.95
19.75%	925.15	507.74	370.36	302.97	263.55	238.08	220.56	207.98	198.66	191.60
20.00%	926.35	508.96	371.64	304.30	264.94	239.53	222.06	209.53	200.27	193.26
20.25%	927.54	510.18	372.91	305.64	266.33	240.98	223.57	211.09	201.88	194.92
20.50%	928.74	511.40	374.19	306.97	267.73	242.44	225.08	212.66	203.50	196.58
20.75%	929.94	512.63	375.47	308.31	269.13	243.90	226.60	214.23	205.12	198.25

	1	2	3	4	5	6	7	8	9	10
1.00%	921.64	463.12	310.29	233.88	188.03	157.47	135.64	119.28	106.55	96.36
1.25%	922.89	464.33	311.48	235.06	189.22	158.66	136.83	120.47	107.74	97.56
1.50%	924.13	465.53	312.67	236.25	190.41	159.85	138.03	121.67	108.95	98.77
1.75%	925.38	466.74	313.87	237.45	191.60	161.05	139.23	122.87	110.16	99.99
2.00%	926.63	467.94	315.07	238.65	192.81	162.25	140.44	124.09	111.38	101.21
2.25%	927.88	469.15	316.27	239.85	194.01	163.47	141.66	125.31	112.61	102.45
2.50%	929.13	470.36	317.48	241.05	195.22	164.68	142.88	126.54	113.85	103.70
2.75%	930.38	471.58	318.68	242.26	196.44	165.90	144.11	127.78	115.09	104.95
3.00%	931.63	472.79	319.89	243.48	197.66	167.13	145.35	129.03	116.35	106.22
3.25%	932.88	474.01	321.11	244.69	198.88	168.36	146.59	130.28	117.61	107.49
3.50%	934.14	475.23	322.32	245.92	200.11	169.60	147.84	131.54	118.88	108.77
3.75%	935.39	476.45	323.54	247.14	201.34	170.85	149.09	132.81	120.16	110.07
4.00%	936.65	477.67	324.76	248.37	202.58	172.10	150.36	134.08	121.45	111.37
4.25%	937.91	478.90	325.99	249.60	203.83	173.35	151.63	135.37	122.75	112.68
4.50%	939.16	480.13	327.22	250.84	205.07	174.61	152.90	136.66	124.05	114.00
4.75%	940.42	481.35	328.45	252.08	206.33	175.88	154.18	137.95	125.37	115.33
5.00%	941.68	482.59	329.68	253.32	207.58	177.15	155.47	139.26	126.69	116.67
5.25%	942.94	483.82	330.92	254.57	208.85	178.43	156.77	140.57	128.02	118.02
5.50%	944.20	485.05	332.15	255.82	210.11	179.72	158.07	141.89	129.36	119.38
5.75%	945.47	486.29	333.40	257.08	211.38	181.01	159.38	143.22	130.71	120.75
6.00%	946.73	487.53	334.64	258.34	212.66	182.30	160.69	144.56	132.06	122.12
6.25%	948.00	488.77	335.89	259.60	213.94	183.60	162.02	145.90	133.43	123.51
6.50%	949.26	490.01	337.14	260.86	215.23	184.91	163.34	147.25	134.80	124.90
6.75%	950.53	491.25	338.39	262.13	216.52	186.22	164.68	148.61	136.18	126.31
7.00%	951.79	492.50	339.65	263.41	217.81	187.54	166.02	149.97	137.57	127.72
7.25%	953.06	493.75	340.91	264.69	219.11	188.86	167.37	151.34	138.97	129.14
7.50%	954.33	495.00	342.17	265.97	220.42	190.19	168.72	152.72	140.37	130.57
7.75%	955.60	496.25	343.43	267.25	221.73	191.53	170.08	154.11	141.78	132.01
8.00%	956.87	497.50	344.70	268.54	223.04	192.87	171.45	155.50	143.21	133.46
8.25%	958.14	498.76	345.97	269.83	224.36	194.21	172.82	156.90	144.64	134.92
8.50%	959.42	500.01	347.24	271.13	225.68	195.56	174.20	158.31	146.07	136.38
8.75%	960.69	501.27	348.52	272.43	227.01	196.92	175.59	159.73	147.52	137.86
9.00%	961.97	502.53	349.80	273.74	228.34	198.28	176.98	161.15	148.97	139.34
9.25%	963.24	503.79	351.08	275.04	229.68	199.65	178.38	162.58	150.43	140.84
9.50%	964.52	505.06	352.36	276.35	231.02	201.02	179.78	164.02	151.90	142.34
9.75%	965.80	506.33	353.65	277.67	232.37	202.40	181.20	165.46	153.38	143.85
10.00%	967.07	507.59	354.94	278.99	233.72	203.78	182.61	166.92	154.87	145.37
10.25%	968.35	508.86	356.23	280.31	235.07	205.17	184.04	168.37	156.36	146.89
10.50%	969.63	510.14	357.53	281.64	236.43	206.57	185.47	169.84	157.86	148.43
10.75%	970.92	511.41	358.82	282.97	237.80	207.97	186.90	171.31	159.37	149.97

$11,000   11.00 - 20.75%   1 - 10 Years

	1	2	3	4	5	6	7	8	9	10
11.00%	972.20	512.69	360.13	284.30	239.17	209.37	188.35	172.79	160.88	151.53
11.25%	973.48	513.96	361.43	285.64	240.54	210.79	189.80	174.28	162.41	153.09
11.50%	974.77	515.24	362.74	286.98	241.92	212.20	191.25	175.77	163.94	154.65
11.75%	976.05	516.52	364.05	288.32	243.30	213.62	192.71	177.27	165.48	156.23
12.00%	977.34	517.81	365.36	289.67	244.69	215.05	194.18	178.78	167.03	157.82
12.25%	978.62	519.09	366.67	291.02	246.08	216.48	195.65	180.30	168.58	159.41
12.50%	979.91	520.38	367.99	292.38	247.48	217.92	197.13	181.82	170.14	161.01
12.75%	981.20	521.67	369.31	293.74	248.88	219.37	198.62	183.34	171.71	162.62
13.00%	982.49	522.96	370.63	295.10	250.28	220.82	200.11	184.88	173.29	164.24
13.25%	983.78	524.25	371.96	296.47	251.69	222.27	201.61	186.42	174.87	165.87
13.50%	985.07	525.55	373.29	297.84	253.11	223.73	203.11	187.97	176.47	167.50
13.75%	986.36	526.84	374.62	299.21	254.53	225.19	204.62	189.52	178.06	169.14
14.00%	987.66	528.14	375.95	300.59	255.95	226.66	206.14	191.09	179.67	170.79
14.25%	988.95	529.44	377.29	301.97	257.38	228.14	207.66	192.65	181.28	172.45
14.50%	990.25	530.74	378.63	303.36	258.81	229.62	209.19	194.23	182.90	174.12
14.75%	991.54	532.05	379.97	304.75	260.25	231.10	210.72	195.81	184.53	175.79
15.00%	992.84	533.35	381.32	306.14	261.69	232.60	212.26	197.40	186.17	177.47
15.25%	994.14	534.66	382.67	307.53	263.13	234.09	213.81	198.99	187.81	179.16
15.50%	995.44	535.97	384.02	308.93	264.59	235.59	215.36	200.60	189.46	180.85
15.75%	996.74	537.28	385.37	310.34	266.04	237.10	216.92	202.20	191.11	182.55
16.00%	998.04	538.59	386.73	311.74	267.50	238.61	218.48	203.82	192.78	184.26
16.25%	999.34	539.91	388.09	313.15	268.96	240.13	220.05	205.44	194.45	185.98
16.50%	1,000.64	541.23	389.45	314.57	270.43	241.65	221.63	207.06	196.12	187.71
16.75%	1,001.95	542.54	390.81	315.98	271.90	243.18	223.21	208.70	197.81	189.44
17.00%	1,003.25	543.86	392.18	317.41	273.38	244.71	224.79	210.34	199.50	191.18
17.25%	1,004.56	545.19	393.55	318.83	274.86	246.24	226.39	211.98	201.20	192.92
17.50%	1,005.86	546.51	394.92	320.26	276.34	247.79	227.98	213.63	202.90	194.68
17.75%	1,007.17	547.84	396.30	321.69	277.83	249.33	229.59	215.29	204.61	196.44
18.00%	1,008.48	549.17	397.68	323.12	279.33	250.89	231.20	216.96	206.33	198.20
18.25%	1,009.79	550.49	399.06	324.56	280.83	252.44	232.81	218.63	208.05	199.98
18.50%	1,011.10	551.83	400.44	326.01	282.33	254.00	234.43	220.30	209.78	201.76
18.75%	1,012.41	553.16	401.83	327.45	283.84	255.57	236.06	221.98	211.52	203.55
19.00%	1,013.72	554.49	403.22	328.90	285.35	257.14	237.69	223.67	213.26	205.34
19.25%	1,015.04	555.83	404.61	330.35	286.86	258.72	239.33	225.37	215.01	207.14
19.50%	1,016.35	557.17	406.00	331.81	288.38	260.30	240.97	227.07	216.76	208.95
19.75%	1,017.66	558.51	407.40	333.27	289.90	261.89	242.62	228.77	218.52	210.76
20.00%	1,018.98	559.85	408.80	334.73	291.43	263.48	244.27	230.49	220.29	212.58
20.25%	1,020.30	561.20	410.20	336.20	292.96	265.08	245.93	232.20	222.07	214.41
20.50%	1,021.61	562.54	411.61	337.67	294.50	266.68	247.59	233.93	223.85	216.24
20.75%	1,022.93	563.89	413.02	339.15	296.04	268.29	249.26	235.66	225.63	218.08

	1	2	3	4	5	6	7	8	9	10
1.00%	1,005.42	505.22	338.50	255.14	205.12	171.79	147.97	130.12	116.23	105.12
1.25%	1,006.78	506.54	339.80	256.43	206.42	173.08	149.27	131.42	117.54	106.43
1.50%	1,008.14	507.85	341.10	257.73	207.72	174.38	150.58	132.73	118.85	107.75
1.75%	1,009.50	509.17	342.40	259.03	209.02	175.69	151.89	134.05	120.17	109.08
2.00%	1,010.87	510.48	343.71	260.34	210.33	177.01	153.21	135.37	121.50	110.42
2.25%	1,012.23	511.80	345.02	261.65	211.65	178.33	154.54	136.70	122.84	111.76
2.50%	1,013.59	513.12	346.34	262.97	212.97	179.65	155.87	138.05	124.19	113.12
2.75%	1,014.96	514.45	347.65	264.29	214.29	180.99	157.21	139.40	125.55	114.49
3.00%	1,016.32	515.77	348.97	265.61	215.62	182.32	158.56	140.75	126.92	115.87
3.25%	1,017.69	517.10	350.30	266.94	216.96	183.67	159.92	142.12	128.30	117.26
3.50%	1,019.06	518.43	351.62	268.27	218.30	185.02	161.28	143.50	129.69	118.66
3.75%	1,020.43	519.76	352.95	269.61	219.65	186.38	162.65	144.88	131.09	120.07
4.00%	1,021.80	521.10	354.29	270.95	221.00	187.74	164.03	146.27	132.49	121.49
4.25%	1,023.17	522.44	355.62	272.29	222.35	189.11	165.41	147.67	133.91	122.93
4.50%	1,024.54	523.77	356.96	273.64	223.72	190.49	166.80	149.08	135.33	124.37
4.75%	1,025.92	525.11	358.31	274.99	225.08	191.87	168.20	150.49	136.76	125.82
5.00%	1,027.29	526.46	359.65	276.35	226.45	193.26	169.61	151.92	138.21	127.28
5.25%	1,028.67	527.80	361.00	277.71	227.83	194.65	171.02	153.35	139.66	128.75
5.50%	1,030.04	529.15	362.35	279.08	229.21	196.05	172.44	154.79	141.12	130.23
5.75%	1,031.42	530.50	363.71	280.45	230.60	197.46	173.87	156.24	142.59	131.72
6.00%	1,032.80	531.85	365.06	281.82	231.99	198.87	175.30	157.70	144.07	133.22
6.25%	1,034.18	533.20	366.42	283.20	233.39	200.29	176.74	159.16	145.56	134.74
6.50%	1,035.56	534.56	367.79	284.58	234.79	201.72	178.19	160.63	147.05	136.26
6.75%	1,036.94	535.91	369.16	285.97	236.20	203.15	179.65	162.12	148.56	137.79
7.00%	1,038.32	537.27	370.53	287.35	237.61	204.59	181.11	163.60	150.08	139.33
7.25%	1,039.70	538.63	371.90	288.75	239.03	206.03	182.58	165.10	151.60	140.88
7.50%	1,041.09	540.00	373.27	290.15	240.46	207.48	184.06	166.61	153.13	142.44
7.75%	1,042.47	541.36	374.65	291.55	241.88	208.94	185.54	168.12	154.67	144.01
8.00%	1,043.86	542.73	376.04	292.96	243.32	210.40	187.03	169.64	156.22	145.59
8.25%	1,045.25	544.10	377.42	294.37	244.76	211.87	188.53	171.17	157.78	147.18
8.50%	1,046.64	545.47	378.81	295.78	246.20	213.34	190.04	172.71	159.35	148.78
8.75%	1,048.03	546.84	380.20	297.20	247.65	214.82	191.55	174.25	160.93	150.39
9.00%	1,049.42	548.22	381.60	298.62	249.10	216.31	193.07	175.80	162.51	152.01
9.25%	1,050.81	549.59	382.99	300.05	250.56	217.80	194.59	177.36	164.11	153.64
9.50%	1,052.20	550.97	384.40	301.48	252.02	219.30	196.13	178.93	165.71	155.28
9.75%	1,053.60	552.36	385.80	302.91	253.49	220.80	197.67	180.51	167.32	156.92
10.00%	1,054.99	553.74	387.21	304.35	254.96	222.31	199.21	182.09	168.94	158.58
10.25%	1,056.39	555.12	388.62	305.79	256.44	223.83	200.77	183.68	170.57	160.25
10.50%	1,057.78	556.51	390.03	307.24	257.93	225.35	202.33	185.28	172.21	161.92
10.75%	1,059.18	557.90	391.45	308.69	259.42	226.88	203.90	186.89	173.86	163.61

$12,000   11.00 - 20.75%   1 - 10 Years

	1	2	3	4	5	6	7	8	9	10
11.00%	1,060.58	559.29	392.86	310.15	260.91	228.41	205.47	188.50	175.51	165.30
11.25%	1,061.98	560.69	394.29	311.61	262.41	229.95	207.05	190.12	177.17	167.00
11.50%	1,063.38	562.08	395.71	313.07	263.91	231.49	208.64	191.75	178.84	168.71
11.75%	1,064.78	563.48	397.14	314.54	265.42	233.05	210.23	193.39	180.52	170.44
12.00%	1,066.19	564.88	398.57	316.01	266.93	234.60	211.83	195.03	182.21	172.17
12.25%	1,067.59	566.28	400.01	317.48	268.45	236.17	213.44	196.69	183.91	173.90
12.50%	1,068.99	567.69	401.44	318.96	269.98	237.73	215.05	198.35	185.61	175.65
12.75%	1,070.40	569.09	402.88	320.44	271.50	239.31	216.68	200.01	187.32	177.41
13.00%	1,071.81	570.50	404.33	321.93	273.04	240.89	218.30	201.69	189.04	179.17
13.25%	1,073.22	571.91	405.77	323.42	274.58	242.48	219.94	203.37	190.77	180.95
13.50%	1,074.62	573.32	407.22	324.92	276.12	244.07	221.58	205.06	192.51	182.73
13.75%	1,076.03	574.74	408.68	326.41	277.67	245.67	223.23	206.75	194.25	184.52
14.00%	1,077.45	576.15	410.13	327.92	279.22	247.27	224.88	208.46	196.00	186.32
14.25%	1,078.86	577.57	411.59	329.42	280.78	248.88	226.54	210.17	197.76	188.13
14.50%	1,080.27	578.99	413.05	330.94	282.34	250.49	228.21	211.89	199.53	189.94
14.75%	1,081.68	580.42	414.52	332.45	283.91	252.11	229.88	213.61	201.31	191.77
15.00%	1,083.10	581.84	415.98	333.97	285.48	253.74	231.56	215.34	203.09	193.60
15.25%	1,084.52	583.27	417.45	335.49	287.06	255.37	233.25	217.08	204.88	195.44
15.50%	1,085.93	584.69	418.93	337.02	288.64	257.01	234.94	218.83	206.68	197.29
15.75%	1,087.35	586.12	420.40	338.55	290.23	258.65	236.64	220.58	208.49	199.15
16.00%	1,088.77	587.56	421.88	340.08	291.82	260.30	238.34	222.35	210.30	201.02
16.25%	1,090.19	588.99	423.37	341.62	293.41	261.96	240.06	224.11	212.12	202.89
16.50%	1,091.61	590.43	424.85	343.16	295.01	263.62	241.77	225.89	213.95	204.77
16.75%	1,093.03	591.87	426.34	344.71	296.62	265.28	243.50	227.67	215.79	206.66
17.00%	1,094.46	593.31	427.83	346.26	298.23	266.95	245.23	229.46	217.63	208.56
17.25%	1,095.88	594.75	429.33	347.81	299.85	268.63	246.97	231.25	219.49	210.46
17.50%	1,097.31	596.19	430.82	349.37	301.47	270.31	248.71	233.05	221.34	212.37
17.75%	1,098.73	597.64	432.33	350.93	303.09	272.00	250.46	234.86	223.21	214.29
18.00%	1,100.16	599.09	433.83	352.50	304.72	273.69	252.21	236.68	225.08	216.22
18.25%	1,101.59	600.54	435.34	354.07	306.36	275.39	253.98	238.50	226.96	218.16
18.50%	1,103.02	601.99	436.84	355.64	307.99	277.10	255.74	240.33	228.85	220.10
18.75%	1,104.45	603.45	438.36	357.22	309.64	278.81	257.52	242.16	230.74	222.05
19.00%	1,105.88	604.90	439.87	358.80	311.29	280.52	259.30	244.01	232.64	224.01
19.25%	1,107.31	606.36	441.39	360.39	312.94	282.24	261.08	245.85	234.55	225.97
19.50%	1,108.74	607.82	442.91	361.98	314.60	283.97	262.87	247.71	236.47	227.94
19.75%	1,110.18	609.29	444.44	363.57	316.26	285.70	264.67	249.57	238.39	229.92
20.00%	1,111.61	610.75	445.96	365.16	317.93	287.43	266.47	251.44	240.32	231.91
20.25%	1,113.05	612.22	447.49	366.76	319.60	289.18	268.28	253.31	242.25	233.90
20.50%	1,114.49	613.68	449.03	368.37	321.27	290.92	270.10	255.19	244.20	235.90
20.75%	1,115.93	615.16	450.56	369.98	322.96	292.67	271.92	257.08	246.14	237.91

	1	2	3	4	5	6	7	8	9	10
1.00%	1,089.21	547.33	366.71	276.40	222.22	186.10	160.31	140.96	125.92	113.89
1.25%	1,090.68	548.75	368.11	277.80	223.62	187.50	161.71	142.37	127.33	115.30
1.50%	1,092.16	550.17	369.52	279.21	225.03	188.92	163.13	143.79	128.75	116.73
1.75%	1,093.63	551.60	370.94	280.62	226.44	190.33	164.55	145.22	130.19	118.17
2.00%	1,095.11	553.02	372.35	282.04	227.86	191.76	165.98	146.65	131.63	119.62
2.25%	1,096.58	554.45	373.77	283.46	229.29	193.19	167.41	148.10	133.08	121.08
2.50%	1,098.06	555.89	375.20	284.88	230.72	194.62	168.86	149.55	134.54	122.55
2.75%	1,099.54	557.32	376.63	286.31	232.15	196.07	170.31	151.01	136.02	124.03
3.00%	1,101.02	558.76	378.06	287.75	233.59	197.52	171.77	152.48	137.50	125.53
3.25%	1,102.50	560.19	379.49	289.18	235.04	198.98	173.24	153.97	138.99	127.03
3.50%	1,103.98	561.64	380.93	290.63	236.49	200.44	174.72	155.45	140.50	128.55
3.75%	1,105.46	563.08	382.37	292.08	237.95	201.91	176.20	156.95	142.01	130.08
4.00%	1,106.95	564.52	383.81	293.53	239.41	203.39	177.69	158.46	143.53	131.62
4.25%	1,108.43	565.97	385.26	294.98	240.88	204.87	179.19	159.98	145.07	133.17
4.50%	1,109.92	567.42	386.71	296.45	242.36	206.36	180.70	161.50	146.61	134.73
4.75%	1,111.41	568.87	388.16	297.91	243.84	207.86	182.22	163.04	148.16	136.30
5.00%	1,112.90	570.33	389.62	299.38	245.33	209.36	183.74	164.58	149.72	137.89
5.25%	1,114.39	571.78	391.08	300.86	246.82	210.87	185.27	166.13	151.30	139.48
5.50%	1,115.88	573.24	392.55	302.33	248.32	212.39	186.81	167.69	152.88	141.08
5.75%	1,117.37	574.70	394.01	303.82	249.82	213.92	188.36	169.26	154.47	142.70
6.00%	1,118.86	576.17	395.49	305.31	251.33	215.45	189.91	170.84	156.07	144.33
6.25%	1,120.36	577.63	396.96	306.80	252.84	216.99	191.47	172.43	157.69	145.96
6.50%	1,121.85	579.10	398.44	308.29	254.36	218.53	193.04	174.02	159.31	147.61
6.75%	1,123.35	580.57	399.92	309.80	255.88	220.08	194.62	175.63	160.94	149.27
7.00%	1,124.85	582.04	401.40	311.30	257.42	221.64	196.20	177.24	162.58	150.94
7.25%	1,126.35	583.52	402.89	312.81	258.95	223.20	197.80	178.86	164.23	152.62
7.50%	1,127.85	584.99	404.38	314.33	260.49	224.77	199.40	180.49	165.89	154.31
7.75%	1,129.35	586.47	405.88	315.84	262.04	226.35	201.01	182.13	167.56	156.01
8.00%	1,130.85	587.95	407.37	317.37	263.59	227.93	202.62	183.78	169.24	157.73
8.25%	1,132.35	589.44	408.87	318.90	265.15	229.52	204.24	185.43	170.93	159.45
8.50%	1,133.86	590.92	410.38	320.43	266.71	231.12	205.87	187.10	172.63	161.18
8.75%	1,135.36	592.41	411.89	321.96	268.28	232.72	207.51	188.77	174.34	162.92
9.00%	1,136.87	593.90	413.40	323.51	269.86	234.33	209.16	190.45	176.06	164.68
9.25%	1,138.38	595.39	414.91	325.05	271.44	235.95	210.81	192.14	177.79	166.44
9.50%	1,139.89	596.89	416.43	326.60	273.02	237.57	212.47	193.84	179.52	168.22
9.75%	1,141.40	598.39	417.95	328.15	274.62	239.20	214.14	195.55	181.27	170.00
10.00%	1,142.91	599.88	419.47	329.71	276.21	240.84	215.82	197.26	183.02	171.80
10.25%	1,144.42	601.39	421.00	331.28	277.81	242.48	217.50	198.99	184.79	173.60
10.50%	1,145.93	602.89	422.53	332.84	279.42	244.13	219.19	200.72	186.56	175.42
10.75%	1,147.45	604.39	424.07	334.42	281.03	245.78	220.89	202.46	188.34	177.24

$13,000   11.00 - 20.75%   1 - 10 Years

	1	2	3	4	5	6	7	8	9	10
11.00%	1,148.96	605.90	425.60	335.99	282.65	247.44	222.59	204.21	190.14	179.08
11.25%	1,150.48	607.41	427.14	337.57	284.28	249.11	224.30	205.97	191.94	180.92
11.50%	1,152.00	608.92	428.69	339.16	285.90	250.79	226.02	207.73	193.75	182.77
11.75%	1,153.51	610.44	430.24	340.75	287.54	252.47	227.75	209.51	195.57	184.64
12.00%	1,155.03	611.96	431.79	342.34	289.18	254.15	229.49	211.29	197.40	186.51
12.25%	1,156.56	613.47	433.34	343.94	290.82	255.85	231.23	213.08	199.23	188.40
12.50%	1,158.08	615.00	434.90	345.54	292.47	257.55	232.98	214.87	201.08	190.29
12.75%	1,159.60	616.52	436.46	347.15	294.13	259.25	234.73	216.68	202.93	192.19
13.00%	1,161.12	618.04	438.02	348.76	295.79	260.96	236.50	218.49	204.80	194.10
13.25%	1,162.65	619.57	439.59	350.37	297.46	262.68	238.27	220.32	206.67	196.03
13.50%	1,164.18	621.10	441.16	351.99	299.13	264.41	240.04	222.15	208.55	197.96
13.75%	1,165.70	622.63	442.73	353.62	300.80	266.14	241.83	223.98	210.44	199.90
14.00%	1,167.23	624.17	444.31	355.24	302.49	267.87	243.62	225.83	212.34	201.85
14.25%	1,168.76	625.70	445.89	356.88	304.17	269.62	245.42	227.68	214.24	203.81
14.50%	1,170.29	627.24	447.47	358.51	305.87	271.37	247.22	229.54	216.16	205.77
14.75%	1,171.83	628.78	449.06	360.15	307.57	273.12	249.04	231.41	218.08	207.75
15.00%	1,173.36	630.33	450.65	361.80	309.27	274.89	250.86	233.29	220.02	209.74
15.25%	1,174.89	631.87	452.24	363.45	310.98	276.65	252.68	235.17	221.96	211.73
15.50%	1,176.43	633.42	453.84	365.10	312.69	278.43	254.52	237.07	223.91	213.73
15.75%	1,177.96	634.97	455.44	366.76	314.41	280.21	256.36	238.97	225.86	215.75
16.00%	1,179.50	636.52	457.04	368.42	316.13	281.99	258.21	240.87	227.83	217.77
16.25%	1,181.04	638.07	458.65	370.09	317.86	283.79	260.06	242.79	229.80	219.80
16.50%	1,182.58	639.63	460.26	371.76	319.60	285.58	261.92	244.71	231.78	221.83
16.75%	1,184.12	641.19	461.87	373.44	321.34	287.39	263.79	246.64	233.77	223.88
17.00%	1,185.66	642.75	463.49	375.12	323.08	289.20	265.67	248.58	235.77	225.94
17.25%	1,187.20	644.31	465.10	376.80	324.83	291.02	267.55	250.52	237.78	228.00
17.50%	1,188.75	645.88	466.73	378.49	326.59	292.84	269.44	252.48	239.79	230.07
17.75%	1,190.29	647.44	468.35	380.18	328.35	294.67	271.33	254.44	241.81	232.15
18.00%	1,191.84	649.01	469.98	381.87	330.11	296.50	273.23	256.40	243.84	234.24
18.25%	1,193.39	650.58	471.61	383.58	331.89	298.34	275.14	258.38	245.88	236.34
18.50%	1,194.94	652.16	473.25	385.28	333.66	300.19	277.05	260.36	247.92	238.44
18.75%	1,196.48	653.73	474.89	386.99	335.44	302.04	278.98	262.34	249.97	240.55
19.00%	1,198.04	655.31	476.53	388.70	337.23	303.90	280.90	264.34	252.03	242.67
19.25%	1,199.59	656.89	478.17	390.42	339.02	305.76	282.84	266.34	254.10	244.80
19.50%	1,201.14	658.47	479.82	392.14	340.81	307.63	284.78	268.35	256.17	246.94
19.75%	1,202.69	660.06	481.47	393.87	342.61	309.51	286.73	270.37	258.26	249.08
20.00%	1,204.25	661.65	483.13	395.59	344.42	311.39	288.68	272.39	260.34	251.23
20.25%	1,205.80	663.23	484.78	397.33	346.23	313.27	290.64	274.42	262.44	253.39
20.50%	1,207.36	664.83	486.44	399.07	348.05	315.17	292.61	276.46	264.54	255.56
20.75%	1,208.92	666.42	488.11	400.81	349.87	317.06	294.58	278.50	266.66	257.73

	1	2	3	4	5	6	7	8	9	10
1.00%	1,173.00	589.43	394.91	297.66	239.31	200.42	172.64	151.81	135.60	122.65
1.25%	1,174.58	590.96	396.43	299.17	240.82	201.93	174.15	153.32	137.13	124.17
1.50%	1,176.17	592.49	397.95	300.69	242.34	203.45	175.67	154.85	138.66	125.71
1.75%	1,177.76	594.03	399.47	302.21	243.86	204.97	177.20	156.39	140.20	127.26
2.00%	1,179.34	595.56	401.00	303.73	245.39	206.51	178.74	157.93	141.75	128.82
2.25%	1,180.93	597.10	402.53	305.26	246.92	208.05	180.29	159.49	143.32	130.39
2.50%	1,182.53	598.65	404.06	306.80	248.46	209.59	181.85	161.05	144.89	131.98
2.75%	1,184.12	600.19	405.60	308.34	250.01	211.15	183.41	162.63	146.48	133.58
3.00%	1,185.71	601.74	407.14	309.88	251.56	212.71	184.99	164.21	148.08	135.19
3.25%	1,187.31	603.29	408.68	311.43	253.12	214.28	186.57	165.81	149.69	136.81
3.50%	1,188.90	604.84	410.23	312.98	254.68	215.86	188.16	167.41	151.30	138.44
3.75%	1,190.50	606.39	411.78	314.54	256.25	217.44	189.76	169.03	152.93	140.09
4.00%	1,192.10	607.95	413.34	316.11	257.83	219.03	191.36	170.65	154.57	141.74
4.25%	1,193.70	609.51	414.89	317.68	259.41	220.63	192.98	172.28	156.22	143.41
4.50%	1,195.30	611.07	416.46	319.25	261.00	222.24	194.60	173.93	157.89	145.09
4.75%	1,196.90	612.63	418.02	320.83	262.60	223.85	196.23	175.58	159.56	146.79
5.00%	1,198.50	614.20	419.59	322.41	264.20	225.47	197.87	177.24	161.24	148.49
5.25%	1,200.11	615.77	421.17	324.00	265.80	227.10	199.52	178.91	162.94	150.21
5.50%	1,201.71	617.34	422.74	325.59	267.42	228.73	201.18	180.59	164.64	151.94
5.75%	1,203.32	618.91	424.32	327.19	269.03	230.37	202.85	182.28	166.35	153.68
6.00%	1,204.93	620.49	425.91	328.79	270.66	232.02	204.52	183.98	168.08	155.43
6.25%	1,206.54	622.07	427.49	330.40	272.29	233.68	206.20	185.69	169.82	157.19
6.50%	1,208.15	623.65	429.09	332.01	273.93	235.34	207.89	187.41	171.56	158.97
6.75%	1,209.76	625.23	430.68	333.63	275.57	237.01	209.59	189.13	173.32	160.75
7.00%	1,211.37	626.82	432.28	335.25	277.22	238.69	211.30	190.87	175.09	162.55
7.25%	1,212.99	628.40	433.88	336.87	278.87	240.37	213.01	192.62	176.87	164.36
7.50%	1,214.60	629.99	435.49	338.50	280.53	242.06	214.74	194.37	178.65	166.18
7.75%	1,216.22	631.59	437.10	340.14	282.20	243.76	216.47	196.14	180.45	168.01
8.00%	1,217.84	633.18	438.71	341.78	283.87	245.47	218.21	197.91	182.26	169.86
8.25%	1,219.46	634.78	440.33	343.43	285.55	247.18	219.95	199.70	184.08	171.71
8.50%	1,221.08	636.38	441.95	345.08	287.23	248.90	221.71	201.49	185.91	173.58
8.75%	1,222.70	637.98	443.57	346.73	288.92	250.62	223.47	203.29	187.75	175.46
9.00%	1,224.32	639.59	445.20	348.39	290.62	252.36	225.25	205.10	189.60	177.35
9.25%	1,225.94	641.19	446.83	350.05	292.32	254.10	227.03	206.92	191.46	179.25
9.50%	1,227.57	642.80	448.46	351.72	294.03	255.85	228.82	208.75	193.33	181.16
9.75%	1,229.20	644.41	450.10	353.40	295.74	257.60	230.61	210.59	195.21	183.08
10.00%	1,230.82	646.03	451.74	355.08	297.46	259.36	232.42	212.44	197.10	185.01
10.25%	1,232.45	647.65	453.39	356.76	299.18	261.13	234.23	214.29	199.00	186.95
10.50%	1,234.08	649.26	455.03	358.45	300.91	262.91	236.05	216.16	200.91	188.91
10.75%	1,235.71	650.89	456.69	360.14	302.65	264.69	237.88	218.03	202.83	190.87

$14,000　　11.00 - 20.75%　　1 - 10 Years

	1	2	3	4	5	6	7	8	9	10
11.00%	1,237.34	652.51	458.34	361.84	304.39	266.48	239.71	219.92	204.76	192.85
11.25%	1,238.98	654.14	460.00	363.54	306.14	268.27	241.56	221.81	206.70	194.84
11.50%	1,240.61	655.76	461.66	365.25	307.90	270.08	243.41	223.71	208.65	196.83
11.75%	1,242.25	657.40	463.33	366.96	309.66	271.89	245.27	225.62	210.61	198.84
12.00%	1,243.88	659.03	465.00	368.67	311.42	273.70	247.14	227.54	212.58	200.86
12.25%	1,245.52	660.66	466.67	370.39	313.19	275.53	249.01	229.47	214.56	202.89
12.50%	1,247.16	662.30	468.35	372.12	314.97	277.36	250.90	231.40	216.55	204.93
12.75%	1,248.80	663.94	470.03	373.85	316.75	279.19	252.79	233.35	218.54	206.98
13.00%	1,250.44	665.59	471.72	375.58	318.54	281.04	254.69	235.30	220.55	209.04
13.25%	1,252.08	667.23	473.40	377.32	320.34	282.89	256.59	237.26	222.57	211.10
13.50%	1,253.73	668.88	475.09	379.07	322.14	284.75	258.51	239.23	224.59	213.18
13.75%	1,255.37	670.53	476.79	380.82	323.94	286.61	260.43	241.21	226.63	215.27
14.00%	1,257.02	672.18	478.49	382.57	325.76	288.48	262.36	243.20	228.67	217.37
14.25%	1,258.67	673.83	480.19	384.33	327.57	290.36	264.30	245.20	230.73	219.48
14.50%	1,260.32	675.49	481.89	386.09	329.40	292.24	266.24	247.20	232.79	221.60
14.75%	1,261.97	677.15	483.60	387.86	331.22	294.13	268.19	249.21	234.86	223.73
15.00%	1,263.62	678.81	485.31	389.63	333.06	296.03	270.15	251.24	236.94	225.87
15.25%	1,265.27	680.48	487.03	391.41	334.90	297.93	272.12	253.27	239.03	228.02
15.50%	1,266.92	682.14	488.75	393.19	336.74	299.84	274.10	255.30	241.13	230.17
15.75%	1,268.58	683.81	490.47	394.97	338.60	301.76	276.08	257.35	243.24	232.34
16.00%	1,270.23	685.48	492.20	396.76	340.45	303.69	278.07	259.40	245.35	234.52
16.25%	1,271.89	687.16	493.93	398.56	342.32	305.62	280.07	261.47	247.48	236.70
16.50%	1,273.55	688.83	495.66	400.36	344.18	307.55	282.07	263.54	249.61	238.90
16.75%	1,275.21	690.51	497.40	402.16	346.06	309.50	284.08	265.61	251.76	241.10
17.00%	1,276.87	692.19	499.14	403.97	347.94	311.45	286.10	267.70	253.91	243.32
17.25%	1,278.53	693.87	500.88	405.78	349.82	313.40	288.13	269.79	256.07	245.54
17.50%	1,280.19	695.56	502.63	407.60	351.71	315.36	290.16	271.90	258.23	247.77
17.75%	1,281.85	697.25	504.38	409.42	353.61	317.33	292.20	274.01	260.41	250.01
18.00%	1,283.52	698.94	506.13	411.25	355.51	319.31	294.25	276.12	262.60	252.26
18.25%	1,285.19	700.63	507.89	413.08	357.41	321.29	296.30	278.25	264.79	254.52
18.50%	1,286.85	702.32	509.65	414.92	359.33	323.28	298.37	280.38	266.99	256.78
18.75%	1,288.52	704.02	511.42	416.76	361.24	325.27	300.44	282.53	269.20	259.06
19.00%	1,290.19	705.72	513.18	418.60	363.17	327.27	302.51	284.67	271.42	261.34
19.25%	1,291.86	707.42	514.96	420.45	365.10	329.28	304.60	286.83	273.65	263.63
19.50%	1,293.54	709.13	516.73	422.30	367.03	331.29	306.69	288.99	275.88	265.93
19.75%	1,295.21	710.83	518.51	424.16	368.97	333.31	308.78	291.17	278.12	268.24
20.00%	1,296.88	712.54	520.29	426.03	370.91	335.34	310.89	293.34	280.37	270.56
20.25%	1,298.56	714.25	522.08	427.89	372.86	337.37	313.00	295.53	282.63	272.88
20.50%	1,300.24	715.97	523.86	429.76	374.82	339.41	315.12	297.72	284.89	275.22
20.75%	1,301.91	717.68	525.66	431.64	376.78	341.45	317.24	299.93	287.17	277.56

	1	2	3	4	5	6	7	8	9	10
1.00%	1,256.78	631.53	423.12	318.92	256.41	214.73	184.97	162.65	145.29	131.41
1.25%	1,258.48	633.17	424.74	320.54	258.02	216.35	186.59	164.27	146.92	133.04
1.50%	1,260.18	634.81	426.37	322.16	259.65	217.98	188.22	165.91	148.56	134.69
1.75%	1,261.88	636.46	428.00	323.79	261.28	219.61	189.86	167.56	150.21	136.35
2.00%	1,263.58	638.10	429.64	325.43	262.92	221.26	191.51	169.21	151.88	138.02
2.25%	1,265.29	639.75	431.28	327.07	264.56	222.91	193.17	170.88	153.56	139.71
2.50%	1,266.99	641.41	432.92	328.71	266.21	224.57	194.84	172.56	155.24	141.40
2.75%	1,268.70	643.06	434.57	330.36	267.87	226.23	196.51	174.25	156.94	143.12
3.00%	1,270.41	644.72	436.22	332.01	269.53	227.91	198.20	175.94	158.65	144.84
3.25%	1,272.11	646.38	437.87	333.67	271.20	229.59	199.89	177.65	160.38	146.58
3.50%	1,273.82	648.04	439.53	335.34	272.88	231.28	201.60	179.37	162.11	148.33
3.75%	1,275.54	649.71	441.19	337.01	274.56	232.97	203.31	181.10	163.86	150.09
4.00%	1,277.25	651.37	442.86	338.69	276.25	234.68	205.03	182.84	165.61	151.87
4.25%	1,278.96	653.04	444.53	340.37	277.94	236.39	206.76	184.59	167.38	153.66
4.50%	1,280.68	654.72	446.20	342.05	279.65	238.11	208.50	186.35	169.16	155.46
4.75%	1,282.39	656.39	447.88	343.74	281.35	239.84	210.25	188.12	170.96	157.27
5.00%	1,284.11	658.07	449.56	345.44	283.07	241.57	212.01	189.90	172.76	159.10
5.25%	1,285.83	659.75	451.25	347.14	284.79	243.32	213.78	191.69	174.57	160.94
5.50%	1,287.55	661.43	452.94	348.85	286.52	245.07	215.55	193.49	176.40	162.79
5.75%	1,289.27	663.12	454.63	350.56	288.25	246.83	217.34	195.30	178.24	164.65
6.00%	1,291.00	664.81	456.33	352.28	289.99	248.59	219.13	197.12	180.09	166.53
6.25%	1,292.72	666.50	458.03	354.00	291.74	250.37	220.93	198.95	181.95	168.42
6.50%	1,294.45	668.19	459.74	355.72	293.49	252.15	222.74	200.79	183.82	170.32
6.75%	1,296.17	669.89	461.44	357.46	295.25	253.94	224.56	202.64	185.70	172.24
7.00%	1,297.90	671.59	463.16	359.19	297.02	255.74	226.39	204.51	187.59	174.16
7.25%	1,299.63	673.29	464.87	360.94	298.79	257.54	228.23	206.38	189.50	176.10
7.50%	1,301.36	674.99	466.59	362.68	300.57	259.35	230.07	208.26	191.42	178.05
7.75%	1,303.09	676.70	468.32	364.44	302.35	261.17	231.93	210.15	193.34	180.02
8.00%	1,304.83	678.41	470.05	366.19	304.15	263.00	233.79	212.05	195.28	181.99
8.25%	1,306.56	680.12	471.78	367.96	305.94	264.83	235.67	213.96	197.23	183.98
8.50%	1,308.30	681.84	473.51	369.72	307.75	266.68	237.55	215.88	199.19	185.98
8.75%	1,310.03	683.55	475.25	371.50	309.56	268.53	239.44	217.81	201.16	187.99
9.00%	1,311.77	685.27	477.00	373.28	311.38	270.38	241.34	219.75	203.14	190.01
9.25%	1,313.51	686.99	478.74	375.06	313.20	272.25	243.24	221.70	205.14	192.05
9.50%	1,315.25	688.72	480.49	376.85	315.03	274.12	245.16	223.66	207.14	194.10
9.75%	1,316.99	690.44	482.25	378.64	316.86	276.00	247.08	225.63	209.15	196.16
10.00%	1,318.74	692.17	484.01	380.44	318.71	277.89	249.02	227.61	211.18	198.23
10.25%	1,320.48	693.91	485.77	382.24	320.55	279.78	250.96	229.60	213.22	200.31
10.50%	1,322.23	695.64	487.54	384.05	322.41	281.68	252.91	231.60	215.26	202.40
10.75%	1,323.98	697.38	489.31	385.86	324.27	283.59	254.87	233.61	217.32	204.51

$15,000   11.00 - 20.75%   1 - 10 Years

	1	2	3	4	5	6	7	8	9	10
11.00%	1,325.72	699.12	491.08	387.68	326.14	285.51	256.84	235.63	219.39	206.63
11.25%	1,327.47	700.86	492.86	389.51	328.01	287.44	258.81	237.65	221.47	208.75
11.50%	1,329.23	702.60	494.64	391.34	329.89	289.37	260.80	239.69	223.55	210.89
11.75%	1,330.98	704.35	496.43	393.17	331.77	291.31	262.79	241.74	225.65	213.04
12.00%	1,332.73	706.10	498.21	395.01	333.67	293.25	264.79	243.79	227.76	215.21
12.25%	1,334.49	707.85	500.01	396.85	335.56	295.21	266.80	245.86	229.88	217.38
12.50%	1,336.24	709.61	501.80	398.70	337.47	297.17	268.82	247.93	232.01	219.56
12.75%	1,338.00	711.37	503.60	400.55	339.38	299.14	270.84	250.02	234.15	221.76
13.00%	1,339.76	713.13	505.41	402.41	341.30	301.11	272.88	252.11	236.30	223.97
13.25%	1,341.52	714.89	507.22	404.28	343.22	303.09	274.92	254.21	238.46	226.18
13.50%	1,343.28	716.66	509.03	406.14	345.15	305.08	276.97	256.32	240.63	228.41
13.75%	1,345.04	718.42	510.84	408.02	347.08	307.08	279.03	258.44	242.82	230.65
14.00%	1,346.81	720.19	512.66	409.90	349.02	309.09	281.10	260.57	245.01	232.90
14.25%	1,348.57	721.97	514.49	411.78	350.97	311.10	283.18	262.71	247.21	235.16
14.50%	1,350.34	723.74	516.31	413.67	352.92	313.12	285.26	264.86	249.42	237.43
14.75%	1,352.11	725.52	518.15	415.56	354.88	315.14	287.35	267.02	251.64	239.71
15.00%	1,353.87	727.30	519.98	417.46	356.85	317.18	289.45	269.18	253.87	242.00
15.25%	1,355.64	729.08	521.82	419.36	358.82	319.22	291.56	271.36	256.10	244.30
15.50%	1,357.42	730.87	523.66	421.27	360.80	321.26	293.68	273.54	258.35	246.62
15.75%	1,359.19	732.66	525.51	423.19	362.78	323.32	295.80	275.73	260.61	248.94
16.00%	1,360.96	734.45	527.36	425.10	364.77	325.38	297.93	277.93	262.88	251.27
16.25%	1,362.74	736.24	529.21	427.03	366.77	327.45	300.07	280.14	265.16	253.61
16.50%	1,364.51	738.04	531.07	428.96	368.77	329.52	302.22	282.36	267.44	255.96
16.75%	1,366.29	739.83	532.93	430.89	370.78	331.60	304.37	284.59	269.74	258.33
17.00%	1,368.07	741.63	534.79	432.83	372.79	333.69	306.54	286.82	272.04	260.70
17.25%	1,369.85	743.44	536.66	434.77	374.81	335.79	308.71	289.07	274.36	263.08
17.50%	1,371.63	745.24	538.53	436.72	376.83	337.89	310.89	291.32	276.68	265.47
17.75%	1,373.42	747.05	540.41	438.67	378.86	340.00	313.07	293.58	279.01	267.87
18.00%	1,375.20	748.86	542.29	440.62	380.90	342.12	315.27	295.85	281.35	270.28
18.25%	1,376.99	750.67	544.17	442.59	382.94	344.24	317.47	298.13	283.70	272.70
18.50%	1,378.77	752.49	546.06	444.55	384.99	346.37	319.68	300.41	286.06	275.12
18.75%	1,380.56	754.31	547.95	446.53	387.05	348.51	321.90	302.71	288.43	277.56
19.00%	1,382.35	756.13	549.84	448.50	389.11	350.65	324.12	305.01	290.81	280.01
19.25%	1,384.14	757.95	551.74	450.48	391.17	352.80	326.35	307.32	293.19	282.46
19.50%	1,385.93	759.78	553.64	452.47	393.25	354.96	328.59	309.64	295.58	284.93
19.75%	1,387.72	761.61	555.54	454.46	395.32	357.12	330.84	311.96	297.99	287.40
20.00%	1,389.52	763.44	557.45	456.46	397.41	359.29	333.09	314.30	300.40	289.88
20.25%	1,391.31	765.27	559.37	458.46	399.50	361.47	335.35	316.64	302.82	292.37
20.50%	1,393.11	767.11	561.28	460.46	401.59	363.65	337.62	318.99	305.24	294.87
20.75%	1,394.91	768.94	563.20	462.47	403.69	365.84	339.90	321.35	307.68	297.38

	1	2	3	4	5	6	7	8	9	10
1.00%	1,340.57	673.63	451.33	340.18	273.50	229.05	197.30	173.49	154.98	140.17
1.25%	1,342.38	675.38	453.06	341.91	275.23	230.78	199.03	175.23	156.71	141.91
1.50%	1,344.19	677.13	454.80	343.64	276.96	232.51	200.77	176.97	158.47	143.67
1.75%	1,346.01	678.89	456.54	345.38	278.70	234.25	202.52	178.73	160.23	145.44
2.00%	1,347.82	680.64	458.28	347.12	280.44	236.01	204.28	180.49	162.00	147.22
2.25%	1,349.64	682.40	460.03	348.87	282.20	237.77	206.05	182.27	163.79	149.02
2.50%	1,351.46	684.17	461.78	350.62	283.96	239.54	207.83	184.06	165.59	150.83
2.75%	1,353.28	685.93	463.54	352.38	285.72	241.31	209.61	185.86	167.41	152.66
3.00%	1,355.10	687.70	465.30	354.15	287.50	243.10	211.41	187.67	169.23	154.50
3.25%	1,356.92	689.47	467.06	355.92	289.28	244.89	213.22	189.50	171.07	156.35
3.50%	1,358.75	691.24	468.83	357.70	291.07	246.69	215.04	191.33	172.92	158.22
3.75%	1,360.57	693.02	470.61	359.48	292.86	248.50	216.86	193.17	174.78	160.10
4.00%	1,362.40	694.80	472.38	361.26	294.66	250.32	218.70	195.03	176.66	161.99
4.25%	1,364.23	696.58	474.17	363.06	296.47	252.15	220.55	196.89	178.54	163.90
4.50%	1,366.06	698.36	475.95	364.86	298.29	253.98	222.40	198.77	180.44	165.82
4.75%	1,367.89	700.15	477.74	366.66	300.11	255.83	224.27	200.66	182.35	167.76
5.00%	1,369.72	701.94	479.53	368.47	301.94	257.68	226.14	202.56	184.28	169.70
5.25%	1,371.55	703.73	481.33	370.28	303.78	259.54	228.03	204.47	186.21	171.67
5.50%	1,373.39	705.53	483.13	372.10	305.62	261.41	229.92	206.39	188.16	173.64
5.75%	1,375.23	707.33	484.94	373.93	307.47	263.28	231.82	208.32	190.12	175.63
6.00%	1,377.06	709.13	486.75	375.76	309.32	265.17	233.74	210.26	192.09	177.63
6.25%	1,378.90	710.93	488.57	377.60	311.19	267.06	235.66	212.22	194.08	179.65
6.50%	1,380.74	712.74	490.38	379.44	313.06	268.96	237.59	214.18	196.07	181.68
6.75%	1,382.58	714.55	492.21	381.29	314.94	270.87	239.53	216.15	198.08	183.72
7.00%	1,384.43	716.36	494.03	383.14	316.82	272.78	241.48	218.14	200.10	185.77
7.25%	1,386.27	718.18	495.86	385.00	318.71	274.71	243.44	220.14	202.13	187.84
7.50%	1,388.12	719.99	497.70	386.86	320.61	276.64	245.41	222.14	204.18	189.92
7.75%	1,389.97	721.81	499.54	388.73	322.51	278.58	247.39	224.16	206.23	192.02
8.00%	1,391.81	723.64	501.38	390.61	324.42	280.53	249.38	226.19	208.30	194.12
8.25%	1,393.67	725.46	503.23	392.49	326.34	282.49	251.38	228.23	210.38	196.24
8.50%	1,395.52	727.29	505.08	394.37	328.26	284.45	253.38	230.27	212.47	198.38
8.75%	1,397.37	729.12	506.94	396.26	330.20	286.43	255.40	232.33	214.57	200.52
9.00%	1,399.22	730.96	508.80	398.16	332.13	288.41	257.43	234.40	216.69	202.68
9.25%	1,401.08	732.79	510.66	400.06	334.08	290.40	259.46	236.48	218.81	204.85
9.50%	1,402.94	734.63	512.53	401.97	336.03	292.40	261.50	238.57	220.95	207.04
9.75%	1,404.79	736.47	514.40	403.88	337.99	294.40	263.56	240.68	223.10	209.23
10.00%	1,406.65	738.32	516.27	405.80	339.95	296.41	265.62	242.79	225.26	211.44
10.25%	1,408.52	740.17	518.16	407.73	341.92	298.43	267.69	244.91	227.43	213.66
10.50%	1,410.38	742.02	520.04	409.65	343.90	300.46	269.77	247.04	229.61	215.90
10.75%	1,412.24	743.87	521.93	411.59	345.89	302.50	271.86	249.18	231.81	218.14

$16,000   11.00 - 20.75%   1 - 10 Years

	1	2	3	4	5	6	7	8	9	10
11.00%	1,414.11	745.73	523.82	413.53	347.88	304.55	273.96	251.33	234.01	220.40
11.25%	1,415.97	747.58	525.72	415.47	349.88	306.60	276.07	253.50	236.23	222.67
11.50%	1,417.84	749.45	527.62	417.42	351.88	308.66	278.18	255.67	238.46	224.95
11.75%	1,419.71	751.31	529.52	419.38	353.89	310.73	280.31	257.85	240.70	227.25
12.00%	1,421.58	753.18	531.43	421.34	355.91	312.80	282.44	260.05	242.95	229.55
12.25%	1,423.45	755.04	533.34	423.31	357.94	314.89	284.59	262.25	245.21	231.87
12.50%	1,425.33	756.92	535.26	425.28	359.97	316.98	286.74	264.46	247.48	234.20
12.75%	1,427.20	758.79	537.18	427.26	362.00	319.08	288.90	266.68	249.76	236.54
13.00%	1,429.08	760.67	539.10	429.24	364.05	321.19	291.07	268.92	252.06	238.90
13.25%	1,430.95	762.55	541.03	431.23	366.10	323.30	293.25	271.16	254.36	241.26
13.50%	1,432.83	764.43	542.96	433.22	368.16	325.42	295.44	273.41	256.68	243.64
13.75%	1,434.71	766.32	544.90	435.22	370.22	327.55	297.63	275.67	259.00	246.03
14.00%	1,436.59	768.21	546.84	437.22	372.29	329.69	299.84	277.94	261.34	248.43
14.25%	1,438.48	770.10	548.79	439.23	374.37	331.84	302.05	280.23	263.69	250.84
14.50%	1,440.36	771.99	550.74	441.25	376.45	333.99	304.28	282.52	266.04	253.26
14.75%	1,442.25	773.89	552.69	443.27	378.54	336.15	306.51	284.82	268.41	255.69
15.00%	1,444.13	775.79	554.65	445.29	380.64	338.32	308.75	287.13	270.79	258.14
15.25%	1,446.02	777.69	556.61	447.32	382.74	340.50	311.00	289.45	273.18	260.59
15.50%	1,447.91	779.59	558.57	449.36	384.85	342.68	313.25	291.77	275.58	263.06
15.75%	1,449.80	781.50	560.54	451.40	386.97	344.87	315.52	294.11	277.99	265.53
16.00%	1,451.69	783.41	562.51	453.44	389.09	347.07	317.79	296.46	280.40	268.02
16.25%	1,453.59	785.32	564.49	455.50	391.22	349.28	320.08	298.82	282.83	270.52
16.50%	1,455.48	787.24	566.47	457.55	393.35	351.49	322.37	301.18	285.27	273.03
16.75%	1,457.38	789.16	568.45	459.61	395.49	353.71	324.67	303.56	287.72	275.55
17.00%	1,459.28	791.08	570.44	461.68	397.64	355.94	326.97	305.94	290.18	278.08
17.25%	1,461.17	793.00	572.44	463.75	399.80	358.17	329.29	308.34	292.65	280.62
17.50%	1,463.08	794.93	574.43	465.83	401.96	360.42	331.61	310.74	295.13	283.17
17.75%	1,464.98	796.85	576.43	467.91	404.12	362.67	333.94	313.15	297.61	285.73
18.00%	1,466.88	798.79	578.44	470.00	406.29	364.92	336.29	315.57	300.11	288.30
18.25%	1,468.78	800.72	580.45	472.09	408.47	367.19	338.63	318.00	302.62	290.88
18.50%	1,470.69	802.66	582.46	474.19	410.66	369.46	340.99	320.44	305.13	293.47
18.75%	1,472.60	804.60	584.48	476.29	412.85	371.74	343.36	322.89	307.66	296.07
19.00%	1,474.51	806.54	586.50	478.40	415.05	374.03	345.73	325.34	310.19	298.68
19.25%	1,476.41	808.48	588.52	480.52	417.25	376.32	348.11	327.81	312.74	301.29
19.50%	1,478.33	810.43	590.55	482.63	419.46	378.62	350.50	330.28	315.29	303.92
19.75%	1,480.24	812.38	592.58	484.76	421.68	380.93	352.89	332.76	317.85	306.56
20.00%	1,482.15	814.33	594.62	486.89	423.90	383.25	355.30	335.25	320.42	309.21
20.25%	1,484.07	816.29	596.66	489.02	426.13	385.57	357.71	337.75	323.00	311.87
20.50%	1,485.98	818.25	598.70	491.16	428.37	387.90	360.13	340.26	325.59	314.53
20.75%	1,487.90	820.21	600.75	493.30	430.61	390.23	362.56	342.77	328.19	317.21

	1	2	3	4	5	6	7	8	9	10
1.00%	1,424.35	715.74	479.54	361.44	290.59	243.36	209.63	184.33	164.66	148.93
1.25%	1,426.28	717.59	481.38	363.28	292.43	245.20	211.47	186.18	166.51	150.78
1.50%	1,428.20	719.45	483.22	365.12	294.27	247.04	213.32	188.03	168.37	152.65
1.75%	1,430.13	721.32	485.07	366.97	296.12	248.90	215.18	189.90	170.24	154.53
2.00%	1,432.06	723.18	486.92	368.82	297.97	250.76	217.05	191.77	172.13	156.42
2.25%	1,433.99	725.05	488.78	370.67	299.83	252.63	218.93	193.66	174.03	158.33
2.50%	1,435.92	726.93	490.64	372.54	301.71	254.51	220.82	195.57	175.94	160.26
2.75%	1,437.86	728.80	492.51	374.41	303.58	256.40	222.72	197.48	177.87	162.20
3.00%	1,439.79	730.68	494.38	376.28	305.47	258.29	224.63	199.40	179.81	164.15
3.25%	1,441.73	732.56	496.26	378.16	307.36	260.20	226.55	201.34	181.76	166.12
3.50%	1,443.67	734.45	498.14	380.05	309.26	262.11	228.48	203.29	183.73	168.11
3.75%	1,445.61	736.33	500.02	381.95	311.17	264.04	230.42	205.25	185.70	170.10
4.00%	1,447.55	738.22	501.91	383.84	313.08	265.97	232.37	207.22	187.70	172.12
4.25%	1,449.49	740.12	503.80	385.75	315.00	267.91	234.33	209.20	189.70	174.14
4.50%	1,451.43	742.01	505.70	387.66	316.93	269.86	236.30	211.19	191.72	176.19
4.75%	1,453.38	743.91	507.60	389.58	318.87	271.82	238.28	213.20	193.75	178.24
5.00%	1,455.33	745.81	509.51	391.50	320.81	273.78	240.28	215.22	195.79	180.31
5.25%	1,457.28	747.72	511.42	393.43	322.76	275.76	242.28	217.25	197.85	182.40
5.50%	1,459.23	749.63	513.33	395.36	324.72	277.74	244.29	219.29	199.92	184.49
5.75%	1,461.18	751.54	515.25	397.30	326.69	279.74	246.31	221.34	202.00	186.61
6.00%	1,463.13	753.45	517.17	399.25	328.66	281.74	248.35	223.40	204.10	188.73
6.25%	1,465.08	755.37	519.10	401.20	330.64	283.75	250.39	225.48	206.21	190.88
6.50%	1,467.04	757.29	521.03	403.15	332.62	285.77	252.44	227.57	208.33	193.03
6.75%	1,469.00	759.21	522.97	405.12	334.62	287.80	254.50	229.66	210.46	195.20
7.00%	1,470.95	761.13	524.91	407.09	336.62	289.83	256.58	231.77	212.61	197.38
7.25%	1,472.91	763.06	526.86	409.06	338.63	291.88	258.66	233.89	214.77	199.58
7.50%	1,474.88	764.99	528.81	411.04	340.65	293.93	260.75	236.03	216.94	201.79
7.75%	1,476.84	766.93	530.76	413.03	342.67	295.99	262.85	238.17	219.12	204.02
8.00%	1,478.80	768.86	532.72	415.02	344.70	298.07	264.97	240.32	221.32	206.26
8.25%	1,480.77	770.80	534.68	417.02	346.74	300.14	267.09	242.49	223.53	208.51
8.50%	1,482.74	772.75	536.65	419.02	348.78	302.23	269.22	244.67	225.75	210.78
8.75%	1,484.70	774.69	538.62	421.03	350.83	304.33	271.36	246.85	227.98	213.06
9.00%	1,486.68	776.64	540.60	423.05	352.89	306.43	273.51	249.05	230.23	215.35
9.25%	1,488.65	778.59	542.58	425.07	354.96	308.55	275.68	251.26	232.49	217.66
9.50%	1,490.62	780.55	544.56	427.09	357.03	310.67	277.85	253.49	234.76	219.98
9.75%	1,492.59	782.50	546.55	429.13	359.11	312.80	280.03	255.72	237.04	222.31
10.00%	1,494.57	784.46	548.54	431.16	361.20	314.94	282.22	257.96	239.34	224.66
10.25%	1,496.55	786.43	550.54	433.21	363.29	317.09	284.42	260.22	241.65	227.02
10.50%	1,498.53	788.39	552.54	435.26	365.40	319.24	286.63	262.48	243.96	229.39
10.75%	1,500.51	790.36	554.55	437.31	367.51	321.41	288.85	264.76	246.30	231.78

$17,000   11.00 - 20.75%   1 - 10 Years

	1	2	3	4	5	6	7	8	9	10
11.00%	1,502.49	792.33	556.56	439.37	369.62	323.58	291.08	267.04	248.64	234.18
11.25%	1,504.47	794.31	558.57	441.44	371.74	325.76	293.32	269.34	251.00	236.59
11.50%	1,506.46	796.29	560.59	443.51	373.87	327.95	295.57	271.65	253.36	239.01
11.75%	1,508.44	798.27	562.62	445.59	376.01	330.15	297.83	273.97	255.74	241.45
12.00%	1,510.43	800.25	564.64	447.68	378.16	332.35	300.10	276.30	258.13	243.90
12.25%	1,512.42	802.24	566.68	449.76	380.31	334.57	302.37	278.64	260.53	246.36
12.50%	1,514.41	804.22	568.71	451.86	382.46	336.79	304.66	280.99	262.95	248.84
12.75%	1,516.40	806.22	570.75	453.96	384.63	339.02	306.96	283.35	265.37	251.33
13.00%	1,518.39	808.21	572.80	456.07	386.80	341.26	309.26	285.72	267.81	253.83
13.25%	1,520.39	810.21	574.85	458.18	388.98	343.51	311.58	288.11	270.26	256.34
13.50%	1,522.38	812.21	576.90	460.30	391.17	345.76	313.90	290.50	272.72	258.87
13.75%	1,524.38	814.21	578.96	462.42	393.36	348.03	316.24	292.90	275.19	261.40
14.00%	1,526.38	816.22	581.02	464.55	395.56	350.30	318.58	295.32	277.67	263.95
14.25%	1,528.38	818.23	583.09	466.68	397.77	352.58	320.93	297.74	280.17	266.51
14.50%	1,530.38	820.24	585.16	468.83	399.98	354.87	323.29	300.17	282.67	269.09
14.75%	1,532.39	822.26	587.23	470.97	402.20	357.16	325.66	302.62	285.19	271.67
15.00%	1,534.39	824.27	589.31	473.12	404.43	359.47	328.04	305.07	287.71	274.27
15.25%	1,536.40	826.29	591.39	475.28	406.66	361.78	330.43	307.54	290.25	276.88
15.50%	1,538.41	828.32	593.48	477.44	408.90	364.10	332.83	310.01	292.80	279.50
15.75%	1,540.41	830.34	595.57	479.61	411.15	366.43	335.24	312.50	295.36	282.13
16.00%	1,542.42	832.37	597.67	481.78	413.41	368.76	337.66	314.99	297.93	284.77
16.25%	1,544.44	834.40	599.77	483.96	415.67	371.11	340.08	317.49	300.51	287.43
16.50%	1,546.45	836.44	601.87	486.15	417.94	373.46	342.51	320.01	303.10	290.09
16.75%	1,548.46	838.48	603.98	488.34	420.21	375.82	344.96	322.53	305.70	292.77
17.00%	1,550.48	840.52	606.10	490.54	422.49	378.18	347.41	325.06	308.32	295.46
17.25%	1,552.50	842.56	608.21	492.74	424.78	380.56	349.87	327.61	310.94	298.15
17.50%	1,554.52	844.61	610.34	494.94	427.08	382.94	352.34	330.16	313.57	300.86
17.75%	1,556.54	846.66	612.46	497.16	429.38	385.33	354.82	332.72	316.21	303.58
18.00%	1,558.56	848.71	614.59	499.37	431.69	387.73	357.30	335.29	318.87	306.31
18.25%	1,560.58	850.76	616.72	501.60	434.00	390.14	359.80	337.88	321.53	309.06
18.50%	1,562.61	852.82	618.86	503.83	436.33	392.55	362.30	340.47	324.20	311.81
18.75%	1,564.63	854.88	621.01	506.06	438.65	394.97	364.82	343.07	326.89	314.57
19.00%	1,566.66	856.95	623.15	508.30	440.99	397.40	367.34	345.68	329.58	317.34
19.25%	1,568.69	859.01	625.30	510.55	443.33	399.84	369.87	348.29	332.28	320.13
19.50%	1,570.72	861.08	627.46	512.80	445.68	402.29	372.40	350.92	335.00	322.92
19.75%	1,572.75	863.15	629.62	515.05	448.03	404.74	374.95	353.56	337.72	325.72
20.00%	1,574.79	865.23	631.78	517.32	450.40	407.20	377.51	356.20	340.45	328.53
20.25%	1,576.82	867.31	633.95	519.58	452.76	409.67	380.07	358.86	343.19	331.36
20.50%	1,578.86	869.39	636.12	521.86	455.14	412.14	382.64	361.52	345.94	334.19
20.75%	1,580.90	871.47	638.30	524.13	457.52	414.62	385.22	364.20	348.70	337.03

	1	2	3	4	5	6	7	8	9	10
1.00%	1,508.14	757.84	507.75	382.71	307.69	257.68	221.96	195.18	174.35	157.69
1.25%	1,510.18	759.80	509.69	384.65	309.63	259.62	223.91	197.13	176.30	159.65
1.50%	1,512.22	761.77	511.65	386.60	311.58	261.57	225.87	199.09	178.27	161.62
1.75%	1,514.26	763.75	513.60	388.55	313.53	263.54	227.83	201.07	180.26	163.62
2.00%	1,516.30	765.72	515.57	390.51	315.50	265.51	229.81	203.06	182.25	165.62
2.25%	1,518.34	767.70	517.53	392.48	317.47	267.49	231.80	205.06	184.27	167.65
2.50%	1,520.39	769.69	519.50	394.45	319.45	269.48	233.80	207.07	186.29	169.69
2.75%	1,522.44	771.67	521.48	396.43	321.44	271.48	235.82	209.09	188.33	171.74
3.00%	1,524.49	773.66	523.46	398.42	323.44	273.49	237.84	211.13	190.38	173.81
3.25%	1,526.54	775.65	525.45	400.41	325.44	275.50	239.87	213.18	192.45	175.89
3.50%	1,528.59	777.65	527.44	402.41	327.45	277.53	241.92	215.24	194.53	177.99
3.75%	1,530.64	779.65	529.43	404.41	329.47	279.57	243.97	217.32	196.63	180.11
4.00%	1,532.70	781.65	531.43	406.42	331.50	281.61	246.04	219.41	198.74	182.24
4.25%	1,534.76	783.65	533.44	408.44	333.53	283.67	248.12	221.51	200.86	184.39
4.50%	1,536.81	785.66	535.44	410.46	335.57	285.73	250.20	223.62	203.00	186.55
4.75%	1,538.87	787.67	537.46	412.49	337.62	287.81	252.30	225.74	205.15	188.73
5.00%	1,540.93	789.69	539.48	414.53	339.68	289.89	254.41	227.88	207.31	190.92
5.25%	1,543.00	791.70	541.50	416.57	341.75	291.98	256.53	230.03	209.49	193.13
5.50%	1,545.06	793.72	543.53	418.62	343.82	294.08	258.66	232.19	211.68	195.35
5.75%	1,547.13	795.74	545.56	420.67	345.90	296.19	260.80	234.36	213.88	197.58
6.00%	1,549.20	797.77	547.59	422.73	347.99	298.31	262.95	236.55	216.10	199.84
6.25%	1,551.26	799.80	549.64	424.80	350.09	300.44	265.12	238.74	218.34	202.10
6.50%	1,553.34	801.83	551.68	426.87	352.19	302.58	267.29	240.95	220.58	204.39
6.75%	1,555.41	803.87	553.73	428.95	354.30	304.73	269.47	243.17	222.84	206.68
7.00%	1,557.48	805.91	555.79	431.03	356.42	306.88	271.67	245.41	225.11	209.00
7.25%	1,559.56	807.95	557.85	433.12	358.55	309.05	273.87	247.65	227.40	211.32
7.50%	1,561.63	809.99	559.91	435.22	360.68	311.22	276.09	249.91	229.70	213.66
7.75%	1,563.71	812.04	561.98	437.32	362.83	313.41	278.32	252.18	232.01	216.02
8.00%	1,565.79	814.09	564.05	439.43	364.98	315.60	280.55	254.46	234.34	218.39
8.25%	1,567.87	816.15	566.13	441.55	367.13	317.80	282.80	256.75	236.68	220.77
8.50%	1,569.96	818.20	568.22	443.67	369.30	320.01	285.06	259.06	239.03	223.17
8.75%	1,572.04	820.26	570.30	445.80	371.47	322.23	287.32	261.38	241.39	225.59
9.00%	1,574.13	822.33	572.40	447.93	373.65	324.46	289.60	263.70	243.77	228.02
9.25%	1,576.21	824.39	574.49	450.07	375.84	326.70	291.89	266.04	246.16	230.46
9.50%	1,578.30	826.46	576.59	452.22	378.03	328.94	294.19	268.40	248.57	232.92
9.75%	1,580.39	828.53	578.70	454.37	380.24	331.20	296.50	270.76	250.99	235.39
10.00%	1,582.49	830.61	580.81	456.53	382.45	333.47	298.82	273.13	253.42	237.87
10.25%	1,584.58	832.69	582.92	458.69	384.66	335.74	301.15	275.52	255.86	240.37
10.50%	1,586.67	834.77	585.04	460.86	386.89	338.02	303.49	277.92	258.32	242.88
10.75%	1,588.77	836.85	587.17	463.04	389.12	340.31	305.84	280.33	260.78	245.41

	1	2	3	4	5	6	7	8	9	10
11.00%	1,590.87	838.94	589.30	465.22	391.36	342.61	308.20	282.75	263.27	247.95
11.25%	1,592.97	841.03	591.43	467.41	393.61	344.92	310.58	285.18	265.76	250.50
11.50%	1,595.07	843.13	593.57	469.60	395.87	347.24	312.96	287.63	268.27	253.07
11.75%	1,597.17	845.22	595.71	471.80	398.13	349.57	315.35	290.08	270.78	255.65
12.00%	1,599.28	847.32	597.86	474.01	400.40	351.90	317.75	292.55	273.32	258.25
12.25%	1,601.38	849.43	600.01	476.22	402.68	354.25	320.16	295.03	275.86	260.86
12.50%	1,603.49	851.53	602.17	478.44	404.96	356.60	322.58	297.52	278.42	263.48
12.75%	1,605.60	853.64	604.33	480.66	407.26	358.96	325.01	300.02	280.98	266.11
13.00%	1,607.71	855.75	606.49	482.89	409.56	361.33	327.46	302.53	283.56	268.76
13.25%	1,609.82	857.87	608.66	485.13	411.86	363.71	329.91	305.05	286.16	271.42
13.50%	1,611.94	859.99	610.84	487.37	414.18	366.10	332.37	307.59	288.76	274.09
13.75%	1,614.05	862.11	613.01	489.62	416.50	368.50	334.84	310.13	291.38	276.78
14.00%	1,616.17	864.23	615.20	491.88	418.83	370.90	337.32	312.69	294.01	279.48
14.25%	1,618.29	866.36	617.39	494.14	421.17	373.32	339.81	315.25	296.65	282.19
14.50%	1,620.41	868.49	619.58	496.40	423.51	375.74	342.31	317.83	299.30	284.92
14.75%	1,622.53	870.62	621.77	498.68	425.86	378.17	344.82	320.42	301.96	287.65
15.00%	1,624.65	872.76	623.98	500.95	428.22	380.61	347.34	323.02	304.64	290.40
15.25%	1,626.77	874.90	626.18	503.24	430.58	383.06	349.87	325.63	307.33	293.16
15.50%	1,628.90	877.04	628.39	505.53	432.96	385.51	352.41	328.25	310.02	295.94
15.75%	1,631.03	879.19	630.61	507.82	435.34	387.98	354.96	330.88	312.73	298.73
16.00%	1,633.16	881.34	632.83	510.13	437.73	390.45	357.52	333.52	315.45	301.52
16.25%	1,635.29	883.49	635.05	512.43	440.12	392.93	360.08	336.17	318.19	304.33
16.50%	1,637.42	885.64	637.28	514.75	442.52	395.43	362.66	338.83	320.93	307.16
16.75%	1,639.55	887.80	639.51	517.07	444.93	397.92	365.25	341.50	323.69	309.99
17.00%	1,641.69	889.96	641.75	519.39	447.35	400.43	367.84	344.19	326.45	312.84
17.25%	1,643.82	892.12	643.99	521.72	449.77	402.95	370.45	346.88	329.23	315.69
17.50%	1,645.96	894.29	646.24	524.06	452.20	405.47	373.06	349.58	332.02	318.56
17.75%	1,648.10	896.46	648.49	526.40	454.64	408.00	375.69	352.29	334.81	321.44
18.00%	1,650.24	898.63	650.74	528.75	457.08	410.54	378.32	355.02	337.62	324.33
18.25%	1,652.38	900.81	653.00	531.10	459.53	413.09	380.96	357.75	340.44	327.24
18.50%	1,654.53	902.99	655.27	533.46	461.99	415.64	383.61	360.49	343.27	330.15
18.75%	1,656.67	905.17	657.54	535.83	464.46	418.21	386.27	363.25	346.12	333.07
19.00%	1,658.82	907.36	659.81	538.20	466.93	420.78	388.94	366.01	348.97	336.01
19.25%	1,660.97	909.54	662.09	540.58	469.41	423.36	391.62	368.78	351.83	338.96
19.50%	1,663.12	911.73	664.37	542.96	471.90	425.95	394.31	371.56	354.70	341.91
19.75%	1,665.27	913.93	666.65	545.35	474.39	428.55	397.01	374.36	357.58	344.88
20.00%	1,667.42	916.12	668.94	547.75	476.89	431.15	399.71	377.16	360.48	347.86
20.25%	1,669.58	918.32	671.24	550.15	479.40	433.76	402.43	379.97	363.38	350.85
20.50%	1,671.73	920.53	673.54	552.55	481.91	436.38	405.15	382.79	366.29	353.85
20.75%	1,673.89	922.73	675.84	554.96	484.43	439.01	407.88	385.62	369.22	356.86

	1	2	3	4	5	6	7	8	9	10
1.00%	1,591.92	799.94	535.95	403.97	324.78	271.99	234.29	206.02	184.03	166.45
1.25%	1,594.07	802.02	538.01	406.02	326.83	274.05	236.35	208.08	186.10	168.52
1.50%	1,596.23	804.10	540.07	408.07	328.89	276.11	238.41	210.15	188.18	170.60
1.75%	1,598.38	806.18	542.14	410.14	330.95	278.18	240.49	212.24	190.27	172.71
2.00%	1,600.54	808.27	544.21	412.21	333.03	280.26	242.58	214.34	192.38	174.83
2.25%	1,602.70	810.35	546.29	414.28	335.11	282.35	244.68	216.45	194.50	176.96
2.50%	1,604.86	812.45	548.37	416.37	337.20	284.45	246.79	218.57	196.64	179.11
2.75%	1,607.02	814.54	550.45	418.46	339.30	286.56	248.92	220.71	198.79	181.28
3.00%	1,609.18	816.64	552.54	420.55	341.41	288.68	251.05	222.86	200.96	183.47
3.25%	1,611.34	818.75	554.64	422.65	343.52	290.81	253.20	225.03	203.14	185.67
3.50%	1,613.51	820.85	556.74	424.76	345.64	292.95	255.36	227.20	205.34	187.88
3.75%	1,615.68	822.96	558.85	426.88	347.77	295.10	257.53	229.39	207.55	190.12
4.00%	1,617.85	825.07	560.96	429.00	349.91	297.26	259.71	231.60	209.78	192.37
4.25%	1,620.02	827.19	563.07	431.13	352.06	299.43	261.90	233.81	212.02	194.63
4.50%	1,622.19	829.31	565.19	433.27	354.22	301.61	264.10	236.04	214.27	196.91
4.75%	1,624.37	831.43	567.32	435.41	356.38	303.80	266.32	238.28	216.54	199.21
5.00%	1,626.54	833.56	569.45	437.56	358.55	305.99	268.54	240.54	218.83	201.52
5.25%	1,628.72	835.69	571.58	439.71	360.73	308.20	270.78	242.81	221.13	203.85
5.50%	1,630.90	837.82	573.72	441.87	362.92	310.42	273.03	245.09	223.44	206.20
5.75%	1,633.08	839.95	575.87	444.04	365.12	312.65	275.29	247.38	225.77	208.56
6.00%	1,635.26	842.09	578.02	446.22	367.32	314.88	277.56	249.69	228.11	210.94
6.25%	1,637.45	844.23	580.17	448.40	369.54	317.13	279.85	252.01	230.47	213.33
6.50%	1,639.63	846.38	582.33	450.58	371.76	319.39	282.14	254.34	232.84	215.74
6.75%	1,641.82	848.53	584.50	452.78	373.99	321.66	284.44	256.68	235.22	218.17
7.00%	1,644.01	850.68	586.66	454.98	376.22	323.93	286.76	259.04	237.62	220.61
7.25%	1,646.20	852.83	588.84	457.19	378.47	326.22	289.09	261.41	240.03	223.06
7.50%	1,648.39	854.99	591.02	459.40	380.72	328.51	291.43	263.79	242.46	225.53
7.75%	1,650.58	857.15	593.20	461.62	382.98	330.82	293.78	266.19	244.90	228.02
8.00%	1,652.78	859.32	595.39	463.85	385.25	333.13	296.14	268.60	247.36	230.52
8.25%	1,654.98	861.49	597.58	466.08	387.53	335.46	298.51	271.02	249.82	233.04
8.50%	1,657.18	863.66	599.78	468.32	389.81	337.79	300.89	273.45	252.31	235.57
8.75%	1,659.38	865.83	601.99	470.56	392.11	340.13	303.29	275.90	254.80	238.12
9.00%	1,661.58	868.01	604.19	472.82	394.41	342.49	305.69	278.35	257.32	240.68
9.25%	1,663.78	870.19	606.41	475.07	396.72	344.85	308.11	280.82	259.84	243.26
9.50%	1,665.99	872.38	608.63	477.34	399.04	347.22	310.54	283.31	262.38	245.86
9.75%	1,668.19	874.56	610.85	479.61	401.36	349.60	312.97	285.80	264.93	248.46
10.00%	1,670.40	876.75	613.08	481.89	403.69	351.99	315.42	288.31	267.50	251.09
10.25%	1,672.61	878.95	615.31	484.17	406.04	354.39	317.88	290.83	270.07	253.72
10.50%	1,674.82	881.14	617.55	486.46	408.38	356.80	320.35	293.36	272.67	256.38
10.75%	1,677.04	883.35	619.79	488.76	410.74	359.22	322.83	295.90	275.27	259.04

	1	2	3	4	5	6	7	8	9	10
11.00%	1,679.25	885.55	622.04	491.06	413.11	361.65	325.33	298.46	277.89	261.73
11.25%	1,681.47	887.76	624.29	493.37	415.48	364.09	327.83	301.03	280.52	264.42
11.50%	1,683.69	889.97	626.54	495.69	417.86	366.53	330.34	303.61	283.17	267.13
11.75%	1,685.91	892.18	628.81	498.01	420.25	368.99	332.87	306.20	285.83	269.86
12.00%	1,688.13	894.40	631.07	500.34	422.64	371.45	335.40	308.80	288.50	272.59
12.25%	1,690.35	896.62	633.34	502.68	425.05	373.93	337.95	311.42	291.19	275.35
12.50%	1,692.57	898.84	635.62	505.02	427.46	376.41	340.50	314.05	293.88	278.11
12.75%	1,694.80	901.07	637.90	507.37	429.88	378.91	343.07	316.69	296.59	280.90
13.00%	1,697.03	903.29	640.19	509.72	432.31	381.41	345.65	319.34	299.32	283.69
13.25%	1,699.26	905.53	642.48	512.08	434.74	383.92	348.23	322.00	302.05	286.50
13.50%	1,701.49	907.76	644.77	514.45	437.19	386.44	350.83	324.68	304.80	289.32
13.75%	1,703.72	910.00	647.07	516.82	439.64	388.97	353.44	327.36	307.57	292.16
14.00%	1,705.96	912.24	649.37	519.20	442.10	391.51	356.06	330.06	310.34	295.01
14.25%	1,708.19	914.49	651.68	521.59	444.56	394.06	358.69	332.77	313.13	297.87
14.50%	1,710.43	916.74	654.00	523.98	447.04	396.61	361.33	335.49	315.93	300.74
14.75%	1,712.67	918.99	656.32	526.38	449.52	399.18	363.98	338.22	318.74	303.63
15.00%	1,714.91	921.25	658.64	528.78	452.01	401.76	366.64	340.96	321.56	306.54
15.25%	1,717.15	923.50	660.97	531.20	454.51	404.34	369.31	343.72	324.40	309.45
15.50%	1,719.39	925.77	663.30	533.61	457.01	406.93	371.99	346.48	327.25	312.38
15.75%	1,721.64	928.03	665.64	536.04	459.52	409.53	374.68	349.26	330.11	315.32
16.00%	1,723.89	930.30	667.98	538.47	462.04	412.14	377.38	352.05	332.98	318.27
16.25%	1,726.13	932.57	670.33	540.90	464.57	414.76	380.09	354.85	335.86	321.24
16.50%	1,728.39	934.84	672.68	543.34	467.11	417.39	382.81	357.66	338.76	324.22
16.75%	1,730.64	937.12	675.04	545.79	469.65	420.03	385.54	360.48	341.67	327.21
17.00%	1,732.89	939.40	677.40	548.25	472.20	422.68	388.28	363.31	344.59	330.22
17.25%	1,735.15	941.69	679.77	550.71	474.76	425.33	391.03	366.15	347.52	333.23
17.50%	1,737.40	943.97	682.14	553.17	477.32	427.99	393.79	369.00	350.46	336.26
17.75%	1,739.66	946.26	684.52	555.65	479.89	430.67	396.56	371.87	353.42	339.30
18.00%	1,741.92	948.56	686.90	558.12	482.48	433.35	399.34	374.74	356.38	342.35
18.25%	1,744.18	950.85	689.28	560.61	485.06	436.04	402.13	377.63	359.36	345.42
18.50%	1,746.44	953.15	691.67	563.10	487.66	438.74	404.93	380.52	362.35	348.49
18.75%	1,748.71	955.46	694.07	565.60	490.26	441.44	407.73	383.43	365.34	351.58
19.00%	1,750.97	957.76	696.46	568.10	492.87	444.16	410.55	386.34	368.35	354.68
19.25%	1,753.24	960.07	698.87	570.61	495.49	446.88	413.38	389.27	371.38	357.79
19.50%	1,755.51	962.39	701.28	573.13	498.11	449.61	416.22	392.21	374.41	360.91
19.75%	1,757.78	964.70	703.69	575.65	500.74	452.35	419.06	395.15	377.45	364.04
20.00%	1,760.06	967.02	706.11	578.18	503.38	455.10	421.92	398.11	380.50	367.19
20.25%	1,762.33	969.34	708.53	580.71	506.03	457.86	424.78	401.08	383.57	370.34
20.50%	1,764.61	971.67	710.96	583.25	508.68	460.63	427.66	404.06	386.64	373.51
20.75%	1,766.88	974.00	713.39	585.80	511.35	463.40	430.54	407.04	389.73	376.68

	1	2	3	4	5	6	7	8	9	10
1.00%	1,675.71	842.04	564.16	425.23	341.87	286.31	246.62	216.86	193.72	175.21
1.25%	1,677.97	844.23	566.33	427.39	344.03	288.47	248.79	219.03	195.89	177.39
1.50%	1,680.24	846.42	568.50	429.55	346.20	290.64	250.96	221.21	198.08	179.58
1.75%	1,682.51	848.61	570.67	431.72	348.37	292.82	253.15	223.41	200.29	181.80
2.00%	1,684.78	850.81	572.85	433.90	350.56	295.01	255.35	225.62	202.51	184.03
2.25%	1,687.05	853.00	575.04	436.09	352.75	297.21	257.56	227.84	204.74	186.27
2.50%	1,689.32	855.21	577.23	438.28	354.95	299.42	259.78	230.08	206.99	188.54
2.75%	1,691.60	857.41	579.42	440.48	357.16	301.64	262.02	232.33	209.26	190.82
3.00%	1,693.87	859.62	581.62	442.69	359.37	303.87	264.27	234.59	211.54	193.12
3.25%	1,696.15	861.84	583.83	444.90	361.60	306.12	266.53	236.87	213.84	195.44
3.50%	1,698.43	864.05	586.04	447.12	363.83	308.37	268.80	239.16	216.15	197.77
3.75%	1,700.71	866.27	588.26	449.35	366.08	310.63	271.08	241.47	218.48	200.12
4.00%	1,703.00	868.50	590.48	451.58	368.33	312.90	273.38	243.79	220.82	202.49
4.25%	1,705.28	870.73	592.71	453.82	370.59	315.19	275.68	246.12	223.18	204.88
4.50%	1,707.57	872.96	594.94	456.07	372.86	317.48	278.00	248.46	225.55	207.28
4.75%	1,709.86	875.19	597.18	458.32	375.14	319.78	280.33	250.82	227.94	209.70
5.00%	1,712.15	877.43	599.42	460.59	377.42	322.10	282.68	253.20	230.35	212.13
5.25%	1,714.44	879.67	601.67	462.85	379.72	324.42	285.03	255.59	232.77	214.58
5.50%	1,716.74	881.91	603.92	465.13	382.02	326.76	287.40	257.99	235.20	217.05
5.75%	1,719.03	884.16	606.18	467.41	384.34	329.10	289.78	260.40	237.65	219.54
6.00%	1,721.33	886.41	608.44	469.70	386.66	331.46	292.17	262.83	240.11	222.04
6.25%	1,723.63	888.67	610.71	472.00	388.99	333.82	294.57	265.27	242.60	224.56
6.50%	1,725.93	890.93	612.98	474.30	391.32	336.20	296.99	267.72	245.09	227.10
6.75%	1,728.23	893.19	615.26	476.61	393.67	338.58	299.42	270.19	247.60	229.65
7.00%	1,730.53	895.45	617.54	478.92	396.02	340.98	301.85	272.67	250.13	232.22
7.25%	1,732.84	897.72	619.83	481.25	398.39	343.39	304.30	275.17	252.67	234.80
7.50%	1,735.15	899.99	622.12	483.58	400.76	345.80	306.77	277.68	255.22	237.40
7.75%	1,737.46	902.27	624.42	485.91	403.14	348.23	309.24	280.20	257.79	240.02
8.00%	1,739.77	904.55	626.73	488.26	405.53	350.66	311.72	282.73	260.37	242.66
8.25%	1,742.08	906.83	629.04	490.61	407.93	353.11	314.22	285.28	262.97	245.31
8.50%	1,744.40	909.11	631.35	492.97	410.33	355.57	316.73	287.84	265.59	247.97
8.75%	1,746.71	911.40	633.67	495.33	412.74	358.03	319.25	290.42	268.22	250.65
9.00%	1,749.03	913.69	635.99	497.70	415.17	360.51	321.78	293.00	270.86	253.35
9.25%	1,751.35	915.99	638.32	500.08	417.60	363.00	324.32	295.60	273.52	256.07
9.50%	1,753.67	918.29	640.66	502.46	420.04	365.49	326.88	298.22	276.19	258.80
9.75%	1,755.99	920.59	643.00	504.85	422.48	368.00	329.45	300.84	278.87	261.54
10.00%	1,758.32	922.90	645.34	507.25	424.94	370.52	332.02	303.48	281.57	264.30
10.25%	1,760.64	925.21	647.69	509.66	427.41	373.04	334.61	306.14	284.29	267.08
10.50%	1,762.97	927.52	650.05	512.07	429.88	375.58	337.21	308.80	287.02	269.87
10.75%	1,765.30	929.84	652.41	514.49	432.36	378.13	339.83	311.48	289.76	272.68

$20,000 11.00 - 20.75% 1 - 10 Years

	1	2	3	4	5	6	7	8	9	10
11.00%	1,767.63	932.16	654.77	516.91	434.85	380.68	342.45	314.17	292.52	275.50
11.25%	1,769.97	934.48	657.14	519.34	437.35	383.25	345.08	316.87	295.29	278.34
11.50%	1,772.30	936.81	659.52	521.78	439.85	385.82	347.73	319.59	298.07	281.19
11.75%	1,774.64	939.14	661.90	524.23	442.37	388.41	350.39	322.32	300.87	284.06
12.00%	1,776.98	941.47	664.29	526.68	444.89	391.00	353.05	325.06	303.68	286.94
12.25%	1,779.32	943.81	666.68	529.14	447.42	393.61	355.73	327.81	306.51	289.84
12.50%	1,781.66	946.15	669.07	531.60	449.96	396.22	358.42	330.58	309.35	292.75
12.75%	1,784.00	948.49	671.47	534.07	452.51	398.85	361.13	333.35	312.20	295.68
13.00%	1,786.35	950.84	673.88	536.55	455.06	401.48	363.84	336.15	315.07	298.62
13.25%	1,788.69	953.19	676.29	539.03	457.63	404.13	366.56	338.95	317.95	301.58
13.50%	1,791.04	955.54	678.71	541.53	460.20	406.78	369.30	341.76	320.85	304.55
13.75%	1,793.39	957.90	681.13	544.02	462.78	409.44	372.04	344.59	323.75	307.53
14.00%	1,795.74	960.26	683.55	546.53	465.37	412.11	374.80	347.43	326.67	310.53
14.25%	1,798.10	962.62	685.98	549.04	467.96	414.80	377.57	350.28	329.61	313.55
14.50%	1,800.45	964.99	688.42	551.56	470.57	417.49	380.35	353.15	332.55	316.57
14.75%	1,802.81	967.36	690.86	554.08	473.18	420.19	383.14	356.02	335.51	319.61
15.00%	1,805.17	969.73	693.31	556.61	475.80	422.90	385.94	358.91	338.49	322.67
15.25%	1,807.53	972.11	695.76	559.15	478.43	425.62	388.75	361.81	341.47	325.74
15.50%	1,809.89	974.49	698.21	561.70	481.06	428.35	391.57	364.72	344.47	328.82
15.75%	1,812.25	976.87	700.67	564.25	483.71	431.09	394.40	367.64	347.48	331.92
16.00%	1,814.62	979.26	703.14	566.81	486.36	433.84	397.24	370.58	350.51	335.03
16.25%	1,816.98	981.65	705.61	569.37	489.02	436.59	400.09	373.52	353.54	338.15
16.50%	1,819.35	984.05	708.09	571.94	491.69	439.36	402.96	376.48	356.59	341.28
16.75%	1,821.72	986.44	710.57	574.52	494.37	442.14	405.83	379.45	359.65	344.43
17.00%	1,824.10	988.85	713.05	577.10	497.05	444.92	408.72	382.43	362.72	347.60
17.25%	1,826.47	991.25	715.55	579.69	499.74	447.72	411.61	385.42	365.81	350.77
17.50%	1,828.84	993.66	718.04	582.29	502.44	450.52	414.52	388.42	368.91	353.96
17.75%	1,831.22	996.07	720.54	584.89	505.15	453.33	417.43	391.44	372.02	357.16
18.00%	1,833.60	998.48	723.05	587.50	507.87	456.16	420.36	394.46	375.14	360.37
18.25%	1,835.98	1,000.90	725.56	590.12	510.59	458.99	423.29	397.50	378.27	363.60
18.50%	1,838.36	1,003.32	728.07	592.74	513.32	461.83	426.24	400.55	381.42	366.83
18.75%	1,840.75	1,005.74	730.59	595.37	516.06	464.68	429.19	403.61	384.57	370.08
19.00%	1,843.13	1,008.17	733.12	598.00	518.81	467.53	432.16	406.68	387.74	373.34
19.25%	1,845.52	1,010.60	735.65	600.64	521.57	470.40	435.14	409.76	390.92	376.62
19.50%	1,847.91	1,013.04	738.19	603.29	524.33	473.28	438.12	412.85	394.11	379.90
19.75%	1,850.30	1,015.48	740.73	605.95	527.10	476.16	441.12	415.95	397.32	383.20
20.00%	1,852.69	1,017.92	743.27	608.61	529.88	479.06	444.12	419.06	400.53	386.51
20.25%	1,855.08	1,020.36	745.82	611.27	532.66	481.96	447.14	422.19	403.76	389.83
20.50%	1,857.48	1,022.81	748.38	613.95	535.46	484.87	450.16	425.32	406.99	393.16
20.75%	1,859.88	1,025.26	750.94	616.63	538.26	487.79	453.20	428.47	410.24	396.51

	1	2	3	4	5	6	7	8	9	10
1.00%	1,759.49	884.14	592.37	446.49	358.97	300.63	258.96	227.71	203.41	183.97
1.25%	1,761.87	886.44	594.64	448.76	361.23	302.89	261.23	229.98	205.69	186.26
1.50%	1,764.25	888.74	596.92	451.03	363.51	305.17	263.51	232.27	207.99	188.56
1.75%	1,766.63	891.04	599.20	453.31	365.79	307.46	265.81	234.58	210.30	190.89
2.00%	1,769.02	893.35	601.49	455.60	368.08	309.76	268.12	236.90	212.63	193.23
2.25%	1,771.40	895.66	603.79	457.89	370.38	312.07	270.44	239.23	214.98	195.59
2.50%	1,773.79	897.97	606.09	460.19	372.69	314.39	272.77	241.58	217.34	197.97
2.75%	1,776.18	900.29	608.39	462.50	375.01	316.72	275.12	243.94	219.72	200.36
3.00%	1,778.57	902.61	610.71	464.82	377.34	319.07	277.48	246.32	222.12	202.78
3.25%	1,780.96	904.93	613.02	467.14	379.68	321.42	279.85	248.71	224.53	205.21
3.50%	1,783.35	907.26	615.34	469.48	382.03	323.79	282.24	251.12	226.96	207.66
3.75%	1,785.75	909.59	617.67	471.81	384.38	326.16	284.63	253.54	229.40	210.13
4.00%	1,788.15	911.92	620.00	474.16	386.75	328.55	287.04	255.97	231.86	212.61
4.25%	1,790.55	914.26	622.34	476.51	389.12	330.95	289.47	258.42	234.34	215.12
4.50%	1,792.95	916.60	624.69	478.87	391.50	333.35	291.90	260.89	236.83	217.64
4.75%	1,795.35	918.95	627.03	481.24	393.90	335.77	294.35	263.37	239.34	220.18
5.00%	1,797.76	921.30	629.39	483.62	396.30	338.20	296.81	265.86	241.86	222.74
5.25%	1,800.16	923.65	631.75	486.00	398.71	340.64	299.29	268.36	244.40	225.31
5.50%	1,802.57	926.01	634.11	488.39	401.12	343.10	301.77	270.89	246.96	227.91
5.75%	1,804.98	928.37	636.48	490.78	403.55	345.56	304.27	273.42	249.53	230.52
6.00%	1,807.40	930.73	638.86	493.19	405.99	348.03	306.78	275.97	252.12	233.14
6.25%	1,809.81	933.10	641.24	495.60	408.43	350.51	309.30	278.53	254.72	235.79
6.50%	1,812.22	935.47	643.63	498.01	410.89	353.01	311.84	281.11	257.34	238.45
6.75%	1,814.64	937.85	646.02	500.44	413.35	355.51	314.39	283.70	259.98	241.13
7.00%	1,817.06	940.22	648.42	502.87	415.83	358.03	316.95	286.31	262.63	243.83
7.25%	1,819.48	942.61	650.82	505.31	418.31	360.56	319.52	288.93	265.30	246.54
7.50%	1,821.91	944.99	653.23	507.76	420.80	363.09	322.10	291.56	267.98	249.27
7.75%	1,824.33	947.38	655.64	510.21	423.30	365.64	324.70	294.21	270.68	252.02
8.00%	1,826.76	949.77	658.06	512.67	425.80	368.20	327.31	296.87	273.39	254.79
8.25%	1,829.19	952.17	660.49	515.14	428.32	370.77	329.93	299.55	276.12	257.57
8.50%	1,831.62	954.57	662.92	517.61	430.85	373.35	332.57	302.23	278.87	260.37
8.75%	1,834.05	956.97	665.35	520.10	433.38	375.94	335.21	304.94	281.63	263.19
9.00%	1,836.48	959.38	667.79	522.59	435.93	378.54	337.87	307.65	284.40	266.02
9.25%	1,838.92	961.79	670.24	525.08	438.48	381.15	340.54	310.38	287.19	268.87
9.50%	1,841.35	964.20	672.69	527.59	441.04	383.77	343.22	313.13	290.00	271.73
9.75%	1,843.79	966.62	675.15	530.10	443.61	386.40	345.92	315.89	292.82	274.62
10.00%	1,846.23	969.04	677.61	532.61	446.19	389.04	348.62	318.66	295.65	277.52
10.25%	1,848.68	971.47	680.08	535.14	448.78	391.70	351.34	321.44	298.50	280.43
10.50%	1,851.12	973.90	682.55	537.67	451.37	394.36	354.07	324.24	301.37	283.36
10.75%	1,853.57	976.33	685.03	540.21	453.98	397.03	356.82	327.05	304.25	286.31

	1	2	3	4	5	6	7	8	9	10
11.00%	1,856.01	978.76	687.51	542.76	456.59	399.72	359.57	329.88	307.14	289.28
11.25%	1,858.46	981.20	690.00	545.31	459.21	402.41	362.34	332.72	310.05	292.25
11.50%	1,860.92	983.65	692.50	547.87	461.84	405.11	365.12	335.57	312.98	295.25
11.75%	1,863.37	986.09	695.00	550.44	464.48	407.83	367.91	338.43	315.92	298.26
12.00%	1,865.82	988.54	697.50	553.01	467.13	410.55	370.71	341.31	318.87	301.29
12.25%	1,868.28	991.00	700.01	555.59	469.79	413.29	373.52	344.20	321.84	304.33
12.50%	1,870.74	993.45	702.53	558.18	472.46	416.03	376.35	347.10	324.82	307.39
12.75%	1,873.20	995.91	705.05	560.78	475.13	418.79	379.18	350.02	327.81	310.46
13.00%	1,875.66	998.38	707.57	563.38	477.81	421.56	382.03	352.95	330.83	313.55
13.25%	1,878.13	1,000.85	710.10	565.99	480.51	424.33	384.89	355.90	333.85	316.66
13.50%	1,880.59	1,003.32	712.64	568.60	483.21	427.12	387.76	358.85	336.89	319.78
13.75%	1,883.06	1,005.79	715.18	571.23	485.92	429.91	390.65	361.82	339.94	322.91
14.00%	1,885.53	1,008.27	717.73	573.86	488.63	432.72	393.54	364.80	343.01	326.06
14.25%	1,888.00	1,010.75	720.28	576.49	491.36	435.54	396.45	367.80	346.09	329.22
14.50%	1,890.47	1,013.24	722.84	579.14	494.09	438.36	399.36	370.80	349.18	332.40
14.75%	1,892.95	1,015.73	725.40	581.79	496.84	441.20	402.29	373.82	352.29	335.60
15.00%	1,895.42	1,018.22	727.97	584.45	499.59	444.05	405.23	376.85	355.41	338.80
15.25%	1,897.90	1,020.72	730.55	587.11	502.35	446.90	408.18	379.90	358.55	342.03
15.50%	1,900.38	1,023.22	733.12	589.78	505.12	449.77	411.15	382.95	361.69	345.26
15.75%	1,902.86	1,025.72	735.71	592.46	507.89	452.64	414.12	386.02	364.86	348.51
16.00%	1,905.35	1,028.23	738.30	595.15	510.68	455.53	417.10	389.10	368.03	351.78
16.25%	1,907.83	1,030.74	740.89	597.84	513.47	458.42	420.10	392.20	371.22	355.06
16.50%	1,910.32	1,033.25	743.49	600.54	516.27	461.33	423.11	395.30	374.42	358.35
16.75%	1,912.81	1,035.77	746.10	603.24	519.09	464.24	426.12	398.42	377.63	361.66
17.00%	1,915.30	1,038.29	748.71	605.96	521.90	467.17	429.15	401.55	380.86	364.98
17.25%	1,917.79	1,040.81	751.32	608.68	524.73	470.10	432.19	404.69	384.10	368.31
17.50%	1,920.29	1,043.34	753.94	611.40	527.57	473.05	435.24	407.85	387.35	371.66
17.75%	1,922.78	1,045.87	756.57	614.14	530.41	476.00	438.30	411.01	390.62	375.02
18.00%	1,925.28	1,048.41	759.20	616.87	533.26	478.96	441.37	414.19	393.89	378.39
18.25%	1,927.78	1,050.94	761.84	619.62	536.12	481.94	444.46	417.38	397.18	381.78
18.50%	1,930.28	1,053.49	764.48	622.38	538.99	484.92	447.55	420.58	400.49	385.17
18.75%	1,932.78	1,056.03	767.12	625.14	541.87	487.91	450.65	423.79	403.80	388.59
19.00%	1,935.29	1,058.58	769.78	627.90	544.75	490.91	453.77	427.01	407.13	392.01
19.25%	1,937.79	1,061.13	772.43	630.68	547.64	493.92	456.89	430.25	410.47	395.45
19.50%	1,940.30	1,063.69	775.10	633.46	550.55	496.94	460.03	433.49	413.82	398.90
19.75%	1,942.81	1,066.25	777.76	636.24	553.45	499.97	463.17	436.75	417.18	402.36
20.00%	1,945.32	1,068.81	780.44	639.04	556.37	503.01	466.33	440.02	420.56	405.84
20.25%	1,947.84	1,071.38	783.11	641.84	559.30	506.06	469.50	443.30	423.94	409.32
20.50%	1,950.35	1,073.95	785.80	644.65	562.23	509.11	472.67	446.59	427.34	412.82
20.75%	1,952.87	1,076.52	788.48	647.46	565.17	512.18	475.86	449.89	430.75	416.33

	1	2	3	4	5	6	7	8	9	10
1.00%	1,843.28	926.25	620.58	467.75	376.06	314.94	271.29	238.55	213.09	192.73
1.25%	1,845.77	928.65	622.96	470.13	378.44	317.32	273.67	240.94	215.48	195.13
1.50%	1,848.26	931.06	625.35	472.51	380.82	319.70	276.06	243.33	217.89	197.54
1.75%	1,850.76	933.47	627.74	474.90	383.21	322.10	278.46	245.75	220.31	199.98
2.00%	1,853.26	935.89	630.14	477.29	385.61	324.51	280.88	248.18	222.76	202.43
2.25%	1,855.75	938.31	632.54	479.70	388.02	326.93	283.32	250.62	225.21	204.90
2.50%	1,858.25	940.73	634.95	482.11	390.44	329.36	285.76	253.08	227.69	207.39
2.75%	1,860.76	943.16	637.37	484.53	392.87	331.81	288.22	255.56	230.18	209.90
3.00%	1,863.26	945.59	639.79	486.96	395.31	334.26	290.69	258.05	232.69	212.43
3.25%	1,865.77	948.02	642.21	489.39	397.76	336.73	293.18	260.56	235.22	214.98
3.50%	1,868.28	950.46	644.65	491.83	400.22	339.20	295.68	263.08	237.76	217.55
3.75%	1,870.79	952.90	647.08	494.28	402.69	341.69	298.19	265.61	240.32	220.13
4.00%	1,873.30	955.35	649.53	496.74	405.16	344.19	300.71	268.16	242.90	222.74
4.25%	1,875.81	957.80	651.98	499.20	407.65	346.71	303.25	270.73	245.50	225.36
4.50%	1,878.33	960.25	654.43	501.68	410.15	349.23	305.80	273.31	248.11	228.00
4.75%	1,880.85	962.71	656.89	504.16	412.65	351.76	308.37	275.91	250.74	230.67
5.00%	1,883.36	965.17	659.36	506.64	415.17	354.31	310.95	278.52	253.38	233.34
5.25%	1,885.89	967.64	661.83	509.14	417.69	356.87	313.54	281.14	256.04	236.04
5.50%	1,888.41	970.10	664.31	511.64	420.23	359.43	316.14	283.79	258.72	238.76
5.75%	1,890.93	972.58	666.79	514.15	422.77	362.01	318.76	286.44	261.41	241.49
6.00%	1,893.46	975.05	669.28	516.67	425.32	364.60	321.39	289.11	264.13	244.25
6.25%	1,895.99	977.53	671.78	519.20	427.88	367.21	324.03	291.80	266.85	247.02
6.50%	1,898.52	980.02	674.28	521.73	430.46	369.82	326.69	294.50	269.60	249.81
6.75%	1,901.05	982.51	676.78	524.27	433.04	372.44	329.36	297.21	272.36	252.61
7.00%	1,903.59	985.00	679.30	526.82	435.63	375.08	332.04	299.94	275.14	255.44
7.25%	1,906.12	987.49	681.81	529.37	438.23	377.72	334.73	302.69	277.93	258.28
7.50%	1,908.66	989.99	684.34	531.94	440.83	380.38	337.44	305.45	280.74	261.14
7.75%	1,911.20	992.49	686.87	534.51	443.45	383.05	340.16	308.22	283.57	264.02
8.00%	1,913.75	995.00	689.40	537.08	446.08	385.73	342.90	311.01	286.41	266.92
8.25%	1,916.29	997.51	691.94	539.67	448.72	388.42	345.64	313.81	289.27	269.84
8.50%	1,918.84	1,000.02	694.49	542.26	451.36	391.12	348.40	316.63	292.15	272.77
8.75%	1,921.38	1,002.54	697.04	544.86	454.02	393.84	351.17	319.46	295.04	275.72
9.00%	1,923.93	1,005.06	699.59	547.47	456.68	396.56	353.96	322.30	297.94	278.69
9.25%	1,926.48	1,007.59	702.16	550.09	459.36	399.30	356.76	325.16	300.87	281.67
9.50%	1,929.04	1,010.12	704.72	552.71	462.04	402.04	359.57	328.04	303.81	284.67
9.75%	1,931.59	1,012.65	707.30	555.34	464.73	404.80	362.39	330.93	306.76	287.69
10.00%	1,934.15	1,015.19	709.88	557.98	467.43	407.57	365.23	333.83	309.73	290.73
10.25%	1,936.71	1,017.73	712.46	560.62	470.15	410.35	368.07	336.75	312.72	293.79
10.50%	1,939.27	1,020.27	715.05	563.27	472.87	413.14	370.93	339.68	315.72	296.86
10.75%	1,941.83	1,022.82	717.65	565.93	475.59	415.94	373.81	342.63	318.74	299.95

$22,000   11.00 - 20.75%   1 - 10 Years

	1	2	3	4	5	6	7	8	9	10
11.00%	1,944.40	1,025.37	720.25	568.60	478.33	418.75	376.69	345.59	321.77	303.05
11.25%	1,946.96	1,027.93	722.86	571.28	481.08	421.57	379.59	348.56	324.82	306.17
11.50%	1,949.53	1,030.49	725.47	573.96	483.84	424.41	382.50	351.55	327.88	309.31
11.75%	1,952.10	1,033.05	728.09	576.65	486.60	427.25	385.42	354.55	330.96	312.46
12.00%	1,954.67	1,035.62	730.71	579.34	489.38	430.10	388.36	357.56	334.05	315.64
12.25%	1,957.25	1,038.19	733.34	582.05	492.16	432.97	391.31	360.59	337.16	318.82
12.50%	1,959.82	1,040.76	735.98	584.76	494.95	435.85	394.27	363.63	340.29	322.03
12.75%	1,962.40	1,043.34	738.62	587.48	497.76	438.73	397.24	366.69	343.43	325.25
13.00%	1,964.98	1,045.92	741.27	590.20	500.57	441.63	400.22	369.76	346.58	328.48
13.25%	1,967.56	1,048.51	743.92	592.94	503.39	444.54	403.22	372.84	349.75	331.74
13.50%	1,970.14	1,051.09	746.58	595.68	506.22	447.46	406.23	375.94	352.93	335.00
13.75%	1,972.73	1,053.69	749.24	598.43	509.05	450.39	409.25	379.05	356.13	338.29
14.00%	1,975.32	1,056.28	751.91	601.18	511.90	453.33	412.28	382.17	359.34	341.59
14.25%	1,977.91	1,058.88	754.58	603.95	514.76	456.28	415.32	385.31	362.57	344.90
14.50%	1,980.50	1,061.49	757.26	606.71	517.62	459.24	418.38	388.46	365.81	348.23
14.75%	1,983.09	1,064.09	759.95	609.49	520.50	462.21	421.45	391.62	369.07	351.58
15.00%	1,985.68	1,066.71	762.64	612.28	523.38	465.19	424.53	394.80	372.34	354.94
15.25%	1,988.28	1,069.32	765.33	615.07	526.27	468.18	427.62	397.99	375.62	358.31
15.50%	1,990.88	1,071.94	768.03	617.87	529.17	471.18	430.72	401.19	378.92	361.70
15.75%	1,993.48	1,074.56	770.74	620.67	532.08	474.20	433.84	404.41	382.23	365.11
16.00%	1,996.08	1,077.19	773.45	623.49	535.00	477.22	436.97	407.63	385.56	368.53
16.25%	1,998.68	1,079.82	776.17	626.31	537.92	480.25	440.10	410.87	388.90	371.96
16.50%	2,001.29	1,082.45	778.90	629.13	540.86	483.30	443.25	414.13	392.25	375.41
16.75%	2,003.90	1,085.09	781.63	631.97	543.80	486.35	446.41	417.39	395.62	378.88
17.00%	2,006.50	1,087.73	784.36	634.81	546.76	489.41	449.59	420.67	399.00	382.35
17.25%	2,009.12	1,090.37	787.10	637.66	549.72	492.49	452.77	423.96	402.39	385.85
17.50%	2,011.73	1,093.02	789.85	640.52	552.69	495.57	455.97	427.27	405.80	389.35
17.75%	2,014.34	1,095.67	792.60	643.38	555.67	498.67	459.17	430.58	409.22	392.87
18.00%	2,016.96	1,098.33	795.35	646.25	558.66	501.77	462.39	433.91	412.65	396.41
18.25%	2,019.58	1,100.99	798.11	649.13	561.65	504.89	465.62	437.25	416.10	399.96
18.50%	2,022.20	1,103.65	800.88	652.01	564.66	508.01	468.86	440.60	419.56	403.52
18.75%	2,024.82	1,106.32	803.65	654.90	567.67	511.14	472.11	443.97	423.03	407.09
19.00%	2,027.44	1,108.99	806.43	657.80	570.69	514.29	475.38	447.35	426.52	410.68
19.25%	2,030.07	1,111.66	809.22	660.71	573.72	517.44	478.65	450.73	430.01	414.28
19.50%	2,032.70	1,114.34	812.00	663.62	576.76	520.61	481.93	454.13	433.52	417.89
19.75%	2,035.33	1,117.02	814.80	666.54	579.81	523.78	485.23	457.55	437.05	421.52
20.00%	2,037.96	1,119.71	817.60	669.47	582.87	526.96	488.54	460.97	440.58	425.16
20.25%	2,040.59	1,122.40	820.40	672.40	585.93	530.16	491.85	464.41	444.13	428.82
20.50%	2,043.23	1,125.09	823.21	675.34	589.00	533.36	495.18	467.85	447.69	432.48
20.75%	2,045.86	1,127.78	826.03	678.29	592.08	536.57	498.52	471.31	451.26	436.16

	1	2	3	4	5	6	7	8	9	10
1.00%	1,927.06	968.35	648.79	489.01	393.16	329.26	283.62	249.39	222.78	201.49
1.25%	1,929.67	970.86	651.28	491.50	395.64	331.74	286.11	251.89	225.28	204.00
1.50%	1,932.28	973.38	653.77	493.98	398.13	334.23	288.61	254.40	227.79	206.52
1.75%	1,934.88	975.90	656.27	496.48	400.63	336.74	291.12	256.92	230.33	209.07
2.00%	1,937.49	978.43	658.78	498.99	403.14	339.26	293.65	259.46	232.88	211.63
2.25%	1,940.11	980.96	661.29	501.50	405.66	341.79	296.19	262.02	235.45	214.22
2.50%	1,942.72	983.49	663.81	504.02	408.19	344.33	298.75	264.59	238.04	216.82
2.75%	1,945.34	986.03	666.34	506.55	410.73	346.89	301.32	267.18	240.65	219.45
3.00%	1,947.96	988.57	668.87	509.09	413.28	349.45	303.91	269.78	243.27	222.09
3.25%	1,950.58	991.11	671.40	511.63	415.84	352.03	306.50	272.40	245.91	224.75
3.50%	1,953.20	993.66	673.95	514.19	418.41	354.62	309.12	275.04	248.57	227.44
3.75%	1,955.82	996.22	676.50	516.75	420.99	357.23	311.74	277.69	251.25	230.14
4.00%	1,958.45	998.77	679.05	519.32	423.58	359.84	314.38	280.35	253.94	232.86
4.25%	1,961.08	1,001.33	681.61	521.90	426.18	362.47	317.04	283.04	256.65	235.61
4.50%	1,963.71	1,003.90	684.18	524.48	428.79	365.10	319.70	285.73	259.38	238.37
4.75%	1,966.34	1,006.47	686.75	527.07	431.41	367.75	322.38	288.45	262.13	241.15
5.00%	1,968.97	1,009.04	689.33	529.67	434.04	370.41	325.08	291.18	264.90	243.95
5.25%	1,971.61	1,011.62	691.92	532.28	436.68	373.09	327.79	293.92	267.68	246.77
5.50%	1,974.25	1,014.20	694.51	534.90	439.33	375.77	330.51	296.68	270.48	249.61
5.75%	1,976.89	1,016.79	697.10	537.52	441.99	378.47	333.25	299.46	273.30	252.47
6.00%	1,979.53	1,019.37	699.70	540.16	444.65	381.18	336.00	302.25	276.13	255.35
6.25%	1,982.17	1,021.97	702.31	542.80	447.33	383.90	338.76	305.06	278.98	258.24
6.50%	1,984.82	1,024.56	704.93	545.44	450.02	386.63	341.54	307.88	281.85	261.16
6.75%	1,987.47	1,027.16	707.55	548.10	452.72	389.37	344.33	310.72	284.74	264.10
7.00%	1,990.12	1,029.77	710.17	550.76	455.43	392.13	347.13	313.58	287.64	267.05
7.25%	1,992.77	1,032.38	712.81	553.44	458.15	394.89	349.95	316.44	290.57	270.02
7.50%	1,995.42	1,034.99	715.44	556.11	460.87	397.67	352.78	319.33	293.50	273.01
7.75%	1,998.08	1,037.61	718.09	558.80	463.61	400.46	355.62	322.23	296.46	276.02
8.00%	2,000.73	1,040.23	720.74	561.50	466.36	403.26	358.48	325.14	299.43	279.05
8.25%	2,003.39	1,042.85	723.39	564.20	469.11	406.08	361.35	328.07	302.42	282.10
8.50%	2,006.05	1,045.48	726.05	566.91	471.88	408.90	364.24	331.02	305.43	285.17
8.75%	2,008.72	1,048.11	728.72	569.63	474.66	411.74	367.14	333.98	308.45	288.25
9.00%	2,011.38	1,050.75	731.39	572.36	477.44	414.59	370.05	336.95	311.49	291.35
9.25%	2,014.05	1,053.39	734.07	575.09	480.24	417.45	372.97	339.95	314.54	294.48
9.50%	2,016.72	1,056.03	736.76	577.83	483.04	420.32	375.91	342.95	317.62	297.61
9.75%	2,019.39	1,058.68	739.45	580.58	485.86	423.20	378.86	345.97	320.70	300.77
10.00%	2,022.07	1,061.33	742.15	583.34	488.68	426.09	381.83	349.01	323.81	303.95
10.25%	2,024.74	1,063.99	744.85	586.10	491.52	429.00	384.80	352.06	326.93	307.14
10.50%	2,027.42	1,066.65	747.56	588.88	494.36	431.92	387.80	355.12	330.07	310.35
10.75%	2,030.10	1,069.31	750.27	591.66	497.21	434.84	390.80	358.20	333.22	313.58

$23,000   11.00 - 20.75%   1 - 10 Years

	1	2	3	4	5	6	7	8	9	10
11.00%	2,032.78	1,071.98	752.99	594.45	500.08	437.78	393.82	361.29	336.39	316.83
11.25%	2,035.46	1,074.65	755.72	597.24	502.95	440.73	396.85	364.40	339.58	320.09
11.50%	2,038.15	1,077.33	758.45	600.05	505.83	443.70	399.89	367.53	342.78	323.37
11.75%	2,040.83	1,080.01	761.19	602.86	508.72	446.67	402.94	370.66	346.00	326.67
12.00%	2,043.52	1,082.69	763.93	605.68	511.62	449.65	406.01	373.82	349.24	329.98
12.25%	2,046.21	1,085.38	766.68	608.51	514.53	452.65	409.09	376.98	352.49	333.32
12.50%	2,048.91	1,088.07	769.43	611.34	517.45	455.66	412.19	380.16	355.75	336.67
12.75%	2,051.60	1,090.76	772.19	614.18	520.38	458.68	415.30	383.36	359.04	340.03
13.00%	2,054.30	1,093.46	774.96	617.03	523.32	461.70	418.42	386.57	362.33	343.41
13.25%	2,057.00	1,096.16	777.73	619.89	526.27	464.74	421.55	389.79	365.65	346.81
13.50%	2,059.70	1,098.87	780.51	622.76	529.23	467.80	424.69	393.03	368.97	350.23
13.75%	2,062.40	1,101.58	783.30	625.63	532.19	470.86	427.85	396.28	372.32	353.66
14.00%	2,065.10	1,104.30	786.09	628.51	535.17	473.93	431.02	399.54	375.68	357.11
14.25%	2,067.81	1,107.01	788.88	631.40	538.16	477.02	434.20	402.82	379.05	360.58
14.50%	2,070.52	1,109.74	791.68	634.29	541.15	480.11	437.40	406.12	382.44	364.06
14.75%	2,073.23	1,112.46	794.49	637.20	544.15	483.22	440.61	409.42	385.84	367.56
15.00%	2,075.94	1,115.19	797.30	640.11	547.17	486.34	443.83	412.74	389.26	371.07
15.25%	2,078.66	1,117.93	800.12	643.03	550.19	489.46	447.06	416.08	392.69	374.60
15.50%	2,081.37	1,120.66	802.95	645.95	553.22	492.60	450.30	419.43	396.14	378.14
15.75%	2,084.09	1,123.41	805.78	648.89	556.26	495.75	453.56	422.79	399.60	381.70
16.00%	2,086.81	1,126.15	808.61	651.83	559.32	498.91	456.83	426.16	403.08	385.28
16.25%	2,089.53	1,128.90	811.45	654.78	562.38	502.08	460.11	429.55	406.57	388.87
16.50%	2,092.26	1,131.65	814.30	657.73	565.44	505.27	463.40	432.95	410.08	392.48
16.75%	2,094.98	1,134.41	817.15	660.69	568.52	508.46	466.71	436.37	413.60	396.10
17.00%	2,097.71	1,137.17	820.01	663.67	571.61	511.66	470.02	439.79	417.13	399.73
17.25%	2,100.44	1,139.94	822.88	666.64	574.71	514.87	473.35	443.23	420.68	403.39
17.50%	2,103.17	1,142.71	825.75	669.63	577.81	518.10	476.69	446.69	424.24	407.05
17.75%	2,105.90	1,145.48	828.62	672.62	580.93	521.33	480.05	450.15	427.82	410.73
18.00%	2,108.64	1,148.25	831.51	675.62	584.05	524.58	483.41	453.63	431.41	414.43
18.25%	2,111.38	1,151.03	834.39	678.63	587.18	527.83	486.79	457.13	435.01	418.13
18.50%	2,114.12	1,153.82	837.29	681.65	590.32	531.10	490.17	460.63	438.63	421.86
18.75%	2,116.86	1,156.61	840.18	684.67	593.47	534.38	493.57	464.15	442.26	425.60
19.00%	2,119.60	1,159.40	843.09	687.70	596.63	537.66	496.98	467.68	445.90	429.35
19.25%	2,122.35	1,162.19	846.00	690.74	599.80	540.96	500.41	471.22	449.56	433.11
19.50%	2,125.09	1,164.99	848.91	693.79	602.98	544.27	503.84	474.78	453.23	436.89
19.75%	2,127.84	1,167.80	851.84	696.84	606.16	547.59	507.29	478.34	456.91	440.68
20.00%	2,130.59	1,170.60	854.76	699.90	609.36	550.91	510.74	481.92	460.61	444.49
20.25%	2,133.35	1,173.41	857.70	702.97	612.56	554.25	514.21	485.52	464.32	448.31
20.50%	2,136.10	1,176.23	860.63	706.04	615.78	557.60	517.69	489.12	468.04	452.14
20.75%	2,138.86	1,179.05	863.58	709.12	619.00	560.96	521.18	492.74	471.77	455.98

	1	2	3	4	5	6	7	8	9	10
1.00%	2,010.85	1,010.45	676.99	510.27	410.25	343.57	295.95	260.24	232.46	210.25
1.25%	2,013.57	1,013.07	679.59	512.86	412.84	346.16	298.55	262.84	235.07	212.86
1.50%	2,016.29	1,015.70	682.20	515.46	415.44	348.77	301.16	265.46	237.70	215.50
1.75%	2,019.01	1,018.33	684.81	518.07	418.05	351.38	303.78	268.09	240.34	218.16
2.00%	2,021.73	1,020.97	687.42	520.68	420.67	354.01	306.42	270.74	243.01	220.83
2.25%	2,024.46	1,023.61	690.04	523.31	423.30	356.65	309.07	273.41	245.69	223.53
2.50%	2,027.19	1,026.25	692.67	525.94	425.94	359.30	311.74	276.09	248.39	226.25
2.75%	2,029.92	1,028.90	695.31	528.58	428.59	361.97	314.42	278.79	251.11	228.99
3.00%	2,032.65	1,031.55	697.95	531.22	431.25	364.65	317.12	281.51	253.85	231.75
3.25%	2,035.38	1,034.21	700.60	533.88	433.92	367.34	319.83	284.24	256.60	234.53
3.50%	2,038.12	1,036.87	703.25	536.54	436.60	370.04	322.56	286.99	259.38	237.33
3.75%	2,040.86	1,039.53	705.91	539.22	439.29	372.76	325.30	289.76	262.17	240.15
4.00%	2,043.60	1,042.20	708.58	541.90	442.00	375.48	328.05	292.54	264.98	242.99
4.25%	2,046.34	1,044.87	711.25	544.59	444.71	378.22	330.82	295.34	267.81	245.85
4.50%	2,049.08	1,047.55	713.93	547.28	447.43	380.98	333.60	298.16	270.66	248.73
4.75%	2,051.83	1,050.23	716.61	549.99	450.17	383.74	336.40	300.99	273.53	251.63
5.00%	2,054.58	1,052.91	719.30	552.70	452.91	386.52	339.21	303.84	276.41	254.56
5.25%	2,057.33	1,055.60	722.00	555.43	455.66	389.31	342.04	306.70	279.32	257.50
5.50%	2,060.08	1,058.30	724.70	558.16	458.43	392.11	344.88	309.58	282.24	260.46
5.75%	2,062.84	1,060.99	727.41	560.89	461.20	394.92	347.74	312.48	285.18	263.45
6.00%	2,065.59	1,063.69	730.13	563.64	463.99	397.75	350.61	315.39	288.14	266.45
6.25%	2,068.35	1,066.40	732.85	566.40	466.78	400.59	353.49	318.32	291.11	269.47
6.50%	2,071.11	1,069.11	735.58	569.16	469.59	403.44	356.39	321.27	294.11	272.52
6.75%	2,073.88	1,071.82	738.31	571.93	472.40	406.30	359.30	324.23	297.12	275.58
7.00%	2,076.64	1,074.54	741.05	574.71	475.23	409.18	362.22	327.21	300.15	278.66
7.25%	2,079.41	1,077.26	743.80	577.50	478.06	412.06	365.16	330.20	303.20	281.76
7.50%	2,082.18	1,079.99	746.55	580.29	480.91	414.96	368.12	333.21	306.26	284.88
7.75%	2,084.95	1,082.72	749.31	583.10	483.77	417.87	371.09	336.24	309.35	288.03
8.00%	2,087.72	1,085.45	752.07	585.91	486.63	420.80	374.07	339.28	312.45	291.19
8.25%	2,090.50	1,088.19	754.84	588.73	489.51	423.73	377.07	342.34	315.57	294.37
8.50%	2,093.27	1,090.94	757.62	591.56	492.40	426.68	380.08	345.41	318.70	297.57
8.75%	2,096.05	1,093.68	760.40	594.40	495.29	429.64	383.10	348.50	321.86	300.78
9.00%	2,098.84	1,096.43	763.19	597.24	498.20	432.61	386.14	351.60	325.03	304.02
9.25%	2,101.62	1,099.19	765.99	600.09	501.12	435.60	389.19	354.73	328.22	307.28
9.50%	2,104.40	1,101.95	768.79	602.96	504.04	438.59	392.26	357.86	331.42	310.55
9.75%	2,107.19	1,104.71	771.60	605.82	506.98	441.60	395.34	361.01	334.65	313.85
10.00%	2,109.98	1,107.48	774.41	608.70	509.93	444.62	398.43	364.18	337.89	317.16
10.25%	2,112.77	1,110.25	777.23	611.59	512.89	447.65	401.54	367.36	341.15	320.49
10.50%	2,115.57	1,113.02	780.06	614.48	515.85	450.70	404.66	370.56	344.42	323.84
10.75%	2,118.36	1,115.80	782.89	617.38	518.83	453.75	407.79	373.77	347.71	327.21

$24,000   11.00 - 20.75%   1 - 10 Years

	1	2	3	4	5	6	7	8	9	10
11.00%	2,121.16	1,118.59	785.73	620.29	521.82	456.82	410.94	377.00	351.02	330.60
11.25%	2,123.96	1,121.38	788.57	623.21	524.82	459.90	414.10	380.25	354.35	334.01
11.50%	2,126.76	1,124.17	791.42	626.14	527.82	462.99	417.28	383.50	357.69	337.43
11.75%	2,129.57	1,126.96	794.28	629.07	530.84	466.09	420.46	386.78	361.05	340.87
12.00%	2,132.37	1,129.76	797.14	632.01	533.87	469.20	423.67	390.07	364.42	344.33
12.25%	2,135.18	1,132.57	800.01	634.96	536.90	472.33	426.88	393.37	367.81	347.81
12.50%	2,137.99	1,135.38	802.89	637.92	539.95	475.47	430.11	396.69	371.22	351.30
12.75%	2,140.80	1,138.19	805.77	640.89	543.01	478.62	433.35	400.03	374.65	354.82
13.00%	2,143.61	1,141.00	808.65	643.86	546.07	481.78	436.61	403.37	378.09	358.35
13.25%	2,146.43	1,143.82	811.55	646.84	549.15	484.95	439.88	406.74	381.54	361.89
13.50%	2,149.25	1,146.65	814.45	649.83	552.24	488.14	443.16	410.12	385.02	365.46
13.75%	2,152.07	1,149.48	817.35	652.83	555.33	491.33	446.45	413.51	388.50	369.04
14.00%	2,154.89	1,152.31	820.26	655.84	558.44	494.54	449.76	416.92	392.01	372.64
14.25%	2,157.71	1,155.15	823.18	658.85	561.55	497.76	453.08	420.34	395.53	376.26
14.50%	2,160.54	1,157.99	826.10	661.87	564.68	500.99	456.42	423.77	399.07	379.89
14.75%	2,163.37	1,160.83	829.03	664.90	567.81	504.23	459.76	427.22	402.62	383.54
15.00%	2,166.20	1,163.68	831.97	667.94	570.96	507.48	463.12	430.69	406.18	387.20
15.25%	2,169.03	1,166.53	834.91	670.98	574.11	510.74	466.49	434.17	409.77	390.89
15.50%	2,171.87	1,169.39	837.86	674.04	577.28	514.02	469.88	437.66	413.36	394.59
15.75%	2,174.70	1,172.25	840.81	677.10	580.45	517.31	473.28	441.17	416.98	398.30
16.00%	2,177.54	1,175.11	843.77	680.17	583.63	520.60	476.69	444.69	420.61	402.03
16.25%	2,180.38	1,177.98	846.73	683.24	586.83	523.91	480.11	448.23	424.25	405.78
16.50%	2,183.22	1,180.86	849.71	686.33	590.03	527.23	483.55	451.78	427.91	409.54
16.75%	2,186.07	1,183.73	852.68	689.42	593.24	530.56	487.00	455.34	431.58	413.32
17.00%	2,188.91	1,186.61	855.67	692.52	596.46	533.91	490.46	458.91	435.27	417.11
17.25%	2,191.76	1,189.50	858.65	695.63	599.69	537.26	493.93	462.51	438.97	420.92
17.50%	2,194.61	1,192.39	861.65	698.74	602.93	540.63	497.42	466.11	442.69	424.75
17.75%	2,197.47	1,195.28	864.65	701.87	606.18	544.00	500.92	469.73	446.42	428.59
18.00%	2,200.32	1,198.18	867.66	705.00	609.44	547.39	504.43	473.36	450.17	432.44
18.25%	2,203.18	1,201.08	870.67	708.14	612.71	550.78	507.95	477.00	453.93	436.31
18.50%	2,206.03	1,203.98	873.69	711.29	615.99	554.19	511.49	480.66	457.70	440.20
18.75%	2,208.90	1,206.89	876.71	714.44	619.28	557.61	515.03	484.33	461.49	444.10
19.00%	2,211.76	1,209.81	879.74	717.60	622.57	561.04	518.59	488.01	465.29	448.01
19.25%	2,214.62	1,212.72	882.78	720.77	625.88	564.48	522.16	491.71	469.11	451.94
19.50%	2,217.49	1,215.65	885.82	723.95	629.19	567.93	525.75	495.42	472.94	455.89
19.75%	2,220.36	1,218.57	888.87	727.14	632.52	571.40	529.34	499.14	476.78	459.84
20.00%	2,223.23	1,221.50	891.93	730.33	635.85	574.87	532.95	502.88	480.64	463.81
20.25%	2,226.10	1,224.43	894.99	733.53	639.20	578.35	536.57	506.62	484.51	467.80
20.50%	2,228.98	1,227.37	898.05	736.74	642.55	581.84	540.20	510.39	488.39	471.80
20.75%	2,231.85	1,230.31	901.12	739.95	645.91	585.35	543.84	514.16	492.29	475.81

	1	2	3	4	5	6	7	8	9	10
1.00%	2,094.64	1,052.55	705.20	531.54	427.34	357.89	308.28	271.08	242.15	219.01
1.25%	2,097.47	1,055.28	707.91	534.23	430.04	360.59	310.98	273.79	244.87	221.73
1.50%	2,100.30	1,058.02	710.62	536.94	432.75	363.30	313.70	276.52	247.60	224.48
1.75%	2,103.13	1,060.76	713.34	539.65	435.47	366.02	316.44	279.26	250.36	227.25
2.00%	2,105.97	1,063.51	716.06	542.38	438.19	368.76	319.19	282.02	253.13	230.03
2.25%	2,108.81	1,066.26	718.80	545.11	440.93	371.51	321.95	284.80	255.93	232.84
2.50%	2,111.65	1,069.01	721.53	547.85	443.68	374.28	324.73	287.60	258.74	235.67
2.75%	2,114.50	1,071.77	724.28	550.60	446.45	377.05	327.52	290.41	261.57	238.53
3.00%	2,117.34	1,074.53	727.03	553.36	449.22	379.84	330.33	293.24	264.42	241.40
3.25%	2,120.19	1,077.30	729.79	556.12	452.00	382.64	333.16	296.09	267.29	244.30
3.50%	2,123.04	1,080.07	732.55	558.90	454.79	385.46	336.00	298.95	270.19	247.21
3.75%	2,125.89	1,082.84	735.32	561.68	457.60	388.29	338.85	301.83	273.10	250.15
4.00%	2,128.75	1,085.62	738.10	564.48	460.41	391.13	341.72	304.73	276.02	253.11
4.25%	2,131.60	1,088.41	740.88	567.28	463.24	393.98	344.60	307.65	278.97	256.09
4.50%	2,134.46	1,091.20	743.67	570.09	466.08	396.85	347.50	310.58	281.94	259.10
4.75%	2,137.32	1,093.99	746.47	572.91	468.92	399.73	350.42	313.53	284.93	262.12
5.00%	2,140.19	1,096.78	749.27	575.73	471.78	402.62	353.35	316.50	287.93	265.16
5.25%	2,143.05	1,099.59	752.08	578.57	474.65	405.53	356.29	319.48	290.96	268.23
5.50%	2,145.92	1,102.39	754.90	581.41	477.53	408.45	359.25	322.48	294.00	271.32
5.75%	2,148.79	1,105.20	757.72	584.26	480.42	411.38	362.23	325.50	297.06	274.42
6.00%	2,151.66	1,108.02	760.55	587.13	483.32	414.32	365.21	328.54	300.14	277.55
6.25%	2,154.53	1,110.83	763.38	590.00	486.23	417.28	368.22	331.59	303.24	280.70
6.50%	2,157.41	1,113.66	766.23	592.87	489.15	420.25	371.24	334.66	306.36	283.87
6.75%	2,160.29	1,116.48	769.07	595.76	492.09	423.23	374.27	337.74	309.50	287.06
7.00%	2,163.17	1,119.31	771.93	598.66	495.03	426.23	377.32	340.84	312.66	290.27
7.25%	2,166.05	1,122.15	774.79	601.56	497.98	429.23	380.38	343.96	315.83	293.50
7.50%	2,168.94	1,124.99	777.66	604.47	500.95	432.25	383.46	347.10	319.03	296.75
7.75%	2,171.82	1,127.83	780.53	607.39	503.92	435.29	386.55	350.25	322.24	300.03
8.00%	2,174.71	1,130.68	783.41	610.32	506.91	438.33	389.66	353.42	325.47	303.32
8.25%	2,177.60	1,133.53	786.30	613.26	509.91	441.39	392.78	356.60	328.72	306.63
8.50%	2,180.49	1,136.39	789.19	616.21	512.91	444.46	395.91	359.80	331.98	309.96
8.75%	2,183.39	1,139.25	792.09	619.16	515.93	447.54	399.06	363.02	335.27	313.32
9.00%	2,186.29	1,142.12	794.99	622.13	518.96	450.64	402.23	366.26	338.57	316.69
9.25%	2,189.19	1,144.99	797.91	625.10	522.00	453.75	405.41	369.51	341.89	320.08
9.50%	2,192.09	1,147.86	800.82	628.08	525.05	456.87	408.60	372.77	345.23	323.49
9.75%	2,194.99	1,150.74	803.75	631.07	528.11	460.00	411.81	376.06	348.59	326.93
10.00%	2,197.90	1,153.62	806.68	634.06	531.18	463.15	415.03	379.35	351.97	330.38
10.25%	2,200.81	1,156.51	809.62	637.07	534.26	466.30	418.27	382.67	355.36	333.85
10.50%	2,203.72	1,159.40	812.56	640.08	537.35	469.47	421.52	386.00	358.77	337.34
10.75%	2,206.63	1,162.30	815.51	643.11	540.45	472.66	424.78	389.35	362.20	340.85

$25,000   11.00 - 20.75%   1 - 10 Years

	1	2	3	4	5	6	7	8	9	10
11.00%	2,209.54	1,165.20	818.47	646.14	543.56	475.85	428.06	392.71	365.65	344.38
11.25%	2,212.46	1,168.10	821.43	649.18	546.68	479.06	431.35	396.09	369.11	347.92
11.50%	2,215.38	1,171.01	824.40	652.23	549.82	482.28	434.66	399.48	372.59	351.49
11.75%	2,218.30	1,173.92	827.38	655.28	552.96	485.51	437.98	402.89	376.09	355.07
12.00%	2,221.22	1,176.84	830.36	658.35	556.11	488.75	441.32	406.32	379.61	358.68
12.25%	2,224.14	1,179.76	833.35	661.42	559.27	492.01	444.67	409.76	383.14	362.30
12.50%	2,227.07	1,182.68	836.34	664.50	562.45	495.28	448.03	413.22	386.69	365.94
12.75%	2,230.00	1,185.61	839.34	667.59	565.63	498.56	451.41	416.69	390.26	369.60
13.00%	2,232.93	1,188.55	842.35	670.69	568.83	501.85	454.80	420.18	393.84	373.28
13.25%	2,235.87	1,191.48	845.36	673.79	572.03	505.16	458.20	423.69	397.44	376.97
13.50%	2,238.80	1,194.43	848.38	676.91	575.25	508.47	461.62	427.20	401.06	380.69
13.75%	2,241.74	1,197.37	851.41	680.03	578.47	511.80	465.05	430.74	404.69	384.42
14.00%	2,244.68	1,200.32	854.44	683.16	581.71	515.14	468.50	434.29	408.34	388.17
14.25%	2,247.62	1,203.28	857.48	686.30	584.95	518.50	471.96	437.85	412.01	391.93
14.50%	2,250.56	1,206.24	860.52	689.45	588.21	521.86	475.43	441.43	415.69	395.72
14.75%	2,253.51	1,209.20	863.58	692.60	591.47	525.24	478.92	445.03	419.39	399.52
15.00%	2,256.46	1,212.17	866.63	695.77	594.75	528.63	482.42	448.64	423.11	403.34
15.25%	2,259.41	1,215.14	869.70	698.94	598.03	532.03	485.93	452.26	426.84	407.17
15.50%	2,262.36	1,218.11	872.77	702.12	601.33	535.44	489.46	455.90	430.59	411.03
15.75%	2,265.31	1,221.09	875.84	705.31	604.64	538.86	493.00	459.55	434.35	414.90
16.00%	2,268.27	1,224.08	878.93	708.51	607.95	542.30	496.55	463.22	438.13	418.78
16.25%	2,271.23	1,227.07	882.01	711.71	611.28	545.74	500.12	466.90	441.93	422.69
16.50%	2,274.19	1,230.06	885.11	714.93	614.61	549.20	503.70	470.60	445.74	426.61
16.75%	2,277.15	1,233.06	888.21	718.15	617.96	552.67	507.29	474.31	449.56	430.54
17.00%	2,280.12	1,236.06	891.32	721.38	621.31	556.15	510.90	478.04	453.40	434.49
17.25%	2,283.09	1,239.06	894.43	724.61	624.68	559.65	514.51	481.78	457.26	438.46
17.50%	2,286.06	1,242.07	897.55	727.86	628.06	563.15	518.14	485.53	461.13	442.45
17.75%	2,289.03	1,245.08	900.68	731.11	631.44	566.67	521.79	489.30	465.02	446.45
18.00%	2,292.00	1,248.10	903.81	734.37	634.84	570.19	525.45	493.08	468.92	450.46
18.25%	2,294.98	1,251.12	906.95	737.64	638.24	573.73	529.12	496.88	472.84	454.49
18.50%	2,297.95	1,254.15	910.09	740.92	641.66	577.28	532.80	500.69	476.77	458.54
18.75%	2,300.93	1,257.18	913.24	744.21	645.08	580.85	536.49	504.51	480.72	462.60
19.00%	2,303.91	1,260.22	916.40	747.50	648.51	584.42	540.20	508.35	484.68	466.68
19.25%	2,306.90	1,263.25	919.56	750.81	651.96	588.00	543.92	512.20	488.65	470.77
19.50%	2,309.88	1,266.30	922.73	754.12	655.41	591.60	547.65	516.06	492.64	474.88
19.75%	2,312.87	1,269.34	925.91	757.43	658.87	595.20	551.40	519.94	496.64	479.00
20.00%	2,315.86	1,272.40	929.09	760.76	662.35	598.82	555.15	523.83	500.66	483.14
20.25%	2,318.85	1,275.45	932.28	764.09	665.83	602.45	558.92	527.73	504.69	487.29
20.50%	2,321.85	1,278.51	935.47	767.43	669.32	606.09	562.71	531.65	508.74	491.46
20.75%	2,324.85	1,281.57	938.67	770.78	672.82	609.74	566.50	535.58	512.80	495.64

$26,000   1.00 - 10.75%   1 - 10 Years

	1	2	3	4	5	6	7	8	9	10
1.00%	2,178.42	1,094.65	733.41	552.80	444.44	372.20	320.61	281.92	251.84	227.77
1.25%	2,181.36	1,097.50	736.22	555.60	447.24	375.01	323.42	284.74	254.66	230.60
1.50%	2,184.31	1,100.34	739.05	558.42	450.06	377.83	326.25	287.58	257.51	233.46
1.75%	2,187.26	1,103.19	741.87	561.24	452.88	380.66	329.09	290.43	260.37	236.34
2.00%	2,190.21	1,106.05	744.71	564.07	455.72	383.51	331.95	293.30	263.26	239.23
2.25%	2,193.16	1,108.91	747.55	566.91	458.57	386.37	334.83	296.19	266.16	242.16
2.50%	2,196.12	1,111.77	750.40	569.76	461.43	389.25	337.72	299.10	269.09	245.10
2.75%	2,199.08	1,114.64	753.25	572.62	464.30	392.13	340.62	302.03	272.03	248.07
3.00%	2,202.04	1,117.51	756.11	575.49	467.19	395.04	343.55	304.97	275.00	251.06
3.25%	2,205.00	1,120.39	758.98	578.37	470.08	397.95	346.48	307.93	277.99	254.07
3.50%	2,207.96	1,123.27	761.85	581.26	472.99	400.88	349.44	310.91	280.99	257.10
3.75%	2,210.93	1,126.16	764.74	584.15	475.90	403.82	352.40	313.91	284.02	260.16
4.00%	2,213.90	1,129.05	767.62	587.06	478.83	406.77	355.39	316.92	287.07	263.24
4.25%	2,216.87	1,131.94	770.52	589.97	481.77	409.74	358.39	319.95	290.13	266.34
4.50%	2,219.84	1,134.84	773.42	592.89	484.72	412.72	361.40	323.00	293.22	269.46
4.75%	2,222.82	1,137.75	776.33	595.82	487.68	415.72	364.44	326.07	296.32	272.60
5.00%	2,225.79	1,140.66	779.24	598.76	490.65	418.73	367.48	329.16	299.45	275.77
5.25%	2,228.77	1,143.57	782.17	601.71	493.64	421.75	370.54	332.26	302.59	278.96
5.50%	2,231.76	1,146.49	785.09	604.67	496.63	424.79	373.62	335.38	305.76	282.17
5.75%	2,234.74	1,149.41	788.03	607.64	499.64	427.83	376.71	338.52	308.94	285.40
6.00%	2,237.73	1,152.34	790.97	610.61	502.65	430.90	379.82	341.68	312.15	288.65
6.25%	2,240.72	1,155.27	793.92	613.60	505.68	433.97	382.95	344.85	315.37	291.93
6.50%	2,243.71	1,158.20	796.87	616.59	508.72	437.06	386.09	348.04	318.62	295.22
6.75%	2,246.70	1,161.14	799.84	619.59	511.77	440.16	389.24	351.25	321.88	298.54
7.00%	2,249.70	1,164.09	802.80	622.60	514.83	443.27	392.41	354.48	325.16	301.88
7.25%	2,252.69	1,167.04	805.78	625.62	517.90	446.40	395.59	357.72	328.47	305.24
7.50%	2,255.69	1,169.99	808.76	628.65	520.99	449.54	398.80	360.98	331.79	308.62
7.75%	2,258.69	1,172.95	811.75	631.69	524.08	452.70	402.01	364.26	335.13	312.03
8.00%	2,261.70	1,175.91	814.75	634.74	527.19	455.86	405.24	367.55	338.49	315.45
8.25%	2,264.71	1,178.88	817.75	637.79	530.30	459.04	408.49	370.87	341.87	318.90
8.50%	2,267.71	1,181.85	820.76	640.86	533.43	462.24	411.75	374.20	345.26	322.36
8.75%	2,270.73	1,184.82	823.77	643.93	536.57	465.44	415.02	377.54	348.68	325.85
9.00%	2,273.74	1,187.80	826.79	647.01	539.72	468.66	418.32	380.91	352.12	329.36
9.25%	2,276.75	1,190.79	829.82	650.10	542.88	471.90	421.62	384.29	355.57	332.89
9.50%	2,279.77	1,193.78	832.86	653.20	546.05	475.14	424.94	387.68	359.04	336.43
9.75%	2,282.79	1,196.77	835.90	656.31	549.23	478.40	428.28	391.10	362.54	340.00
10.00%	2,285.81	1,199.77	838.95	659.43	552.42	481.67	431.63	394.53	366.05	343.59
10.25%	2,288.84	1,202.77	842.00	662.55	555.63	484.96	435.00	397.98	369.57	347.20
10.50%	2,291.86	1,205.78	845.06	665.69	558.84	488.25	438.38	401.44	373.12	350.83
10.75%	2,294.89	1,208.79	848.13	668.83	562.07	491.56	441.77	404.92	376.69	354.48

$26,000   11.00 - 20.75%   1 - 10 Years

	1	2	3	4	5	6	7	8	9	10
11.00%	2,297.92	1,211.80	851.21	671.98	565.30	494.89	445.18	408.42	380.27	358.15
11.25%	2,300.96	1,214.82	854.29	675.14	568.55	498.22	448.61	411.93	383.87	361.84
11.50%	2,303.99	1,217.85	857.38	678.31	571.81	501.57	452.05	415.46	387.50	365.55
11.75%	2,307.03	1,220.88	860.47	681.49	575.08	504.93	455.50	419.01	391.13	369.28
12.00%	2,310.07	1,223.91	863.57	684.68	578.36	508.31	458.97	422.57	394.79	373.02
12.25%	2,313.11	1,226.95	866.68	687.88	581.65	511.69	462.45	426.15	398.46	376.79
12.50%	2,316.15	1,229.99	869.79	691.08	584.95	515.09	465.95	429.75	402.16	380.58
12.75%	2,319.20	1,233.04	872.92	694.29	588.26	518.50	469.46	433.36	405.87	384.38
13.00%	2,322.25	1,236.09	876.04	697.51	591.58	521.93	472.99	436.99	409.59	388.21
13.25%	2,325.30	1,239.14	879.18	700.75	594.91	525.36	476.53	440.63	413.34	392.05
13.50%	2,328.35	1,242.20	882.32	703.98	598.26	528.81	480.09	444.29	417.10	395.91
13.75%	2,331.41	1,245.27	885.46	707.23	601.61	532.27	483.66	447.97	420.88	399.79
14.00%	2,334.47	1,248.33	888.62	710.49	604.97	535.75	487.24	451.66	424.68	403.69
14.25%	2,337.52	1,251.41	891.78	713.75	608.35	539.24	490.84	455.37	428.49	407.61
14.50%	2,340.59	1,254.49	894.95	717.03	611.74	542.74	494.45	459.09	432.32	411.55
14.75%	2,343.65	1,257.57	898.12	720.31	615.13	546.25	498.08	462.83	436.17	415.50
15.00%	2,346.72	1,260.65	901.30	723.60	618.54	549.77	501.72	466.58	440.03	419.47
15.25%	2,349.78	1,263.74	904.48	726.90	621.96	553.31	505.37	470.35	443.91	423.46
15.50%	2,352.85	1,266.84	907.68	730.21	625.38	556.85	509.04	474.13	447.81	427.47
15.75%	2,355.93	1,269.94	910.88	733.52	628.82	560.42	512.72	477.93	451.73	431.49
16.00%	2,359.00	1,273.04	914.08	736.85	632.27	563.99	516.41	481.75	455.66	435.53
16.25%	2,362.08	1,276.15	917.30	740.18	635.73	567.57	520.12	485.58	459.60	439.59
16.50%	2,365.16	1,279.26	920.51	743.52	639.20	571.17	523.85	489.42	463.57	443.67
16.75%	2,368.24	1,282.38	923.74	746.87	642.68	574.78	527.58	493.28	467.55	447.76
17.00%	2,371.32	1,285.50	926.97	750.23	646.17	578.40	531.33	497.16	471.54	451.87
17.25%	2,374.41	1,288.62	930.21	753.60	649.67	582.03	535.09	501.05	475.55	456.00
17.50%	2,377.50	1,291.75	933.45	756.97	653.18	585.68	538.87	504.95	479.58	460.14
17.75%	2,380.59	1,294.89	936.70	760.36	656.70	589.33	542.66	508.87	483.62	464.30
18.00%	2,383.68	1,298.03	939.96	763.75	660.23	593.00	546.46	512.80	487.68	468.48
18.25%	2,386.77	1,301.17	943.23	767.15	663.77	596.68	550.28	516.75	491.75	472.67
18.50%	2,389.87	1,304.32	946.50	770.56	667.32	600.38	554.11	520.71	495.84	476.88
18.75%	2,392.97	1,307.47	949.77	773.98	670.88	604.08	557.95	524.69	499.95	481.11
19.00%	2,396.07	1,310.62	953.06	777.40	674.45	607.79	561.81	528.68	504.06	485.35
19.25%	2,399.17	1,313.78	956.35	780.84	678.04	611.52	565.68	532.69	508.20	489.60
19.50%	2,402.28	1,316.95	959.64	784.28	681.63	615.26	569.56	536.70	512.35	493.88
19.75%	2,405.39	1,320.12	962.94	787.73	685.23	619.01	573.45	540.74	516.51	498.16
20.00%	2,408.50	1,323.29	966.25	791.19	688.84	622.77	577.36	544.78	520.69	502.46
20.25%	2,411.61	1,326.47	969.57	794.66	692.46	626.55	581.28	548.84	524.88	506.78
20.50%	2,414.72	1,329.65	972.89	798.13	696.09	630.33	585.21	552.92	529.09	511.11
20.75%	2,417.84	1,332.84	976.22	801.62	699.74	634.13	589.16	557.01	533.31	515.46

	1	2	3	4	5	6	7	8	9	10
1.00%	2,262.21	1,136.76	761.62	574.06	461.53	386.52	332.94	292.77	261.52	236.53
1.25%	2,265.26	1,139.71	764.54	576.97	464.44	389.43	335.86	295.69	264.46	239.47
1.50%	2,268.32	1,142.66	767.47	579.90	467.37	392.36	338.80	298.64	267.41	242.44
1.75%	2,271.39	1,145.62	770.41	582.83	470.30	395.31	341.75	301.60	270.39	245.43
2.00%	2,274.45	1,148.59	773.35	585.77	473.25	398.26	344.72	304.58	273.38	248.44
2.25%	2,277.52	1,151.56	776.30	588.72	476.21	401.23	347.71	307.58	276.40	251.47
2.50%	2,280.59	1,154.53	779.26	591.68	479.18	404.22	350.71	310.60	279.44	254.53
2.75%	2,283.66	1,157.51	782.22	594.65	482.16	407.22	353.73	313.64	282.50	257.61
3.00%	2,286.73	1,160.49	785.19	597.63	485.15	410.23	356.76	316.70	285.58	260.71
3.25%	2,289.81	1,163.48	788.17	600.61	488.16	413.26	359.81	319.77	288.68	263.84
3.50%	2,292.88	1,166.47	791.16	603.61	491.18	416.30	362.88	322.87	291.80	266.99
3.75%	2,295.96	1,169.47	794.15	606.62	494.21	419.35	365.96	325.98	294.94	270.17
4.00%	2,299.05	1,172.47	797.15	609.63	497.25	422.42	369.06	329.11	298.11	273.36
4.25%	2,302.13	1,175.48	800.15	612.66	500.30	425.50	372.17	332.26	301.29	276.58
4.50%	2,305.22	1,178.49	803.17	615.69	503.36	428.60	375.30	335.43	304.50	279.82
4.75%	2,308.31	1,181.51	806.19	618.74	506.44	431.71	378.45	338.61	307.72	283.09
5.00%	2,311.40	1,184.53	809.21	621.79	509.52	434.83	381.62	341.82	310.97	286.38
5.25%	2,314.50	1,187.55	812.25	624.85	512.62	437.97	384.80	345.04	314.23	289.69
5.50%	2,317.59	1,190.58	815.29	627.92	515.73	441.12	387.99	348.28	317.52	293.02
5.75%	2,320.69	1,193.62	818.34	631.01	518.85	444.29	391.20	351.54	320.83	296.38
6.00%	2,323.79	1,196.66	821.39	634.10	521.99	447.47	394.43	354.82	324.16	299.76
6.25%	2,326.90	1,199.70	824.45	637.20	525.13	450.66	397.67	358.11	327.50	303.16
6.50%	2,330.00	1,202.75	827.52	640.30	528.29	453.87	400.93	361.43	330.87	306.58
6.75%	2,333.11	1,205.80	830.60	643.42	531.45	457.09	404.21	364.76	334.26	310.03
7.00%	2,336.22	1,208.86	833.68	646.55	534.63	460.32	407.50	368.11	337.67	313.49
7.25%	2,339.34	1,211.92	836.77	649.68	537.82	463.57	410.81	371.48	341.10	316.98
7.50%	2,342.45	1,214.99	839.87	652.83	541.02	466.83	414.13	374.86	344.55	320.49
7.75%	2,345.57	1,218.06	842.97	655.99	544.24	470.11	417.47	378.27	348.02	324.03
8.00%	2,348.69	1,221.14	846.08	659.15	547.46	473.40	420.83	381.69	351.51	327.58
8.25%	2,351.81	1,224.22	849.20	662.32	550.70	476.70	424.20	385.13	355.01	331.16
8.50%	2,354.93	1,227.30	852.32	665.50	553.95	480.02	427.59	388.59	358.54	334.76
8.75%	2,358.06	1,230.39	855.45	668.70	557.21	483.35	430.99	392.06	362.09	338.38
9.00%	2,361.19	1,233.49	858.59	671.90	560.48	486.69	434.41	395.56	365.66	342.02
9.25%	2,364.32	1,236.59	861.74	675.11	563.76	490.05	437.84	399.07	369.25	345.69
9.50%	2,367.45	1,239.69	864.89	678.32	567.05	493.42	441.29	402.59	372.85	349.37
9.75%	2,370.59	1,242.80	868.05	681.55	570.35	496.80	444.75	406.14	376.48	353.08
10.00%	2,373.73	1,245.91	871.21	684.79	573.67	500.20	448.23	409.70	380.12	356.81
10.25%	2,376.87	1,249.03	874.39	688.04	577.00	503.61	451.73	413.28	383.79	360.56
10.50%	2,380.01	1,252.15	877.57	691.29	580.34	507.03	455.24	416.88	387.47	364.32
10.75%	2,383.16	1,255.28	880.75	694.56	583.68	510.47	458.76	420.50	391.18	368.11

$27,000   11.00 - 20.75%   1 - 10 Years

	1	2	3	4	5	6	7	8	9	10
11.00%	2,386.30	1,258.41	883.95	697.83	587.05	513.92	462.31	424.13	394.90	371.93
11.25%	2,389.45	1,261.55	887.15	701.11	590.42	517.38	465.86	427.78	398.64	375.76
11.50%	2,392.61	1,264.69	890.35	704.40	593.80	520.86	469.43	431.44	402.40	379.61
11.75%	2,395.76	1,267.83	893.57	707.70	597.19	524.35	473.02	435.13	406.18	383.48
12.00%	2,398.92	1,270.98	896.79	711.01	600.60	527.86	476.62	438.83	409.97	387.37
12.25%	2,402.08	1,274.14	900.01	714.33	604.02	531.37	480.24	442.54	413.79	391.28
12.50%	2,405.24	1,277.30	903.25	717.66	607.44	534.90	483.87	446.28	417.62	395.22
12.75%	2,408.40	1,280.46	906.49	721.00	610.88	538.44	487.52	450.03	421.48	399.17
13.00%	2,411.57	1,283.63	909.74	724.34	614.33	542.00	491.18	453.80	425.35	403.14
13.25%	2,414.73	1,286.80	912.99	727.70	617.79	545.57	494.86	457.58	429.24	407.13
13.50%	2,417.90	1,289.98	916.25	731.06	621.27	549.15	498.55	461.38	433.14	411.14
13.75%	2,421.08	1,293.16	919.52	734.43	624.75	552.75	502.26	465.20	437.07	415.17
14.00%	2,424.25	1,296.35	922.80	737.81	628.24	556.35	505.98	469.03	441.01	419.22
14.25%	2,427.43	1,299.54	926.08	741.21	631.75	559.98	509.72	472.88	444.97	423.29
14.50%	2,430.61	1,302.73	929.37	744.60	635.26	563.61	513.47	476.75	448.95	427.37
14.75%	2,433.79	1,305.93	932.66	748.01	638.79	567.26	517.23	480.63	452.94	431.48
15.00%	2,436.97	1,309.14	935.96	751.43	642.33	570.92	521.01	484.53	456.96	435.60
15.25%	2,440.16	1,312.35	939.27	754.86	645.88	574.59	524.81	488.44	460.99	439.75
15.50%	2,443.35	1,315.56	942.59	758.29	649.44	578.27	528.62	492.37	465.04	443.91
15.75%	2,446.54	1,318.78	945.91	761.73	653.01	581.97	532.44	496.32	469.10	448.09
16.00%	2,449.73	1,322.00	949.24	765.19	656.59	585.68	536.28	500.28	473.18	452.29
16.25%	2,452.93	1,325.23	952.58	768.65	660.18	589.40	540.13	504.25	477.28	456.50
16.50%	2,456.13	1,328.46	955.92	772.12	663.78	593.14	543.99	508.25	481.40	460.73
16.75%	2,459.33	1,331.70	959.27	775.60	667.40	596.89	547.87	512.26	485.53	464.99
17.00%	2,462.53	1,334.94	962.62	779.09	671.02	600.65	551.77	516.28	489.68	469.25
17.25%	2,465.73	1,338.19	965.99	782.58	674.65	604.42	555.67	520.32	493.84	473.54
17.50%	2,468.94	1,341.44	969.36	786.09	678.30	608.20	559.60	524.37	498.02	477.84
17.75%	2,472.15	1,344.69	972.73	789.60	681.96	612.00	563.53	528.44	502.22	482.16
18.00%	2,475.36	1,347.95	976.11	793.12	685.62	615.81	567.48	532.53	506.44	486.50
18.25%	2,478.57	1,351.21	979.50	796.66	689.30	619.63	571.44	536.63	510.67	490.85
18.50%	2,481.79	1,354.48	982.90	800.20	692.99	623.47	575.42	540.74	514.91	495.22
18.75%	2,485.01	1,357.76	986.30	803.75	696.69	627.31	579.41	544.87	519.17	499.61
19.00%	2,488.23	1,361.03	989.71	807.30	700.39	631.17	583.42	549.01	523.45	504.02
19.25%	2,491.45	1,364.31	993.13	810.87	704.11	635.04	587.43	553.17	527.74	508.44
19.50%	2,494.68	1,367.60	996.55	814.44	707.84	638.92	591.47	557.35	532.05	512.87
19.75%	2,497.90	1,370.89	999.98	818.03	711.58	642.82	595.51	561.53	536.38	517.32
20.00%	2,501.13	1,374.19	1,003.42	821.62	715.33	646.73	599.57	565.74	540.72	521.79
20.25%	2,504.36	1,377.49	1,006.86	825.22	719.10	650.64	603.64	569.95	545.07	526.27
20.50%	2,507.60	1,380.79	1,010.31	828.83	722.87	654.58	607.72	574.18	549.44	530.77
20.75%	2,510.83	1,384.10	1,013.76	832.45	726.65	658.52	611.82	578.43	553.82	535.29

	1	2	3	4	5	6	7	8	9	10
1.00%	2,345.99	1,178.86	789.83	595.32	478.62	400.83	345.27	303.61	271.21	245.29
1.25%	2,349.16	1,181.92	792.86	598.34	481.64	403.86	348.30	306.64	274.25	248.34
1.50%	2,352.34	1,184.98	795.89	601.37	484.68	406.89	351.35	309.70	277.31	251.42
1.75%	2,355.51	1,188.05	798.94	604.41	487.72	409.95	354.41	312.77	280.40	254.51
2.00%	2,358.69	1,191.13	801.99	607.46	490.78	413.01	357.49	315.86	283.51	257.64
2.25%	2,361.87	1,194.21	805.05	610.52	493.85	416.09	360.58	318.98	286.64	260.78
2.50%	2,365.05	1,197.29	808.12	613.59	496.93	419.19	363.70	322.11	289.79	263.96
2.75%	2,368.24	1,200.38	811.19	616.67	500.02	422.30	366.83	325.26	292.96	267.15
3.00%	2,371.42	1,203.47	814.27	619.76	503.12	425.42	369.97	328.43	296.15	270.37
3.25%	2,374.61	1,206.57	817.36	622.86	506.24	428.56	373.14	331.62	299.37	273.61
3.50%	2,377.81	1,209.68	820.46	625.97	509.37	431.72	376.32	334.83	302.61	276.88
3.75%	2,381.00	1,212.78	823.56	629.09	512.51	434.88	379.51	338.05	305.87	280.17
4.00%	2,384.20	1,215.90	826.67	632.21	515.66	438.07	382.73	341.30	309.15	283.49
4.25%	2,387.40	1,219.02	829.79	635.35	518.83	441.26	385.96	344.57	312.45	286.83
4.50%	2,390.60	1,222.14	832.91	638.50	522.00	444.47	389.20	347.85	315.77	290.19
4.75%	2,393.80	1,225.27	836.05	641.65	525.19	447.70	392.47	351.15	319.12	293.57
5.00%	2,397.01	1,228.40	839.19	644.82	528.39	450.94	395.75	354.48	322.48	296.98
5.25%	2,400.22	1,231.54	842.33	648.00	531.61	454.19	399.05	357.82	325.87	300.42
5.50%	2,403.43	1,234.68	845.49	651.18	534.83	457.46	402.36	361.18	329.28	303.87
5.75%	2,406.64	1,237.83	848.65	654.38	538.07	460.74	405.69	364.56	332.71	307.35
6.00%	2,409.86	1,240.98	851.81	657.58	541.32	464.04	409.04	367.96	336.16	310.86
6.25%	2,413.08	1,244.13	854.99	660.79	544.58	467.35	412.40	371.38	339.63	314.38
6.50%	2,416.30	1,247.30	858.17	664.02	547.85	470.68	415.78	374.81	343.13	317.93
6.75%	2,419.52	1,250.46	861.36	667.25	551.14	474.02	419.18	378.27	346.64	321.51
7.00%	2,422.75	1,253.63	864.56	670.49	554.43	477.37	422.60	381.74	350.18	325.10
7.25%	2,425.98	1,256.81	867.76	673.75	557.74	480.74	426.03	385.24	353.73	328.72
7.50%	2,429.21	1,259.99	870.97	677.01	561.06	484.12	429.47	388.75	357.31	332.36
7.75%	2,432.44	1,263.17	874.19	680.28	564.39	487.52	432.93	392.28	360.91	336.03
8.00%	2,435.68	1,266.36	877.42	683.56	567.74	490.93	436.41	395.83	364.52	339.72
8.25%	2,438.91	1,269.56	880.65	686.85	571.10	494.36	439.91	399.39	368.16	343.43
8.50%	2,442.15	1,272.76	883.89	690.15	574.46	497.79	443.42	402.98	371.82	347.16
8.75%	2,445.40	1,275.96	887.14	693.46	577.84	501.25	446.95	406.58	375.50	350.91
9.00%	2,448.64	1,279.17	890.39	696.78	581.23	504.72	450.49	410.21	379.20	354.69
9.25%	2,451.89	1,282.39	893.65	700.11	584.64	508.20	454.05	413.85	382.92	358.49
9.50%	2,455.14	1,285.61	896.92	703.45	588.05	511.69	457.63	417.50	386.66	362.31
9.75%	2,458.39	1,288.83	900.20	706.80	591.48	515.20	461.22	421.18	390.42	366.16
10.00%	2,461.64	1,292.06	903.48	710.15	594.92	518.72	464.83	424.88	394.20	370.02
10.25%	2,464.90	1,295.29	906.77	713.52	598.37	522.26	468.46	428.59	398.00	373.91
10.50%	2,468.16	1,298.53	910.07	716.89	601.83	525.81	472.10	432.32	401.82	377.82
10.75%	2,471.42	1,301.77	913.37	720.28	605.30	529.38	475.76	436.07	405.66	381.75

$28,000　　11.00 - 20.75%　　1 - 10 Years

	1	2	3	4	5	6	7	8	9	10
11.00%	2,474.69	1,305.02	916.68	723.67	608.79	532.95	479.43	439.84	409.52	385.70
11.25%	2,477.95	1,308.27	920.00	727.08	612.28	536.55	483.12	443.62	413.40	389.67
11.50%	2,481.22	1,311.53	923.33	730.49	615.79	540.15	486.82	447.42	417.30	393.67
11.75%	2,484.49	1,314.79	926.66	733.92	619.31	543.77	490.54	451.24	421.22	397.68
12.00%	2,487.77	1,318.06	930.00	737.35	622.84	547.41	494.28	455.08	425.16	401.72
12.25%	2,491.04	1,321.33	933.35	740.79	626.39	551.05	498.03	458.93	429.12	405.78
12.50%	2,494.32	1,324.60	936.70	744.24	629.94	554.71	501.79	462.81	433.09	409.85
12.75%	2,497.60	1,327.89	940.06	747.70	633.51	558.39	505.58	466.70	437.09	413.95
13.00%	2,500.88	1,331.17	943.43	751.17	637.09	562.07	509.37	470.60	441.10	418.07
13.25%	2,504.17	1,334.46	946.81	754.65	640.68	565.78	513.19	474.53	445.13	422.21
13.50%	2,507.46	1,337.76	950.19	758.14	644.28	569.49	517.02	478.47	449.18	426.37
13.75%	2,510.75	1,341.06	953.58	761.63	647.89	573.22	520.86	482.43	453.25	430.55
14.00%	2,514.04	1,344.36	956.97	765.14	651.51	576.96	524.72	486.40	457.34	434.75
14.25%	2,517.33	1,347.67	960.38	768.66	655.15	580.72	528.59	490.39	461.45	438.96
14.50%	2,520.63	1,350.98	963.79	772.18	658.79	584.48	532.48	494.40	465.58	443.20
14.75%	2,523.93	1,354.30	967.20	775.72	662.45	588.27	536.39	498.43	469.72	447.46
15.00%	2,527.23	1,357.63	970.63	779.26	666.12	592.06	540.31	502.47	473.88	451.74
15.25%	2,530.54	1,360.95	974.06	782.81	669.80	595.87	544.24	506.53	478.06	456.03
15.50%	2,533.84	1,364.29	977.50	786.38	673.49	599.69	548.19	510.61	482.26	460.35
15.75%	2,537.15	1,367.62	980.94	789.95	677.19	603.52	552.16	514.70	486.47	464.68
16.00%	2,540.46	1,370.97	984.40	793.53	680.91	607.37	556.14	518.81	490.71	469.04
16.25%	2,543.78	1,374.31	987.86	797.12	684.63	611.23	560.13	522.93	494.96	473.41
16.50%	2,547.09	1,377.67	991.32	800.72	688.37	615.11	564.14	527.07	499.23	477.80
16.75%	2,550.41	1,381.02	994.80	804.32	692.11	618.99	568.16	531.23	503.51	482.21
17.00%	2,553.73	1,384.38	998.28	807.94	695.87	622.89	572.20	535.40	507.81	486.63
17.25%	2,557.06	1,387.75	1,001.76	811.57	699.64	626.80	576.26	539.59	512.13	491.08
17.50%	2,560.38	1,391.12	1,005.26	815.20	703.42	630.73	580.32	543.79	516.47	495.54
17.75%	2,563.71	1,394.49	1,008.76	818.85	707.21	634.67	584.40	548.01	520.82	500.02
18.00%	2,567.04	1,397.87	1,012.27	822.50	711.02	638.62	588.50	552.25	525.19	504.52
18.25%	2,570.37	1,401.26	1,015.78	826.16	714.83	642.58	592.61	556.50	529.58	509.03
18.50%	2,573.71	1,404.65	1,019.30	829.83	718.65	646.56	596.73	560.77	533.98	513.57
18.75%	2,577.04	1,408.04	1,022.83	833.51	722.49	650.55	600.87	565.05	538.40	518.12
19.00%	2,580.38	1,411.44	1,026.37	837.20	726.34	654.55	605.02	569.35	542.84	522.68
19.25%	2,583.73	1,414.84	1,029.91	840.90	730.19	658.56	609.19	573.66	547.29	527.27
19.50%	2,587.07	1,418.25	1,033.46	844.61	734.06	662.59	613.37	577.99	551.76	531.87
19.75%	2,590.42	1,421.67	1,037.02	848.33	737.94	666.63	617.57	582.33	556.24	536.48
20.00%	2,593.77	1,425.08	1,040.58	852.05	741.83	670.68	621.77	586.69	560.74	541.12
20.25%	2,597.12	1,428.50	1,044.15	855.78	745.73	674.74	626.00	591.06	565.26	545.77
20.50%	2,600.47	1,431.93	1,047.73	859.53	749.64	678.82	630.23	595.45	569.79	550.43
20.75%	2,603.83	1,435.36	1,051.31	863.28	753.56	682.91	634.48	599.85	574.33	555.11

	1	2	3	4	5	6	7	8	9	10
1.00%	2,429.78	1,220.96	818.03	616.58	495.72	415.15	357.61	314.45	280.89	254.05
1.25%	2,433.06	1,224.13	821.17	619.71	498.85	418.28	360.74	317.60	284.05	257.21
1.50%	2,436.35	1,227.30	824.32	622.85	501.99	421.43	363.90	320.76	287.22	260.40
1.75%	2,439.64	1,230.48	827.47	626.00	505.14	424.59	367.07	323.94	290.41	263.60
2.00%	2,442.93	1,233.67	830.63	629.16	508.31	427.76	370.26	327.15	293.63	266.84
2.25%	2,446.22	1,236.86	833.80	632.33	511.48	430.95	373.46	330.37	296.87	270.10
2.50%	2,449.52	1,240.05	836.98	635.51	514.67	434.16	376.69	333.61	300.14	273.38
2.75%	2,452.82	1,243.25	840.16	638.70	517.88	437.38	379.93	336.87	303.42	276.69
3.00%	2,456.12	1,246.46	843.36	641.90	521.09	440.62	383.19	340.16	306.73	280.03
3.25%	2,459.42	1,249.66	846.55	645.10	524.32	443.87	386.46	343.46	310.06	283.39
3.50%	2,462.73	1,252.88	849.76	648.32	527.56	447.13	389.76	346.78	313.42	286.77
3.75%	2,466.04	1,256.10	852.97	651.55	530.81	450.41	393.07	350.13	316.79	290.18
4.00%	2,469.35	1,259.32	856.20	654.79	534.08	453.71	396.40	353.49	320.19	293.61
4.25%	2,472.66	1,262.55	859.42	658.04	537.36	457.02	399.74	356.87	323.61	297.07
4.50%	2,475.98	1,265.79	862.66	661.30	540.65	460.35	403.10	360.27	327.05	300.55
4.75%	2,479.30	1,269.03	865.90	664.57	543.95	463.69	406.49	363.70	330.51	304.06
5.00%	2,482.62	1,272.27	869.16	667.85	547.27	467.04	409.88	367.14	334.00	307.59
5.25%	2,485.94	1,275.52	872.41	671.14	550.59	470.41	413.30	370.60	337.51	311.15
5.50%	2,489.27	1,278.77	875.68	674.44	553.93	473.80	416.73	374.08	341.04	314.73
5.75%	2,492.60	1,282.03	878.95	677.75	557.29	477.20	420.18	377.58	344.59	318.33
6.00%	2,495.93	1,285.30	882.24	681.07	560.65	480.61	423.65	381.10	348.17	321.96
6.25%	2,499.26	1,288.57	885.52	684.39	564.03	484.04	427.13	384.64	351.76	325.61
6.50%	2,502.60	1,291.84	888.82	687.73	567.42	487.49	430.63	388.20	355.38	329.29
6.75%	2,505.93	1,295.12	892.12	691.08	570.82	490.95	434.15	391.78	359.02	332.99
7.00%	2,509.28	1,298.40	895.44	694.44	574.23	494.42	437.69	395.38	362.68	336.71
7.25%	2,512.62	1,301.69	898.75	697.81	577.66	497.91	441.24	399.00	366.36	340.46
7.50%	2,515.97	1,304.99	902.08	701.19	581.10	501.41	444.81	402.63	370.07	344.24
7.75%	2,519.31	1,308.29	905.41	704.58	584.55	504.93	448.40	406.29	373.80	348.03
8.00%	2,522.66	1,311.59	908.75	707.97	588.02	508.46	452.00	409.96	377.54	351.85
8.25%	2,526.02	1,314.90	912.10	711.38	591.49	512.01	455.62	413.66	381.31	355.69
8.50%	2,529.37	1,318.21	915.46	714.80	594.98	515.57	459.26	417.37	385.10	359.56
8.75%	2,532.73	1,321.53	918.82	718.23	598.48	519.15	462.91	421.10	388.91	363.45
9.00%	2,536.09	1,324.86	922.19	721.67	601.99	522.74	466.58	424.86	392.74	367.36
9.25%	2,539.46	1,328.19	925.57	725.11	605.52	526.35	470.27	428.63	396.60	371.29
9.50%	2,542.82	1,331.52	928.96	728.57	609.05	529.97	473.98	432.42	400.47	375.25
9.75%	2,546.19	1,334.86	932.35	732.04	612.60	533.60	477.70	436.22	404.37	379.23
10.00%	2,549.56	1,338.20	935.75	735.51	616.16	537.25	481.43	440.05	408.28	383.24
10.25%	2,552.93	1,341.55	939.16	739.00	619.74	540.91	485.19	443.90	412.22	387.26
10.50%	2,556.31	1,344.91	942.57	742.50	623.32	544.59	488.96	447.76	416.17	391.31
10.75%	2,559.69	1,348.26	945.99	746.00	626.92	548.28	492.75	451.64	420.15	395.38

$29,000   11.00 - 20.75%   1 - 10 Years

	1	2	3	4	5	6	7	8	9	10
11.00%	2,563.07	1,351.63	949.42	749.52	630.53	551.99	496.55	455.54	424.15	399.48
11.25%	2,566.45	1,355.00	952.86	753.05	634.15	555.71	500.37	459.46	428.17	403.59
11.50%	2,569.84	1,358.37	956.30	756.58	637.79	559.44	504.21	463.40	432.21	407.73
11.75%	2,573.22	1,361.75	959.76	760.13	641.43	563.19	508.06	467.36	436.26	411.89
12.00%	2,576.61	1,365.13	963.21	763.68	645.09	566.96	511.93	471.33	440.34	416.07
12.25%	2,580.01	1,368.52	966.68	767.25	648.76	570.73	515.81	475.32	444.44	420.27
12.50%	2,583.40	1,371.91	970.16	770.82	652.44	574.52	519.72	479.34	448.56	424.49
12.75%	2,586.80	1,375.31	973.64	774.40	656.13	578.33	523.63	483.36	452.70	428.74
13.00%	2,590.20	1,378.71	977.12	778.00	659.84	582.15	527.57	487.41	456.85	433.00
13.25%	2,593.60	1,382.12	980.62	781.60	663.56	585.98	531.52	491.47	461.03	437.29
13.50%	2,597.01	1,385.53	984.12	785.21	667.29	589.83	535.48	495.56	465.23	441.60
13.75%	2,600.42	1,388.95	987.63	788.84	671.03	593.69	539.46	499.66	469.44	445.92
14.00%	2,603.83	1,392.37	991.15	792.47	674.78	597.57	543.46	503.77	473.68	450.27
14.25%	2,607.24	1,395.80	994.68	796.11	678.54	601.46	547.47	507.91	477.93	454.64
14.50%	2,610.65	1,399.23	998.21	799.76	682.32	605.36	551.50	512.06	482.20	459.03
14.75%	2,614.07	1,402.67	1,001.75	803.42	686.11	609.28	555.55	516.23	486.50	463.44
15.00%	2,617.49	1,406.11	1,005.29	807.09	689.91	613.21	559.61	520.42	490.81	467.87
15.25%	2,620.91	1,409.56	1,008.85	810.77	693.72	617.15	563.68	524.62	495.13	472.32
15.50%	2,624.34	1,413.01	1,012.41	814.46	697.54	621.11	567.77	528.84	499.48	476.79
15.75%	2,627.77	1,416.47	1,015.98	818.16	701.38	625.08	571.88	533.08	503.85	481.28
16.00%	2,631.19	1,419.93	1,019.55	821.87	705.22	629.06	576.00	537.33	508.23	485.79
16.25%	2,634.63	1,423.40	1,023.14	825.59	709.08	633.06	580.14	541.61	512.63	490.32
16.50%	2,638.06	1,426.87	1,026.73	829.31	712.95	637.07	584.29	545.90	517.05	494.86
16.75%	2,641.50	1,430.34	1,030.32	833.05	716.83	641.10	588.46	550.20	521.49	499.43
17.00%	2,644.94	1,433.83	1,033.93	836.80	720.72	645.14	592.64	554.52	525.95	504.01
17.25%	2,648.38	1,437.31	1,037.54	840.55	724.63	649.19	596.84	558.86	530.42	508.62
17.50%	2,651.82	1,440.80	1,041.16	844.32	728.54	653.26	601.05	563.22	534.91	513.24
17.75%	2,655.27	1,444.30	1,044.79	848.09	732.47	657.33	605.28	567.59	539.42	517.88
18.00%	2,658.72	1,447.80	1,048.42	851.87	736.41	661.43	609.52	571.97	543.95	522.54
18.25%	2,662.17	1,451.30	1,052.06	855.67	740.36	665.53	613.77	576.38	548.49	527.21
18.50%	2,665.63	1,454.81	1,055.71	859.47	744.32	669.65	618.05	580.80	553.05	531.91
18.75%	2,669.08	1,458.33	1,059.36	863.28	748.29	673.78	622.33	585.23	557.63	536.62
19.00%	2,672.54	1,461.85	1,063.02	867.10	752.28	677.92	626.63	589.68	562.23	541.35
19.25%	2,676.00	1,465.37	1,066.69	870.93	756.27	682.08	630.95	594.15	566.84	546.10
19.50%	2,679.47	1,468.90	1,070.37	874.77	760.28	686.25	635.28	598.63	571.46	550.86
19.75%	2,682.93	1,472.44	1,074.05	878.62	764.29	690.44	639.62	603.13	576.11	555.64
20.00%	2,686.40	1,475.98	1,077.74	882.48	768.32	694.63	643.98	607.64	580.77	560.44
20.25%	2,689.87	1,479.52	1,081.44	886.35	772.36	698.84	648.35	612.17	585.45	565.26
20.50%	2,693.35	1,483.07	1,085.15	890.22	776.41	703.06	652.74	616.72	590.14	570.09
20.75%	2,696.82	1,486.63	1,088.86	894.11	780.47	707.30	657.14	621.27	594.85	574.94

	1	2	3	4	5	6	7	8	9	10
1.00%	2,513.56	1,263.06	846.24	637.84	512.81	429.47	369.94	325.30	290.58	262.81
1.25%	2,516.96	1,266.34	849.49	641.08	516.05	432.70	373.18	328.55	293.84	266.08
1.50%	2,520.36	1,269.62	852.74	644.33	519.30	435.96	376.44	331.82	297.12	269.37
1.75%	2,523.76	1,272.91	856.01	647.59	522.56	439.23	379.72	335.11	300.43	272.69
2.00%	2,527.17	1,276.21	859.28	650.85	525.83	442.51	383.02	338.43	303.76	276.04
2.25%	2,530.57	1,279.51	862.56	654.13	529.12	445.81	386.34	341.76	307.11	279.41
2.50%	2,533.98	1,282.81	865.84	657.42	532.42	449.13	389.67	345.12	310.49	282.81
2.75%	2,537.40	1,286.12	869.13	660.72	535.73	452.46	393.03	348.49	313.89	286.23
3.00%	2,540.81	1,289.44	872.44	664.03	539.06	455.81	396.40	351.89	317.31	289.68
3.25%	2,544.23	1,292.76	875.75	667.35	542.40	459.17	399.79	355.30	320.75	293.16
3.50%	2,547.65	1,296.08	879.06	670.68	545.75	462.55	403.20	358.74	324.22	296.66
3.75%	2,551.07	1,299.41	882.39	674.02	549.12	465.95	406.62	362.20	327.71	300.18
4.00%	2,554.50	1,302.75	885.72	677.37	552.50	469.36	410.06	365.68	331.23	303.74
4.25%	2,557.93	1,306.09	889.06	680.73	555.89	472.78	413.53	369.18	334.77	307.31
4.50%	2,561.36	1,309.43	892.41	684.10	559.29	476.22	417.00	372.70	338.33	310.92
4.75%	2,564.79	1,312.79	895.76	687.49	562.71	479.68	420.50	376.24	341.91	314.54
5.00%	2,568.22	1,316.14	899.13	690.88	566.14	483.15	424.02	379.80	345.52	318.20
5.25%	2,571.66	1,319.50	902.50	694.28	569.58	486.63	427.55	383.38	349.15	321.88
5.50%	2,575.10	1,322.87	905.88	697.69	573.03	490.14	431.10	386.98	352.80	325.58
5.75%	2,578.55	1,326.24	909.26	701.12	576.50	493.65	434.67	390.60	356.47	329.31
6.00%	2,581.99	1,329.62	912.66	704.55	579.98	497.19	438.26	394.24	360.17	333.06
6.25%	2,585.44	1,333.00	916.06	707.99	583.48	500.73	441.86	397.90	363.89	336.84
6.50%	2,588.89	1,336.39	919.47	711.45	586.98	504.30	445.48	401.59	367.64	340.64
6.75%	2,592.35	1,339.78	922.89	714.91	590.50	507.88	449.12	405.29	371.40	344.47
7.00%	2,595.80	1,343.18	926.31	718.39	594.04	511.47	452.78	409.01	375.19	348.33
7.25%	2,599.26	1,346.58	929.75	721.87	597.58	515.08	456.46	412.75	379.00	352.20
7.50%	2,602.72	1,349.99	933.19	725.37	601.14	518.70	460.15	416.52	382.83	356.11
7.75%	2,606.19	1,353.40	936.63	728.87	604.71	522.34	463.86	420.30	386.68	360.03
8.00%	2,609.65	1,356.82	940.09	732.39	608.29	526.00	467.59	424.10	390.56	363.98
8.25%	2,613.12	1,360.24	943.55	735.91	611.89	529.67	471.33	427.92	394.46	367.96
8.50%	2,616.59	1,363.67	947.03	739.45	615.50	533.35	475.09	431.76	398.38	371.96
8.75%	2,620.07	1,367.10	950.51	743.00	619.12	537.05	478.87	435.63	402.32	375.98
9.00%	2,623.54	1,370.54	953.99	746.55	622.75	540.77	482.67	439.51	406.29	380.03
9.25%	2,627.02	1,373.99	957.49	750.12	626.40	544.50	486.49	443.41	410.27	384.10
9.50%	2,630.51	1,377.43	960.99	753.69	630.06	548.24	490.32	447.33	414.28	388.19
9.75%	2,633.99	1,380.89	964.50	757.28	633.73	552.00	494.17	451.27	418.31	392.31
10.00%	2,637.48	1,384.35	968.02	760.88	637.41	555.78	498.04	455.22	422.36	396.45
10.25%	2,640.97	1,387.81	971.54	764.48	641.11	559.56	501.92	459.20	426.43	400.62
10.50%	2,644.46	1,391.28	975.07	768.10	644.82	563.37	505.82	463.20	430.53	404.80
10.75%	2,647.95	1,394.76	978.61	771.73	648.54	567.19	509.74	467.22	434.64	409.02

$30,000   11.00 - 20.75%   1 - 10 Years

	1	2	3	4	5	6	7	8	9	10
11.00%	2,651.45	1,398.24	982.16	775.37	652.27	571.02	513.67	471.25	438.78	413.25
11.25%	2,654.95	1,401.72	985.72	779.01	656.02	574.87	517.63	475.31	442.93	417.51
11.50%	2,658.45	1,405.21	989.28	782.67	659.78	578.73	521.59	479.38	447.11	421.79
11.75%	2,661.96	1,408.70	992.85	786.34	663.55	582.61	525.58	483.47	451.31	426.09
12.00%	2,665.46	1,412.20	996.43	790.02	667.33	586.51	529.58	487.59	455.53	430.41
12.25%	2,668.97	1,415.71	1,000.02	793.70	671.13	590.41	533.60	491.72	459.77	434.76
12.50%	2,672.49	1,419.22	1,003.61	797.40	674.94	594.34	537.64	495.86	464.03	439.13
12.75%	2,676.00	1,422.73	1,007.21	801.11	678.76	598.27	541.69	500.03	468.31	443.52
13.00%	2,679.52	1,426.25	1,010.82	804.82	682.59	602.22	545.76	504.22	472.61	447.93
13.25%	2,683.04	1,429.78	1,014.43	808.55	686.44	606.19	549.84	508.42	476.93	452.37
13.50%	2,686.56	1,433.31	1,018.06	812.29	690.30	610.17	553.95	512.64	481.27	456.82
13.75%	2,690.09	1,436.85	1,021.69	816.04	694.17	614.16	558.07	516.89	485.63	461.30
14.00%	2,693.61	1,440.39	1,025.33	819.79	698.05	618.17	562.20	521.15	490.01	465.80
14.25%	2,697.14	1,443.93	1,028.98	823.56	701.94	622.20	566.35	525.42	494.41	470.32
14.50%	2,700.68	1,447.48	1,032.63	827.34	705.85	626.23	570.52	529.72	498.83	474.86
14.75%	2,704.21	1,451.04	1,036.29	831.13	709.77	630.28	574.70	534.03	503.27	479.42
15.00%	2,707.75	1,454.60	1,039.96	834.92	713.70	634.35	578.90	538.36	507.73	484.00
15.25%	2,711.29	1,458.17	1,043.64	838.73	717.64	638.43	583.12	542.71	512.21	488.61
15.50%	2,714.83	1,461.74	1,047.32	842.55	721.60	642.52	587.35	547.08	516.71	493.23
15.75%	2,718.38	1,465.31	1,051.01	846.37	725.56	646.63	591.60	551.46	521.22	497.88
16.00%	2,721.93	1,468.89	1,054.71	850.21	729.54	650.76	595.86	555.86	525.76	502.54
16.25%	2,725.48	1,472.48	1,058.42	854.05	733.53	654.89	600.14	560.28	530.31	507.22
16.50%	2,729.03	1,476.07	1,062.13	857.91	737.54	659.04	604.44	564.72	534.88	511.93
16.75%	2,732.58	1,479.67	1,065.85	861.78	741.55	663.21	608.75	569.17	539.48	516.65
17.00%	2,736.14	1,483.27	1,069.58	865.65	745.58	667.38	613.07	573.64	544.09	521.39
17.25%	2,739.70	1,486.87	1,073.32	869.54	749.62	671.58	617.42	578.13	548.71	526.16
17.50%	2,743.27	1,490.49	1,077.06	873.43	753.67	675.78	621.77	582.64	553.36	530.94
17.75%	2,746.83	1,494.10	1,080.81	877.34	757.73	680.00	626.15	587.16	558.02	535.74
18.00%	2,750.40	1,497.72	1,084.57	881.25	761.80	684.23	630.54	591.70	562.71	540.56
18.25%	2,753.97	1,501.35	1,088.34	885.17	765.89	688.48	634.94	596.25	567.41	545.39
18.50%	2,757.54	1,504.98	1,092.11	889.11	769.99	692.74	639.36	600.82	572.12	550.25
18.75%	2,761.12	1,508.62	1,095.89	893.05	774.10	697.01	643.79	605.41	576.86	555.12
19.00%	2,764.70	1,512.26	1,099.68	897.00	778.22	701.30	648.24	610.02	581.61	560.02
19.25%	2,768.28	1,515.90	1,103.48	900.97	782.35	705.60	652.70	614.64	586.38	564.93
19.50%	2,771.86	1,519.56	1,107.28	904.94	786.49	709.92	657.18	619.27	591.17	569.86
19.75%	2,775.45	1,523.21	1,111.09	908.92	790.65	714.24	661.68	623.93	595.97	574.80
20.00%	2,779.04	1,526.87	1,114.91	912.91	794.82	718.58	666.19	628.60	600.80	579.77
20.25%	2,782.63	1,530.54	1,118.73	916.91	799.00	722.94	670.71	633.28	605.63	584.75
20.50%	2,786.22	1,534.21	1,122.57	920.92	803.19	727.31	675.25	637.98	610.49	589.75
20.75%	2,789.81	1,537.89	1,126.40	924.94	807.39	731.69	679.80	642.70	615.36	594.76

	1	2	3	4	5	6	7	8	9	10
1.00%	2,723.03	1,368.32	916.76	691.00	555.55	465.25	400.77	352.40	314.80	284.71
1.25%	2,726.71	1,371.87	920.28	694.50	559.05	468.76	404.28	355.93	318.33	288.25
1.50%	2,730.39	1,375.43	923.81	698.02	562.57	472.29	407.81	359.47	321.88	291.82
1.75%	2,734.07	1,378.99	927.34	701.55	566.10	475.83	411.37	363.04	325.46	295.42
2.00%	2,737.76	1,382.56	930.88	705.09	569.65	479.39	414.94	366.63	329.07	299.04
2.25%	2,741.45	1,386.13	934.44	708.64	573.21	482.97	418.53	370.24	332.70	302.70
2.50%	2,745.15	1,389.71	937.99	712.21	576.79	486.56	422.15	373.87	336.36	306.38
2.75%	2,748.85	1,393.30	941.56	715.78	580.38	490.17	425.78	377.53	340.04	310.09
3.00%	2,752.55	1,396.89	945.14	719.37	583.98	493.79	429.43	381.21	343.75	313.82
3.25%	2,756.25	1,400.49	948.72	722.96	587.60	497.44	433.10	384.91	347.48	317.59
3.50%	2,759.95	1,404.09	952.32	726.57	591.23	501.10	436.80	388.64	351.24	321.38
3.75%	2,763.66	1,407.70	955.92	730.19	594.88	504.77	440.51	392.38	355.02	325.20
4.00%	2,767.37	1,411.31	959.53	733.82	598.54	508.47	444.24	396.15	358.83	329.05
4.25%	2,771.09	1,414.93	963.15	737.46	602.21	512.18	447.99	399.94	362.66	332.92
4.50%	2,774.80	1,418.55	966.78	741.11	605.90	515.91	451.76	403.76	366.52	336.82
4.75%	2,778.52	1,422.18	970.41	744.78	609.60	519.65	455.54	407.59	370.40	340.76
5.00%	2,782.24	1,425.82	974.05	748.45	613.32	523.41	459.35	411.45	374.31	344.71
5.25%	2,785.97	1,429.46	977.71	752.14	617.04	527.19	463.18	415.33	378.24	348.70
5.50%	2,789.70	1,433.11	981.37	755.84	620.79	530.98	467.03	419.23	382.20	352.71
5.75%	2,793.43	1,436.76	985.04	759.54	624.54	534.79	470.89	423.15	386.18	356.75
6.00%	2,797.16	1,440.42	988.71	763.26	628.32	538.62	474.78	427.10	390.19	360.82
6.25%	2,800.89	1,444.08	992.40	766.99	632.10	542.46	478.68	431.06	394.22	364.91
6.50%	2,804.63	1,447.75	996.09	770.74	635.90	546.32	482.61	435.05	398.27	369.03
6.75%	2,808.38	1,451.43	999.79	774.49	639.71	550.20	486.55	439.06	402.35	373.18
7.00%	2,812.12	1,455.11	1,003.51	778.25	643.54	554.09	490.51	443.10	406.45	377.35
7.25%	2,815.87	1,458.80	1,007.22	782.03	647.38	558.00	494.49	447.15	410.58	381.55
7.50%	2,819.62	1,462.49	1,010.95	785.81	651.23	561.93	498.49	451.23	414.73	385.78
7.75%	2,823.37	1,466.18	1,014.69	789.61	655.10	565.87	502.51	455.32	418.91	390.03
8.00%	2,827.12	1,469.89	1,018.43	793.42	658.98	569.83	506.55	459.44	423.11	394.31
8.25%	2,830.88	1,473.60	1,022.18	797.24	662.88	573.81	510.61	463.58	427.33	398.62
8.50%	2,834.64	1,477.31	1,025.94	801.07	666.79	577.80	514.69	467.74	431.58	402.95
8.75%	2,838.41	1,481.03	1,029.71	804.91	670.71	581.81	518.78	471.93	435.85	407.31
9.00%	2,842.17	1,484.75	1,033.49	808.76	674.65	585.83	522.90	476.13	440.14	411.70
9.25%	2,845.94	1,488.48	1,037.28	812.63	678.60	589.87	527.03	480.36	444.46	416.11
9.50%	2,849.71	1,492.22	1,041.07	816.50	682.56	593.93	531.18	484.60	448.80	420.54
9.75%	2,853.49	1,495.96	1,044.87	820.39	686.54	598.00	535.35	488.87	453.17	425.00
10.00%	2,857.27	1,499.71	1,048.68	824.28	690.53	602.09	539.54	493.16	457.56	429.49
10.25%	2,861.05	1,503.46	1,052.50	828.19	694.53	606.20	543.75	497.47	461.97	434.00
10.50%	2,864.83	1,507.22	1,056.33	832.11	698.55	610.32	547.97	501.80	466.40	438.54
10.75%	2,868.62	1,510.99	1,060.16	836.04	702.58	614.45	552.22	506.15	470.86	443.10

$32,500　　11.00 - 20.75%　　1 - 10 Years

	1	2	3	4	5	6	7	8	9	10
11.00%	2,872.40	1,514.75	1,064.01	839.98	706.63	618.61	556.48	510.52	475.34	447.69
11.25%	2,876.20	1,518.53	1,067.86	843.93	710.69	622.78	560.76	514.92	479.84	452.30
11.50%	2,879.99	1,522.31	1,071.72	847.89	714.76	626.96	565.06	519.33	484.37	456.94
11.75%	2,883.79	1,526.10	1,075.59	851.87	718.85	631.16	569.38	523.76	488.92	461.60
12.00%	2,887.59	1,529.89	1,079.47	855.85	722.94	635.38	573.71	528.22	493.49	466.28
12.25%	2,891.39	1,533.68	1,083.35	859.84	727.06	639.61	578.07	532.69	498.08	470.99
12.50%	2,895.19	1,537.49	1,087.24	863.85	731.18	643.86	582.44	537.19	502.70	475.72
12.75%	2,899.00	1,541.30	1,091.14	867.87	735.32	648.13	586.83	541.70	507.33	480.48
13.00%	2,902.81	1,545.11	1,095.05	871.89	739.47	652.41	591.24	546.24	511.99	485.26
13.25%	2,906.62	1,548.93	1,098.97	875.93	743.64	656.70	595.66	550.79	516.67	490.06
13.50%	2,910.44	1,552.75	1,102.90	879.98	747.82	661.02	600.11	555.37	521.38	494.89
13.75%	2,914.26	1,556.58	1,106.83	884.04	752.01	665.34	604.57	559.96	526.10	499.74
14.00%	2,918.08	1,560.42	1,110.77	888.11	756.22	669.69	609.05	564.57	530.85	504.62
14.25%	2,921.91	1,564.26	1,114.72	892.19	760.44	674.04	613.55	569.21	535.61	509.51
14.50%	2,925.73	1,568.11	1,118.68	896.28	764.67	678.42	618.06	573.86	540.40	514.43
14.75%	2,929.56	1,571.96	1,122.65	900.39	768.91	682.81	622.59	578.53	545.21	519.37
15.00%	2,933.40	1,575.82	1,126.62	904.50	773.17	687.21	627.14	583.23	550.04	524.34
15.25%	2,937.23	1,579.68	1,130.61	908.62	777.44	691.63	631.71	587.94	554.89	529.33
15.50%	2,941.07	1,583.55	1,134.60	912.76	781.73	696.07	636.30	592.67	559.76	534.33
15.75%	2,944.91	1,587.42	1,138.60	916.90	786.03	700.52	640.90	597.42	564.66	539.37
16.00%	2,948.75	1,591.30	1,142.60	921.06	790.34	704.98	645.52	602.19	569.57	544.42
16.25%	2,952.60	1,595.19	1,146.62	925.23	794.66	709.47	650.15	606.97	574.50	549.49
16.50%	2,956.45	1,599.08	1,150.64	929.40	799.00	713.96	654.81	611.78	579.46	554.59
16.75%	2,960.30	1,602.97	1,154.67	933.59	803.35	718.47	659.48	616.60	584.43	559.70
17.00%	2,964.15	1,606.87	1,158.71	937.79	807.71	723.00	664.16	621.45	589.43	564.84
17.25%	2,968.01	1,610.78	1,162.76	942.00	812.08	727.54	668.87	626.31	594.44	570.00
17.50%	2,971.87	1,614.69	1,166.82	946.22	816.47	732.10	673.59	631.19	599.47	575.18
17.75%	2,975.73	1,618.61	1,170.88	950.45	820.87	736.67	678.33	636.09	604.53	580.38
18.00%	2,979.60	1,622.53	1,174.95	954.69	825.29	741.25	683.08	641.00	609.60	585.60
18.25%	2,983.47	1,626.46	1,179.03	958.94	829.71	745.85	687.85	645.94	614.69	590.84
18.50%	2,987.34	1,630.40	1,183.12	963.20	834.15	750.47	692.64	650.89	619.80	596.10
18.75%	2,991.21	1,634.34	1,187.22	967.47	838.60	755.10	697.44	655.86	624.93	601.38
19.00%	2,995.09	1,638.28	1,191.32	971.75	843.07	759.74	702.26	660.85	630.08	606.69
19.25%	2,998.97	1,642.23	1,195.43	976.05	847.54	764.40	707.10	665.86	635.25	612.01
19.50%	3,002.85	1,646.19	1,199.55	980.35	852.03	769.08	711.95	670.88	640.43	617.34
19.75%	3,006.73	1,650.15	1,203.68	984.66	856.54	773.76	716.82	675.92	645.64	622.70
20.00%	3,010.62	1,654.11	1,207.82	988.99	861.05	778.47	721.70	680.98	650.86	628.08
20.25%	3,014.51	1,658.09	1,211.96	993.32	865.58	783.18	726.60	686.05	656.10	633.48
20.50%	3,018.40	1,662.06	1,216.11	997.67	870.12	787.91	731.52	691.15	661.36	638.89
20.75%	3,022.30	1,666.05	1,220.27	1,002.02	874.67	792.66	736.45	696.26	666.64	644.33

	1	2	3	4	5	6	7	8	9	10
1.00%	2,932.49	1,473.57	987.28	744.15	598.28	501.04	431.59	379.51	339.01	306.61
1.25%	2,936.45	1,477.40	991.07	747.93	602.06	504.82	435.38	383.31	342.81	310.43
1.50%	2,940.42	1,481.23	994.87	751.72	605.85	508.62	439.18	387.12	346.64	314.27
1.75%	2,944.39	1,485.07	998.67	755.52	609.65	512.43	443.01	390.96	350.50	318.14
2.00%	2,948.36	1,488.91	1,002.49	759.33	613.47	516.27	446.86	394.83	354.38	322.05
2.25%	2,952.34	1,492.76	1,006.31	763.15	617.31	520.12	450.73	398.72	358.30	325.98
2.50%	2,956.31	1,496.61	1,010.15	766.99	621.16	523.99	454.62	402.63	362.23	329.94
2.75%	2,960.30	1,500.48	1,013.99	770.84	625.02	527.87	458.53	406.57	366.20	333.94
3.00%	2,964.28	1,504.34	1,017.84	774.70	628.90	531.78	462.47	410.54	370.19	337.96
3.25%	2,968.27	1,508.22	1,021.70	778.57	632.80	535.70	466.42	414.52	374.21	342.02
3.50%	2,972.26	1,512.10	1,025.57	782.46	636.71	539.64	470.39	418.53	378.26	346.10
3.75%	2,976.25	1,515.98	1,029.45	786.36	640.64	543.60	474.39	422.57	382.33	350.21
4.00%	2,980.25	1,519.87	1,033.34	790.27	644.58	547.58	478.41	426.62	386.43	354.36
4.25%	2,984.25	1,523.77	1,037.24	794.19	648.53	551.58	482.45	430.71	390.56	358.53
4.50%	2,988.25	1,527.67	1,041.14	798.12	652.51	555.59	486.51	434.81	394.72	362.73
4.75%	2,992.25	1,531.58	1,045.06	802.07	656.49	559.62	490.59	438.94	398.90	366.97
5.00%	2,996.26	1,535.50	1,048.98	806.03	660.49	563.67	494.69	443.10	403.10	371.23
5.25%	3,000.27	1,539.42	1,052.91	809.99	664.51	567.74	498.81	447.27	407.34	375.52
5.50%	3,004.29	1,543.35	1,056.86	813.98	668.54	571.83	502.95	451.48	411.60	379.84
5.75%	3,008.30	1,547.28	1,060.81	817.97	672.59	575.93	507.12	455.70	415.89	384.19
6.00%	3,012.33	1,551.22	1,064.77	821.98	676.65	580.05	511.30	459.95	420.20	388.57
6.25%	3,016.35	1,555.17	1,068.74	825.99	680.72	584.19	515.50	464.22	424.54	392.98
6.50%	3,020.37	1,559.12	1,072.72	830.02	684.82	588.35	519.73	468.52	428.91	397.42
6.75%	3,024.40	1,563.08	1,076.70	834.06	688.92	592.52	523.98	472.84	433.30	401.88
7.00%	3,028.44	1,567.04	1,080.70	838.12	693.04	596.72	528.24	477.18	437.72	406.38
7.25%	3,032.47	1,571.01	1,084.70	842.18	697.18	600.93	532.53	481.55	442.16	410.90
7.50%	3,036.51	1,574.99	1,088.72	846.26	701.33	605.15	536.84	485.94	446.64	415.46
7.75%	3,040.55	1,578.97	1,092.74	850.35	705.49	609.40	541.17	490.35	451.13	420.04
8.00%	3,044.60	1,582.96	1,096.77	854.45	709.67	613.66	545.52	494.78	455.66	424.65
8.25%	3,048.64	1,586.95	1,100.81	858.57	713.87	617.94	549.89	499.24	460.20	429.28
8.50%	3,052.69	1,590.95	1,104.86	862.69	718.08	622.24	554.28	503.72	464.78	433.95
8.75%	3,056.75	1,594.95	1,108.92	866.83	722.30	626.56	558.69	508.23	469.38	438.64
9.00%	3,060.80	1,598.97	1,112.99	870.98	726.54	630.89	563.12	512.76	474.00	443.37
9.25%	3,064.86	1,602.98	1,117.07	875.14	730.80	635.25	567.57	517.31	478.65	448.11
9.50%	3,068.92	1,607.01	1,121.15	879.31	735.07	639.61	572.04	521.88	483.33	452.89
9.75%	3,072.99	1,611.04	1,125.25	883.49	739.35	644.00	576.53	526.48	488.03	457.70
10.00%	3,077.06	1,615.07	1,129.35	887.69	743.65	648.40	581.04	531.10	492.75	462.53
10.25%	3,081.13	1,619.11	1,133.46	891.90	747.96	652.83	585.57	535.74	497.50	467.39
10.50%	3,085.20	1,623.16	1,137.59	896.12	752.29	657.26	590.12	540.40	502.28	472.27
10.75%	3,089.28	1,627.21	1,141.72	900.35	756.63	661.72	594.69	545.09	507.08	477.19

$35,000   11.00 - 20.75%   1 - 10 Years

	1	2	3	4	5	6	7	8	9	10
11.00%	3,093.36	1,631.27	1,145.86	904.59	760.98	666.19	599.29	549.79	511.91	482.13
11.25%	3,097.44	1,635.34	1,150.00	908.85	765.36	670.68	603.90	554.53	516.75	487.09
11.50%	3,101.53	1,639.41	1,154.16	913.12	769.74	675.19	608.53	559.28	521.63	492.08
11.75%	3,105.62	1,643.49	1,158.33	917.39	774.14	679.72	613.18	564.05	526.53	497.10
12.00%	3,109.71	1,647.57	1,162.50	921.68	778.56	684.26	617.85	568.85	531.45	502.15
12.25%	3,113.80	1,651.66	1,166.68	925.99	782.98	688.82	622.53	573.67	536.39	507.22
12.50%	3,117.90	1,655.76	1,170.88	930.30	787.43	693.39	627.24	578.51	541.36	512.32
12.75%	3,122.00	1,659.86	1,175.08	934.63	791.89	697.98	631.97	583.37	546.36	517.44
13.00%	3,126.10	1,663.96	1,179.29	938.96	796.36	702.59	636.72	588.25	551.38	522.59
13.25%	3,130.21	1,668.08	1,183.51	943.31	800.84	707.22	641.49	593.16	556.42	527.76
13.50%	3,134.32	1,672.20	1,187.74	947.67	805.34	711.86	646.27	598.09	561.48	532.96
13.75%	3,138.43	1,676.32	1,191.97	952.04	809.86	716.52	651.08	603.03	566.57	538.18
14.00%	3,142.55	1,680.45	1,196.22	956.43	814.39	721.20	655.90	608.00	571.68	543.43
14.25%	3,146.67	1,684.59	1,200.47	960.82	818.93	725.89	660.74	612.99	576.81	548.71
14.50%	3,150.79	1,688.73	1,204.73	965.23	823.49	730.60	665.61	618.00	581.97	554.00
14.75%	3,154.91	1,692.88	1,209.01	969.65	828.06	735.33	670.49	623.04	587.15	559.33
15.00%	3,159.04	1,697.03	1,213.29	974.08	832.65	740.08	675.39	628.09	592.35	564.67
15.25%	3,163.17	1,701.19	1,217.58	978.52	837.25	744.84	680.30	633.16	597.58	570.04
15.50%	3,167.30	1,705.36	1,221.87	982.97	841.86	749.61	685.24	638.26	602.82	575.44
15.75%	3,171.44	1,709.53	1,226.18	987.43	846.49	754.41	690.20	643.37	608.09	580.85
16.00%	3,175.58	1,713.71	1,230.50	991.91	851.13	759.21	695.17	648.51	613.38	586.30
16.25%	3,179.72	1,717.89	1,234.82	996.40	855.79	764.04	700.16	653.66	618.70	591.76
16.50%	3,183.87	1,722.08	1,239.15	1,000.90	860.46	768.88	705.18	658.84	624.03	597.25
16.75%	3,188.02	1,726.28	1,243.50	1,005.41	865.14	773.74	710.21	664.03	629.39	602.76
17.00%	3,192.17	1,730.48	1,247.85	1,009.93	869.84	778.61	715.25	669.25	634.77	608.29
17.25%	3,196.32	1,734.69	1,252.20	1,014.46	874.55	783.51	720.32	674.49	640.17	613.85
17.50%	3,200.48	1,738.90	1,256.57	1,019.00	879.28	788.41	725.40	679.74	645.59	619.43
17.75%	3,204.64	1,743.12	1,260.95	1,023.56	884.02	793.33	730.50	685.02	651.03	625.03
18.00%	3,208.80	1,747.34	1,265.33	1,028.12	888.77	798.27	735.62	690.31	656.49	630.65
18.25%	3,212.97	1,751.57	1,269.73	1,032.70	893.54	803.23	740.76	695.63	661.97	636.29
18.50%	3,217.13	1,755.81	1,274.13	1,037.29	898.32	808.20	745.92	700.96	667.48	641.96
18.75%	3,221.31	1,760.05	1,278.54	1,041.89	903.11	813.18	751.09	706.31	673.00	647.64
19.00%	3,225.48	1,764.30	1,282.96	1,046.50	907.92	818.19	756.28	711.69	678.55	653.35
19.25%	3,229.66	1,768.56	1,287.39	1,051.13	912.74	823.20	761.49	717.08	684.11	659.08
19.50%	3,233.84	1,772.82	1,291.83	1,055.76	917.58	828.24	766.71	722.49	689.70	664.83
19.75%	3,238.02	1,777.08	1,296.27	1,060.41	922.42	833.28	771.96	727.91	695.30	670.60
20.00%	3,242.21	1,781.35	1,300.73	1,065.06	927.29	838.35	777.22	733.36	700.93	676.39
20.25%	3,246.40	1,785.63	1,305.19	1,069.73	932.16	843.43	782.49	738.83	706.57	682.21
20.50%	3,250.59	1,789.91	1,309.66	1,074.41	937.05	848.52	787.79	744.31	712.24	688.04
20.75%	3,254.78	1,794.20	1,314.14	1,079.10	941.95	853.63	793.10	749.81	717.92	693.89

	1	2	3	4	5	6	7	8	9	10
1.00%	3,141.95	1,578.83	1,057.80	797.30	641.02	536.83	462.42	406.62	363.23	328.52
1.25%	3,146.20	1,582.93	1,061.86	801.35	645.06	540.88	466.48	410.68	367.30	332.60
1.50%	3,150.45	1,587.03	1,065.93	805.41	649.12	544.95	470.55	414.77	371.40	336.72
1.75%	3,154.70	1,591.14	1,070.01	809.48	653.20	549.03	474.66	418.89	375.54	340.87
2.00%	3,158.96	1,595.26	1,074.10	813.57	657.29	553.14	478.78	423.03	379.70	345.05
2.25%	3,163.22	1,599.38	1,078.19	817.67	661.40	557.27	482.92	427.20	383.89	349.27
2.50%	3,167.48	1,603.51	1,082.30	821.78	665.53	561.41	487.09	431.39	388.11	353.51
2.75%	3,171.74	1,607.65	1,086.42	825.90	669.67	565.58	491.28	435.61	392.36	357.79
3.00%	3,176.01	1,611.80	1,090.55	830.04	673.83	569.76	495.50	439.86	396.64	362.10
3.25%	3,180.29	1,615.95	1,094.68	834.19	678.00	573.97	499.74	444.13	400.94	366.45
3.50%	3,184.56	1,620.10	1,098.83	838.35	682.19	578.19	503.99	448.43	405.28	370.82
3.75%	3,188.84	1,624.27	1,102.98	842.53	686.40	582.43	508.28	452.75	409.64	375.23
4.00%	3,193.12	1,628.43	1,107.15	846.71	690.62	586.69	512.58	457.10	414.04	379.67
4.25%	3,197.41	1,632.61	1,111.32	850.92	694.86	590.98	516.91	461.47	418.46	384.14
4.50%	3,201.69	1,636.79	1,115.51	855.13	699.11	595.28	521.26	465.87	422.91	388.64
4.75%	3,205.99	1,640.98	1,119.70	859.36	703.38	599.60	525.63	470.30	427.39	393.18
5.00%	3,210.28	1,645.18	1,123.91	863.60	707.67	603.93	530.02	474.75	431.90	397.75
5.25%	3,214.58	1,649.38	1,128.12	867.85	711.97	608.29	534.44	479.22	436.43	402.34
5.50%	3,218.88	1,653.59	1,132.35	872.12	716.29	612.67	538.88	483.72	441.00	406.97
5.75%	3,223.18	1,657.80	1,136.58	876.40	720.63	617.07	543.34	488.25	445.59	411.63
6.00%	3,227.49	1,662.02	1,140.82	880.69	724.98	621.48	547.82	492.80	450.22	416.33
6.25%	3,231.80	1,666.25	1,145.08	884.99	729.35	625.92	552.33	497.38	454.87	421.05
6.50%	3,236.12	1,670.48	1,149.34	889.31	733.73	630.37	556.85	501.98	459.54	425.80
6.75%	3,240.43	1,674.72	1,153.61	893.64	738.13	634.85	561.40	506.61	464.25	430.59
7.00%	3,244.75	1,678.97	1,157.89	897.98	742.54	639.34	565.98	511.26	468.99	435.41
7.25%	3,249.08	1,683.23	1,162.18	902.34	746.98	643.85	570.57	515.94	473.75	440.25
7.50%	3,253.40	1,687.48	1,166.48	906.71	751.42	648.38	575.19	520.65	478.54	445.13
7.75%	3,257.73	1,691.75	1,170.79	911.09	755.89	652.93	579.82	525.37	483.36	450.04
8.00%	3,262.07	1,696.02	1,175.11	915.48	760.36	657.50	584.48	530.13	488.20	454.98
8.25%	3,266.40	1,700.30	1,179.44	919.89	764.86	662.08	589.16	534.90	493.08	459.95
8.50%	3,270.74	1,704.59	1,183.78	924.31	769.37	666.69	593.87	539.70	497.98	464.95
8.75%	3,275.08	1,708.88	1,188.13	928.74	773.90	671.31	598.59	544.53	502.90	469.98
9.00%	3,279.43	1,713.18	1,192.49	933.19	778.44	675.96	603.34	549.38	507.86	475.03
9.25%	3,283.78	1,717.48	1,196.86	937.65	783.00	680.62	608.11	554.26	512.84	480.12
9.50%	3,288.13	1,721.79	1,201.24	942.12	787.57	685.30	612.90	559.16	517.85	485.24
9.75%	3,292.49	1,726.11	1,205.62	946.60	792.16	690.00	617.71	564.08	522.89	490.39
10.00%	3,296.85	1,730.43	1,210.02	951.10	796.76	694.72	622.54	569.03	527.95	495.57
10.25%	3,301.21	1,734.76	1,214.43	955.61	801.38	699.46	627.40	574.00	533.04	500.77
10.50%	3,305.57	1,739.10	1,218.84	960.13	806.02	704.21	632.28	579.00	538.16	506.01
10.75%	3,309.94	1,743.44	1,223.27	964.66	810.67	708.99	637.17	584.02	543.30	511.27

$37,500   11.00 - 20.75%   1 - 10 Years

	1	2	3	4	5	6	7	8	9	10
11.00%	3,314.31	1,747.79	1,227.70	969.21	815.34	713.78	642.09	589.07	548.47	516.56
11.25%	3,318.69	1,752.15	1,232.15	973.77	820.02	718.59	647.03	594.13	553.67	521.88
11.50%	3,323.06	1,756.51	1,236.60	978.34	824.72	723.42	651.99	599.23	558.89	527.23
11.75%	3,327.45	1,760.88	1,241.06	982.92	829.44	728.27	656.97	604.34	564.14	532.61
12.00%	3,331.83	1,765.26	1,245.54	987.52	834.17	733.13	661.98	609.48	569.41	538.02
12.25%	3,336.22	1,769.64	1,250.02	992.13	838.91	738.02	667.00	614.64	574.71	543.45
12.50%	3,340.61	1,774.02	1,254.51	996.75	843.67	742.92	672.05	619.83	580.03	548.91
12.75%	3,345.00	1,778.42	1,259.01	1,001.38	848.45	747.84	677.11	625.04	585.38	554.40
13.00%	3,349.40	1,782.82	1,263.52	1,006.03	853.24	752.78	682.20	630.27	590.76	559.92
13.25%	3,353.80	1,787.23	1,268.04	1,010.69	858.05	757.74	687.31	635.53	596.16	565.46
13.50%	3,358.20	1,791.64	1,272.57	1,015.36	862.87	762.71	692.43	640.81	601.59	571.03
13.75%	3,362.61	1,796.06	1,277.11	1,020.05	867.71	767.70	697.58	646.11	607.04	576.63
14.00%	3,367.02	1,800.48	1,281.66	1,024.74	872.56	772.72	702.75	651.43	612.51	582.25
14.25%	3,371.43	1,804.92	1,286.22	1,029.45	877.43	777.74	707.94	656.78	618.01	587.90
14.50%	3,375.85	1,809.35	1,290.79	1,034.17	882.31	782.79	713.15	662.15	623.54	593.58
14.75%	3,380.26	1,813.80	1,295.36	1,038.91	887.21	787.86	718.38	667.54	629.09	599.28
15.00%	3,384.69	1,818.25	1,299.95	1,043.65	892.12	792.94	723.63	672.95	634.66	605.01
15.25%	3,389.11	1,822.71	1,304.55	1,048.41	897.05	798.04	728.90	678.39	640.26	610.76
15.50%	3,393.54	1,827.17	1,309.15	1,053.18	901.99	803.16	734.19	683.85	645.88	616.54
15.75%	3,397.97	1,831.64	1,313.76	1,057.97	906.95	808.29	739.50	689.33	651.53	622.34
16.00%	3,402.41	1,836.12	1,318.39	1,062.76	911.93	813.44	744.83	694.83	657.20	628.17
16.25%	3,406.85	1,840.60	1,323.02	1,067.57	916.92	818.61	750.18	700.35	662.89	634.03
16.50%	3,411.29	1,845.09	1,327.66	1,072.39	921.92	823.80	755.55	705.90	668.61	639.91
16.75%	3,415.73	1,849.58	1,332.32	1,077.22	926.94	829.01	760.93	711.47	674.34	645.81
17.00%	3,420.18	1,854.08	1,336.98	1,082.06	931.97	834.23	766.34	717.05	680.11	651.74
17.25%	3,424.63	1,858.59	1,341.65	1,086.92	937.02	839.47	771.77	722.66	685.89	657.69
17.50%	3,429.08	1,863.11	1,346.33	1,091.79	942.08	844.73	777.22	728.30	691.70	663.67
17.75%	3,433.54	1,867.63	1,351.02	1,096.67	947.16	850.00	782.68	733.95	697.53	669.67
18.00%	3,438.00	1,872.15	1,355.71	1,101.56	952.25	855.29	788.17	739.62	703.38	675.69
18.25%	3,442.46	1,876.69	1,360.42	1,106.47	957.36	860.60	793.67	745.31	709.26	681.74
18.50%	3,446.93	1,881.23	1,365.14	1,111.38	962.48	865.93	799.20	751.03	715.16	687.81
18.75%	3,451.40	1,885.77	1,369.87	1,116.31	967.62	871.27	804.74	756.76	721.07	693.91
19.00%	3,455.87	1,890.32	1,374.60	1,121.25	972.77	876.63	810.30	762.52	727.02	700.02
19.25%	3,460.35	1,894.88	1,379.35	1,126.21	977.94	882.00	815.88	768.30	732.98	706.16
19.50%	3,464.83	1,899.45	1,384.10	1,131.17	983.12	887.40	821.48	774.09	738.96	712.32
19.75%	3,469.31	1,904.02	1,388.86	1,136.15	988.31	892.81	827.10	779.91	744.97	718.50
20.00%	3,473.79	1,908.59	1,393.63	1,141.14	993.52	898.23	832.73	785.75	750.99	724.71
20.25%	3,478.28	1,913.18	1,398.42	1,146.14	998.74	903.67	838.39	791.60	757.04	730.94
20.50%	3,482.77	1,917.76	1,403.21	1,151.15	1,003.98	909.13	844.06	797.48	763.11	737.18
20.75%	3,487.27	1,922.36	1,408.01	1,156.18	1,009.23	914.61	849.75	803.37	769.20	743.45

	1	2	3	4	5	6	7	8	9	10
1.00%	3,351.42	1,684.08	1,128.32	850.46	683.75	572.62	493.25	433.73	387.44	350.42
1.25%	3,355.95	1,688.45	1,132.65	854.77	688.06	576.94	497.58	438.06	391.79	354.77
1.50%	3,360.48	1,692.83	1,136.99	859.10	692.40	581.28	501.93	442.43	396.16	359.17
1.75%	3,365.01	1,697.22	1,141.34	863.45	696.74	585.64	506.30	446.82	400.57	363.59
2.00%	3,369.55	1,701.61	1,145.70	867.80	701.11	590.02	510.70	451.23	405.01	368.05
2.25%	3,374.10	1,706.01	1,150.07	872.18	705.49	594.42	515.12	455.68	409.48	372.55
2.50%	3,378.64	1,710.42	1,154.46	876.56	709.89	598.84	519.57	460.15	413.98	377.08
2.75%	3,383.19	1,714.83	1,158.85	880.96	714.31	603.28	524.04	464.65	418.51	381.64
3.00%	3,387.75	1,719.25	1,163.25	885.37	718.75	607.75	528.53	469.18	423.08	386.24
3.25%	3,392.30	1,723.68	1,167.66	889.80	723.20	612.23	533.05	473.74	427.67	390.88
3.50%	3,396.87	1,728.11	1,172.08	894.24	727.67	616.74	537.59	478.32	432.30	395.54
3.75%	3,401.43	1,732.55	1,176.52	898.69	732.16	621.26	542.16	482.93	436.95	400.24
4.00%	3,406.00	1,737.00	1,180.96	903.16	736.66	625.81	546.75	487.57	441.64	404.98
4.25%	3,410.57	1,741.45	1,185.41	907.64	741.18	630.37	551.37	492.24	446.36	409.75
4.50%	3,415.14	1,745.91	1,189.88	912.14	745.72	634.96	556.01	496.93	451.10	414.55
4.75%	3,419.72	1,750.38	1,194.35	916.65	750.28	639.57	560.67	501.65	455.88	419.39
5.00%	3,424.30	1,754.86	1,198.84	921.17	754.85	644.20	565.36	506.40	460.69	424.26
5.25%	3,428.88	1,759.34	1,203.33	925.71	759.44	648.85	570.07	511.17	465.53	429.17
5.50%	3,433.47	1,763.83	1,207.84	930.26	764.05	653.52	574.80	515.97	470.40	434.11
5.75%	3,438.06	1,768.32	1,212.35	934.82	768.67	658.21	579.56	520.80	475.30	439.08
6.00%	3,442.66	1,772.82	1,216.88	939.40	773.31	662.92	584.34	525.66	480.23	444.08
6.25%	3,447.26	1,777.33	1,221.41	943.99	777.97	667.65	589.15	530.54	485.19	449.12
6.50%	3,451.86	1,781.85	1,225.96	948.60	782.65	672.40	593.98	535.45	490.18	454.19
6.75%	3,456.46	1,786.37	1,230.52	953.22	787.34	677.17	598.83	540.39	495.20	459.30
7.00%	3,461.07	1,790.90	1,235.08	957.85	792.05	681.96	603.71	545.35	500.25	464.43
7.25%	3,465.68	1,795.44	1,239.66	962.50	796.77	686.77	608.61	550.34	505.33	469.60
7.50%	3,470.30	1,799.98	1,244.25	967.16	801.52	691.60	613.53	555.35	510.44	474.81
7.75%	3,474.92	1,804.53	1,248.85	971.83	806.28	696.46	618.48	560.40	515.58	480.04
8.00%	3,479.54	1,809.09	1,253.45	976.52	811.06	701.33	623.45	565.47	520.75	485.31
8.25%	3,484.16	1,813.66	1,258.07	981.22	815.85	706.22	628.44	570.56	525.95	490.61
8.50%	3,488.79	1,818.23	1,262.70	985.93	820.66	711.14	633.46	575.69	531.17	495.94
8.75%	3,493.42	1,822.80	1,267.34	990.66	825.49	716.07	638.50	580.83	536.43	501.31
9.00%	3,498.06	1,827.39	1,271.99	995.40	830.33	721.02	643.56	586.01	541.72	506.70
9.25%	3,502.70	1,831.98	1,276.65	1,000.16	835.20	725.99	648.65	591.21	547.03	512.13
9.50%	3,507.34	1,836.58	1,281.32	1,004.93	840.07	730.99	653.76	596.44	552.37	517.59
9.75%	3,511.99	1,841.18	1,286.00	1,009.71	844.97	736.00	658.89	601.69	557.75	523.08
10.00%	3,516.64	1,845.80	1,290.69	1,014.50	849.88	741.03	664.05	606.97	563.15	528.60
10.25%	3,521.29	1,850.42	1,295.39	1,019.31	854.81	746.09	669.23	612.27	568.58	534.16
10.50%	3,525.94	1,855.04	1,300.10	1,024.14	859.76	751.16	674.43	617.60	574.03	539.74
10.75%	3,530.60	1,859.67	1,304.82	1,028.97	864.72	756.25	679.65	622.96	579.52	545.35

	1	2	3	4	5	6	7	8	9	10
11.00%	3,535.27	1,864.31	1,309.55	1,033.82	869.70	761.36	684.90	628.34	585.03	551.00
11.25%	3,539.93	1,868.96	1,314.29	1,038.68	874.69	766.49	690.17	633.74	590.58	556.68
11.50%	3,544.60	1,873.61	1,319.04	1,043.56	879.70	771.65	695.46	639.17	596.15	562.38
11.75%	3,549.28	1,878.27	1,323.80	1,048.45	884.73	776.82	700.77	644.63	601.74	568.12
12.00%	3,553.95	1,882.94	1,328.57	1,053.35	889.78	782.01	706.11	650.11	607.37	573.88
12.25%	3,558.63	1,887.61	1,333.35	1,058.27	894.84	787.22	711.47	655.62	613.02	579.68
12.50%	3,563.31	1,892.29	1,338.15	1,063.20	899.92	792.45	716.85	661.15	618.70	585.50
12.75%	3,568.00	1,896.98	1,342.95	1,068.14	905.01	797.70	722.25	666.71	624.41	591.36
13.00%	3,572.69	1,901.67	1,347.76	1,073.10	910.12	802.96	727.68	672.29	630.14	597.24
13.25%	3,577.38	1,906.37	1,352.58	1,078.07	915.25	808.25	733.13	677.90	635.90	603.16
13.50%	3,582.08	1,911.08	1,357.41	1,083.05	920.39	813.56	738.60	683.53	641.69	609.10
13.75%	3,586.78	1,915.79	1,362.25	1,088.05	925.55	818.88	744.09	689.18	647.51	615.07
14.00%	3,591.48	1,920.52	1,367.11	1,093.06	930.73	824.23	749.60	694.86	653.35	621.07
14.25%	3,596.19	1,925.24	1,371.97	1,098.08	935.92	829.59	755.14	700.56	659.22	627.09
14.50%	3,600.90	1,929.98	1,376.84	1,103.12	941.13	834.98	760.69	706.29	665.11	633.15
14.75%	3,605.62	1,934.72	1,381.72	1,108.17	946.36	840.38	766.27	712.04	671.03	639.23
15.00%	3,610.33	1,939.47	1,386.61	1,113.23	951.60	845.80	771.87	717.82	676.97	645.34
15.25%	3,615.05	1,944.22	1,391.52	1,118.31	956.85	851.24	777.49	723.61	682.94	651.48
15.50%	3,619.78	1,948.98	1,396.43	1,123.39	962.13	856.70	783.13	729.44	688.94	657.64
15.75%	3,624.50	1,953.75	1,401.35	1,128.50	967.42	862.18	788.80	735.28	694.96	663.83
16.00%	3,629.23	1,958.52	1,406.28	1,133.61	972.72	867.67	794.48	741.15	701.01	670.05
16.25%	3,633.97	1,963.31	1,411.22	1,138.74	978.04	873.19	800.19	747.04	707.08	676.30
16.50%	3,638.71	1,968.09	1,416.18	1,143.88	983.38	878.72	805.92	752.96	713.18	682.57
16.75%	3,643.45	1,972.89	1,421.14	1,149.03	988.73	884.27	811.66	758.90	719.30	688.87
17.00%	3,648.19	1,977.69	1,426.11	1,154.20	994.10	889.85	817.43	764.86	725.45	695.19
17.25%	3,652.94	1,982.50	1,431.09	1,159.38	999.49	895.43	823.22	770.84	731.62	701.54
17.50%	3,657.69	1,987.31	1,436.08	1,164.57	1,004.89	901.04	829.03	776.85	737.81	707.92
17.75%	3,662.44	1,992.14	1,441.08	1,169.78	1,010.30	906.67	834.86	782.88	744.03	714.32
18.00%	3,667.20	1,996.96	1,446.10	1,175.00	1,015.74	912.31	840.71	788.93	750.28	720.74
18.25%	3,671.96	2,001.80	1,451.12	1,180.23	1,021.18	917.97	846.59	795.00	756.54	727.19
18.50%	3,676.72	2,006.64	1,456.15	1,185.48	1,026.65	923.65	852.48	801.10	762.83	733.67
18.75%	3,681.49	2,011.49	1,461.19	1,190.73	1,032.13	929.35	858.39	807.22	769.15	740.17
19.00%	3,686.26	2,016.34	1,466.24	1,196.00	1,037.62	935.07	864.32	813.35	775.48	746.69
19.25%	3,691.04	2,021.21	1,471.30	1,201.29	1,043.13	940.80	870.27	819.52	781.84	753.24
19.50%	3,695.81	2,026.08	1,476.37	1,206.58	1,048.66	946.56	876.24	825.70	788.23	759.81
19.75%	3,700.60	2,030.95	1,481.45	1,211.89	1,054.20	952.33	882.24	831.90	794.63	766.40
20.00%	3,705.38	2,035.83	1,486.54	1,217.21	1,059.76	958.11	888.25	838.13	801.06	773.02
20.25%	3,710.17	2,040.72	1,491.64	1,222.55	1,065.33	963.92	894.28	844.37	807.51	779.66
20.50%	3,714.96	2,045.62	1,496.75	1,227.90	1,070.91	969.74	900.33	850.64	813.98	786.33
20.75%	3,719.75	2,050.52	1,501.87	1,233.26	1,076.52	975.58	906.40	856.93	820.48	793.02

	1	2	3	4	5	6	7	8	9	10
1.00%	3,560.88	1,789.34	1,198.84	903.61	726.48	608.41	524.08	460.84	411.66	372.32
1.25%	3,565.69	1,793.98	1,203.44	908.20	731.07	613.00	528.67	465.44	416.27	376.95
1.50%	3,570.51	1,798.64	1,208.05	912.80	735.67	617.61	533.30	470.08	420.92	381.61
1.75%	3,575.33	1,803.29	1,212.68	917.41	740.29	622.24	537.94	474.74	425.61	386.32
2.00%	3,580.15	1,807.96	1,217.31	922.04	744.93	626.89	542.62	479.44	430.32	391.06
2.25%	3,584.98	1,812.64	1,221.95	926.69	749.59	631.57	547.31	484.16	435.07	395.83
2.50%	3,589.81	1,817.32	1,226.61	931.35	754.26	636.27	552.04	488.91	439.86	400.65
2.75%	3,594.64	1,822.01	1,231.27	936.02	758.96	640.99	556.79	493.70	444.67	405.50
3.00%	3,599.48	1,826.70	1,235.95	940.71	763.67	645.73	561.57	498.51	449.52	410.38
3.25%	3,604.32	1,831.40	1,240.64	945.41	768.40	650.50	566.37	503.35	454.40	415.31
3.50%	3,609.17	1,836.12	1,245.34	950.13	773.15	655.28	571.19	508.22	459.32	420.26
3.75%	3,614.02	1,840.83	1,250.05	954.86	777.92	660.09	576.05	513.12	464.26	425.26
4.00%	3,618.87	1,845.56	1,254.77	959.61	782.70	664.92	580.92	518.04	469.24	430.29
4.25%	3,623.73	1,850.29	1,259.50	964.37	787.51	669.77	585.83	523.00	474.25	435.36
4.50%	3,628.59	1,855.03	1,264.24	969.15	792.33	674.65	590.76	527.99	479.30	440.46
4.75%	3,633.45	1,859.78	1,269.00	973.94	797.17	679.54	595.71	533.00	484.37	445.60
5.00%	3,638.32	1,864.53	1,273.76	978.74	802.03	684.46	600.69	538.05	489.48	450.78
5.25%	3,643.19	1,869.30	1,278.54	983.57	806.90	689.40	605.70	543.12	494.63	455.99
5.50%	3,648.06	1,874.07	1,283.33	988.40	811.80	694.36	610.73	548.22	499.80	461.24
5.75%	3,652.94	1,878.84	1,288.12	993.25	816.71	699.34	615.78	553.35	505.01	466.52
6.00%	3,657.82	1,883.63	1,292.93	998.11	821.64	704.35	620.86	558.51	510.24	471.84
6.25%	3,662.71	1,888.42	1,297.75	1,002.99	826.59	709.37	625.97	563.70	515.51	477.19
6.50%	3,667.60	1,893.22	1,302.58	1,007.89	831.56	714.42	631.10	568.91	520.82	482.58
6.75%	3,672.49	1,898.02	1,307.42	1,012.79	836.55	719.49	636.26	574.16	526.15	488.00
7.00%	3,677.39	1,902.83	1,312.28	1,017.72	841.55	724.58	641.44	579.43	531.52	493.46
7.25%	3,682.29	1,907.66	1,317.14	1,022.65	846.57	729.70	646.65	584.73	536.91	498.95
7.50%	3,687.19	1,912.48	1,322.01	1,027.60	851.61	734.83	651.88	590.06	542.34	504.48
7.75%	3,692.10	1,917.32	1,326.90	1,032.57	856.67	739.99	657.13	595.42	547.80	510.05
8.00%	3,697.01	1,922.16	1,331.80	1,037.55	861.75	745.16	662.41	600.81	553.30	515.64
8.25%	3,701.92	1,927.01	1,336.70	1,042.54	866.84	750.36	667.72	606.22	558.82	521.27
8.50%	3,706.84	1,931.87	1,341.62	1,047.55	871.95	755.58	673.05	611.67	564.37	526.94
8.75%	3,711.76	1,936.73	1,346.55	1,052.58	877.08	760.82	678.41	617.14	569.96	532.64
9.00%	3,716.69	1,941.60	1,351.49	1,057.61	882.23	766.09	683.79	622.63	575.57	538.37
9.25%	3,721.62	1,946.48	1,356.44	1,062.67	887.40	771.37	689.19	628.16	581.22	544.14
9.50%	3,726.55	1,951.37	1,361.40	1,067.73	892.58	776.67	694.62	633.71	586.90	549.94
9.75%	3,731.49	1,956.26	1,366.37	1,072.81	897.78	782.00	700.07	639.29	592.61	555.77
10.00%	3,736.43	1,961.16	1,371.36	1,077.91	903.00	787.35	705.55	644.90	598.34	561.64
10.25%	3,741.37	1,966.07	1,376.35	1,083.02	908.24	792.72	711.05	650.54	604.11	567.54
10.50%	3,746.32	1,970.98	1,381.35	1,088.14	913.49	798.11	716.58	656.20	609.91	573.47
10.75%	3,751.27	1,975.90	1,386.37	1,093.28	918.76	803.52	722.13	661.89	615.74	579.44

	1	2	3	4	5	6	7	8	9	10
11.00%	3,756.22	1,980.83	1,391.40	1,098.43	924.05	808.95	727.70	667.61	621.60	585.44
11.25%	3,761.18	1,985.77	1,396.43	1,103.60	929.36	814.40	733.30	673.35	627.49	591.47
11.50%	3,766.14	1,990.71	1,401.48	1,108.78	934.69	819.87	738.92	679.12	633.41	597.53
11.75%	3,771.10	1,995.66	1,406.54	1,113.98	940.03	825.37	744.57	684.92	639.35	603.63
12.00%	3,776.07	2,000.62	1,411.61	1,119.19	945.39	830.88	750.24	690.75	645.33	609.75
12.25%	3,781.05	2,005.59	1,416.69	1,124.41	950.77	836.42	755.94	696.60	651.34	615.91
12.50%	3,786.02	2,010.56	1,421.78	1,129.65	956.16	841.98	761.65	702.47	657.37	622.10
12.75%	3,791.00	2,015.54	1,426.88	1,134.90	961.58	847.55	767.39	708.38	663.43	628.32
13.00%	3,795.98	2,020.53	1,431.99	1,140.17	967.01	853.15	773.16	714.31	669.53	634.57
13.25%	3,800.97	2,025.52	1,437.12	1,145.45	972.45	858.77	778.95	720.26	675.65	640.85
13.50%	3,805.96	2,030.52	1,442.25	1,150.74	977.92	864.41	784.76	726.25	681.80	647.17
13.75%	3,810.96	2,035.53	1,447.39	1,156.05	983.40	870.06	790.59	732.25	687.98	653.51
14.00%	3,815.95	2,040.55	1,452.55	1,161.38	988.90	875.74	796.45	738.29	694.18	659.88
14.25%	3,820.95	2,045.57	1,457.72	1,166.71	994.42	881.44	802.33	744.35	700.42	666.29
14.50%	3,825.96	2,050.60	1,462.89	1,172.06	999.95	887.16	808.24	750.43	706.68	672.72
14.75%	3,830.97	2,055.64	1,468.08	1,177.43	1,005.50	892.90	814.16	756.54	712.97	679.18
15.00%	3,835.98	2,060.68	1,473.28	1,182.81	1,011.07	898.66	820.11	762.68	719.28	685.67
15.25%	3,840.99	2,065.73	1,478.48	1,188.20	1,016.66	904.44	826.08	768.84	725.63	692.19
15.50%	3,846.01	2,070.79	1,483.70	1,193.61	1,022.26	910.24	832.08	775.03	732.00	698.74
15.75%	3,851.04	2,075.86	1,488.93	1,199.03	1,027.88	916.06	838.10	781.24	738.40	705.32
16.00%	3,856.06	2,080.93	1,494.17	1,204.46	1,033.52	921.90	844.14	787.47	744.82	711.93
16.25%	3,861.09	2,086.01	1,499.42	1,209.91	1,039.17	927.76	850.20	793.73	751.27	718.57
16.50%	3,866.12	2,091.10	1,504.69	1,215.37	1,044.84	933.64	856.29	800.02	757.75	725.23
16.75%	3,871.16	2,096.19	1,509.96	1,220.85	1,050.53	939.54	862.39	806.33	764.26	731.92
17.00%	3,876.20	2,101.30	1,515.24	1,226.34	1,056.23	945.46	868.52	812.66	770.79	738.64
17.25%	3,881.25	2,106.41	1,520.53	1,231.84	1,061.96	951.40	874.67	819.02	777.34	745.39
17.50%	3,886.29	2,111.52	1,525.84	1,237.36	1,067.69	957.36	880.85	825.40	783.93	752.16
17.75%	3,891.34	2,116.64	1,531.15	1,242.89	1,073.45	963.33	887.04	831.81	790.53	758.96
18.00%	3,896.40	2,121.77	1,536.48	1,248.44	1,079.22	969.33	893.26	838.24	797.17	765.79
18.25%	3,901.46	2,126.91	1,541.81	1,254.00	1,085.01	975.35	899.50	844.69	803.83	772.64
18.50%	3,906.52	2,132.06	1,547.16	1,259.57	1,090.81	981.38	905.76	851.17	810.51	779.52
18.75%	3,911.59	2,137.21	1,552.51	1,265.16	1,096.64	987.44	912.04	857.67	817.22	786.43
19.00%	3,916.65	2,142.37	1,557.88	1,270.76	1,102.47	993.51	918.34	864.19	823.95	793.36
19.25%	3,921.73	2,147.53	1,563.26	1,276.37	1,108.33	999.60	924.66	870.74	830.71	800.31
19.50%	3,926.80	2,152.70	1,568.65	1,282.00	1,114.20	1,005.72	931.01	877.30	837.49	807.30
19.75%	3,931.88	2,157.88	1,574.04	1,287.64	1,120.09	1,011.85	937.38	883.90	844.30	814.30
20.00%	3,936.97	2,163.07	1,579.45	1,293.29	1,125.99	1,018.00	943.76	890.51	851.13	821.34
20.25%	3,942.05	2,168.27	1,584.87	1,298.96	1,131.91	1,024.16	950.17	897.15	857.98	828.39
20.50%	3,947.14	2,173.47	1,590.30	1,304.64	1,137.85	1,030.35	956.60	903.81	864.86	835.47
20.75%	3,952.24	2,178.67	1,595.74	1,310.33	1,143.80	1,036.56	963.05	910.49	871.76	842.58

	1	2	3	4	5	6	7	8	9	10
1.00%	3,770.34	1,894.59	1,269.36	956.77	769.22	644.20	554.91	487.95	435.87	394.22
1.25%	3,775.44	1,899.51	1,274.23	961.62	774.07	649.06	559.77	492.82	440.76	399.12
1.50%	3,780.54	1,904.44	1,279.12	966.49	778.94	653.94	564.67	497.73	445.68	404.06
1.75%	3,785.64	1,909.37	1,284.01	971.38	783.84	658.84	569.59	502.67	450.64	409.04
2.00%	3,790.75	1,914.31	1,288.92	976.28	788.75	663.77	574.53	507.64	455.64	414.06
2.25%	3,795.86	1,919.26	1,293.83	981.20	793.68	668.72	579.51	512.64	460.67	419.12
2.50%	3,800.98	1,924.22	1,298.76	986.13	798.63	673.70	584.51	517.67	465.73	424.21
2.75%	3,806.09	1,929.18	1,303.70	991.08	803.60	678.69	589.54	522.74	470.83	429.35
3.00%	3,811.22	1,934.15	1,308.65	996.04	808.59	683.72	594.60	527.83	475.96	434.52
3.25%	3,816.34	1,939.13	1,313.62	1,001.02	813.60	688.76	599.68	532.96	481.13	439.74
3.50%	3,821.47	1,944.12	1,318.59	1,006.02	818.63	693.83	604.79	538.11	486.33	444.99
3.75%	3,826.61	1,949.12	1,323.58	1,011.03	823.68	698.92	609.93	543.30	491.57	450.28
4.00%	3,831.75	1,954.12	1,328.58	1,016.06	828.74	704.03	615.10	548.52	496.84	455.60
4.25%	3,836.89	1,959.13	1,333.59	1,021.10	833.83	709.17	620.29	553.77	502.15	460.97
4.50%	3,842.03	1,964.15	1,338.61	1,026.16	838.94	714.33	625.51	559.05	507.49	466.37
4.75%	3,847.18	1,969.18	1,343.65	1,031.23	844.06	719.52	630.75	564.36	512.87	471.81
5.00%	3,852.34	1,974.21	1,348.69	1,036.32	849.21	724.72	636.03	569.70	518.28	477.29
5.25%	3,857.49	1,979.25	1,353.75	1,041.42	854.37	729.95	641.33	575.07	523.72	482.81
5.50%	3,862.66	1,984.30	1,358.82	1,046.54	859.55	735.20	646.65	580.47	529.20	488.37
5.75%	3,867.82	1,989.36	1,363.90	1,051.68	864.75	740.48	652.01	585.90	534.71	493.96
6.00%	3,872.99	1,994.43	1,368.99	1,056.83	869.98	745.78	657.38	591.36	540.26	499.59
6.25%	3,878.16	1,999.50	1,374.09	1,061.99	875.22	751.10	662.79	596.86	545.84	505.26
6.50%	3,883.34	2,004.58	1,379.21	1,067.17	880.48	756.45	668.22	602.38	551.45	510.97
6.75%	3,888.52	2,009.67	1,384.33	1,072.37	885.76	761.81	673.68	607.93	557.10	516.71
7.00%	3,893.70	2,014.77	1,389.47	1,077.58	891.05	767.21	679.17	613.52	562.78	522.49
7.25%	3,898.89	2,019.87	1,394.62	1,082.81	896.37	772.62	684.68	619.13	568.50	528.30
7.50%	3,904.08	2,024.98	1,399.78	1,088.05	901.71	778.06	690.22	624.77	574.25	534.16
7.75%	3,909.28	2,030.10	1,404.95	1,093.31	907.06	783.51	695.79	630.45	580.03	540.05
8.00%	3,914.48	2,035.23	1,410.14	1,098.58	912.44	789.00	701.38	636.15	585.84	545.97
8.25%	3,919.68	2,040.36	1,415.33	1,103.87	917.83	794.50	707.00	641.88	591.69	551.94
8.50%	3,924.89	2,045.51	1,420.54	1,109.17	923.24	800.03	712.64	647.65	597.57	557.94
8.75%	3,930.10	2,050.66	1,425.76	1,114.49	928.68	805.58	718.31	653.44	603.48	563.97
9.00%	3,935.32	2,055.81	1,430.99	1,119.83	934.13	811.15	724.01	659.26	609.43	570.04
9.25%	3,940.54	2,060.98	1,436.23	1,125.18	939.60	816.74	729.73	665.11	615.41	576.15
9.50%	3,945.76	2,066.15	1,441.48	1,130.54	945.08	822.36	735.48	670.99	621.42	582.29
9.75%	3,950.98	2,071.33	1,446.75	1,135.92	950.59	828.00	741.25	676.90	627.46	588.47
10.00%	3,956.21	2,076.52	1,452.02	1,141.32	956.12	833.66	747.05	682.84	633.54	594.68
10.25%	3,961.45	2,081.72	1,457.31	1,146.73	961.66	839.35	752.88	688.80	639.65	600.93
10.50%	3,966.69	2,086.92	1,462.61	1,152.15	967.23	845.05	758.73	694.80	645.79	607.21
10.75%	3,971.93	2,092.13	1,467.92	1,157.59	972.81	850.78	764.61	700.83	651.96	613.52

$45,000   11.00 - 20.75%   1 - 10 Years

	1	2	3	4	5	6	7	8	9	10
11.00%	3,977.17	2,097.35	1,473.24	1,163.05	978.41	856.53	770.51	706.88	658.16	619.88
11.25%	3,982.42	2,102.58	1,478.58	1,168.52	984.03	862.31	776.44	712.96	664.40	626.26
11.50%	3,987.68	2,107.81	1,483.92	1,174.01	989.67	868.10	782.39	719.07	670.66	632.68
11.75%	3,992.93	2,113.06	1,489.28	1,179.51	995.32	873.92	788.37	725.21	676.96	639.13
12.00%	3,998.20	2,118.31	1,494.64	1,185.02	1,001.00	879.76	794.37	731.38	683.29	645.62
12.25%	4,003.46	2,123.56	1,500.02	1,190.55	1,006.69	885.62	800.40	737.57	689.65	652.14
12.50%	4,008.73	2,128.83	1,505.41	1,196.10	1,012.41	891.50	806.46	743.80	696.04	658.69
12.75%	4,014.00	2,134.10	1,510.81	1,201.66	1,018.14	897.41	812.53	750.05	702.46	665.28
13.00%	4,019.28	2,139.38	1,516.23	1,207.24	1,023.89	903.33	818.64	756.33	708.91	671.90
13.25%	4,024.56	2,144.67	1,521.65	1,212.83	1,029.66	909.28	824.77	762.63	715.39	678.55
13.50%	4,029.84	2,149.97	1,527.09	1,218.43	1,035.44	915.25	830.92	768.97	721.90	685.23
13.75%	4,035.13	2,155.27	1,532.53	1,224.06	1,041.25	921.25	837.10	775.33	728.45	691.95
14.00%	4,040.42	2,160.58	1,537.99	1,229.69	1,047.07	927.26	843.30	781.72	735.02	698.70
14.25%	4,045.72	2,165.90	1,543.46	1,235.34	1,052.91	933.29	849.53	788.13	741.62	705.48
14.50%	4,051.01	2,171.22	1,548.94	1,241.01	1,058.77	939.35	855.78	794.58	748.25	712.29
14.75%	4,056.32	2,176.56	1,554.44	1,246.69	1,064.65	945.43	862.05	801.05	754.91	719.13
15.00%	4,061.62	2,181.90	1,559.94	1,252.38	1,070.55	951.53	868.35	807.54	761.60	726.01
15.25%	4,066.93	2,187.25	1,565.45	1,258.09	1,076.46	957.65	874.68	814.07	768.31	732.91
15.50%	4,072.25	2,192.60	1,570.98	1,263.82	1,082.39	963.79	881.03	820.62	775.06	739.85
15.75%	4,077.57	2,197.97	1,576.52	1,269.56	1,088.34	969.95	887.40	827.19	781.83	746.81
16.00%	4,082.89	2,203.34	1,582.07	1,275.31	1,094.31	976.13	893.79	833.80	788.64	753.81
16.25%	4,088.21	2,208.72	1,587.63	1,281.08	1,100.30	982.34	900.21	840.42	795.47	760.83
16.50%	4,093.54	2,214.11	1,593.20	1,286.87	1,106.30	988.56	906.66	847.08	802.33	767.89
16.75%	4,098.88	2,219.50	1,598.78	1,292.66	1,112.33	994.81	913.12	853.76	809.21	774.98
17.00%	4,104.21	2,224.90	1,604.37	1,298.48	1,118.37	1,001.08	919.61	860.47	816.13	782.09
17.25%	4,109.55	2,230.31	1,609.98	1,304.30	1,124.42	1,007.36	926.12	867.20	823.07	789.23
17.50%	4,114.90	2,235.73	1,615.59	1,310.15	1,130.50	1,013.67	932.66	873.95	830.04	796.40
17.75%	4,120.25	2,241.15	1,621.22	1,316.00	1,136.59	1,020.00	939.22	880.74	837.04	803.60
18.00%	4,125.60	2,246.58	1,626.86	1,321.87	1,142.70	1,026.35	945.80	887.54	844.06	810.83
18.25%	4,130.96	2,252.02	1,632.51	1,327.76	1,148.83	1,032.72	952.41	894.38	851.11	818.09
18.50%	4,136.32	2,257.47	1,638.17	1,333.66	1,154.98	1,039.11	959.04	901.23	858.19	825.37
18.75%	4,141.68	2,262.93	1,643.84	1,339.58	1,161.14	1,045.52	965.69	908.12	865.29	832.69
19.00%	4,147.05	2,268.39	1,649.52	1,345.51	1,167.32	1,051.95	972.36	915.02	872.42	840.03
19.25%	4,152.42	2,273.86	1,655.21	1,351.45	1,173.52	1,058.40	979.06	921.96	879.57	847.39
19.50%	4,157.79	2,279.33	1,660.92	1,357.41	1,179.74	1,064.87	985.78	928.91	886.75	854.78
19.75%	4,163.17	2,284.82	1,666.63	1,363.38	1,185.97	1,071.37	992.52	935.89	893.96	862.20
20.00%	4,168.55	2,290.31	1,672.36	1,369.37	1,192.22	1,077.88	999.28	942.89	901.19	869.65
20.25%	4,173.94	2,295.81	1,678.10	1,375.37	1,198.49	1,084.41	1,006.06	949.92	908.45	877.12
20.50%	4,179.33	2,301.32	1,683.85	1,381.38	1,204.78	1,090.96	1,012.87	956.97	915.73	884.62
20.75%	4,184.72	2,306.83	1,689.61	1,387.41	1,211.08	1,097.53	1,019.70	964.05	923.04	892.14

	1	2	3	4	5	6	7	8	9	10
1.00%	3,979.81	1,999.85	1,339.88	1,009.92	811.95	679.99	585.73	515.05	460.09	416.12
1.25%	3,985.19	2,005.04	1,345.03	1,015.04	817.08	685.11	590.87	520.20	465.25	421.29
1.50%	3,990.57	2,010.24	1,350.18	1,020.19	822.22	690.27	596.04	525.38	470.44	426.51
1.75%	3,995.96	2,015.45	1,355.34	1,025.34	827.38	695.44	601.23	530.60	475.68	431.77
2.00%	4,001.35	2,020.66	1,360.52	1,030.52	832.57	700.65	606.45	535.84	480.95	437.06
2.25%	4,006.74	2,025.89	1,365.71	1,035.71	837.77	705.87	611.70	541.12	486.26	442.40
2.50%	4,012.14	2,031.12	1,370.92	1,040.92	843.00	711.12	616.99	546.43	491.60	447.78
2.75%	4,017.54	2,036.36	1,376.13	1,046.14	848.25	716.40	622.29	551.78	496.99	453.20
3.00%	4,022.95	2,041.61	1,381.36	1,051.38	853.51	721.70	627.63	557.15	502.40	458.66
3.25%	4,028.36	2,046.86	1,386.60	1,056.64	858.80	727.02	633.00	562.56	507.86	464.17
3.50%	4,033.78	2,052.13	1,391.85	1,061.91	864.11	732.37	638.39	568.01	513.35	469.71
3.75%	4,039.20	2,057.40	1,397.11	1,067.20	869.44	737.75	643.82	573.48	518.88	475.29
4.00%	4,044.62	2,062.68	1,402.39	1,072.51	874.78	743.15	649.27	578.99	524.45	480.91
4.25%	4,050.05	2,067.97	1,407.68	1,077.83	880.15	748.57	654.75	584.53	530.05	486.58
4.50%	4,055.48	2,073.27	1,412.98	1,083.17	885.54	754.02	660.26	590.10	535.69	492.28
4.75%	4,060.92	2,078.58	1,418.29	1,088.52	890.95	759.49	665.79	595.71	541.36	498.03
5.00%	4,066.36	2,083.89	1,423.62	1,093.89	896.38	764.98	671.36	601.35	547.07	503.81
5.25%	4,071.80	2,089.21	1,428.96	1,099.28	901.83	770.50	676.95	607.02	552.82	509.64
5.50%	4,077.25	2,094.54	1,434.31	1,104.68	907.31	776.05	682.58	612.72	558.60	515.50
5.75%	4,082.70	2,099.88	1,439.67	1,110.10	912.80	781.62	688.23	618.45	564.42	521.40
6.00%	4,088.16	2,105.23	1,445.04	1,115.54	918.31	787.21	693.91	624.22	570.27	527.35
6.25%	4,093.62	2,110.58	1,450.43	1,120.99	923.84	792.83	699.61	630.02	576.16	533.33
6.50%	4,099.08	2,115.95	1,455.83	1,126.46	929.39	798.47	705.35	635.85	582.09	539.35
6.75%	4,104.55	2,121.32	1,461.24	1,131.95	934.96	804.14	711.11	641.71	588.05	545.41
7.00%	4,110.02	2,126.70	1,466.66	1,137.45	940.56	809.83	716.90	647.60	594.05	551.52
7.25%	4,115.50	2,132.09	1,472.10	1,142.96	946.17	815.54	722.72	653.53	600.08	557.65
7.50%	4,120.98	2,137.48	1,477.55	1,148.50	951.80	821.28	728.57	659.48	606.15	563.83
7.75%	4,126.46	2,142.88	1,483.01	1,154.05	957.46	827.04	734.44	665.47	612.25	570.05
8.00%	4,131.95	2,148.30	1,488.48	1,159.61	963.13	832.83	740.35	671.49	618.39	576.31
8.25%	4,137.44	2,153.72	1,493.96	1,165.20	968.82	838.64	746.28	677.54	624.56	582.60
8.50%	4,142.94	2,159.14	1,499.46	1,170.79	974.54	844.47	752.23	683.63	630.77	588.93
8.75%	4,148.44	2,164.58	1,504.97	1,176.41	980.27	850.33	758.22	689.74	637.01	595.30
9.00%	4,153.95	2,170.03	1,510.49	1,182.04	986.02	856.21	764.23	695.88	643.29	601.71
9.25%	4,159.45	2,175.48	1,516.02	1,187.69	991.80	862.12	770.27	702.06	649.60	608.16
9.50%	4,164.97	2,180.94	1,521.57	1,193.35	997.59	868.05	776.34	708.27	655.94	614.64
9.75%	4,170.48	2,186.41	1,527.12	1,199.03	1,003.40	874.00	782.43	714.50	662.32	621.16
10.00%	4,176.00	2,191.88	1,532.69	1,204.72	1,009.23	879.98	788.56	720.77	668.74	627.72
10.25%	4,181.53	2,197.37	1,538.27	1,210.43	1,015.09	885.98	794.71	727.07	675.18	634.31
10.50%	4,187.06	2,202.86	1,543.87	1,216.16	1,020.96	892.00	800.88	733.40	681.67	640.94
10.75%	4,192.59	2,208.36	1,549.47	1,221.90	1,026.85	898.05	807.09	739.76	688.18	647.61

	1	2	3	4	5	6	7	8	9	10
11.00%	4,198.13	2,213.87	1,555.09	1,227.66	1,032.77	904.12	813.32	746.15	694.73	654.31
11.25%	4,203.67	2,219.39	1,560.72	1,233.44	1,038.70	910.21	819.57	752.57	701.31	661.05
11.50%	4,209.22	2,224.91	1,566.36	1,239.23	1,044.65	916.33	825.86	759.02	707.92	667.83
11.75%	4,214.76	2,230.45	1,572.01	1,245.03	1,050.62	922.47	832.17	765.50	714.57	674.64
12.00%	4,220.32	2,235.99	1,577.68	1,250.86	1,056.61	928.63	838.50	772.01	721.25	681.49
12.25%	4,225.87	2,241.54	1,583.36	1,256.70	1,062.62	934.82	844.87	778.55	727.96	688.37
12.50%	4,231.44	2,247.10	1,589.05	1,262.55	1,068.65	941.03	851.26	785.12	734.71	695.29
12.75%	4,237.00	2,252.66	1,594.75	1,268.42	1,074.70	947.26	857.68	791.72	741.49	702.24
13.00%	4,242.57	2,258.24	1,600.46	1,274.31	1,080.77	953.52	864.12	798.34	748.30	709.23
13.25%	4,248.14	2,263.82	1,606.19	1,280.21	1,086.86	959.80	870.59	805.00	755.14	716.25
13.50%	4,253.72	2,269.41	1,611.93	1,286.13	1,092.97	966.10	877.08	811.69	762.01	723.30
13.75%	4,259.30	2,275.01	1,617.68	1,292.06	1,099.10	972.43	883.60	818.40	768.91	730.39
14.00%	4,264.89	2,280.61	1,623.44	1,298.01	1,105.24	978.77	890.15	825.15	775.85	737.52
14.25%	4,270.48	2,286.23	1,629.21	1,303.97	1,111.41	985.14	896.72	831.92	782.82	744.67
14.50%	4,276.07	2,291.85	1,635.00	1,309.95	1,117.59	991.54	903.32	838.72	789.82	751.86
14.75%	4,281.67	2,297.48	1,640.79	1,315.95	1,123.80	997.95	909.95	845.55	796.85	759.09
15.00%	4,287.27	2,303.12	1,646.60	1,321.96	1,130.02	1,004.39	916.60	852.41	803.91	766.34
15.25%	4,292.88	2,308.76	1,652.42	1,327.99	1,136.26	1,010.85	923.27	859.29	811.00	773.63
15.50%	4,298.48	2,314.42	1,658.26	1,334.03	1,142.53	1,017.33	929.97	866.21	818.12	780.95
15.75%	4,304.10	2,320.08	1,664.10	1,340.09	1,148.81	1,023.84	936.70	873.15	825.27	788.30
16.00%	4,309.72	2,325.75	1,669.96	1,346.16	1,155.11	1,030.36	943.45	880.12	832.45	795.69
16.25%	4,315.34	2,331.43	1,675.83	1,352.25	1,161.43	1,036.91	950.22	887.11	839.66	803.10
16.50%	4,320.96	2,337.11	1,681.71	1,358.36	1,167.76	1,043.48	957.02	894.14	846.90	810.55
16.75%	4,326.59	2,342.81	1,687.60	1,364.48	1,174.12	1,050.08	963.85	901.19	854.17	818.03
17.00%	4,332.23	2,348.51	1,693.50	1,370.61	1,180.50	1,056.69	970.70	908.27	861.47	825.54
17.25%	4,337.86	2,354.22	1,699.42	1,376.77	1,186.89	1,063.33	977.58	915.37	868.80	833.08
17.50%	4,343.50	2,359.94	1,705.35	1,382.93	1,193.31	1,069.99	984.48	922.51	876.15	840.65
17.75%	4,349.15	2,365.66	1,711.29	1,389.11	1,199.74	1,076.67	991.40	929.67	883.54	848.25
18.00%	4,354.80	2,371.39	1,717.24	1,395.31	1,206.19	1,083.37	998.35	936.85	890.95	855.88
18.25%	4,360.45	2,377.14	1,723.20	1,401.53	1,212.66	1,090.09	1,005.32	944.06	898.39	863.54
18.50%	4,366.11	2,382.89	1,729.18	1,407.75	1,219.14	1,096.84	1,012.32	951.30	905.86	871.23
18.75%	4,371.77	2,388.64	1,735.16	1,414.00	1,225.65	1,103.61	1,019.34	958.57	913.36	878.95
19.00%	4,377.44	2,394.41	1,741.16	1,420.26	1,232.18	1,110.39	1,026.38	965.86	920.89	886.69
19.25%	4,383.11	2,400.18	1,747.17	1,426.53	1,238.72	1,117.20	1,033.45	973.17	928.44	894.47
19.50%	4,388.78	2,405.96	1,753.19	1,432.82	1,245.28	1,124.03	1,040.54	980.52	936.02	902.27
19.75%	4,394.46	2,411.75	1,759.23	1,439.12	1,251.86	1,130.89	1,047.66	987.88	943.63	910.10
20.00%	4,400.14	2,417.55	1,765.27	1,445.44	1,258.46	1,137.76	1,054.79	995.28	951.26	917.96
20.25%	4,405.82	2,423.36	1,771.33	1,451.78	1,265.08	1,144.65	1,061.96	1,002.69	958.92	925.85
20.50%	4,411.51	2,429.17	1,777.39	1,458.13	1,271.71	1,151.57	1,069.14	1,010.14	966.61	933.77
20.75%	4,417.21	2,434.99	1,783.47	1,464.49	1,278.36	1,158.50	1,076.35	1,017.61	974.32	941.71

	1	2	3	4	5	6	7	8	9	10
1.00%	4,189.27	2,105.10	1,410.40	1,063.07	854.69	715.78	616.56	542.16	484.30	438.02
1.25%	4,194.93	2,110.57	1,415.82	1,068.47	860.08	721.17	621.97	547.58	489.73	443.47
1.50%	4,200.60	2,116.04	1,421.24	1,073.88	865.49	726.60	627.41	553.03	495.20	448.96
1.75%	4,206.27	2,121.52	1,426.68	1,079.31	870.93	732.05	632.87	558.52	500.71	454.49
2.00%	4,211.94	2,127.01	1,432.13	1,084.76	876.39	737.52	638.37	564.04	506.26	460.07
2.25%	4,217.62	2,132.51	1,437.59	1,090.22	881.87	743.02	643.90	569.60	511.85	465.69
2.50%	4,223.31	2,138.02	1,443.07	1,095.70	887.37	748.55	649.46	575.19	517.48	471.35
2.75%	4,228.99	2,143.54	1,448.56	1,101.20	892.89	754.10	655.05	580.82	523.14	477.06
3.00%	4,234.68	2,149.06	1,454.06	1,106.72	898.43	759.68	660.67	586.48	528.85	482.80
3.25%	4,240.38	2,154.59	1,459.58	1,112.25	904.00	765.29	666.31	592.17	534.59	488.60
3.50%	4,246.08	2,160.14	1,465.10	1,117.80	909.59	770.92	671.99	597.90	540.37	494.43
3.75%	4,251.79	2,165.69	1,470.65	1,123.37	915.20	776.58	677.70	603.67	546.19	500.31
4.00%	4,257.50	2,171.25	1,476.20	1,128.95	920.83	782.26	683.44	609.46	552.05	506.23
4.25%	4,263.21	2,176.81	1,481.77	1,134.55	926.48	787.97	689.21	615.30	557.94	512.19
4.50%	4,268.93	2,182.39	1,487.35	1,140.17	932.15	793.70	695.01	621.16	563.88	518.19
4.75%	4,274.65	2,187.98	1,492.94	1,145.81	937.85	799.46	700.84	627.06	569.85	524.24
5.00%	4,280.37	2,193.57	1,498.54	1,151.46	943.56	805.25	706.70	633.00	575.86	530.33
5.25%	4,286.10	2,199.17	1,504.16	1,157.14	949.30	811.06	712.58	638.96	581.91	536.46
5.50%	4,291.84	2,204.78	1,509.80	1,162.82	955.06	816.89	718.50	644.97	588.00	542.63
5.75%	4,297.58	2,210.40	1,515.44	1,168.53	960.84	822.76	724.45	651.00	594.12	548.85
6.00%	4,303.32	2,216.03	1,521.10	1,174.25	966.64	828.64	730.43	657.07	600.29	555.10
6.25%	4,309.07	2,221.67	1,526.77	1,179.99	972.46	834.56	736.43	663.17	606.49	561.40
6.50%	4,314.82	2,227.31	1,532.45	1,185.75	978.31	840.50	742.47	669.31	612.73	567.74
6.75%	4,320.58	2,232.97	1,538.15	1,191.52	984.17	846.46	748.54	675.48	619.00	574.12
7.00%	4,326.34	2,238.63	1,543.85	1,197.31	990.06	852.45	754.63	681.69	625.31	580.54
7.25%	4,332.10	2,244.30	1,549.58	1,203.12	995.97	858.47	760.76	687.92	631.66	587.01
7.50%	4,337.87	2,249.98	1,555.31	1,208.95	1,001.90	864.51	766.91	694.19	638.05	593.51
7.75%	4,343.64	2,255.67	1,561.06	1,214.79	1,007.85	870.57	773.10	700.50	644.47	600.05
8.00%	4,349.42	2,261.36	1,566.82	1,220.65	1,013.82	876.66	779.31	706.83	650.94	606.64
8.25%	4,355.20	2,267.07	1,572.59	1,226.52	1,019.81	882.78	785.55	713.20	657.43	613.26
8.50%	4,360.99	2,272.78	1,578.38	1,232.42	1,025.83	888.92	791.82	719.61	663.97	619.93
8.75%	4,366.78	2,278.51	1,584.18	1,238.33	1,031.86	895.09	798.12	726.04	670.54	626.63
9.00%	4,372.57	2,284.24	1,589.99	1,244.25	1,037.92	901.28	804.45	732.51	677.15	633.38
9.25%	4,378.37	2,289.98	1,595.81	1,250.20	1,043.99	907.49	810.81	739.01	683.79	640.16
9.50%	4,384.18	2,295.72	1,601.65	1,256.16	1,050.09	913.73	817.20	745.54	690.47	646.99
9.75%	4,389.98	2,301.48	1,607.50	1,262.13	1,056.21	920.00	823.61	752.11	697.18	653.85
10.00%	4,395.79	2,307.25	1,613.36	1,268.13	1,062.35	926.29	830.06	758.71	703.93	660.75
10.25%	4,401.61	2,313.02	1,619.23	1,274.14	1,068.51	932.61	836.53	765.34	710.72	667.70
10.50%	4,407.43	2,318.80	1,625.12	1,280.17	1,074.70	938.95	843.03	772.00	717.54	674.67
10.75%	4,413.25	2,324.59	1,631.02	1,286.21	1,080.90	945.31	849.56	778.70	724.40	681.69

$50,000   11.00 - 20.75%   1 - 10 Years

	1	2	3	4	5	6	7	8	9	10
11.00%	4,419.08	2,330.39	1,636.94	1,292.28	1,087.12	951.70	856.12	785.42	731.29	688.75
11.25%	4,424.92	2,336.20	1,642.86	1,298.35	1,093.37	958.12	862.71	792.18	738.22	695.84
11.50%	4,430.75	2,342.02	1,648.80	1,304.45	1,099.63	964.56	869.32	798.97	745.18	702.98
11.75%	4,436.59	2,347.84	1,654.75	1,310.56	1,105.92	971.02	875.97	805.79	752.18	710.15
12.00%	4,442.44	2,353.67	1,660.72	1,316.69	1,112.22	977.51	882.64	812.64	759.21	717.35
12.25%	4,448.29	2,359.52	1,666.69	1,322.84	1,118.55	984.02	889.34	819.53	766.28	724.60
12.50%	4,454.14	2,365.37	1,672.68	1,329.00	1,124.90	990.56	896.06	826.44	773.38	731.88
12.75%	4,460.00	2,371.22	1,678.68	1,335.18	1,131.27	997.12	902.82	833.39	780.51	739.20
13.00%	4,465.86	2,377.09	1,684.70	1,341.37	1,137.65	1,003.71	909.60	840.36	787.68	746.55
13.25%	4,471.73	2,382.97	1,690.72	1,347.59	1,144.06	1,010.31	916.41	847.37	794.88	753.94
13.50%	4,477.60	2,388.85	1,696.76	1,353.82	1,150.49	1,016.95	923.24	854.41	802.12	761.37
13.75%	4,483.48	2,394.74	1,702.82	1,360.06	1,156.94	1,023.61	930.11	861.48	809.38	768.83
14.00%	4,489.36	2,400.64	1,708.88	1,366.32	1,163.41	1,030.29	937.00	868.58	816.69	776.33
14.25%	4,495.24	2,406.55	1,714.96	1,372.60	1,169.90	1,036.99	943.92	875.70	824.02	783.87
14.50%	4,501.13	2,412.47	1,721.05	1,378.90	1,176.41	1,043.72	950.87	882.86	831.39	791.43
14.75%	4,507.02	2,418.40	1,727.15	1,385.21	1,182.95	1,050.47	957.84	890.05	838.79	799.04
15.00%	4,512.92	2,424.33	1,733.27	1,391.54	1,189.50	1,057.25	964.84	897.27	846.22	806.67
15.25%	4,518.82	2,430.28	1,739.39	1,397.88	1,196.07	1,064.05	971.86	904.52	853.68	814.35
15.50%	4,524.72	2,436.23	1,745.53	1,404.24	1,202.66	1,070.87	978.92	911.80	861.18	822.05
15.75%	4,530.63	2,442.19	1,751.69	1,410.62	1,209.27	1,077.72	986.00	919.10	868.70	829.79
16.00%	4,536.54	2,448.16	1,757.85	1,417.01	1,215.90	1,084.59	993.10	926.44	876.26	837.57
16.25%	4,542.46	2,454.13	1,764.03	1,423.42	1,222.55	1,091.49	1,000.24	933.80	883.85	845.37
16.50%	4,548.38	2,460.12	1,770.22	1,429.85	1,229.23	1,098.40	1,007.39	941.20	891.47	853.21
16.75%	4,554.31	2,466.11	1,776.42	1,436.29	1,235.92	1,105.34	1,014.58	948.62	899.13	861.08
17.00%	4,560.24	2,472.11	1,782.64	1,442.75	1,242.63	1,112.31	1,021.79	956.07	906.81	868.99
17.25%	4,566.17	2,478.12	1,788.86	1,449.23	1,249.36	1,119.29	1,029.03	963.55	914.52	876.93
17.50%	4,572.11	2,484.14	1,795.10	1,455.72	1,256.11	1,126.30	1,036.29	971.06	922.27	884.89
17.75%	4,578.05	2,490.17	1,801.36	1,462.23	1,262.88	1,133.33	1,043.58	978.60	930.04	892.89
18.00%	4,584.00	2,496.21	1,807.62	1,468.75	1,269.67	1,140.39	1,050.89	986.16	937.84	900.93
18.25%	4,589.95	2,502.25	1,813.90	1,475.29	1,276.48	1,147.47	1,058.23	993.75	945.68	908.99
18.50%	4,595.91	2,508.30	1,820.19	1,481.85	1,283.31	1,154.57	1,065.60	1,001.37	953.54	917.08
18.75%	4,601.87	2,514.36	1,826.49	1,488.42	1,290.16	1,161.69	1,072.99	1,009.02	961.43	925.21
19.00%	4,607.83	2,520.43	1,832.80	1,495.01	1,297.03	1,168.84	1,080.40	1,016.69	969.35	933.36
19.25%	4,613.80	2,526.51	1,839.13	1,501.61	1,303.92	1,176.00	1,087.84	1,024.39	977.30	941.55
19.50%	4,619.77	2,532.59	1,845.47	1,508.23	1,310.82	1,183.19	1,095.31	1,032.12	985.28	949.76
19.75%	4,625.74	2,538.69	1,851.82	1,514.87	1,317.75	1,190.41	1,102.80	1,039.88	993.29	958.01
20.00%	4,631.73	2,544.79	1,858.18	1,521.52	1,324.69	1,197.64	1,110.31	1,047.66	1,001.33	966.28
20.25%	4,637.71	2,550.90	1,864.55	1,528.19	1,331.66	1,204.90	1,117.85	1,055.47	1,009.39	974.58
20.50%	4,643.70	2,557.02	1,870.94	1,534.87	1,338.64	1,212.18	1,125.41	1,063.30	1,017.48	982.91
20.75%	4,649.69	2,563.15	1,877.34	1,541.57	1,345.65	1,219.48	1,133.00	1,071.16	1,025.60	991.27

	1	2	3	4	5	6	7	8	9	10
1.00%	4,398.73	2,210.36	1,480.93	1,116.23	897.42	751.56	647.39	569.27	508.52	459.92
1.25%	4,404.68	2,216.10	1,486.61	1,121.89	903.08	757.23	653.07	574.96	514.22	465.64
1.50%	4,410.63	2,221.84	1,492.30	1,127.57	908.77	762.93	658.78	580.68	519.96	471.41
1.75%	4,416.58	2,227.60	1,498.01	1,133.27	914.48	768.65	664.52	586.45	525.75	477.22
2.00%	4,422.54	2,233.36	1,503.74	1,138.99	920.21	774.40	670.29	592.25	531.58	483.07
2.25%	4,428.50	2,239.14	1,509.47	1,144.73	925.96	780.17	676.09	598.08	537.44	488.97
2.50%	4,434.47	2,244.92	1,515.22	1,150.49	931.74	785.98	681.93	603.95	543.35	494.92
2.75%	4,440.44	2,250.71	1,520.99	1,156.26	937.54	791.81	687.80	609.86	549.30	500.91
3.00%	4,446.42	2,256.51	1,526.76	1,162.05	943.36	797.67	693.70	615.80	555.29	506.94
3.25%	4,452.40	2,262.32	1,532.55	1,167.86	949.20	803.55	699.63	621.78	561.32	513.02
3.50%	4,458.39	2,268.14	1,538.36	1,173.69	955.07	809.47	705.59	627.80	567.39	519.15
3.75%	4,464.38	2,273.97	1,544.18	1,179.54	960.96	815.41	711.59	633.85	573.50	525.32
4.00%	4,470.37	2,279.81	1,550.01	1,185.40	966.87	821.37	717.61	639.94	579.65	531.54
4.25%	4,476.37	2,285.65	1,555.85	1,191.28	972.80	827.37	723.67	646.06	585.84	537.80
4.50%	4,482.37	2,291.51	1,561.71	1,197.18	978.76	833.39	729.76	652.22	592.07	544.10
4.75%	4,488.38	2,297.37	1,567.59	1,203.10	984.74	839.43	735.88	658.41	598.35	550.45
5.00%	4,494.39	2,303.25	1,573.47	1,209.04	990.74	845.51	742.03	664.65	604.66	556.84
5.25%	4,500.41	2,309.13	1,579.37	1,214.99	996.76	851.61	748.21	670.91	611.01	563.28
5.50%	4,506.43	2,315.02	1,585.28	1,220.96	1,002.81	857.74	754.43	677.21	617.40	569.76
5.75%	4,512.46	2,320.92	1,591.21	1,226.96	1,008.88	863.89	760.67	683.55	623.83	576.29
6.00%	4,518.49	2,326.83	1,597.15	1,232.96	1,014.97	870.08	766.95	689.93	630.30	582.86
6.25%	4,524.52	2,332.75	1,603.11	1,238.99	1,021.09	876.29	773.26	696.33	636.81	589.47
6.50%	4,530.56	2,338.68	1,609.07	1,245.04	1,027.22	882.52	779.60	702.78	643.36	596.13
6.75%	4,536.61	2,344.61	1,615.05	1,251.10	1,033.38	888.78	785.97	709.26	649.95	602.83
7.00%	4,542.65	2,350.56	1,621.05	1,257.18	1,039.56	895.07	792.37	715.77	656.58	609.57
7.25%	4,548.71	2,356.52	1,627.06	1,263.28	1,045.77	901.39	798.80	722.32	663.25	616.36
7.50%	4,554.76	2,362.48	1,633.08	1,269.39	1,051.99	907.73	805.26	728.90	669.95	623.18
7.75%	4,560.83	2,368.45	1,639.11	1,275.53	1,058.24	914.10	811.75	735.52	676.70	630.06
8.00%	4,566.89	2,374.43	1,645.16	1,281.68	1,064.51	920.50	818.28	742.18	683.48	636.97
8.25%	4,572.96	2,380.42	1,651.22	1,287.85	1,070.80	926.92	824.83	748.86	690.31	643.93
8.50%	4,579.04	2,386.42	1,657.30	1,294.04	1,077.12	933.37	831.42	755.59	697.17	650.92
8.75%	4,585.12	2,392.43	1,663.38	1,300.24	1,083.45	939.84	838.03	762.34	704.07	657.97
9.00%	4,591.20	2,398.45	1,669.49	1,306.46	1,089.81	946.34	844.68	769.14	711.00	665.05
9.25%	4,597.29	2,404.48	1,675.60	1,312.71	1,096.19	952.87	851.35	775.96	717.98	672.17
9.50%	4,603.38	2,410.51	1,681.73	1,318.96	1,102.60	959.42	858.06	782.82	724.99	679.34
9.75%	4,609.48	2,416.56	1,687.87	1,325.24	1,109.02	966.00	864.80	789.72	732.04	686.54
10.00%	4,615.58	2,422.61	1,694.03	1,331.54	1,115.47	972.61	871.56	796.64	739.13	693.79
10.25%	4,621.69	2,428.67	1,700.20	1,337.85	1,121.94	979.24	878.36	803.61	746.26	701.08
10.50%	4,627.80	2,434.74	1,706.38	1,344.18	1,128.43	985.90	885.19	810.60	753.42	708.41
10.75%	4,633.92	2,440.82	1,712.57	1,350.52	1,134.94	992.58	892.04	817.63	760.62	715.78

$52,500   11.00 - 20.75%   1 - 10 Years

	1	2	3	4	5	6	7	8	9	10
11.00%	4,640.04	2,446.91	1,718.78	1,356.89	1,141.48	999.29	898.93	824.69	767.86	723.19
11.25%	4,646.16	2,453.01	1,725.00	1,363.27	1,148.03	1,006.02	905.84	831.79	775.13	730.64
11.50%	4,652.29	2,459.12	1,731.24	1,369.67	1,154.61	1,012.79	912.79	838.92	782.44	738.13
11.75%	4,658.42	2,465.23	1,737.49	1,376.09	1,161.21	1,019.57	919.76	846.08	789.79	745.65
12.00%	4,664.56	2,471.36	1,743.75	1,382.53	1,167.83	1,026.39	926.77	853.27	797.17	753.22
12.25%	4,670.70	2,477.49	1,750.03	1,388.98	1,174.48	1,033.22	933.80	860.50	804.59	760.83
12.50%	4,676.85	2,483.63	1,756.32	1,395.45	1,181.14	1,040.09	940.87	867.76	812.05	768.47
12.75%	4,683.00	2,489.79	1,762.62	1,401.94	1,187.83	1,046.98	947.96	875.06	819.54	776.16
13.00%	4,689.16	2,495.95	1,768.93	1,408.44	1,194.54	1,053.89	955.08	882.38	827.06	783.88
13.25%	4,695.32	2,502.12	1,775.26	1,414.97	1,201.27	1,060.83	962.23	889.74	834.62	791.64
13.50%	4,701.48	2,508.29	1,781.60	1,421.51	1,208.02	1,067.80	969.41	897.13	842.22	799.44
13.75%	4,707.65	2,514.48	1,787.96	1,428.06	1,214.79	1,074.79	976.61	904.55	849.85	807.28
14.00%	4,713.82	2,520.68	1,794.33	1,434.64	1,221.58	1,081.80	983.85	912.00	857.52	815.15
14.25%	4,720.00	2,526.88	1,800.71	1,441.23	1,228.40	1,088.84	991.12	919.49	865.22	823.06
14.50%	4,726.18	2,533.09	1,807.10	1,447.84	1,235.23	1,095.91	998.41	927.01	872.96	831.01
14.75%	4,732.37	2,539.32	1,813.51	1,454.47	1,242.09	1,103.00	1,005.73	934.55	880.72	838.99
15.00%	4,738.56	2,545.55	1,819.93	1,461.11	1,248.97	1,110.11	1,013.08	942.13	888.53	847.01
15.25%	4,744.76	2,551.79	1,826.36	1,467.78	1,255.87	1,117.25	1,020.46	949.74	896.36	855.06
15.50%	4,750.96	2,558.04	1,832.81	1,474.46	1,262.79	1,124.42	1,027.86	957.39	904.24	863.16
15.75%	4,757.16	2,564.30	1,839.27	1,481.15	1,269.73	1,131.61	1,035.30	965.06	912.14	871.28
16.00%	4,763.37	2,570.56	1,845.74	1,487.86	1,276.70	1,138.82	1,042.76	972.76	920.08	879.44
16.25%	4,769.58	2,576.84	1,852.23	1,494.60	1,283.68	1,146.06	1,050.25	980.49	928.05	887.64
16.50%	4,775.80	2,583.12	1,858.73	1,501.34	1,290.69	1,153.32	1,057.76	988.26	936.05	895.87
16.75%	4,782.02	2,589.42	1,865.24	1,508.11	1,297.71	1,160.61	1,065.31	996.05	944.08	904.14
17.00%	4,788.25	2,595.72	1,871.77	1,514.89	1,304.76	1,167.92	1,072.88	1,003.88	952.15	912.44
17.25%	4,794.48	2,602.03	1,878.31	1,521.69	1,311.83	1,175.26	1,080.48	1,011.73	960.25	920.77
17.50%	4,800.72	2,608.35	1,884.86	1,528.50	1,318.92	1,182.62	1,088.10	1,019.61	968.38	929.14
17.75%	4,806.96	2,614.68	1,891.42	1,535.34	1,326.03	1,190.00	1,095.76	1,027.53	976.54	937.54
18.00%	4,813.20	2,621.02	1,898.00	1,542.19	1,333.15	1,197.41	1,103.44	1,035.47	984.74	945.97
18.25%	4,819.45	2,627.36	1,904.59	1,549.05	1,340.31	1,204.84	1,111.14	1,043.44	992.96	954.44
18.50%	4,825.70	2,633.72	1,911.20	1,555.94	1,347.48	1,212.30	1,118.88	1,051.44	1,001.22	962.94
18.75%	4,831.96	2,640.08	1,917.81	1,562.84	1,354.67	1,219.78	1,126.64	1,059.47	1,009.50	971.47
19.00%	4,838.22	2,646.45	1,924.44	1,569.76	1,361.88	1,227.28	1,134.42	1,067.53	1,017.82	980.03
19.25%	4,844.49	2,652.83	1,931.08	1,576.69	1,369.11	1,234.80	1,142.23	1,075.61	1,026.17	988.62
19.50%	4,850.76	2,659.22	1,937.74	1,583.64	1,376.36	1,242.35	1,150.07	1,083.73	1,034.55	997.25
19.75%	4,857.03	2,665.62	1,944.41	1,590.61	1,383.64	1,249.93	1,157.94	1,091.87	1,042.95	1,005.91
20.00%	4,863.31	2,672.03	1,951.09	1,597.59	1,390.93	1,257.52	1,165.83	1,100.04	1,051.39	1,014.59
20.25%	4,869.60	2,678.45	1,957.78	1,604.60	1,398.24	1,265.14	1,173.74	1,108.24	1,059.86	1,023.31
20.50%	4,875.88	2,684.87	1,964.49	1,611.61	1,405.58	1,272.79	1,181.68	1,116.47	1,068.35	1,032.06
20.75%	4,882.18	2,691.30	1,971.21	1,618.65	1,412.93	1,280.45	1,189.65	1,124.72	1,076.88	1,040.83

	1	2	3	4	5	6	7	8	9	10
1.00%	4,608.20	2,315.61	1,551.45	1,169.38	940.16	787.35	678.22	596.38	532.73	481.82
1.25%	4,614.43	2,321.63	1,557.40	1,175.31	946.09	793.29	684.17	602.34	538.71	487.81
1.50%	4,620.66	2,327.65	1,563.37	1,181.27	952.04	799.26	690.15	608.34	544.73	493.85
1.75%	4,626.90	2,333.68	1,569.35	1,187.24	958.02	805.25	696.16	614.37	550.79	499.94
2.00%	4,633.14	2,339.71	1,575.34	1,193.23	964.03	811.27	702.21	620.45	556.89	506.07
2.25%	4,639.38	2,345.76	1,581.35	1,199.24	970.05	817.33	708.29	626.56	563.04	512.26
2.50%	4,645.64	2,351.82	1,587.38	1,205.27	976.10	823.41	714.40	632.71	569.23	518.48
2.75%	4,651.89	2,357.89	1,593.41	1,211.32	982.18	829.51	720.55	638.90	575.46	524.76
3.00%	4,658.15	2,363.97	1,599.47	1,217.39	988.28	835.65	726.73	645.13	581.73	531.08
3.25%	4,664.42	2,370.05	1,605.53	1,223.47	994.40	841.82	732.95	651.39	588.05	537.45
3.50%	4,670.69	2,376.15	1,611.61	1,229.58	1,000.55	848.01	739.19	657.69	594.41	543.87
3.75%	4,676.96	2,382.26	1,617.71	1,235.70	1,006.72	854.23	745.47	664.03	600.81	550.34
4.00%	4,683.24	2,388.37	1,623.82	1,241.85	1,012.91	860.49	751.78	670.41	607.25	556.85
4.25%	4,689.53	2,394.50	1,629.94	1,248.01	1,019.13	866.76	758.13	676.83	613.74	563.41
4.50%	4,695.82	2,400.63	1,636.08	1,254.19	1,025.37	873.07	764.51	683.28	620.27	570.01
4.75%	4,702.11	2,406.77	1,642.23	1,260.39	1,031.63	879.41	770.92	689.77	626.84	576.66
5.00%	4,708.41	2,412.93	1,648.40	1,266.61	1,037.92	885.77	777.36	696.30	633.45	583.36
5.25%	4,714.71	2,419.09	1,654.58	1,272.85	1,044.23	892.16	783.84	702.86	640.10	590.10
5.50%	4,721.02	2,425.26	1,660.77	1,279.11	1,050.56	898.58	790.35	709.46	646.80	596.89
5.75%	4,727.34	2,431.44	1,666.98	1,285.38	1,056.92	905.03	796.90	716.10	653.54	603.73
6.00%	4,733.65	2,437.63	1,673.21	1,291.68	1,063.30	911.51	803.47	722.78	660.32	610.61
6.25%	4,739.98	2,443.83	1,679.44	1,297.99	1,069.71	918.01	810.08	729.49	667.14	617.54
6.50%	4,746.30	2,450.04	1,685.70	1,304.32	1,076.14	924.55	816.72	736.24	674.00	624.51
6.75%	4,752.63	2,456.26	1,691.96	1,310.67	1,082.59	931.11	823.39	743.03	680.90	631.53
7.00%	4,758.97	2,462.49	1,698.24	1,317.04	1,089.07	937.70	830.10	749.85	687.85	638.60
7.25%	4,765.31	2,468.73	1,704.53	1,323.43	1,095.56	944.31	836.84	756.72	694.83	645.71
7.50%	4,771.66	2,474.98	1,710.84	1,329.84	1,102.09	950.96	843.61	763.61	701.86	652.86
7.75%	4,778.01	2,481.23	1,717.16	1,336.27	1,108.63	957.63	850.41	770.55	708.92	660.06
8.00%	4,784.36	2,487.50	1,723.50	1,342.71	1,115.20	964.33	857.24	777.52	716.03	667.30
8.25%	4,790.72	2,493.78	1,729.85	1,349.17	1,121.79	971.06	864.11	784.52	723.18	674.59
8.50%	4,797.09	2,500.06	1,736.21	1,355.66	1,128.41	977.81	871.01	791.57	730.36	681.92
8.75%	4,803.46	2,506.36	1,742.59	1,362.16	1,135.05	984.59	877.94	798.65	737.59	689.30
9.00%	4,809.83	2,512.66	1,748.99	1,368.68	1,141.71	991.40	884.90	805.76	744.86	696.72
9.25%	4,816.21	2,518.97	1,755.39	1,375.22	1,148.39	998.24	891.89	812.91	752.17	704.18
9.50%	4,822.59	2,525.30	1,761.81	1,381.77	1,155.10	1,005.11	898.92	820.10	759.51	711.69
9.75%	4,828.98	2,531.63	1,768.25	1,388.35	1,161.83	1,012.00	905.98	827.32	766.90	719.24
10.00%	4,835.37	2,537.97	1,774.70	1,394.94	1,168.59	1,018.92	913.07	834.58	774.33	726.83
10.25%	4,841.77	2,544.32	1,781.16	1,401.55	1,175.36	1,025.87	920.19	841.87	781.79	734.46
10.50%	4,848.17	2,550.68	1,787.63	1,408.19	1,182.16	1,032.84	927.34	849.20	789.30	742.14
10.75%	4,854.58	2,557.05	1,794.12	1,414.84	1,188.99	1,039.85	934.52	856.56	796.84	749.86

$55,000   11.00 - 20.75%   1 - 10 Years

	1	2	3	4	5	6	7	8	9	10
11.00%	4,860.99	2,563.43	1,800.63	1,421.50	1,195.83	1,046.87	941.73	863.96	804.42	757.63
11.25%	4,867.41	2,569.82	1,807.15	1,428.19	1,202.70	1,053.93	948.98	871.40	812.04	765.43
11.50%	4,873.83	2,576.22	1,813.68	1,434.90	1,209.59	1,061.01	956.26	878.87	819.70	773.27
11.75%	4,880.25	2,582.62	1,820.23	1,441.62	1,216.51	1,068.12	963.56	886.37	827.40	781.16
12.00%	4,886.68	2,589.04	1,826.79	1,448.36	1,223.44	1,075.26	970.90	893.91	835.13	789.09
12.25%	4,893.12	2,595.47	1,833.36	1,455.12	1,230.40	1,082.42	978.27	901.48	842.91	797.06
12.50%	4,899.56	2,601.90	1,839.95	1,461.90	1,237.39	1,089.61	985.67	909.08	850.72	805.07
12.75%	4,906.00	2,608.35	1,846.55	1,468.70	1,244.39	1,096.83	993.10	916.72	858.56	813.12
13.00%	4,912.45	2,614.80	1,853.17	1,475.51	1,251.42	1,104.08	1,000.56	924.40	866.45	821.21
13.25%	4,918.90	2,621.26	1,859.80	1,482.35	1,258.47	1,111.35	1,008.05	932.11	874.37	829.34
13.50%	4,925.36	2,627.74	1,866.44	1,489.20	1,265.54	1,118.64	1,015.57	939.85	882.33	837.51
13.75%	4,931.82	2,634.22	1,873.10	1,496.07	1,272.64	1,125.97	1,023.12	947.62	890.32	845.72
14.00%	4,938.29	2,640.71	1,879.77	1,502.96	1,279.75	1,133.32	1,030.70	955.43	898.35	853.97
14.25%	4,944.76	2,647.21	1,886.45	1,509.86	1,286.89	1,140.69	1,038.31	963.27	906.42	862.25
14.50%	4,951.24	2,653.72	1,893.15	1,516.79	1,294.06	1,148.09	1,045.95	971.15	914.52	870.58
14.75%	4,957.72	2,660.24	1,899.87	1,523.73	1,301.24	1,155.52	1,053.62	979.06	922.66	878.94
15.00%	4,964.21	2,666.77	1,906.59	1,530.69	1,308.45	1,162.98	1,061.32	987.00	930.84	887.34
15.25%	4,970.70	2,673.30	1,913.33	1,537.67	1,315.67	1,170.46	1,069.05	994.97	939.05	895.78
15.50%	4,977.19	2,679.85	1,920.09	1,544.67	1,322.93	1,177.96	1,076.81	1,002.98	947.29	904.26
15.75%	4,983.69	2,686.41	1,926.86	1,551.68	1,330.20	1,185.49	1,084.60	1,011.01	955.57	912.77
16.00%	4,990.20	2,692.97	1,933.64	1,558.72	1,337.49	1,193.05	1,092.41	1,019.08	963.89	921.32
16.25%	4,996.71	2,699.55	1,940.43	1,565.77	1,344.81	1,200.63	1,100.26	1,027.18	972.24	929.91
16.50%	5,003.22	2,706.13	1,947.24	1,572.84	1,352.15	1,208.24	1,108.13	1,035.32	980.62	938.53
16.75%	5,009.74	2,712.72	1,954.06	1,579.92	1,359.51	1,215.88	1,116.04	1,043.48	989.04	947.19
17.00%	5,016.26	2,719.32	1,960.90	1,587.03	1,366.89	1,223.54	1,123.97	1,051.68	997.49	955.89
17.25%	5,022.79	2,725.94	1,967.75	1,594.15	1,374.30	1,231.22	1,131.93	1,059.91	1,005.98	964.62
17.50%	5,029.32	2,732.56	1,974.61	1,601.29	1,381.72	1,238.93	1,139.92	1,068.17	1,014.49	973.38
17.75%	5,035.86	2,739.19	1,981.49	1,608.45	1,389.17	1,246.67	1,147.94	1,076.46	1,023.04	982.18
18.00%	5,042.40	2,745.83	1,988.38	1,615.62	1,396.64	1,254.43	1,155.98	1,084.78	1,031.63	991.02
18.25%	5,048.95	2,752.47	1,995.29	1,622.82	1,404.13	1,262.21	1,164.05	1,093.13	1,040.25	999.89
18.50%	5,055.50	2,759.13	2,002.20	1,630.03	1,411.64	1,270.02	1,172.16	1,101.51	1,048.89	1,008.79
18.75%	5,062.05	2,765.80	2,009.14	1,637.26	1,419.18	1,277.86	1,180.28	1,109.92	1,057.58	1,017.73
19.00%	5,068.61	2,772.47	2,016.08	1,644.51	1,426.73	1,285.72	1,188.44	1,118.36	1,066.29	1,026.70
19.25%	5,075.18	2,779.16	2,023.04	1,651.77	1,434.31	1,293.60	1,196.63	1,126.83	1,075.03	1,035.70
19.50%	5,081.75	2,785.85	2,030.01	1,659.05	1,441.90	1,301.51	1,204.84	1,135.34	1,083.81	1,044.74
19.75%	5,088.32	2,792.56	2,037.00	1,666.35	1,449.52	1,309.45	1,213.08	1,143.87	1,092.62	1,053.81
20.00%	5,094.90	2,799.27	2,044.00	1,673.67	1,457.16	1,317.41	1,221.34	1,152.43	1,101.46	1,062.91
20.25%	5,101.48	2,805.99	2,051.01	1,681.00	1,464.82	1,325.39	1,229.63	1,161.02	1,110.33	1,072.04
20.50%	5,108.07	2,812.72	2,058.04	1,688.36	1,472.51	1,333.39	1,237.95	1,169.63	1,119.23	1,081.20
20.75%	5,114.66	2,819.46	2,065.08	1,695.73	1,480.21	1,341.43	1,246.30	1,178.28	1,128.16	1,090.40

	1	2	3	4	5	6	7	8	9	10
1.00%	4,817.66	2,420.87	1,621.97	1,222.53	982.89	823.14	709.05	623.49	556.95	503.72
1.25%	4,824.17	2,427.15	1,628.19	1,228.74	989.09	829.35	715.26	629.72	563.19	509.99
1.50%	4,830.69	2,433.45	1,634.43	1,234.96	995.32	835.59	721.52	635.99	569.49	516.30
1.75%	4,837.21	2,439.75	1,640.68	1,241.21	1,001.57	841.85	727.81	642.30	575.82	522.66
2.00%	4,843.73	2,446.07	1,646.95	1,247.47	1,007.85	848.15	734.13	648.65	582.20	529.08
2.25%	4,850.27	2,452.39	1,653.23	1,253.75	1,014.15	854.48	740.48	655.04	588.63	535.54
2.50%	4,856.80	2,458.72	1,659.53	1,260.06	1,020.47	860.83	746.88	661.47	595.10	542.05
2.75%	4,863.34	2,465.07	1,665.84	1,266.38	1,026.82	867.22	753.30	667.94	601.61	548.61
3.00%	4,869.89	2,471.42	1,672.17	1,272.72	1,033.20	873.64	759.76	674.45	608.17	555.22
3.25%	4,876.44	2,477.78	1,678.51	1,279.09	1,039.60	880.08	766.26	681.00	614.78	561.88
3.50%	4,882.99	2,484.16	1,684.87	1,285.47	1,046.03	886.56	772.79	687.59	621.43	568.59
3.75%	4,889.55	2,490.54	1,691.24	1,291.87	1,052.48	893.06	779.36	694.22	628.12	575.35
4.00%	4,896.12	2,496.93	1,697.63	1,298.30	1,058.95	899.60	785.96	700.88	634.86	582.16
4.25%	4,902.69	2,503.34	1,704.03	1,304.74	1,065.45	906.16	792.59	707.59	641.64	589.02
4.50%	4,909.26	2,509.75	1,710.45	1,311.20	1,071.97	912.76	799.26	714.34	648.46	595.92
4.75%	4,915.85	2,516.17	1,716.88	1,317.68	1,078.52	919.38	805.96	721.12	655.33	602.87
5.00%	4,922.43	2,522.60	1,723.33	1,324.18	1,085.10	926.03	812.70	727.95	662.24	609.88
5.25%	4,929.02	2,529.05	1,729.79	1,330.71	1,091.69	932.72	819.47	734.81	669.20	616.93
5.50%	4,935.62	2,535.50	1,736.26	1,337.25	1,098.32	939.43	826.28	741.71	676.20	624.03
5.75%	4,942.21	2,541.96	1,742.76	1,343.81	1,104.96	946.17	833.12	748.65	683.24	631.17
6.00%	4,948.82	2,548.44	1,749.26	1,350.39	1,111.64	952.94	839.99	755.63	690.33	638.37
6.25%	4,955.43	2,554.92	1,755.78	1,356.99	1,118.33	959.74	846.90	762.65	697.46	645.61
6.50%	4,962.04	2,561.41	1,762.32	1,363.61	1,125.05	966.57	853.84	769.71	704.63	652.90
6.75%	4,968.66	2,567.91	1,768.87	1,370.25	1,131.80	973.43	860.82	776.80	711.85	660.24
7.00%	4,975.29	2,574.42	1,775.43	1,376.91	1,138.57	980.32	867.83	783.94	719.11	667.62
7.25%	4,981.92	2,580.95	1,782.01	1,383.59	1,145.36	987.24	874.87	791.11	726.41	675.06
7.50%	4,988.55	2,587.48	1,788.61	1,390.29	1,152.18	994.18	881.95	798.32	733.76	682.54
7.75%	4,995.19	2,594.02	1,795.22	1,397.01	1,159.03	1,001.16	889.06	805.57	741.15	690.06
8.00%	5,001.83	2,600.57	1,801.84	1,403.74	1,165.89	1,008.16	896.21	812.86	748.58	697.63
8.25%	5,008.48	2,607.13	1,808.48	1,410.50	1,172.78	1,015.19	903.39	820.18	756.05	705.25
8.50%	5,015.14	2,613.70	1,815.13	1,417.28	1,179.70	1,022.26	910.60	827.55	763.56	712.92
8.75%	5,021.80	2,620.28	1,821.80	1,424.07	1,186.64	1,029.35	917.84	834.95	771.12	720.63
9.00%	5,028.46	2,626.87	1,828.48	1,430.89	1,193.61	1,036.47	925.12	842.39	778.72	728.39
9.25%	5,035.13	2,633.47	1,835.18	1,437.73	1,200.59	1,043.62	932.43	849.86	786.36	736.19
9.50%	5,041.80	2,640.08	1,841.89	1,444.58	1,207.61	1,050.79	939.78	857.38	794.04	744.04
9.75%	5,048.48	2,646.70	1,848.62	1,451.45	1,214.64	1,058.00	947.16	864.93	801.76	751.93
10.00%	5,055.16	2,653.33	1,855.36	1,458.35	1,221.71	1,065.24	954.57	872.51	809.52	759.87
10.25%	5,061.85	2,659.97	1,862.12	1,465.26	1,228.79	1,072.50	962.01	880.14	817.33	767.85
10.50%	5,068.54	2,666.62	1,868.89	1,472.19	1,235.90	1,079.79	969.49	887.80	825.17	775.88
10.75%	5,075.24	2,673.28	1,875.68	1,479.15	1,243.03	1,087.11	977.00	895.50	833.06	783.95

$57,500　　11.00 - 20.75%　　1 - 10 Years

	1	2	3	4	5	6	7	8	9	10
11.00%	5,081.95	2,679.95	1,882.48	1,486.12	1,250.19	1,094.46	984.54	903.23	840.99	792.06
11.25%	5,088.65	2,686.63	1,889.29	1,493.11	1,257.37	1,101.84	992.11	911.01	848.95	800.22
11.50%	5,095.37	2,693.32	1,896.12	1,500.12	1,264.57	1,109.24	999.72	918.81	856.96	808.42
11.75%	5,102.08	2,700.02	1,902.96	1,507.15	1,271.80	1,116.67	1,007.36	926.66	865.01	816.67
12.00%	5,108.81	2,706.72	1,909.82	1,514.20	1,279.06	1,124.14	1,015.03	934.54	873.09	824.96
12.25%	5,115.53	2,713.44	1,916.70	1,521.26	1,286.33	1,131.63	1,022.74	942.45	881.22	833.29
12.50%	5,122.26	2,720.17	1,923.58	1,528.35	1,293.63	1,139.14	1,030.47	950.41	889.38	841.66
12.75%	5,129.00	2,726.91	1,930.49	1,535.46	1,300.95	1,146.69	1,038.24	958.39	897.59	850.08
13.00%	5,135.74	2,733.65	1,937.40	1,542.58	1,308.30	1,154.26	1,046.04	966.42	905.83	858.54
13.25%	5,142.49	2,740.41	1,944.33	1,549.73	1,315.67	1,161.86	1,053.87	974.48	914.11	867.04
13.50%	5,149.24	2,747.18	1,951.28	1,556.89	1,323.07	1,169.49	1,061.73	982.57	922.43	875.58
13.75%	5,156.00	2,753.95	1,958.24	1,564.07	1,330.48	1,177.15	1,069.63	990.70	930.79	884.16
14.00%	5,162.76	2,760.74	1,965.21	1,571.27	1,337.92	1,184.83	1,077.55	998.86	939.19	892.78
14.25%	5,169.53	2,767.54	1,972.20	1,578.49	1,345.39	1,192.54	1,085.51	1,007.06	947.62	901.45
14.50%	5,176.30	2,774.34	1,979.21	1,585.73	1,352.88	1,200.28	1,093.49	1,015.29	956.09	910.15
14.75%	5,183.07	2,781.16	1,986.22	1,592.99	1,360.39	1,208.05	1,101.51	1,023.56	964.60	918.89
15.00%	5,189.85	2,787.98	1,993.26	1,600.27	1,367.92	1,215.84	1,109.56	1,031.86	973.15	927.68
15.25%	5,196.64	2,794.82	2,000.30	1,607.56	1,375.48	1,223.66	1,117.64	1,040.20	981.73	936.50
15.50%	5,203.43	2,801.66	2,007.36	1,614.88	1,383.06	1,231.51	1,125.75	1,048.57	990.35	945.36
15.75%	5,210.22	2,808.52	2,014.44	1,622.21	1,390.66	1,239.38	1,133.90	1,056.97	999.01	954.26
16.00%	5,217.02	2,815.38	2,021.53	1,629.57	1,398.29	1,247.28	1,142.07	1,065.41	1,007.70	963.20
16.25%	5,223.83	2,822.25	2,028.63	1,636.94	1,405.94	1,255.21	1,150.27	1,073.88	1,016.43	972.18
16.50%	5,230.64	2,829.14	2,035.75	1,644.33	1,413.61	1,263.16	1,158.50	1,082.38	1,025.20	981.19
16.75%	5,237.45	2,836.03	2,042.88	1,651.74	1,421.31	1,271.14	1,166.77	1,090.91	1,034.00	990.25
17.00%	5,244.27	2,842.93	2,050.03	1,659.16	1,429.02	1,279.15	1,175.06	1,099.48	1,042.83	999.34
17.25%	5,251.10	2,849.84	2,057.19	1,666.61	1,436.76	1,287.19	1,183.38	1,108.09	1,051.70	1,008.46
17.50%	5,257.93	2,856.76	2,064.37	1,674.08	1,444.53	1,295.25	1,191.73	1,116.72	1,060.61	1,017.63
17.75%	5,264.76	2,863.69	2,071.56	1,681.56	1,452.31	1,303.33	1,200.11	1,125.39	1,069.55	1,026.83
18.00%	5,271.60	2,870.64	2,078.76	1,689.06	1,460.12	1,311.45	1,208.53	1,134.08	1,078.52	1,036.06
18.25%	5,278.44	2,877.59	2,085.98	1,696.58	1,467.95	1,319.59	1,216.97	1,142.82	1,087.53	1,045.34
18.50%	5,285.29	2,884.55	2,093.21	1,704.12	1,475.81	1,327.75	1,225.44	1,151.58	1,096.57	1,054.65
18.75%	5,292.15	2,891.52	2,100.46	1,711.68	1,483.68	1,335.94	1,233.93	1,160.37	1,105.65	1,063.99
19.00%	5,299.00	2,898.50	2,107.72	1,719.26	1,491.58	1,344.16	1,242.46	1,169.20	1,114.76	1,073.37
19.25%	5,305.87	2,905.48	2,115.00	1,726.85	1,499.50	1,352.40	1,251.02	1,178.05	1,123.90	1,082.78
19.50%	5,312.73	2,912.48	2,122.29	1,734.46	1,507.45	1,360.67	1,259.60	1,186.94	1,133.08	1,092.23
19.75%	5,319.61	2,919.49	2,129.59	1,742.10	1,515.41	1,368.97	1,268.21	1,195.86	1,142.28	1,101.71
20.00%	5,326.48	2,926.51	2,136.91	1,749.75	1,523.40	1,377.29	1,276.86	1,204.81	1,151.52	1,111.22
20.25%	5,333.37	2,933.54	2,144.24	1,757.41	1,531.41	1,385.63	1,285.53	1,213.79	1,160.80	1,120.77
20.50%	5,340.25	2,940.57	2,151.58	1,765.10	1,539.44	1,394.00	1,294.22	1,222.80	1,170.10	1,130.35
20.75%	5,347.15	2,947.62	2,158.94	1,772.80	1,547.49	1,402.40	1,302.95	1,231.84	1,179.44	1,139.96

$60,000   1.00 - 10.75%   1 - 10 Years

	1	2	3	4	5	6	7	8	9	10
1.00%	5,027.12	2,526.12	1,692.49	1,275.69	1,025.62	858.93	739.87	650.59	581.16	525.62
1.25%	5,033.92	2,532.68	1,698.98	1,282.16	1,032.10	865.41	746.36	657.10	587.68	532.16
1.50%	5,040.72	2,539.25	1,705.49	1,288.66	1,038.59	871.92	752.89	663.64	594.25	538.75
1.75%	5,047.52	2,545.83	1,712.01	1,295.17	1,045.12	878.46	759.45	670.23	600.86	545.39
2.00%	5,054.33	2,552.42	1,718.55	1,301.71	1,051.67	885.03	766.05	676.85	607.52	552.08
2.25%	5,061.15	2,559.01	1,725.11	1,308.26	1,058.24	891.63	772.68	683.52	614.22	558.82
2.50%	5,067.97	2,565.62	1,731.68	1,314.84	1,064.84	898.26	779.35	690.23	620.97	565.62
2.75%	5,074.79	2,572.24	1,738.27	1,321.44	1,071.47	904.93	786.06	696.98	627.77	572.47
3.00%	5,081.62	2,578.87	1,744.87	1,328.06	1,078.12	911.62	792.80	703.77	634.62	579.36
3.25%	5,088.46	2,585.51	1,751.49	1,334.70	1,084.80	918.35	799.58	710.61	641.51	586.31
3.50%	5,095.30	2,592.16	1,758.12	1,341.36	1,091.50	925.10	806.39	717.48	648.44	593.32
3.75%	5,102.14	2,598.82	1,764.77	1,348.04	1,098.24	931.89	813.24	724.40	655.43	600.37
4.00%	5,108.99	2,605.50	1,771.44	1,354.74	1,104.99	938.71	820.13	731.36	662.46	607.47
4.25%	5,115.85	2,612.18	1,778.12	1,361.47	1,111.77	945.56	827.05	738.35	669.53	614.63
4.50%	5,122.71	2,618.87	1,784.82	1,368.21	1,118.58	952.44	834.01	745.39	676.66	621.83
4.75%	5,129.58	2,625.57	1,791.53	1,374.97	1,125.41	959.35	841.00	752.47	683.82	629.09
5.00%	5,136.45	2,632.28	1,798.25	1,381.76	1,132.27	966.30	848.03	759.60	691.04	636.39
5.25%	5,143.33	2,639.01	1,805.00	1,388.56	1,139.16	973.27	855.10	766.76	698.30	643.75
5.50%	5,150.21	2,645.74	1,811.75	1,395.39	1,146.07	980.27	862.20	773.96	705.60	651.16
5.75%	5,157.09	2,652.48	1,818.53	1,402.23	1,153.01	987.31	869.34	781.20	712.95	658.62
6.00%	5,163.99	2,659.24	1,825.32	1,409.10	1,159.97	994.37	876.51	788.49	720.34	666.12
6.25%	5,170.88	2,666.00	1,832.12	1,415.99	1,166.96	1,001.47	883.72	795.81	727.79	673.68
6.50%	5,177.79	2,672.78	1,838.94	1,422.90	1,173.97	1,008.60	890.97	803.17	735.27	681.29
6.75%	5,184.69	2,679.56	1,845.78	1,429.83	1,181.01	1,015.75	898.25	810.58	742.80	688.94
7.00%	5,191.60	2,686.35	1,852.63	1,436.77	1,188.07	1,022.94	905.56	818.02	750.38	696.65
7.25%	5,198.52	2,693.16	1,859.49	1,443.74	1,195.16	1,030.16	912.91	825.51	758.00	704.41
7.50%	5,205.45	2,699.98	1,866.37	1,450.73	1,202.28	1,037.41	920.30	833.03	765.66	712.21
7.75%	5,212.37	2,706.80	1,873.27	1,457.74	1,209.42	1,044.69	927.72	840.60	773.37	720.06
8.00%	5,219.31	2,713.64	1,880.18	1,464.78	1,216.58	1,051.99	935.17	848.20	781.12	727.97
8.25%	5,226.24	2,720.48	1,887.11	1,471.83	1,223.78	1,059.33	942.66	855.84	788.92	735.92
8.50%	5,233.19	2,727.34	1,894.05	1,478.90	1,230.99	1,066.70	950.19	863.53	796.76	743.91
8.75%	5,240.14	2,734.21	1,901.01	1,485.99	1,238.23	1,074.10	957.75	871.25	804.65	751.96
9.00%	5,247.09	2,741.08	1,907.98	1,493.10	1,245.50	1,081.53	965.34	879.01	812.57	760.05
9.25%	5,254.05	2,747.97	1,914.97	1,500.24	1,252.79	1,088.99	972.97	886.81	820.55	768.20
9.50%	5,261.01	2,754.87	1,921.98	1,507.39	1,260.11	1,096.48	980.64	894.65	828.56	776.39
9.75%	5,267.98	2,761.78	1,929.00	1,514.56	1,267.45	1,104.00	988.34	902.53	836.62	784.62
10.00%	5,274.95	2,768.70	1,936.03	1,521.76	1,274.82	1,111.55	996.07	910.45	844.72	792.90
10.25%	5,281.93	2,775.62	1,943.08	1,528.97	1,282.22	1,119.13	1,003.84	918.41	852.87	801.23
10.50%	5,288.92	2,782.56	1,950.15	1,536.20	1,289.63	1,126.74	1,011.64	926.40	861.05	809.61
10.75%	5,295.91	2,789.51	1,957.23	1,543.46	1,297.08	1,134.38	1,019.48	934.43	869.28	818.03

$60,000   11.00 - 20.75%   1 - 10 Years

	1	2	3	4	5	6	7	8	9	10
11.00%	5,302.90	2,796.47	1,964.32	1,550.73	1,304.55	1,142.04	1,027.35	942.51	877.55	826.50
11.25%	5,309.90	2,803.44	1,971.43	1,558.03	1,312.04	1,149.74	1,035.25	950.62	885.86	835.01
11.50%	5,316.90	2,810.42	1,978.56	1,565.34	1,319.56	1,157.47	1,043.19	958.76	894.22	843.57
11.75%	5,323.91	2,817.41	1,985.70	1,572.68	1,327.10	1,165.23	1,051.16	966.95	902.62	852.18
12.00%	5,330.93	2,824.41	1,992.86	1,580.03	1,334.67	1,173.01	1,059.16	975.17	911.05	860.83
12.25%	5,337.95	2,831.42	2,000.03	1,587.41	1,342.26	1,180.83	1,067.20	983.43	919.53	869.52
12.50%	5,344.97	2,838.44	2,007.22	1,594.80	1,349.88	1,188.67	1,075.27	991.73	928.05	878.26
12.75%	5,352.00	2,845.47	2,014.42	1,602.21	1,357.52	1,196.54	1,083.38	1,000.06	936.61	887.04
13.00%	5,359.04	2,852.51	2,021.64	1,609.65	1,365.18	1,204.45	1,091.52	1,008.44	945.22	895.86
13.25%	5,366.08	2,859.56	2,028.87	1,617.10	1,372.88	1,212.38	1,099.69	1,016.84	953.86	904.73
13.50%	5,373.12	2,866.62	2,036.12	1,624.58	1,380.59	1,220.34	1,107.89	1,025.29	962.54	913.65
13.75%	5,380.17	2,873.69	2,043.38	1,632.07	1,388.33	1,228.33	1,116.13	1,033.77	971.26	922.60
14.00%	5,387.23	2,880.77	2,050.66	1,639.59	1,396.10	1,236.34	1,124.40	1,042.29	980.02	931.60
14.25%	5,394.29	2,887.86	2,057.95	1,647.12	1,403.88	1,244.39	1,132.70	1,050.84	988.82	940.64
14.50%	5,401.35	2,894.97	2,065.26	1,654.68	1,411.70	1,252.47	1,141.04	1,059.44	997.66	949.72
14.75%	5,408.42	2,902.08	2,072.58	1,662.25	1,419.53	1,260.57	1,149.41	1,068.06	1,006.54	958.84
15.00%	5,415.50	2,909.20	2,079.92	1,669.84	1,427.40	1,268.70	1,157.81	1,076.72	1,015.46	968.01
15.25%	5,422.58	2,916.33	2,087.27	1,677.46	1,435.28	1,276.86	1,166.24	1,085.42	1,024.42	977.22
15.50%	5,429.66	2,923.47	2,094.64	1,685.09	1,443.19	1,285.05	1,174.70	1,094.16	1,033.41	986.46
15.75%	5,436.76	2,930.62	2,102.02	1,692.74	1,451.13	1,293.27	1,183.20	1,102.92	1,042.44	995.75
16.00%	5,443.85	2,937.79	2,109.42	1,700.42	1,459.08	1,301.51	1,191.72	1,111.73	1,051.52	1,005.08
16.25%	5,450.95	2,944.96	2,116.83	1,708.11	1,467.07	1,309.78	1,200.28	1,120.57	1,060.62	1,014.45
16.50%	5,458.06	2,952.14	2,124.26	1,715.82	1,475.07	1,318.08	1,208.87	1,129.44	1,069.77	1,023.85
16.75%	5,465.17	2,959.33	2,131.71	1,723.55	1,483.10	1,326.41	1,217.50	1,138.35	1,078.95	1,033.30
17.00%	5,472.29	2,966.54	2,139.16	1,731.30	1,491.15	1,334.77	1,226.15	1,147.29	1,088.17	1,042.79
17.25%	5,479.41	2,973.75	2,146.64	1,739.07	1,499.23	1,343.15	1,234.83	1,156.26	1,097.43	1,052.31
17.50%	5,486.53	2,980.97	2,154.12	1,746.86	1,507.33	1,351.56	1,243.55	1,165.27	1,106.72	1,061.87
17.75%	5,493.66	2,988.20	2,161.63	1,754.67	1,515.46	1,360.00	1,252.29	1,174.32	1,116.05	1,071.47
18.00%	5,500.80	2,995.45	2,169.14	1,762.50	1,523.61	1,368.47	1,261.07	1,183.39	1,125.41	1,081.11
18.25%	5,507.94	3,002.70	2,176.68	1,770.35	1,531.78	1,376.96	1,269.88	1,192.50	1,134.81	1,090.79
18.50%	5,515.09	3,009.96	2,184.22	1,778.21	1,539.97	1,385.48	1,278.72	1,201.65	1,144.25	1,100.50
18.75%	5,522.24	3,017.23	2,191.78	1,786.10	1,548.19	1,394.03	1,287.58	1,210.82	1,153.72	1,110.25
19.00%	5,529.39	3,024.52	2,199.36	1,794.01	1,556.43	1,402.60	1,296.48	1,220.03	1,163.22	1,120.03
19.25%	5,536.56	3,031.81	2,206.95	1,801.93	1,564.70	1,411.20	1,305.41	1,229.27	1,172.77	1,129.86
19.50%	5,543.72	3,039.11	2,214.56	1,809.88	1,572.99	1,419.83	1,314.37	1,238.55	1,182.34	1,139.71
19.75%	5,550.89	3,046.43	2,222.18	1,817.84	1,581.30	1,428.49	1,323.35	1,247.85	1,191.95	1,149.61
20.00%	5,558.07	3,053.75	2,229.82	1,825.82	1,589.63	1,437.17	1,332.37	1,257.19	1,201.59	1,159.53
20.25%	5,565.25	3,061.08	2,237.47	1,833.82	1,597.99	1,445.88	1,341.42	1,266.56	1,211.27	1,169.50
20.50%	5,572.44	3,068.42	2,245.13	1,841.84	1,606.37	1,454.61	1,350.49	1,275.96	1,220.98	1,179.49
20.75%	5,579.63	3,075.78	2,252.81	1,849.88	1,614.78	1,463.37	1,359.60	1,285.40	1,230.72	1,189.53

	1	2	3	4	5	6	7	8	9	10
1.00%	5,236.59	2,631.38	1,763.01	1,328.84	1,068.36	894.72	770.70	677.70	605.38	547.53
1.25%	5,243.67	2,638.21	1,769.77	1,335.58	1,075.10	901.47	777.46	684.47	612.17	554.33
1.50%	5,250.75	2,645.05	1,776.55	1,342.35	1,081.87	908.25	784.26	691.29	619.01	561.20
1.75%	5,257.84	2,651.90	1,783.35	1,349.14	1,088.66	915.06	791.09	698.15	625.89	568.11
2.00%	5,264.93	2,658.77	1,790.16	1,355.95	1,095.49	921.90	797.96	705.05	632.83	575.08
2.25%	5,272.03	2,665.64	1,796.99	1,362.78	1,102.33	928.78	804.87	712.00	639.81	582.11
2.50%	5,279.13	2,672.52	1,803.84	1,369.63	1,109.21	935.69	811.82	718.99	646.85	589.19
2.75%	5,286.24	2,679.42	1,810.70	1,376.50	1,116.11	942.63	818.81	726.02	653.93	596.32
3.00%	5,293.36	2,686.33	1,817.58	1,383.40	1,123.04	949.60	825.83	733.10	661.06	603.50
3.25%	5,300.48	2,693.24	1,824.47	1,390.31	1,130.00	956.61	832.89	740.22	668.24	610.74
3.50%	5,307.60	2,700.17	1,831.38	1,397.25	1,136.98	963.65	839.99	747.38	675.46	618.04
3.75%	5,314.73	2,707.11	1,838.31	1,404.21	1,143.99	970.72	847.13	754.58	682.74	625.38
4.00%	5,321.87	2,714.06	1,845.25	1,411.19	1,151.03	977.82	854.30	761.83	690.06	632.78
4.25%	5,329.01	2,721.02	1,852.21	1,418.19	1,158.10	984.96	861.51	769.12	697.43	640.23
4.50%	5,336.16	2,727.99	1,859.18	1,425.22	1,165.19	992.13	868.76	776.45	704.85	647.74
4.75%	5,343.31	2,734.97	1,866.17	1,432.26	1,172.31	999.33	876.05	783.83	712.32	655.30
5.00%	5,350.47	2,741.96	1,873.18	1,439.33	1,179.45	1,006.56	883.37	791.25	719.83	662.91
5.25%	5,357.63	2,748.96	1,880.20	1,446.42	1,186.62	1,013.82	890.73	798.71	727.39	670.57
5.50%	5,364.80	2,755.98	1,887.24	1,453.53	1,193.82	1,021.12	898.13	806.21	735.00	678.29
5.75%	5,371.97	2,763.00	1,894.30	1,460.66	1,201.05	1,028.45	905.56	813.75	742.66	686.06
6.00%	5,379.15	2,770.04	1,901.37	1,467.81	1,208.30	1,035.81	913.03	821.34	750.36	693.88
6.25%	5,386.34	2,777.08	1,908.46	1,474.99	1,215.58	1,043.20	920.54	828.97	758.11	701.75
6.50%	5,393.53	2,784.14	1,915.56	1,482.18	1,222.88	1,050.62	928.09	836.64	765.91	709.67
6.75%	5,400.72	2,791.21	1,922.68	1,489.40	1,230.22	1,058.08	935.67	844.35	773.75	717.65
7.00%	5,407.92	2,798.29	1,929.82	1,496.64	1,237.57	1,065.56	943.29	852.11	781.64	725.68
7.25%	5,415.13	2,805.38	1,936.97	1,503.90	1,244.96	1,073.08	950.95	859.90	789.58	733.76
7.50%	5,422.34	2,812.47	1,944.14	1,511.18	1,252.37	1,080.63	958.64	867.74	797.56	741.89
7.75%	5,429.56	2,819.58	1,951.32	1,518.48	1,259.81	1,088.21	966.37	875.62	805.59	750.07
8.00%	5,436.78	2,826.71	1,958.52	1,525.81	1,267.27	1,095.83	974.14	883.54	813.67	758.30
8.25%	5,444.00	2,833.84	1,965.74	1,533.15	1,274.77	1,103.47	981.94	891.50	821.79	766.58
8.50%	5,451.24	2,840.98	1,972.97	1,540.52	1,282.28	1,111.15	989.78	899.51	829.96	774.91
8.75%	5,458.47	2,848.13	1,980.22	1,547.91	1,289.83	1,118.86	997.66	907.55	838.17	783.29
9.00%	5,465.72	2,855.30	1,987.48	1,555.32	1,297.40	1,126.60	1,005.57	915.64	846.43	791.72
9.25%	5,472.97	2,862.47	1,994.76	1,562.75	1,304.99	1,134.37	1,013.52	923.76	854.74	800.20
9.50%	5,480.22	2,869.66	2,002.06	1,570.20	1,312.62	1,142.17	1,021.50	931.93	863.09	808.73
9.75%	5,487.48	2,876.85	2,009.37	1,577.67	1,320.27	1,150.00	1,029.52	940.14	871.48	817.31
10.00%	5,494.74	2,884.06	2,016.70	1,585.16	1,327.94	1,157.86	1,037.57	948.39	879.92	825.94
10.25%	5,502.01	2,891.27	2,024.04	1,592.68	1,335.64	1,165.76	1,045.67	956.67	888.40	834.62
10.50%	5,509.29	2,898.50	2,031.40	1,600.21	1,343.37	1,173.69	1,053.79	965.00	896.93	843.34
10.75%	5,516.57	2,905.74	2,038.78	1,607.77	1,351.12	1,181.64	1,061.95	973.37	905.50	852.12

$62,500   11.00 - 20.75%   1 - 10 Years

	1	2	3	4	5	6	7	8	9	10
11.00%	5,523.85	2,912.99	2,046.17	1,615.35	1,358.90	1,189.63	1,070.15	981.78	914.12	860.94
11.25%	5,531.14	2,920.25	2,053.58	1,622.94	1,366.71	1,197.65	1,078.39	990.22	922.78	869.81
11.50%	5,538.44	2,927.52	2,061.00	1,630.56	1,374.54	1,205.70	1,086.65	998.71	931.48	878.72
11.75%	5,545.74	2,934.80	2,068.44	1,638.20	1,382.40	1,213.78	1,094.96	1,007.24	940.23	887.68
12.00%	5,553.05	2,942.09	2,075.89	1,645.86	1,390.28	1,221.89	1,103.30	1,015.80	949.01	896.69
12.25%	5,560.36	2,949.39	2,083.37	1,653.55	1,398.19	1,230.03	1,111.67	1,024.41	957.85	905.75
12.50%	5,567.68	2,956.71	2,090.85	1,661.25	1,406.12	1,238.20	1,120.08	1,033.05	966.72	914.85
12.75%	5,575.00	2,964.03	2,098.35	1,668.97	1,414.08	1,246.40	1,128.52	1,041.73	975.64	924.00
13.00%	5,582.33	2,971.36	2,105.87	1,676.72	1,422.07	1,254.63	1,137.00	1,050.45	984.60	933.19
13.25%	5,589.66	2,978.71	2,113.41	1,684.48	1,430.08	1,262.89	1,145.51	1,059.21	993.60	942.43
13.50%	5,597.00	2,986.06	2,120.96	1,692.27	1,438.12	1,271.19	1,154.06	1,068.01	1,002.64	951.71
13.75%	5,604.35	2,993.43	2,128.52	1,700.08	1,446.18	1,279.51	1,162.64	1,076.85	1,011.73	961.04
14.00%	5,611.69	3,000.81	2,136.10	1,707.90	1,454.27	1,287.86	1,171.25	1,085.72	1,020.86	970.42
14.25%	5,619.05	3,008.19	2,143.70	1,715.75	1,462.38	1,296.24	1,179.90	1,094.63	1,030.02	979.83
14.50%	5,626.41	3,015.59	2,151.31	1,723.62	1,470.52	1,304.65	1,188.58	1,103.58	1,039.23	989.29
14.75%	5,633.77	3,023.00	2,158.94	1,731.51	1,478.68	1,313.09	1,197.30	1,112.56	1,048.48	998.80
15.00%	5,641.14	3,030.42	2,166.58	1,739.42	1,486.87	1,321.56	1,206.05	1,121.59	1,057.77	1,008.34
15.25%	5,648.52	3,037.84	2,174.24	1,747.35	1,495.08	1,330.06	1,214.83	1,130.65	1,067.10	1,017.93
15.50%	5,655.90	3,045.28	2,181.92	1,755.30	1,503.32	1,338.59	1,223.65	1,139.75	1,076.47	1,027.57
15.75%	5,663.29	3,052.73	2,189.61	1,763.28	1,511.59	1,347.15	1,232.50	1,148.88	1,085.88	1,037.24
16.00%	5,670.68	3,060.19	2,197.31	1,771.27	1,519.88	1,355.74	1,241.38	1,158.05	1,095.33	1,046.96
16.25%	5,678.08	3,067.67	2,205.04	1,779.28	1,528.19	1,364.36	1,250.29	1,167.26	1,104.82	1,056.72
16.50%	5,685.48	3,075.15	2,212.77	1,787.31	1,536.53	1,373.00	1,259.24	1,176.50	1,114.34	1,066.51
16.75%	5,692.88	3,082.64	2,220.53	1,795.37	1,544.90	1,381.68	1,268.22	1,185.78	1,123.91	1,076.35
17.00%	5,700.30	3,090.14	2,228.30	1,803.44	1,553.29	1,390.38	1,277.24	1,195.09	1,133.51	1,086.24
17.25%	5,707.71	3,097.65	2,236.08	1,811.53	1,561.70	1,399.12	1,286.28	1,204.44	1,143.15	1,096.16
17.50%	5,715.14	3,105.18	2,243.88	1,819.65	1,570.14	1,407.88	1,295.36	1,213.83	1,152.83	1,106.12
17.75%	5,722.57	3,112.71	2,251.69	1,827.78	1,578.60	1,416.67	1,304.47	1,223.25	1,162.55	1,116.12
18.00%	5,730.00	3,120.26	2,259.52	1,835.94	1,587.09	1,425.49	1,313.61	1,232.70	1,172.31	1,126.16
18.25%	5,737.44	3,127.81	2,267.37	1,844.11	1,595.60	1,434.33	1,322.79	1,242.19	1,182.10	1,136.24
18.50%	5,744.88	3,135.38	2,275.23	1,852.31	1,604.14	1,443.21	1,331.99	1,251.72	1,191.93	1,146.35
18.75%	5,752.33	3,142.95	2,283.11	1,860.52	1,612.70	1,452.11	1,341.23	1,261.27	1,201.79	1,156.51
19.00%	5,759.79	3,150.54	2,291.00	1,868.76	1,621.28	1,461.05	1,350.50	1,270.87	1,211.69	1,166.70
19.25%	5,767.25	3,158.14	2,298.91	1,877.01	1,629.89	1,470.01	1,359.80	1,280.49	1,221.63	1,176.93
19.50%	5,774.71	3,165.74	2,306.83	1,885.29	1,638.53	1,478.99	1,369.13	1,290.15	1,231.60	1,187.20
19.75%	5,782.18	3,173.36	2,314.77	1,893.58	1,647.19	1,488.01	1,378.49	1,299.85	1,241.61	1,197.51
20.00%	5,789.66	3,180.99	2,322.72	1,901.90	1,655.87	1,497.05	1,387.89	1,309.58	1,251.66	1,207.85
20.25%	5,797.14	3,188.63	2,330.69	1,910.23	1,664.57	1,506.12	1,397.31	1,319.34	1,261.74	1,218.23
20.50%	5,804.62	3,196.27	2,338.68	1,918.59	1,673.30	1,515.22	1,406.77	1,329.13	1,271.85	1,228.64
20.75%	5,812.11	3,203.93	2,346.68	1,926.96	1,682.06	1,524.35	1,416.25	1,338.95	1,282.00	1,239.09

	1	2	3	4	5	6	7	8	9	10
1.00%	5,446.05	2,736.64	1,833.53	1,381.99	1,111.09	930.51	801.53	704.81	629.59	569.43
1.25%	5,453.41	2,743.74	1,840.56	1,389.01	1,118.10	937.52	808.56	711.85	636.65	576.51
1.50%	5,460.78	2,750.85	1,847.61	1,396.04	1,125.14	944.58	815.63	718.94	643.77	583.64
1.75%	5,468.15	2,757.98	1,854.68	1,403.10	1,132.21	951.66	822.74	726.08	650.93	590.84
2.00%	5,475.53	2,765.12	1,861.77	1,410.18	1,139.30	958.78	829.88	733.26	658.14	598.09
2.25%	5,482.91	2,772.27	1,868.87	1,417.29	1,146.43	965.93	837.07	740.48	665.41	605.39
2.50%	5,490.30	2,779.43	1,875.99	1,424.41	1,153.58	973.12	844.30	747.75	672.72	612.75
2.75%	5,497.69	2,786.60	1,883.13	1,431.56	1,160.76	980.34	851.56	755.06	680.09	620.17
3.00%	5,505.09	2,793.78	1,890.28	1,438.73	1,167.96	987.59	858.86	762.42	687.50	627.64
3.25%	5,512.50	2,800.97	1,897.45	1,445.92	1,175.20	994.88	866.21	769.83	694.97	635.17
3.50%	5,519.91	2,808.18	1,904.64	1,453.14	1,182.46	1,002.20	873.59	777.27	702.48	642.76
3.75%	5,527.32	2,815.39	1,911.84	1,460.38	1,189.75	1,009.55	881.01	784.77	710.05	650.40
4.00%	5,534.74	2,822.62	1,919.06	1,467.64	1,197.07	1,016.94	888.47	792.30	717.66	658.09
4.25%	5,542.17	2,829.86	1,926.30	1,474.92	1,204.42	1,024.36	895.97	799.88	725.33	665.84
4.50%	5,549.60	2,837.11	1,933.55	1,482.23	1,211.80	1,031.81	903.51	807.51	733.04	673.65
4.75%	5,557.04	2,844.37	1,940.82	1,489.55	1,219.20	1,039.30	911.09	815.18	740.81	681.51
5.00%	5,564.49	2,851.64	1,948.11	1,496.90	1,226.63	1,046.82	918.70	822.89	748.62	689.43
5.25%	5,571.94	2,858.92	1,955.41	1,504.28	1,234.09	1,054.37	926.36	830.65	756.49	697.40
5.50%	5,579.39	2,866.22	1,962.73	1,511.67	1,241.58	1,061.96	934.05	838.46	764.40	705.42
5.75%	5,586.85	2,873.52	1,970.07	1,519.09	1,249.09	1,069.58	941.79	846.30	772.36	713.50
6.00%	5,594.32	2,880.84	1,977.43	1,526.53	1,256.63	1,077.24	949.56	854.19	780.37	721.63
6.25%	5,601.79	2,888.17	1,984.80	1,533.99	1,264.20	1,084.93	957.37	862.13	788.43	729.82
6.50%	5,609.27	2,895.51	1,992.19	1,541.47	1,271.80	1,092.65	965.21	870.11	796.54	738.06
6.75%	5,616.75	2,902.86	1,999.59	1,548.98	1,279.42	1,100.40	973.10	878.13	804.70	746.36
7.00%	5,624.24	2,910.22	2,007.01	1,556.51	1,287.08	1,108.19	981.02	886.19	812.91	754.71
7.25%	5,631.73	2,917.59	2,014.45	1,564.06	1,294.76	1,116.00	988.99	894.30	821.16	763.11
7.50%	5,639.23	2,924.97	2,021.90	1,571.63	1,302.47	1,123.86	996.99	902.45	829.47	771.56
7.75%	5,646.74	2,932.37	2,029.38	1,579.22	1,310.20	1,131.74	1,005.03	910.65	837.82	780.07
8.00%	5,654.25	2,939.77	2,036.86	1,586.84	1,317.97	1,139.66	1,013.10	918.88	846.22	788.63
8.25%	5,661.76	2,947.19	2,044.37	1,594.48	1,325.76	1,147.61	1,021.22	927.16	854.66	797.24
8.50%	5,669.29	2,954.62	2,051.89	1,602.14	1,333.57	1,155.59	1,029.37	935.49	863.16	805.91
8.75%	5,676.81	2,962.06	2,059.43	1,609.82	1,341.42	1,163.61	1,037.56	943.85	871.70	814.62
9.00%	5,684.35	2,969.51	2,066.98	1,617.53	1,349.29	1,171.66	1,045.79	952.26	880.29	823.39
9.25%	5,691.88	2,976.97	2,074.55	1,625.25	1,357.19	1,179.74	1,054.06	960.71	888.93	832.21
9.50%	5,699.43	2,984.44	2,082.14	1,633.00	1,365.12	1,187.85	1,062.36	969.21	897.61	841.08
9.75%	5,706.98	2,991.93	2,089.75	1,640.77	1,373.08	1,196.00	1,070.70	977.74	906.34	850.01
10.00%	5,714.53	2,999.42	2,097.37	1,648.57	1,381.06	1,204.18	1,079.08	986.32	915.11	858.98
10.25%	5,722.09	3,006.93	2,105.00	1,656.38	1,389.07	1,212.39	1,087.49	994.94	923.94	868.00
10.50%	5,729.66	3,014.44	2,112.66	1,664.22	1,397.10	1,220.63	1,095.94	1,003.60	932.81	877.08
10.75%	5,737.23	3,021.97	2,120.33	1,672.08	1,405.17	1,228.91	1,104.43	1,012.30	941.72	886.20

$65,000   11.00 - 20.75%   1 - 10 Years

	1	2	3	4	5	6	7	8	9	10
11.00%	5,744.81	3,029.51	2,128.02	1,679.96	1,413.26	1,237.22	1,112.96	1,021.05	950.68	895.38
11.25%	5,752.39	3,037.06	2,135.72	1,687.86	1,421.38	1,245.55	1,121.52	1,029.83	959.69	904.60
11.50%	5,759.98	3,044.62	2,143.44	1,695.79	1,429.52	1,253.93	1,130.12	1,038.66	968.74	913.87
11.75%	5,767.57	3,052.19	2,151.18	1,703.73	1,437.69	1,262.33	1,138.76	1,047.53	977.83	923.19
12.00%	5,775.17	3,059.78	2,158.93	1,711.70	1,445.89	1,270.76	1,147.43	1,056.43	986.98	932.56
12.25%	5,782.78	3,067.37	2,166.70	1,719.69	1,454.11	1,279.23	1,156.14	1,065.38	996.16	941.98
12.50%	5,790.39	3,074.98	2,174.49	1,727.70	1,462.37	1,287.73	1,164.88	1,074.37	1,005.39	951.45
12.75%	5,798.00	3,082.59	2,182.29	1,735.73	1,470.64	1,296.26	1,173.66	1,083.40	1,014.67	960.96
13.00%	5,805.62	3,090.22	2,190.11	1,743.79	1,478.95	1,304.82	1,182.48	1,092.47	1,023.98	970.52
13.25%	5,813.25	3,097.86	2,197.94	1,751.86	1,487.28	1,313.41	1,191.33	1,101.58	1,033.35	980.13
13.50%	5,820.88	3,105.51	2,205.79	1,759.96	1,495.64	1,322.03	1,200.22	1,110.73	1,042.75	989.78
13.75%	5,828.52	3,113.17	2,213.66	1,768.08	1,504.02	1,330.69	1,209.14	1,119.92	1,052.20	999.48
14.00%	5,836.16	3,120.84	2,221.55	1,776.22	1,512.44	1,339.37	1,218.10	1,129.15	1,061.69	1,009.23
14.25%	5,843.81	3,128.52	2,229.45	1,784.38	1,520.87	1,348.09	1,227.10	1,138.42	1,071.22	1,019.03
14.50%	5,851.47	3,136.21	2,237.36	1,792.57	1,529.34	1,356.84	1,236.12	1,147.72	1,080.80	1,028.86
14.75%	5,859.13	3,143.92	2,245.30	1,800.77	1,537.83	1,365.62	1,245.19	1,157.07	1,090.42	1,038.75
15.00%	5,866.79	3,151.63	2,253.25	1,809.00	1,546.35	1,374.43	1,254.29	1,166.45	1,100.08	1,048.68
15.25%	5,874.46	3,159.36	2,261.21	1,817.25	1,554.89	1,383.27	1,263.42	1,175.87	1,109.78	1,058.65
15.50%	5,882.14	3,167.10	2,269.19	1,825.52	1,563.46	1,392.14	1,272.59	1,185.33	1,119.53	1,068.67
15.75%	5,889.82	3,174.84	2,277.19	1,833.81	1,572.05	1,401.04	1,281.80	1,194.83	1,129.31	1,078.73
16.00%	5,897.51	3,182.60	2,285.21	1,842.12	1,580.67	1,409.97	1,291.03	1,204.37	1,139.14	1,088.84
16.25%	5,905.20	3,190.37	2,293.24	1,850.45	1,589.32	1,418.93	1,300.31	1,213.95	1,149.01	1,098.98
16.50%	5,912.90	3,198.15	2,301.28	1,858.81	1,597.99	1,427.92	1,309.61	1,223.56	1,158.92	1,109.17
16.75%	5,920.60	3,205.94	2,309.35	1,867.18	1,606.69	1,436.95	1,318.95	1,233.21	1,168.86	1,119.41
17.00%	5,928.31	3,213.75	2,317.43	1,875.58	1,615.42	1,446.00	1,328.33	1,242.89	1,178.85	1,129.68
17.25%	5,936.02	3,221.56	2,325.52	1,884.00	1,624.17	1,455.08	1,337.74	1,252.62	1,188.88	1,140.00
17.50%	5,943.74	3,229.39	2,333.63	1,892.43	1,632.94	1,464.19	1,347.18	1,262.38	1,198.95	1,150.36
17.75%	5,951.47	3,237.22	2,341.76	1,900.89	1,641.75	1,473.33	1,356.65	1,272.18	1,209.05	1,160.76
18.00%	5,959.20	3,245.07	2,349.91	1,909.37	1,650.57	1,482.51	1,366.16	1,282.01	1,219.20	1,171.20
18.25%	5,966.94	3,252.92	2,358.07	1,917.88	1,659.43	1,491.71	1,375.70	1,291.88	1,229.38	1,181.69
18.50%	5,974.68	3,260.79	2,366.24	1,926.40	1,668.30	1,500.94	1,385.27	1,301.78	1,239.60	1,192.21
18.75%	5,982.42	3,268.67	2,374.43	1,934.94	1,677.21	1,510.20	1,394.88	1,311.72	1,249.86	1,202.77
19.00%	5,990.18	3,276.56	2,382.64	1,943.51	1,686.14	1,519.49	1,404.52	1,321.70	1,260.16	1,213.37
19.25%	5,997.94	3,284.46	2,390.87	1,952.09	1,695.09	1,528.81	1,414.19	1,331.71	1,270.50	1,224.01
19.50%	6,005.70	3,292.37	2,399.11	1,960.70	1,704.07	1,538.15	1,423.90	1,341.76	1,280.87	1,234.69
19.75%	6,013.47	3,300.29	2,407.36	1,969.33	1,713.07	1,547.53	1,433.63	1,351.84	1,291.28	1,245.41
20.00%	6,021.24	3,308.23	2,415.63	1,977.97	1,722.10	1,556.93	1,443.40	1,361.96	1,301.72	1,256.16
20.25%	6,029.02	3,316.17	2,423.92	1,986.64	1,731.16	1,566.37	1,453.20	1,372.11	1,312.20	1,266.95
20.50%	6,036.81	3,324.13	2,432.22	1,995.33	1,740.24	1,575.83	1,463.04	1,382.29	1,322.72	1,277.78
20.75%	6,044.60	3,332.09	2,440.54	2,004.04	1,749.34	1,585.32	1,472.90	1,392.51	1,333.28	1,288.65

	1	2	3	4	5	6	7	8	9	10
1.00%	5,655.52	2,841.89	1,904.05	1,435.15	1,153.83	966.30	832.36	731.92	653.81	591.33
1.25%	5,663.16	2,849.27	1,911.35	1,442.43	1,161.11	973.58	839.66	739.23	661.14	598.68
1.50%	5,670.81	2,856.66	1,918.68	1,449.74	1,168.42	980.91	847.00	746.59	668.53	606.09
1.75%	5,678.46	2,864.06	1,926.02	1,457.07	1,175.76	988.26	854.38	754.00	675.96	613.56
2.00%	5,686.12	2,871.47	1,933.37	1,464.42	1,183.12	995.65	861.80	761.46	683.46	621.09
2.25%	5,693.79	2,878.89	1,940.75	1,471.80	1,190.52	1,003.08	869.26	768.96	691.00	628.68
2.50%	5,701.46	2,886.33	1,948.14	1,479.20	1,197.95	1,010.54	876.77	776.51	698.60	636.32
2.75%	5,709.14	2,893.77	1,955.55	1,486.62	1,205.40	1,018.04	884.31	784.10	706.24	644.02
3.00%	5,716.82	2,901.23	1,962.98	1,494.07	1,212.89	1,025.57	891.90	791.75	713.94	651.79
3.25%	5,724.51	2,908.70	1,970.43	1,501.54	1,220.40	1,033.14	899.52	799.43	721.70	659.60
3.50%	5,732.21	2,916.18	1,977.89	1,509.03	1,227.94	1,040.74	907.19	807.17	729.50	667.48
3.75%	5,739.91	2,923.68	1,985.37	1,516.55	1,235.51	1,048.38	914.90	814.95	737.36	675.41
4.00%	5,747.62	2,931.18	1,992.87	1,524.09	1,243.12	1,056.05	922.64	822.78	745.27	683.40
4.25%	5,755.33	2,938.70	2,000.38	1,531.65	1,250.75	1,063.76	930.43	830.65	753.23	691.45
4.50%	5,763.05	2,946.23	2,007.92	1,539.24	1,258.40	1,071.50	938.26	838.57	761.24	699.56
4.75%	5,770.77	2,953.77	2,015.47	1,546.84	1,266.09	1,079.27	946.13	846.53	769.30	707.72
5.00%	5,778.51	2,961.32	2,023.04	1,554.48	1,273.81	1,087.08	954.04	854.54	777.42	715.94
5.25%	5,786.24	2,968.88	2,030.62	1,562.13	1,281.55	1,094.93	961.99	862.60	785.58	724.22
5.50%	5,793.98	2,976.46	2,038.22	1,569.81	1,289.33	1,102.81	969.98	870.70	793.80	732.55
5.75%	5,801.73	2,984.04	2,045.84	1,577.51	1,297.13	1,110.72	978.01	878.85	802.07	740.94
6.00%	5,809.48	2,991.64	2,053.48	1,585.24	1,304.96	1,118.67	986.08	887.05	810.39	749.39
6.25%	5,817.24	2,999.25	2,061.14	1,592.99	1,312.83	1,126.65	994.19	895.29	818.76	757.89
6.50%	5,825.01	3,006.87	2,068.81	1,600.76	1,320.72	1,134.67	1,002.34	903.57	827.18	766.45
6.75%	5,832.78	3,014.50	2,076.50	1,608.55	1,328.63	1,142.72	1,010.53	911.90	835.65	775.06
7.00%	5,840.56	3,022.15	2,084.20	1,616.37	1,336.58	1,150.81	1,018.76	920.28	844.17	783.73
7.25%	5,848.34	3,029.81	2,091.93	1,624.21	1,344.56	1,158.93	1,027.02	928.70	852.75	792.46
7.50%	5,856.13	3,037.47	2,099.67	1,632.08	1,352.56	1,167.08	1,035.33	937.16	861.37	801.24
7.75%	5,863.92	3,045.15	2,107.43	1,639.96	1,360.59	1,175.27	1,043.68	945.67	870.04	810.07
8.00%	5,871.72	3,052.84	2,115.20	1,647.87	1,368.66	1,183.49	1,052.07	954.23	878.76	818.96
8.25%	5,879.52	3,060.54	2,123.00	1,655.80	1,376.75	1,191.75	1,060.50	962.83	887.54	827.91
8.50%	5,887.34	3,068.26	2,130.81	1,663.76	1,384.87	1,200.04	1,068.96	971.47	896.36	836.90
8.75%	5,895.15	3,075.98	2,138.64	1,671.74	1,393.01	1,208.37	1,077.47	980.16	905.23	845.96
9.00%	5,902.97	3,083.72	2,146.48	1,679.74	1,401.19	1,216.72	1,086.01	988.89	914.15	855.06
9.25%	5,910.80	3,091.47	2,154.34	1,687.76	1,409.39	1,225.12	1,094.60	997.66	923.11	864.22
9.50%	5,918.64	3,099.23	2,162.22	1,695.81	1,417.63	1,233.54	1,103.22	1,006.48	932.13	873.43
9.75%	5,926.48	3,107.00	2,170.12	1,703.88	1,425.89	1,242.00	1,111.88	1,015.35	941.20	882.70
10.00%	5,934.32	3,114.78	2,178.04	1,711.97	1,434.18	1,250.49	1,120.58	1,024.26	950.31	892.02
10.25%	5,942.17	3,122.58	2,185.97	1,720.09	1,442.49	1,259.02	1,129.32	1,033.21	959.47	901.39
10.50%	5,950.03	3,130.38	2,193.91	1,728.23	1,450.84	1,267.58	1,138.10	1,042.20	968.68	910.81
10.75%	5,957.89	3,138.20	2,201.88	1,736.39	1,459.21	1,276.17	1,146.91	1,051.24	977.94	920.29

	1	2	3	4	5	6	7	8	9	10
11.00%	5,965.76	3,146.03	2,209.86	1,744.57	1,467.61	1,284.80	1,155.76	1,060.32	987.25	929.81
11.25%	5,973.64	3,153.87	2,217.86	1,752.78	1,476.04	1,293.46	1,164.66	1,069.44	996.60	939.39
11.50%	5,981.52	3,161.72	2,225.88	1,761.01	1,484.50	1,302.15	1,173.59	1,078.61	1,006.00	949.02
11.75%	5,989.40	3,169.58	2,233.91	1,769.26	1,492.99	1,310.88	1,182.55	1,087.82	1,015.44	958.70
12.00%	5,997.29	3,177.46	2,241.97	1,777.53	1,501.50	1,319.64	1,191.56	1,097.07	1,024.94	968.43
12.25%	6,005.19	3,185.35	2,250.03	1,785.83	1,510.04	1,328.43	1,200.60	1,106.36	1,034.47	978.21
12.50%	6,013.09	3,193.24	2,258.12	1,794.15	1,518.61	1,337.25	1,209.68	1,115.69	1,044.06	988.04
12.75%	6,021.00	3,201.15	2,266.22	1,802.49	1,527.21	1,346.11	1,218.80	1,125.07	1,053.69	997.92
13.00%	6,028.92	3,209.07	2,274.34	1,810.86	1,535.83	1,355.00	1,227.96	1,134.49	1,063.37	1,007.85
13.25%	6,036.84	3,217.01	2,282.48	1,819.24	1,544.48	1,363.92	1,237.15	1,143.95	1,073.09	1,017.83
13.50%	6,044.76	3,224.95	2,290.63	1,827.65	1,553.16	1,372.88	1,246.38	1,153.45	1,082.86	1,027.85
13.75%	6,052.69	3,232.90	2,298.80	1,836.08	1,561.87	1,381.87	1,255.65	1,162.99	1,092.67	1,037.93
14.00%	6,060.63	3,240.87	2,306.99	1,844.54	1,570.61	1,390.89	1,264.95	1,172.58	1,102.52	1,048.05
14.25%	6,068.57	3,248.85	2,315.19	1,853.01	1,579.37	1,399.94	1,274.29	1,182.20	1,112.43	1,058.22
14.50%	6,076.52	3,256.84	2,323.42	1,861.51	1,588.16	1,409.02	1,283.67	1,191.86	1,122.37	1,068.44
14.75%	6,084.48	3,264.84	2,331.65	1,870.03	1,596.98	1,418.14	1,293.08	1,201.57	1,132.36	1,078.70
15.00%	6,092.44	3,272.85	2,339.91	1,878.58	1,605.82	1,427.29	1,302.53	1,211.31	1,142.39	1,089.01
15.25%	6,100.40	3,280.87	2,348.18	1,887.14	1,614.69	1,436.47	1,312.02	1,221.10	1,152.47	1,099.37
15.50%	6,108.37	3,288.91	2,356.47	1,895.73	1,623.59	1,445.68	1,321.54	1,230.92	1,162.59	1,109.77
15.75%	6,116.35	3,296.95	2,364.78	1,904.34	1,632.52	1,454.92	1,331.10	1,240.79	1,172.75	1,120.22
16.00%	6,124.33	3,305.01	2,373.10	1,912.97	1,641.47	1,464.20	1,340.69	1,250.69	1,182.95	1,130.71
16.25%	6,132.32	3,313.08	2,381.44	1,921.62	1,650.45	1,473.51	1,350.32	1,260.64	1,193.20	1,141.25
16.50%	6,140.32	3,321.16	2,389.80	1,930.30	1,659.46	1,482.84	1,359.98	1,270.62	1,203.49	1,151.84
16.75%	6,148.32	3,329.25	2,398.17	1,939.00	1,668.49	1,492.21	1,369.68	1,280.64	1,213.82	1,162.46
17.00%	6,156.32	3,337.35	2,406.56	1,947.72	1,677.55	1,501.61	1,379.42	1,290.70	1,224.19	1,173.13
17.25%	6,164.33	3,345.47	2,414.97	1,956.46	1,686.64	1,511.05	1,389.19	1,300.80	1,234.61	1,183.85
17.50%	6,172.35	3,353.59	2,423.39	1,965.22	1,695.75	1,520.51	1,398.99	1,310.93	1,245.06	1,194.61
17.75%	6,180.37	3,361.73	2,431.83	1,974.01	1,704.89	1,530.00	1,408.83	1,321.11	1,255.55	1,205.41
18.00%	6,188.40	3,369.88	2,440.29	1,982.81	1,714.06	1,539.53	1,418.70	1,331.32	1,266.09	1,216.25
18.25%	6,196.43	3,378.04	2,448.76	1,991.64	1,723.25	1,549.08	1,428.61	1,341.57	1,276.67	1,227.14
18.50%	6,204.47	3,386.21	2,457.25	2,000.49	1,732.47	1,558.67	1,438.55	1,351.85	1,287.28	1,238.06
18.75%	6,212.52	3,394.39	2,465.76	2,009.36	1,741.72	1,568.28	1,448.53	1,362.18	1,297.93	1,249.03
19.00%	6,220.57	3,402.58	2,474.28	2,018.26	1,750.99	1,577.93	1,458.54	1,372.54	1,308.63	1,260.04
19.25%	6,228.63	3,410.79	2,482.82	2,027.17	1,760.29	1,587.61	1,468.59	1,382.93	1,319.36	1,271.09
19.50%	6,236.69	3,419.00	2,491.38	2,036.11	1,769.61	1,597.31	1,478.66	1,393.37	1,330.13	1,282.18
19.75%	6,244.76	3,427.23	2,499.95	2,045.07	1,778.96	1,607.05	1,488.77	1,403.84	1,340.94	1,293.31
20.00%	6,252.83	3,435.47	2,508.54	2,054.05	1,788.34	1,616.82	1,498.92	1,414.34	1,351.79	1,304.48
20.25%	6,260.91	3,443.72	2,517.15	2,063.05	1,797.74	1,626.61	1,509.10	1,424.88	1,362.67	1,315.68
20.50%	6,268.99	3,451.98	2,525.77	2,072.07	1,807.17	1,636.44	1,519.31	1,435.46	1,373.60	1,326.93
20.75%	6,277.08	3,460.25	2,534.41	2,081.12	1,816.62	1,646.29	1,529.55	1,446.07	1,384.56	1,338.22

	1	2	3	4	5	6	7	8	9	10
1.00%	5,864.98	2,947.15	1,974.57	1,488.30	1,196.56	1,002.09	863.19	759.03	678.02	613.23
1.25%	5,872.91	2,954.80	1,982.14	1,495.85	1,204.11	1,009.64	870.76	766.61	685.63	620.85
1.50%	5,880.84	2,962.46	1,989.74	1,503.43	1,211.69	1,017.24	878.37	774.25	693.29	628.54
1.75%	5,888.78	2,970.13	1,997.35	1,511.03	1,219.30	1,024.87	886.02	781.93	701.00	636.29
2.00%	5,896.72	2,977.82	2,004.98	1,518.66	1,226.94	1,032.53	893.72	789.66	708.77	644.09
2.25%	5,904.67	2,985.52	2,012.63	1,526.31	1,234.61	1,040.23	901.46	797.44	716.59	651.96
2.50%	5,912.63	2,993.23	2,020.30	1,533.98	1,242.32	1,047.97	909.24	805.27	724.47	659.89
2.75%	5,920.59	3,000.95	2,027.98	1,541.68	1,250.05	1,055.75	917.06	813.15	732.40	667.88
3.00%	5,928.56	3,008.68	2,035.68	1,549.40	1,257.81	1,063.56	924.93	821.07	740.39	675.93
3.25%	5,936.53	3,016.43	2,043.41	1,557.15	1,265.60	1,071.40	932.84	829.04	748.43	684.03
3.50%	5,944.51	3,024.19	2,051.15	1,564.92	1,273.42	1,079.29	940.79	837.06	756.52	692.20
3.75%	5,952.50	3,031.96	2,058.90	1,572.71	1,281.27	1,087.21	948.78	845.13	764.67	700.43
4.00%	5,960.49	3,039.74	2,066.68	1,580.53	1,289.16	1,095.16	956.82	853.25	772.87	708.72
4.25%	5,968.49	3,047.54	2,074.47	1,588.38	1,297.07	1,103.15	964.89	861.41	781.12	717.06
4.50%	5,976.50	3,055.35	2,082.28	1,596.24	1,305.01	1,111.18	973.01	869.63	789.43	725.47
4.75%	5,984.51	3,063.17	2,090.11	1,604.14	1,312.98	1,119.25	981.17	877.89	797.79	733.93
5.00%	5,992.52	3,071.00	2,097.96	1,612.05	1,320.99	1,127.35	989.37	886.19	806.21	742.46
5.25%	6,000.55	3,078.84	2,105.83	1,619.99	1,329.02	1,135.48	997.62	894.55	814.68	751.04
5.50%	6,008.57	3,086.70	2,113.71	1,627.95	1,337.08	1,143.65	1,005.90	902.95	823.20	759.68
5.75%	6,016.61	3,094.56	2,121.62	1,635.94	1,345.17	1,151.86	1,014.23	911.40	831.77	768.38
6.00%	6,024.65	3,102.44	2,129.54	1,643.95	1,353.30	1,160.10	1,022.60	919.90	840.40	777.14
6.25%	6,032.70	3,110.33	2,137.47	1,651.99	1,361.45	1,168.38	1,031.01	928.44	849.08	785.96
6.50%	6,040.75	3,118.24	2,145.43	1,660.05	1,369.63	1,176.70	1,039.46	937.04	857.82	794.84
6.75%	6,048.81	3,126.15	2,153.40	1,668.13	1,377.84	1,185.04	1,047.95	945.67	866.60	803.77
7.00%	6,056.87	3,134.08	2,161.40	1,676.24	1,386.08	1,193.43	1,056.49	954.36	875.44	812.76
7.25%	6,064.94	3,142.02	2,169.41	1,684.37	1,394.36	1,201.85	1,065.06	963.09	884.33	821.81
7.50%	6,073.02	3,149.97	2,177.44	1,692.52	1,402.66	1,210.31	1,073.68	971.87	893.27	830.91
7.75%	6,081.10	3,157.93	2,185.48	1,700.70	1,410.99	1,218.80	1,082.34	980.70	902.26	840.07
8.00%	6,089.19	3,165.91	2,193.55	1,708.90	1,419.35	1,227.33	1,091.04	989.57	911.31	849.29
8.25%	6,097.28	3,173.90	2,201.63	1,717.13	1,427.74	1,235.89	1,099.77	998.49	920.41	858.57
8.50%	6,105.38	3,181.90	2,209.73	1,725.38	1,436.16	1,244.49	1,108.55	1,007.45	929.55	867.90
8.75%	6,113.49	3,189.91	2,217.85	1,733.66	1,444.61	1,253.12	1,117.37	1,016.46	938.75	877.29
9.00%	6,121.60	3,197.93	2,225.98	1,741.95	1,453.08	1,261.79	1,126.24	1,025.51	948.00	886.73
9.25%	6,129.72	3,205.97	2,234.13	1,750.27	1,461.59	1,270.49	1,135.14	1,034.62	957.30	896.23
9.50%	6,137.85	3,214.01	2,242.31	1,758.62	1,470.13	1,279.23	1,144.08	1,043.76	966.66	905.78
9.75%	6,145.98	3,222.07	2,250.50	1,766.99	1,478.70	1,288.00	1,153.06	1,052.95	976.06	915.39
10.00%	6,154.11	3,230.14	2,258.70	1,775.38	1,487.29	1,296.81	1,162.08	1,062.19	985.51	925.06
10.25%	6,162.25	3,238.23	2,266.93	1,783.80	1,495.92	1,305.65	1,171.15	1,071.47	995.01	934.77
10.50%	6,170.40	3,246.32	2,275.17	1,792.24	1,504.57	1,314.53	1,180.25	1,080.80	1,004.56	944.54
10.75%	6,178.56	3,254.43	2,283.43	1,800.70	1,513.26	1,323.44	1,189.39	1,090.17	1,014.16	954.37

	1	2	3	4	5	6	7	8	9	10
11.00%	6,186.72	3,262.55	2,291.71	1,809.19	1,521.97	1,332.39	1,198.57	1,099.59	1,023.81	964.25
11.25%	6,194.88	3,270.68	2,300.01	1,817.70	1,530.71	1,341.37	1,207.79	1,109.05	1,033.51	974.18
11.50%	6,203.05	3,278.82	2,308.32	1,826.23	1,539.48	1,350.38	1,217.05	1,118.56	1,043.26	984.17
11.75%	6,211.23	3,286.98	2,316.65	1,834.79	1,548.28	1,359.43	1,226.35	1,128.11	1,053.05	994.21
12.00%	6,219.42	3,295.14	2,325.00	1,843.37	1,557.11	1,368.51	1,235.69	1,137.70	1,062.90	1,004.30
12.25%	6,227.60	3,303.32	2,333.37	1,851.97	1,565.97	1,377.63	1,245.07	1,147.34	1,072.79	1,014.44
12.50%	6,235.80	3,311.51	2,341.75	1,860.60	1,574.86	1,386.78	1,254.49	1,157.02	1,082.73	1,024.63
12.75%	6,244.00	3,319.71	2,350.16	1,869.25	1,583.77	1,395.97	1,263.94	1,166.74	1,092.72	1,034.88
13.00%	6,252.21	3,327.93	2,358.58	1,877.92	1,592.72	1,405.19	1,273.44	1,176.51	1,102.75	1,045.18
13.25%	6,260.42	3,336.15	2,367.01	1,886.62	1,601.69	1,414.44	1,282.97	1,186.32	1,112.83	1,055.52
13.50%	6,268.64	3,344.39	2,375.47	1,895.34	1,610.69	1,423.73	1,292.54	1,196.17	1,122.96	1,065.92
13.75%	6,276.87	3,352.64	2,383.94	1,904.09	1,619.72	1,433.05	1,302.15	1,206.07	1,133.14	1,076.37
14.00%	6,285.10	3,360.90	2,392.43	1,912.85	1,628.78	1,442.40	1,311.80	1,216.01	1,143.36	1,086.87
14.25%	6,293.34	3,369.17	2,400.94	1,921.64	1,637.86	1,451.79	1,321.49	1,225.99	1,153.63	1,097.41
14.50%	6,301.58	3,377.46	2,409.47	1,930.46	1,646.98	1,461.21	1,331.21	1,236.01	1,163.94	1,108.01
14.75%	6,309.83	3,385.76	2,418.01	1,939.29	1,656.12	1,470.66	1,340.97	1,246.07	1,174.30	1,118.65
15.00%	6,318.08	3,394.07	2,426.57	1,948.15	1,665.30	1,480.15	1,350.77	1,256.18	1,184.70	1,129.34
15.25%	6,326.34	3,402.39	2,435.15	1,957.03	1,674.50	1,489.67	1,360.61	1,266.33	1,195.15	1,140.09
15.50%	6,334.61	3,410.72	2,443.75	1,965.94	1,683.72	1,499.22	1,370.48	1,276.51	1,205.65	1,150.87
15.75%	6,342.88	3,419.06	2,452.36	1,974.87	1,692.98	1,508.81	1,380.40	1,286.74	1,216.19	1,161.71
16.00%	6,351.16	3,427.42	2,460.99	1,983.82	1,702.26	1,518.43	1,390.34	1,297.02	1,226.77	1,172.59
16.25%	6,359.44	3,435.79	2,469.64	1,992.79	1,711.58	1,528.08	1,400.33	1,307.33	1,237.39	1,183.52
16.50%	6,367.73	3,444.16	2,478.31	2,001.79	1,720.92	1,537.76	1,410.35	1,317.68	1,248.06	1,194.50
16.75%	6,376.03	3,452.56	2,486.99	2,010.81	1,730.28	1,547.48	1,420.41	1,328.07	1,258.78	1,205.52
17.00%	6,384.33	3,460.96	2,495.69	2,019.85	1,739.68	1,557.23	1,430.51	1,338.50	1,269.53	1,216.58
17.25%	6,392.64	3,469.37	2,504.41	2,028.92	1,749.10	1,567.01	1,440.64	1,348.97	1,280.33	1,227.70
17.50%	6,400.95	3,477.80	2,513.14	2,038.01	1,758.55	1,576.82	1,450.81	1,359.48	1,291.17	1,238.85
17.75%	6,409.27	3,486.24	2,521.90	2,047.12	1,768.03	1,586.67	1,461.01	1,370.04	1,302.06	1,250.05
18.00%	6,417.60	3,494.69	2,530.67	2,056.25	1,777.54	1,596.55	1,471.25	1,380.62	1,312.98	1,261.30
18.25%	6,425.93	3,503.15	2,539.46	2,065.41	1,787.07	1,606.45	1,481.52	1,391.25	1,323.95	1,272.58
18.50%	6,434.27	3,511.62	2,548.26	2,074.58	1,796.63	1,616.39	1,491.83	1,401.92	1,334.96	1,283.92
18.75%	6,442.61	3,520.11	2,557.08	2,083.78	1,806.22	1,626.37	1,502.18	1,412.63	1,346.01	1,295.29
19.00%	6,450.96	3,528.60	2,565.92	2,093.01	1,815.84	1,636.37	1,512.56	1,423.37	1,357.10	1,306.71
19.25%	6,459.32	3,537.11	2,574.78	2,102.25	1,825.48	1,646.41	1,522.98	1,434.15	1,368.23	1,318.17
19.50%	6,467.68	3,545.63	2,583.65	2,111.52	1,835.15	1,656.47	1,533.43	1,444.97	1,379.40	1,329.67
19.75%	6,476.04	3,554.16	2,592.54	2,120.81	1,844.85	1,666.57	1,543.91	1,455.83	1,390.61	1,341.21
20.00%	6,484.42	3,562.71	2,601.45	2,130.13	1,854.57	1,676.70	1,554.43	1,466.72	1,401.86	1,352.79
20.25%	6,492.79	3,571.26	2,610.38	2,139.46	1,864.32	1,686.86	1,564.99	1,477.66	1,413.14	1,364.41
20.50%	6,501.18	3,579.83	2,619.32	2,148.82	1,874.10	1,697.05	1,575.58	1,488.62	1,424.47	1,376.08
20.75%	6,509.57	3,588.41	2,628.28	2,158.20	1,883.90	1,707.27	1,586.20	1,499.63	1,435.84	1,387.78

	1	2	3	4	5	6	7	8	9	10
1.00%	6,074.44	3,052.40	2,045.09	1,541.46	1,239.30	1,037.87	894.02	786.13	702.24	635.13
1.25%	6,082.65	3,060.32	2,052.93	1,549.28	1,247.12	1,045.70	901.86	793.99	710.11	643.03
1.50%	6,090.87	3,068.26	2,060.80	1,557.13	1,254.97	1,053.57	909.74	801.90	718.05	650.99
1.75%	6,099.09	3,076.21	2,068.68	1,565.00	1,262.85	1,061.47	917.67	809.86	726.04	659.01
2.00%	6,107.32	3,084.17	2,076.59	1,572.90	1,270.76	1,069.41	925.64	817.86	734.08	667.10
2.25%	6,115.55	3,092.14	2,084.51	1,580.82	1,278.71	1,077.38	933.65	825.92	742.18	675.25
2.50%	6,123.79	3,100.13	2,092.45	1,588.77	1,286.68	1,085.40	941.71	834.03	750.34	683.46
2.75%	6,132.04	3,108.13	2,100.41	1,596.74	1,294.69	1,093.45	949.82	842.19	758.56	691.73
3.00%	6,140.29	3,116.14	2,108.39	1,604.74	1,302.73	1,101.54	957.96	850.39	766.83	700.07
3.25%	6,148.55	3,124.16	2,116.38	1,612.76	1,310.80	1,109.67	966.15	858.65	775.15	708.46
3.50%	6,156.82	3,132.20	2,124.40	1,620.81	1,318.90	1,117.83	974.39	866.96	783.54	716.92
3.75%	6,165.09	3,140.25	2,132.44	1,628.88	1,327.03	1,126.04	982.67	875.32	791.98	725.44
4.00%	6,173.37	3,148.31	2,140.49	1,636.98	1,335.20	1,134.28	990.99	883.72	800.47	734.03
4.25%	6,181.65	3,156.38	2,148.56	1,645.10	1,343.39	1,142.55	999.35	892.18	809.02	742.67
4.50%	6,189.94	3,164.47	2,156.65	1,653.25	1,351.62	1,150.87	1,007.76	900.68	817.63	751.38
4.75%	6,198.24	3,172.56	2,164.76	1,661.43	1,359.88	1,159.22	1,016.21	909.24	826.29	760.15
5.00%	6,206.54	3,180.68	2,172.89	1,669.62	1,368.16	1,167.61	1,024.71	917.84	835.00	768.97
5.25%	6,214.85	3,188.80	2,181.04	1,677.85	1,376.48	1,176.03	1,033.25	926.50	843.77	777.86
5.50%	6,223.17	3,196.94	2,189.20	1,686.09	1,384.83	1,184.50	1,041.83	935.20	852.60	786.82
5.75%	6,231.49	3,205.08	2,197.39	1,694.37	1,393.22	1,193.00	1,050.45	943.95	861.48	795.83
6.00%	6,239.82	3,213.24	2,205.59	1,702.66	1,401.63	1,201.53	1,059.12	952.75	870.42	804.90
6.25%	6,248.15	3,221.42	2,213.81	1,710.99	1,410.07	1,210.11	1,067.83	961.60	879.41	814.03
6.50%	6,256.49	3,229.60	2,222.05	1,719.33	1,418.55	1,218.72	1,076.58	970.50	888.45	823.22
6.75%	6,264.84	3,237.80	2,230.31	1,727.71	1,427.05	1,227.37	1,085.38	979.45	897.55	832.47
7.00%	6,273.19	3,246.01	2,238.59	1,736.10	1,435.59	1,236.05	1,094.22	988.44	906.71	841.79
7.25%	6,281.55	3,254.24	2,246.89	1,744.52	1,444.15	1,244.77	1,103.10	997.49	915.91	851.16
7.50%	6,289.91	3,262.47	2,255.20	1,752.97	1,452.75	1,253.53	1,112.02	1,006.58	925.17	860.59
7.75%	6,298.28	3,270.72	2,263.53	1,761.44	1,461.38	1,262.33	1,120.99	1,015.72	934.49	870.08
8.00%	6,306.66	3,278.98	2,271.89	1,769.94	1,470.04	1,271.16	1,130.00	1,024.91	943.86	879.63
8.25%	6,315.04	3,287.25	2,280.26	1,778.46	1,478.73	1,280.03	1,139.05	1,034.15	953.28	889.23
8.50%	6,323.43	3,295.54	2,288.65	1,787.00	1,487.45	1,288.93	1,148.15	1,043.43	962.75	898.90
8.75%	6,331.83	3,303.83	2,297.05	1,795.57	1,496.20	1,297.87	1,157.28	1,052.76	972.28	908.62
9.00%	6,340.23	3,312.14	2,305.48	1,804.17	1,504.98	1,306.85	1,166.46	1,062.14	981.86	918.40
9.25%	6,348.64	3,320.47	2,313.93	1,812.78	1,513.79	1,315.87	1,175.68	1,071.57	991.49	928.24
9.50%	6,357.05	3,328.80	2,322.39	1,821.43	1,522.63	1,324.92	1,184.94	1,081.04	1,001.18	938.13
9.75%	6,365.48	3,337.15	2,330.87	1,830.10	1,531.51	1,334.00	1,194.24	1,090.56	1,010.92	948.08
10.00%	6,373.90	3,345.51	2,339.37	1,838.79	1,540.41	1,343.12	1,203.59	1,100.13	1,020.70	958.09
10.25%	6,382.33	3,353.88	2,347.89	1,847.50	1,549.34	1,352.28	1,212.97	1,109.74	1,030.55	968.16
10.50%	6,390.77	3,362.26	2,356.43	1,856.25	1,558.31	1,361.48	1,222.40	1,119.40	1,040.44	978.28
10.75%	6,399.22	3,370.66	2,364.98	1,865.01	1,567.30	1,370.71	1,231.87	1,129.11	1,050.38	988.46

$72,500   11.00 - 20.75%   1 - 10 Years

	1	2	3	4	5	6	7	8	9	10
11.00%	6,407.67	3,379.07	2,373.56	1,873.80	1,576.33	1,379.97	1,241.38	1,138.86	1,060.37	998.69
11.25%	6,416.13	3,387.49	2,382.15	1,882.61	1,585.38	1,389.27	1,250.93	1,148.66	1,070.42	1,008.97
11.50%	6,424.59	3,395.92	2,390.76	1,891.45	1,594.46	1,398.61	1,260.52	1,158.50	1,080.52	1,019.32
11.75%	6,433.06	3,404.37	2,399.39	1,900.32	1,603.58	1,407.98	1,270.15	1,168.40	1,090.66	1,029.71
12.00%	6,441.54	3,412.83	2,408.04	1,909.20	1,612.72	1,417.39	1,279.82	1,178.33	1,100.86	1,040.16
12.25%	6,450.02	3,421.30	2,416.70	1,918.11	1,621.90	1,426.83	1,289.54	1,188.31	1,111.10	1,050.67
12.50%	6,458.51	3,429.78	2,425.39	1,927.05	1,631.10	1,436.31	1,299.29	1,198.34	1,121.40	1,061.23
12.75%	6,467.00	3,438.27	2,434.09	1,936.01	1,640.33	1,445.82	1,309.08	1,208.41	1,131.74	1,071.84
13.00%	6,475.50	3,446.78	2,442.81	1,944.99	1,649.60	1,455.37	1,318.92	1,218.53	1,142.14	1,082.50
13.25%	6,484.01	3,455.30	2,451.55	1,954.00	1,658.89	1,464.96	1,328.79	1,228.69	1,152.58	1,093.22
13.50%	6,492.52	3,463.83	2,460.31	1,963.03	1,668.21	1,474.57	1,338.70	1,238.89	1,163.07	1,103.99
13.75%	6,501.04	3,472.38	2,469.08	1,972.09	1,677.57	1,484.23	1,348.66	1,249.14	1,173.61	1,114.81
14.00%	6,509.57	3,480.93	2,477.88	1,981.17	1,686.95	1,493.92	1,358.65	1,259.43	1,184.19	1,125.68
14.25%	6,518.10	3,489.50	2,486.69	1,990.27	1,696.36	1,503.64	1,368.68	1,269.77	1,194.83	1,136.61
14.50%	6,526.63	3,498.08	2,495.52	1,999.40	1,705.80	1,513.40	1,378.75	1,280.15	1,205.51	1,147.58
14.75%	6,535.18	3,506.68	2,504.37	2,008.55	1,715.27	1,523.19	1,388.87	1,290.57	1,216.24	1,158.60
15.00%	6,543.73	3,515.28	2,513.24	2,017.73	1,724.77	1,533.01	1,399.01	1,301.04	1,227.01	1,169.68
15.25%	6,552.28	3,523.90	2,522.12	2,026.93	1,734.30	1,542.87	1,409.20	1,311.55	1,237.84	1,180.80
15.50%	6,560.85	3,532.53	2,531.02	2,036.15	1,743.86	1,552.77	1,419.43	1,322.10	1,248.71	1,191.98
15.75%	6,569.41	3,541.17	2,539.95	2,045.40	1,753.44	1,562.70	1,429.70	1,332.70	1,259.62	1,203.20
16.00%	6,577.99	3,549.83	2,548.88	2,054.67	1,763.06	1,572.66	1,440.00	1,343.34	1,270.58	1,214.47
16.25%	6,586.57	3,558.49	2,557.84	2,063.96	1,772.70	1,582.65	1,450.34	1,354.02	1,281.59	1,225.79
16.50%	6,595.15	3,567.17	2,566.82	2,073.28	1,782.38	1,592.68	1,460.72	1,364.74	1,292.64	1,237.16
16.75%	6,603.75	3,575.86	2,575.81	2,082.63	1,792.08	1,602.75	1,471.14	1,375.50	1,303.73	1,248.57
17.00%	6,612.34	3,584.56	2,584.82	2,091.99	1,801.81	1,612.84	1,481.60	1,386.31	1,314.87	1,260.03
17.25%	6,620.95	3,593.28	2,593.85	2,101.38	1,811.57	1,622.97	1,492.09	1,397.15	1,326.06	1,271.54
17.50%	6,629.56	3,602.01	2,602.90	2,110.79	1,821.36	1,633.14	1,502.62	1,408.04	1,337.29	1,283.10
17.75%	6,638.18	3,610.75	2,611.97	2,120.23	1,831.18	1,643.34	1,513.19	1,418.97	1,348.56	1,294.70
18.00%	6,646.80	3,619.50	2,621.05	2,129.69	1,841.02	1,653.56	1,523.79	1,429.93	1,359.87	1,306.34
18.25%	6,655.43	3,628.26	2,630.15	2,139.17	1,850.90	1,663.83	1,534.44	1,440.94	1,371.23	1,318.03
18.50%	6,664.06	3,637.04	2,639.27	2,148.68	1,860.80	1,674.12	1,545.11	1,451.99	1,382.63	1,329.77
18.75%	6,672.70	3,645.82	2,648.41	2,158.21	1,870.73	1,684.45	1,555.83	1,463.08	1,394.08	1,341.55
19.00%	6,681.35	3,654.62	2,657.56	2,167.76	1,880.69	1,694.81	1,566.58	1,474.21	1,405.56	1,353.37
19.25%	6,690.01	3,663.44	2,666.73	2,177.33	1,890.68	1,705.21	1,577.37	1,485.37	1,417.09	1,365.24
19.50%	6,698.66	3,672.26	2,675.93	2,186.93	1,900.69	1,715.63	1,588.19	1,496.58	1,428.66	1,377.15
19.75%	6,707.33	3,681.10	2,685.13	2,196.56	1,910.74	1,726.09	1,599.05	1,507.82	1,440.27	1,389.11
20.00%	6,716.00	3,689.95	2,694.36	2,206.20	1,920.81	1,736.58	1,609.95	1,519.11	1,451.92	1,401.10
20.25%	6,724.68	3,698.81	2,703.60	2,215.87	1,930.91	1,747.10	1,620.88	1,530.43	1,463.61	1,413.14
20.50%	6,733.36	3,707.68	2,712.87	2,225.56	1,941.03	1,757.66	1,631.85	1,541.79	1,475.34	1,425.22
20.75%	6,742.05	3,716.56	2,722.15	2,235.28	1,951.19	1,768.24	1,642.85	1,553.19	1,487.12	1,437.34

	1	2	3	4	5	6	7	8	9	10
1.00%	6,283.91	3,157.66	2,115.61	1,594.61	1,282.03	1,073.66	924.84	813.24	726.45	657.03
1.25%	6,292.40	3,165.85	2,123.72	1,602.70	1,290.12	1,081.76	932.95	821.37	734.60	665.20
1.50%	6,300.90	3,174.06	2,131.86	1,610.82	1,298.24	1,089.90	941.11	829.55	742.81	673.44
1.75%	6,309.40	3,182.28	2,140.02	1,618.96	1,306.40	1,098.07	949.31	837.78	751.07	681.74
2.00%	6,317.92	3,190.52	2,148.19	1,627.13	1,314.58	1,106.28	957.56	846.07	759.40	690.10
2.25%	6,326.43	3,198.77	2,156.39	1,635.33	1,322.80	1,114.54	965.85	854.40	767.78	698.53
2.50%	6,334.96	3,207.03	2,164.60	1,643.55	1,331.05	1,122.83	974.19	862.79	776.22	707.02
2.75%	6,343.49	3,215.30	2,172.84	1,651.80	1,339.34	1,131.16	982.57	871.23	784.71	715.58
3.00%	6,352.03	3,223.59	2,181.09	1,660.07	1,347.65	1,139.53	991.00	879.72	793.27	724.21
3.25%	6,360.57	3,231.89	2,189.36	1,668.37	1,356.00	1,147.93	999.47	888.26	801.88	732.89
3.50%	6,369.12	3,240.20	2,197.66	1,676.70	1,364.38	1,156.38	1,007.99	896.85	810.56	741.64
3.75%	6,377.68	3,248.53	2,205.97	1,685.05	1,372.79	1,164.86	1,016.55	905.50	819.29	750.46
4.00%	6,386.24	3,256.87	2,214.30	1,693.43	1,381.24	1,173.39	1,025.16	914.20	828.07	759.34
4.25%	6,394.81	3,265.22	2,222.65	1,701.83	1,389.72	1,181.95	1,033.81	922.94	836.92	768.28
4.50%	6,403.39	3,273.59	2,231.02	1,710.26	1,398.23	1,190.55	1,042.51	931.74	845.82	777.29
4.75%	6,411.97	3,281.96	2,239.41	1,718.72	1,406.77	1,199.19	1,051.26	940.59	854.78	786.36
5.00%	6,420.56	3,290.35	2,247.82	1,727.20	1,415.34	1,207.87	1,060.04	949.49	863.80	795.49
5.25%	6,429.16	3,298.76	2,256.25	1,735.70	1,423.95	1,216.59	1,068.88	958.45	872.87	804.69
5.50%	6,437.76	3,307.17	2,264.69	1,744.24	1,432.59	1,225.34	1,077.75	967.45	882.00	813.95
5.75%	6,446.37	3,315.60	2,273.16	1,752.79	1,441.26	1,234.13	1,086.68	976.50	891.19	823.27
6.00%	6,454.98	3,324.05	2,281.65	1,761.38	1,449.96	1,242.97	1,095.64	985.61	900.43	832.65
6.25%	6,463.60	3,332.50	2,290.15	1,769.99	1,458.69	1,251.84	1,104.65	994.76	909.73	842.10
6.50%	6,472.23	3,340.97	2,298.68	1,778.62	1,467.46	1,260.74	1,113.71	1,003.97	919.09	851.61
6.75%	6,480.87	3,349.45	2,307.22	1,787.28	1,476.26	1,269.69	1,122.81	1,013.22	928.50	861.18
7.00%	6,489.51	3,357.94	2,315.78	1,795.97	1,485.09	1,278.68	1,131.95	1,022.53	937.97	870.81
7.25%	6,498.15	3,366.45	2,324.36	1,804.68	1,493.95	1,287.70	1,141.14	1,031.88	947.50	880.51
7.50%	6,506.81	3,374.97	2,332.97	1,813.42	1,502.85	1,296.76	1,150.37	1,041.29	957.08	890.26
7.75%	6,515.47	3,383.50	2,341.59	1,822.18	1,511.77	1,305.86	1,159.65	1,050.75	966.71	900.08
8.00%	6,524.13	3,392.05	2,350.23	1,830.97	1,520.73	1,314.99	1,168.97	1,060.25	976.40	909.96
8.25%	6,532.80	3,400.60	2,358.89	1,839.78	1,529.72	1,324.17	1,178.33	1,069.81	986.15	919.89
8.50%	6,541.48	3,409.18	2,367.57	1,848.62	1,538.74	1,333.38	1,187.74	1,079.41	995.95	929.89
8.75%	6,550.17	3,417.76	2,376.26	1,857.49	1,547.79	1,342.63	1,197.19	1,089.06	1,005.81	939.95
9.00%	6,558.86	3,426.36	2,384.98	1,866.38	1,556.88	1,351.92	1,206.68	1,098.77	1,015.72	950.07
9.25%	6,567.56	3,434.96	2,393.72	1,875.29	1,565.99	1,361.24	1,216.22	1,108.52	1,025.68	960.25
9.50%	6,576.26	3,443.59	2,402.47	1,884.24	1,575.14	1,370.60	1,225.80	1,118.32	1,035.70	970.48
9.75%	6,584.97	3,452.22	2,411.25	1,893.20	1,584.32	1,380.00	1,235.42	1,128.17	1,045.77	980.78
10.00%	6,593.69	3,460.87	2,420.04	1,902.19	1,593.53	1,389.44	1,245.09	1,138.06	1,055.90	991.13
10.25%	6,602.42	3,469.53	2,428.85	1,911.21	1,602.77	1,398.91	1,254.80	1,148.01	1,066.08	1,001.54
10.50%	6,611.15	3,478.20	2,437.68	1,920.25	1,612.04	1,408.42	1,264.55	1,158.00	1,076.31	1,012.01
10.75%	6,619.88	3,486.89	2,446.53	1,929.32	1,621.35	1,417.97	1,274.35	1,168.04	1,086.60	1,022.54

	1	2	3	4	5	6	7	8	9	10
11.00%	6,628.62	3,495.59	2,455.40	1,938.41	1,630.68	1,427.56	1,284.18	1,178.13	1,096.94	1,033.13
11.25%	6,637.37	3,504.30	2,464.29	1,947.53	1,640.05	1,437.18	1,294.06	1,188.27	1,107.33	1,043.77
11.50%	6,646.13	3,513.02	2,473.20	1,956.68	1,649.45	1,446.84	1,303.98	1,198.45	1,117.77	1,054.47
11.75%	6,654.89	3,521.76	2,482.13	1,965.84	1,658.87	1,456.53	1,313.95	1,208.68	1,128.27	1,065.22
12.00%	6,663.66	3,530.51	2,491.07	1,975.04	1,668.33	1,466.26	1,323.95	1,218.96	1,138.82	1,076.03
12.25%	6,672.43	3,539.27	2,500.04	1,984.26	1,677.82	1,476.03	1,334.00	1,229.29	1,149.42	1,086.90
12.50%	6,681.21	3,548.05	2,509.02	1,993.50	1,687.35	1,485.84	1,344.09	1,239.66	1,160.07	1,097.82
12.75%	6,690.00	3,556.84	2,518.02	2,002.77	1,696.90	1,495.68	1,354.22	1,250.08	1,170.77	1,108.80
13.00%	6,698.80	3,565.64	2,527.05	2,012.06	1,706.48	1,505.56	1,364.40	1,260.54	1,181.52	1,119.83
13.25%	6,707.60	3,574.45	2,536.09	2,021.38	1,716.09	1,515.47	1,374.61	1,271.06	1,192.32	1,130.92
13.50%	6,716.40	3,583.28	2,545.15	2,030.72	1,725.74	1,525.42	1,384.87	1,281.61	1,203.17	1,142.06
13.75%	6,725.21	3,592.11	2,554.22	2,040.09	1,735.41	1,535.41	1,395.16	1,292.21	1,214.08	1,153.25
14.00%	6,734.03	3,600.97	2,563.32	2,049.49	1,745.12	1,545.43	1,405.50	1,302.86	1,225.03	1,164.50
14.25%	6,742.86	3,609.83	2,572.44	2,058.90	1,754.85	1,555.49	1,415.88	1,313.56	1,236.03	1,175.80
14.50%	6,751.69	3,618.71	2,581.57	2,068.35	1,764.62	1,565.58	1,426.30	1,324.29	1,247.08	1,187.15
14.75%	6,760.53	3,627.60	2,590.73	2,077.81	1,774.42	1,575.71	1,436.76	1,335.08	1,258.18	1,198.56
15.00%	6,769.37	3,636.50	2,599.90	2,087.31	1,784.24	1,585.88	1,447.26	1,345.91	1,269.33	1,210.01
15.25%	6,778.22	3,645.41	2,609.09	2,096.82	1,794.10	1,596.08	1,457.80	1,356.78	1,280.52	1,221.52
15.50%	6,787.08	3,654.34	2,618.30	2,106.36	1,803.99	1,606.31	1,468.38	1,367.69	1,291.76	1,233.08
15.75%	6,795.94	3,663.28	2,627.53	2,115.93	1,813.91	1,616.58	1,479.00	1,378.65	1,303.06	1,244.69
16.00%	6,804.81	3,672.23	2,636.78	2,125.52	1,823.85	1,626.89	1,489.65	1,389.66	1,314.39	1,256.35
16.25%	6,813.69	3,681.20	2,646.04	2,135.14	1,833.83	1,637.23	1,500.35	1,400.71	1,325.78	1,268.06
16.50%	6,822.57	3,690.18	2,655.33	2,144.78	1,843.84	1,647.60	1,511.09	1,411.80	1,337.21	1,279.82
16.75%	6,831.46	3,699.17	2,664.63	2,154.44	1,853.88	1,658.01	1,521.87	1,422.93	1,348.69	1,291.63
17.00%	6,840.36	3,708.17	2,673.95	2,164.13	1,863.94	1,668.46	1,532.69	1,434.11	1,360.21	1,303.48
17.25%	6,849.26	3,717.19	2,683.30	2,173.84	1,874.04	1,678.94	1,543.54	1,445.33	1,371.78	1,315.39
17.50%	6,858.17	3,726.21	2,692.65	2,183.58	1,884.17	1,689.45	1,554.43	1,456.59	1,383.40	1,327.34
17.75%	6,867.08	3,735.25	2,702.03	2,193.34	1,894.32	1,700.00	1,565.37	1,467.89	1,395.06	1,339.34
18.00%	6,876.00	3,744.31	2,711.43	2,203.12	1,904.51	1,710.58	1,576.34	1,479.24	1,406.77	1,351.39
18.25%	6,884.93	3,753.37	2,720.84	2,212.93	1,914.72	1,721.20	1,587.35	1,490.63	1,418.52	1,363.48
18.50%	6,893.86	3,762.45	2,730.28	2,222.77	1,924.97	1,731.85	1,598.39	1,502.06	1,430.31	1,375.62
18.75%	6,902.80	3,771.54	2,739.73	2,232.63	1,935.24	1,742.54	1,609.48	1,513.53	1,442.15	1,387.81
19.00%	6,911.74	3,780.65	2,749.20	2,242.51	1,945.54	1,753.25	1,620.60	1,525.04	1,454.03	1,400.04
19.25%	6,920.70	3,789.76	2,758.69	2,252.42	1,955.87	1,764.01	1,631.76	1,536.59	1,465.96	1,412.32
19.50%	6,929.65	3,798.89	2,768.20	2,262.35	1,966.23	1,774.79	1,642.96	1,548.18	1,477.92	1,424.64
19.75%	6,938.62	3,808.03	2,777.72	2,272.30	1,976.62	1,785.61	1,654.19	1,559.82	1,489.93	1,437.01
20.00%	6,947.59	3,817.19	2,787.27	2,282.28	1,987.04	1,796.46	1,665.46	1,571.49	1,501.99	1,449.42
20.25%	6,956.56	3,826.35	2,796.83	2,292.28	1,997.49	1,807.35	1,676.77	1,583.20	1,514.08	1,461.87
20.50%	6,965.55	3,835.53	2,806.41	2,302.30	2,007.96	1,818.27	1,688.12	1,594.95	1,526.22	1,474.37
20.75%	6,974.54	3,844.72	2,816.01	2,312.35	2,018.47	1,829.22	1,699.50	1,606.75	1,538.40	1,486.91

	1	2	3	4	5	6	7	8	9	10
1.00%	6,493.37	3,262.91	2,186.13	1,647.76	1,324.77	1,109.45	955.67	840.35	750.67	678.93
1.25%	6,502.15	3,271.38	2,194.52	1,656.12	1,333.12	1,117.82	964.05	848.75	759.09	687.37
1.50%	6,510.93	3,279.86	2,202.92	1,664.51	1,341.52	1,126.23	972.48	857.20	767.57	695.88
1.75%	6,519.72	3,288.36	2,211.35	1,672.93	1,349.94	1,134.67	980.95	865.71	776.11	704.46
2.00%	6,528.51	3,296.87	2,219.80	1,681.37	1,358.40	1,143.16	989.48	874.27	784.71	713.10
2.25%	6,537.31	3,305.39	2,228.27	1,689.84	1,366.89	1,151.69	998.04	882.88	793.37	721.81
2.50%	6,546.12	3,313.93	2,236.76	1,698.34	1,375.42	1,160.25	1,006.66	891.55	802.09	730.59
2.75%	6,554.94	3,322.48	2,245.27	1,706.86	1,383.98	1,168.86	1,015.32	900.27	810.87	739.44
3.00%	6,563.76	3,331.04	2,253.79	1,715.41	1,392.57	1,177.51	1,024.03	909.04	819.71	748.35
3.25%	6,572.59	3,339.62	2,262.34	1,723.99	1,401.20	1,186.20	1,032.79	917.87	828.61	757.32
3.50%	6,581.43	3,348.21	2,270.91	1,732.59	1,409.86	1,194.93	1,041.59	926.75	837.57	766.37
3.75%	6,590.27	3,356.81	2,279.50	1,741.22	1,418.55	1,203.69	1,050.44	935.68	846.60	775.47
4.00%	6,599.12	3,365.43	2,288.11	1,749.88	1,427.28	1,212.50	1,059.33	944.67	855.68	784.65
4.25%	6,607.97	3,374.06	2,296.74	1,758.56	1,436.04	1,221.35	1,068.27	953.71	864.81	793.89
4.50%	6,616.84	3,382.71	2,305.39	1,767.27	1,444.83	1,230.24	1,077.26	962.80	874.01	803.20
4.75%	6,625.70	3,391.36	2,314.06	1,776.01	1,453.66	1,239.16	1,086.30	971.95	883.27	812.57
5.00%	6,634.58	3,400.03	2,322.74	1,784.77	1,462.52	1,248.13	1,095.38	981.14	892.59	822.01
5.25%	6,643.46	3,408.72	2,331.45	1,793.56	1,471.41	1,257.14	1,104.51	990.39	901.96	831.51
5.50%	6,652.35	3,417.41	2,340.18	1,802.38	1,480.34	1,266.19	1,113.68	999.70	911.40	841.08
5.75%	6,661.25	3,426.12	2,348.93	1,811.22	1,489.30	1,275.27	1,122.90	1,009.05	920.89	850.71
6.00%	6,670.15	3,434.85	2,357.70	1,820.09	1,498.29	1,284.40	1,132.16	1,018.46	930.45	860.41
6.25%	6,679.06	3,443.58	2,366.49	1,828.99	1,507.32	1,293.56	1,141.47	1,027.92	940.06	870.17
6.50%	6,687.97	3,452.33	2,375.30	1,837.91	1,516.38	1,302.77	1,150.83	1,037.43	949.72	880.00
6.75%	6,696.89	3,461.10	2,384.13	1,846.86	1,525.47	1,312.01	1,160.23	1,047.00	959.45	889.89
7.00%	6,705.82	3,469.87	2,392.98	1,855.83	1,534.59	1,321.30	1,169.68	1,056.61	969.24	899.84
7.25%	6,714.76	3,478.67	2,401.84	1,864.84	1,543.75	1,330.62	1,179.18	1,066.28	979.08	909.86
7.50%	6,723.70	3,487.47	2,410.73	1,873.86	1,552.94	1,339.98	1,188.72	1,076.00	988.98	919.94
7.75%	6,732.65	3,496.29	2,419.64	1,882.92	1,562.16	1,349.39	1,198.30	1,085.77	998.94	930.08
8.00%	6,741.60	3,505.12	2,428.57	1,892.00	1,571.42	1,358.83	1,207.93	1,095.59	1,008.95	940.29
8.25%	6,750.56	3,513.96	2,437.52	1,901.11	1,580.71	1,368.31	1,217.61	1,105.47	1,019.02	950.56
8.50%	6,759.53	3,522.81	2,446.48	1,910.24	1,590.03	1,377.82	1,227.33	1,115.39	1,029.15	960.89
8.75%	6,768.51	3,531.68	2,455.47	1,919.40	1,599.39	1,387.38	1,237.09	1,125.37	1,039.33	971.28
9.00%	6,777.49	3,540.57	2,464.48	1,928.59	1,608.77	1,396.98	1,246.90	1,135.39	1,049.58	981.74
9.25%	6,786.48	3,549.46	2,473.51	1,937.80	1,618.19	1,406.61	1,256.76	1,145.47	1,059.87	992.25
9.50%	6,795.47	3,558.37	2,482.55	1,947.04	1,627.64	1,416.29	1,266.66	1,155.59	1,070.23	1,002.83
9.75%	6,804.47	3,567.30	2,491.62	1,956.31	1,637.13	1,426.00	1,276.60	1,165.77	1,080.63	1,013.47
10.00%	6,813.48	3,576.23	2,500.71	1,965.60	1,646.65	1,435.75	1,286.59	1,176.00	1,091.10	1,024.17
10.25%	6,822.50	3,585.18	2,509.81	1,974.92	1,656.20	1,445.54	1,296.62	1,186.27	1,101.62	1,034.93
10.50%	6,831.52	3,594.14	2,518.94	1,984.26	1,665.78	1,455.37	1,306.70	1,196.60	1,112.19	1,045.75
10.75%	6,840.54	3,603.12	2,528.09	1,993.63	1,675.39	1,465.24	1,316.82	1,206.98	1,122.82	1,056.62

$77,500　　　11.00 - 20.75%　　　1 - 10 Years

	1	2	3	4	5	6	7	8	9	10
11.00%	6,849.58	3,612.11	2,537.25	2,003.03	1,685.04	1,475.14	1,326.99	1,217.40	1,133.50	1,067.56
11.25%	6,858.62	3,621.11	2,546.44	2,012.45	1,694.72	1,485.08	1,337.20	1,227.88	1,144.24	1,078.56
11.50%	6,867.67	3,630.12	2,555.64	2,021.90	1,704.43	1,495.06	1,347.45	1,238.40	1,155.03	1,089.61
11.75%	6,876.72	3,639.15	2,564.86	2,031.37	1,714.17	1,505.08	1,357.75	1,248.97	1,165.88	1,100.73
12.00%	6,885.78	3,648.19	2,574.11	2,040.87	1,723.94	1,515.14	1,368.09	1,259.60	1,176.78	1,111.90
12.25%	6,894.85	3,657.25	2,583.37	2,050.40	1,733.75	1,525.23	1,378.47	1,270.26	1,187.73	1,123.13
12.50%	6,903.92	3,666.32	2,592.66	2,059.95	1,743.59	1,535.37	1,388.90	1,280.98	1,198.74	1,134.42
12.75%	6,913.00	3,675.40	2,601.96	2,069.53	1,753.46	1,545.54	1,399.37	1,291.75	1,209.79	1,145.76
13.00%	6,922.09	3,684.49	2,611.28	2,079.13	1,763.36	1,555.74	1,409.88	1,302.56	1,220.90	1,157.16
13.25%	6,931.18	3,693.60	2,620.62	2,088.76	1,773.30	1,565.99	1,420.43	1,313.42	1,232.07	1,168.61
13.50%	6,940.28	3,702.72	2,629.98	2,098.42	1,783.26	1,576.27	1,431.03	1,324.33	1,243.28	1,180.13
13.75%	6,949.39	3,711.85	2,639.37	2,108.10	1,793.26	1,586.59	1,441.67	1,335.29	1,254.54	1,191.69
14.00%	6,958.50	3,721.00	2,648.77	2,117.80	1,803.29	1,596.94	1,452.35	1,346.29	1,265.86	1,203.31
14.25%	6,967.62	3,730.16	2,658.19	2,127.53	1,813.35	1,607.34	1,463.08	1,357.34	1,277.23	1,214.99
14.50%	6,976.75	3,739.33	2,667.63	2,137.29	1,823.44	1,617.77	1,473.84	1,368.44	1,288.65	1,226.72
14.75%	6,985.88	3,748.52	2,677.08	2,147.07	1,833.57	1,628.23	1,484.65	1,379.58	1,300.12	1,238.51
15.00%	6,995.02	3,757.72	2,686.56	2,156.88	1,843.72	1,638.74	1,495.50	1,390.77	1,311.64	1,250.35
15.25%	7,004.16	3,766.93	2,696.06	2,166.72	1,853.91	1,649.28	1,506.39	1,402.00	1,323.20	1,262.24
15.50%	7,013.32	3,776.15	2,705.58	2,176.58	1,864.12	1,659.86	1,517.32	1,413.28	1,334.82	1,274.18
15.75%	7,022.48	3,785.39	2,715.11	2,186.46	1,874.37	1,670.47	1,528.30	1,424.61	1,346.49	1,286.18
16.00%	7,031.64	3,794.64	2,724.67	2,196.37	1,884.65	1,681.12	1,539.31	1,435.98	1,358.21	1,298.23
16.25%	7,040.81	3,803.91	2,734.25	2,206.31	1,894.96	1,691.80	1,550.37	1,447.40	1,369.97	1,310.33
16.50%	7,049.99	3,813.18	2,743.84	2,216.27	1,905.30	1,702.52	1,561.46	1,458.86	1,381.78	1,322.48
16.75%	7,059.18	3,822.47	2,753.45	2,226.25	1,915.67	1,713.28	1,572.60	1,470.36	1,393.65	1,334.68
17.00%	7,068.37	3,831.78	2,763.09	2,236.27	1,926.07	1,724.08	1,583.77	1,481.91	1,405.55	1,346.93
17.25%	7,077.57	3,841.09	2,772.74	2,246.30	1,936.51	1,734.90	1,594.99	1,493.51	1,417.51	1,359.23
17.50%	7,086.77	3,850.42	2,782.41	2,256.36	1,946.97	1,745.77	1,606.25	1,505.14	1,429.51	1,371.59
17.75%	7,095.98	3,859.76	2,792.10	2,266.45	1,957.47	1,756.67	1,617.55	1,516.82	1,441.56	1,383.99
18.00%	7,105.20	3,869.12	2,801.81	2,276.56	1,967.99	1,767.60	1,628.88	1,528.55	1,453.66	1,396.44
18.25%	7,114.42	3,878.49	2,811.54	2,286.70	1,978.55	1,778.57	1,640.26	1,540.32	1,465.80	1,408.93
18.50%	7,123.65	3,887.87	2,821.29	2,296.86	1,989.13	1,789.58	1,651.67	1,552.13	1,477.99	1,421.48
18.75%	7,132.89	3,897.26	2,831.06	2,307.05	1,999.75	1,800.62	1,663.13	1,563.98	1,490.22	1,434.07
19.00%	7,142.13	3,906.67	2,840.84	2,317.26	2,010.39	1,811.70	1,674.62	1,575.87	1,502.50	1,446.71
19.25%	7,151.38	3,916.09	2,850.65	2,327.50	2,021.07	1,822.81	1,686.15	1,587.81	1,514.82	1,459.40
19.50%	7,160.64	3,925.52	2,860.47	2,337.76	2,031.77	1,833.95	1,697.72	1,599.79	1,527.19	1,472.13
19.75%	7,169.90	3,934.97	2,870.32	2,348.04	2,042.51	1,845.13	1,709.33	1,611.81	1,539.60	1,484.91
20.00%	7,179.17	3,944.42	2,880.18	2,358.35	2,053.28	1,856.34	1,720.98	1,623.87	1,552.05	1,497.73
20.25%	7,188.45	3,953.90	2,890.06	2,368.69	2,064.07	1,867.59	1,732.67	1,635.98	1,564.55	1,510.60
20.50%	7,197.73	3,963.38	2,899.96	2,379.05	2,074.90	1,878.87	1,744.39	1,648.12	1,577.09	1,523.51
20.75%	7,207.02	3,972.88	2,909.88	2,389.43	2,085.75	1,890.19	1,756.15	1,660.30	1,589.68	1,536.47

	1	2	3	4	5	6	7	8	9	10
1.00%	6,702.83	3,368.17	2,256.65	1,700.92	1,367.50	1,145.24	986.50	867.46	774.88	700.83
1.25%	6,711.89	3,376.91	2,265.31	1,709.55	1,376.13	1,153.88	995.15	876.13	783.57	709.55
1.50%	6,720.96	3,385.67	2,273.99	1,718.21	1,384.79	1,162.55	1,003.85	884.85	792.33	718.33
1.75%	6,730.03	3,394.44	2,282.69	1,726.89	1,393.49	1,171.27	1,012.60	893.63	801.14	727.19
2.00%	6,739.11	3,403.22	2,291.41	1,735.61	1,402.22	1,180.04	1,021.39	902.47	810.02	736.11
2.25%	6,748.20	3,412.02	2,300.15	1,744.35	1,410.99	1,188.84	1,030.24	911.36	818.96	745.10
2.50%	6,757.29	3,420.83	2,308.91	1,753.12	1,419.79	1,197.68	1,039.13	920.31	827.96	754.16
2.75%	6,766.39	3,429.66	2,317.69	1,761.92	1,428.62	1,206.57	1,048.07	929.31	837.03	763.29
3.00%	6,775.50	3,438.50	2,326.50	1,770.75	1,437.50	1,215.49	1,057.06	938.37	846.16	772.49
3.25%	6,784.61	3,447.35	2,335.32	1,779.60	1,446.40	1,224.46	1,066.10	947.48	855.34	781.75
3.50%	6,793.73	3,456.22	2,344.17	1,788.48	1,455.34	1,233.47	1,075.19	956.64	864.59	791.09
3.75%	6,802.86	3,465.10	2,353.03	1,797.39	1,464.31	1,242.52	1,084.32	965.87	873.90	800.49
4.00%	6,811.99	3,473.99	2,361.92	1,806.32	1,473.32	1,251.61	1,093.50	975.14	883.28	809.96
4.25%	6,821.13	3,482.90	2,370.83	1,815.29	1,482.36	1,260.75	1,102.73	984.47	892.71	819.50
4.50%	6,830.28	3,491.82	2,379.75	1,824.28	1,491.44	1,269.92	1,112.01	993.86	902.21	829.11
4.75%	6,839.44	3,500.76	2,388.70	1,833.30	1,500.55	1,279.14	1,121.34	1,003.30	911.76	838.78
5.00%	6,848.60	3,509.71	2,397.67	1,842.34	1,509.70	1,288.39	1,130.71	1,012.79	921.38	848.52
5.25%	6,857.77	3,518.67	2,406.66	1,851.42	1,518.88	1,297.69	1,140.13	1,022.34	931.06	858.33
5.50%	6,866.94	3,527.65	2,415.67	1,860.52	1,528.09	1,307.03	1,149.60	1,031.95	940.80	868.21
5.75%	6,876.13	3,536.64	2,424.70	1,869.65	1,537.34	1,316.41	1,159.12	1,041.60	950.60	878.15
6.00%	6,885.31	3,545.65	2,433.75	1,878.80	1,546.62	1,325.83	1,168.68	1,051.31	960.46	888.16
6.25%	6,894.51	3,554.67	2,442.83	1,887.99	1,555.94	1,335.29	1,178.30	1,061.08	970.38	898.24
6.50%	6,903.71	3,563.70	2,451.92	1,897.20	1,565.29	1,344.79	1,187.95	1,070.90	980.36	908.38
6.75%	6,912.92	3,572.75	2,461.03	1,906.43	1,574.68	1,354.34	1,197.66	1,080.77	990.40	918.59
7.00%	6,922.14	3,581.81	2,470.17	1,915.70	1,584.10	1,363.92	1,207.41	1,090.70	1,000.50	928.87
7.25%	6,931.36	3,590.88	2,479.32	1,924.99	1,593.55	1,373.54	1,217.21	1,100.68	1,010.66	939.21
7.50%	6,940.59	3,599.97	2,488.50	1,934.31	1,603.04	1,383.21	1,227.06	1,110.71	1,020.88	949.61
7.75%	6,949.83	3,609.07	2,497.69	1,943.66	1,612.56	1,392.91	1,236.96	1,120.80	1,031.16	960.09
8.00%	6,959.07	3,618.18	2,506.91	1,953.03	1,622.11	1,402.66	1,246.90	1,130.93	1,041.50	970.62
8.25%	6,968.33	3,627.31	2,516.15	1,962.44	1,631.70	1,412.44	1,256.88	1,141.13	1,051.89	981.22
8.50%	6,977.58	3,636.45	2,525.40	1,971.86	1,641.32	1,422.27	1,266.92	1,151.37	1,062.35	991.89
8.75%	6,986.85	3,645.61	2,534.68	1,981.32	1,650.98	1,432.14	1,277.00	1,161.67	1,072.86	1,002.61
9.00%	6,996.12	3,654.78	2,543.98	1,990.80	1,660.67	1,442.04	1,287.13	1,172.02	1,083.43	1,013.41
9.25%	7,005.40	3,663.96	2,553.30	2,000.31	1,670.39	1,451.99	1,297.30	1,182.42	1,094.06	1,024.26
9.50%	7,014.68	3,673.16	2,562.64	2,009.85	1,680.15	1,461.98	1,307.52	1,192.87	1,104.75	1,035.18
9.75%	7,023.97	3,682.37	2,572.00	2,019.42	1,689.94	1,472.00	1,317.78	1,203.38	1,115.49	1,046.16
10.00%	7,033.27	3,691.59	2,581.37	2,029.01	1,699.76	1,482.07	1,328.09	1,213.93	1,126.29	1,057.21
10.25%	7,042.58	3,700.83	2,590.78	2,038.63	1,709.62	1,492.17	1,338.45	1,224.54	1,137.15	1,068.31
10.50%	7,051.89	3,710.08	2,600.20	2,048.27	1,719.51	1,502.32	1,348.85	1,235.20	1,148.07	1,079.48
10.75%	7,061.21	3,719.35	2,609.64	2,057.94	1,729.44	1,512.50	1,359.30	1,245.91	1,159.04	1,090.71

	1	2	3	4	5	6	7	8	9	10
11.00%	7,070.53	3,728.63	2,619.10	2,067.64	1,739.39	1,522.73	1,369.79	1,256.67	1,170.07	1,102.00
11.25%	7,079.87	3,737.92	2,628.58	2,077.37	1,749.38	1,532.99	1,380.33	1,267.49	1,181.15	1,113.35
11.50%	7,089.20	3,747.23	2,638.08	2,087.12	1,759.41	1,543.29	1,390.92	1,278.35	1,192.29	1,124.76
11.75%	7,098.55	3,756.54	2,647.60	2,096.90	1,769.47	1,553.63	1,401.55	1,289.26	1,203.49	1,136.24
12.00%	7,107.90	3,765.88	2,657.14	2,106.71	1,779.56	1,564.02	1,412.22	1,300.23	1,214.74	1,147.77
12.25%	7,117.26	3,775.22	2,666.71	2,116.54	1,789.68	1,574.44	1,422.94	1,311.24	1,226.04	1,159.36
12.50%	7,126.63	3,784.58	2,676.29	2,126.40	1,799.84	1,584.89	1,433.70	1,322.30	1,237.40	1,171.01
12.75%	7,136.00	3,793.96	2,685.89	2,136.29	1,810.02	1,595.39	1,444.51	1,333.42	1,248.82	1,182.72
13.00%	7,145.38	3,803.35	2,695.52	2,146.20	1,820.25	1,605.93	1,455.36	1,344.58	1,260.29	1,194.49
13.25%	7,154.77	3,812.75	2,705.16	2,156.14	1,830.50	1,616.50	1,466.25	1,355.79	1,271.81	1,206.31
13.50%	7,164.16	3,822.16	2,714.82	2,166.11	1,840.79	1,627.12	1,477.19	1,367.05	1,283.39	1,218.19
13.75%	7,173.56	3,831.59	2,724.51	2,176.10	1,851.11	1,637.77	1,488.17	1,378.36	1,295.01	1,230.13
14.00%	7,182.97	3,841.03	2,734.21	2,186.12	1,861.46	1,648.46	1,499.20	1,389.72	1,306.70	1,242.13
14.25%	7,192.38	3,850.49	2,743.93	2,196.16	1,871.85	1,659.19	1,510.27	1,401.13	1,318.43	1,254.18
14.50%	7,201.80	3,859.95	2,753.68	2,206.24	1,882.26	1,669.95	1,521.38	1,412.58	1,330.22	1,266.29
14.75%	7,211.23	3,869.44	2,763.44	2,216.33	1,892.71	1,680.76	1,532.54	1,424.08	1,342.06	1,278.46
15.00%	7,220.66	3,878.93	2,773.23	2,226.46	1,903.19	1,691.60	1,543.74	1,435.63	1,353.95	1,290.68
15.25%	7,230.11	3,888.44	2,783.03	2,236.61	1,913.71	1,702.48	1,554.98	1,447.23	1,365.89	1,302.95
15.50%	7,239.55	3,897.96	2,792.85	2,246.79	1,924.26	1,713.40	1,566.27	1,458.87	1,377.88	1,315.28
15.75%	7,249.01	3,907.50	2,802.70	2,256.99	1,934.83	1,724.35	1,577.60	1,470.57	1,389.93	1,327.67
16.00%	7,258.47	3,917.05	2,812.56	2,267.22	1,945.44	1,735.35	1,588.97	1,482.30	1,402.02	1,340.10
16.25%	7,267.94	3,926.61	2,822.45	2,277.48	1,956.09	1,746.38	1,600.38	1,494.09	1,414.16	1,352.60
16.50%	7,277.41	3,936.19	2,832.35	2,287.76	1,966.76	1,757.44	1,611.83	1,505.92	1,426.36	1,365.14
16.75%	7,286.89	3,945.78	2,842.27	2,298.07	1,977.47	1,768.55	1,623.33	1,517.79	1,438.60	1,377.73
17.00%	7,296.38	3,955.38	2,852.22	2,308.40	1,988.21	1,779.69	1,634.86	1,529.72	1,450.90	1,390.38
17.25%	7,305.87	3,965.00	2,862.18	2,318.76	1,998.98	1,790.87	1,646.44	1,541.68	1,463.24	1,403.08
17.50%	7,315.38	3,974.63	2,872.17	2,329.15	2,009.78	1,802.08	1,658.06	1,553.70	1,475.63	1,415.83
17.75%	7,324.88	3,984.27	2,882.17	2,339.56	2,020.61	1,813.34	1,669.72	1,565.75	1,488.06	1,428.63
18.00%	7,334.40	3,993.93	2,892.19	2,350.00	2,031.47	1,824.62	1,681.43	1,577.86	1,500.55	1,441.48
18.25%	7,343.92	4,003.60	2,902.23	2,360.46	2,042.37	1,835.95	1,693.17	1,590.00	1,513.08	1,454.38
18.50%	7,353.45	4,013.28	2,912.30	2,370.95	2,053.30	1,847.31	1,704.95	1,602.20	1,525.67	1,467.33
18.75%	7,362.98	4,022.98	2,922.38	2,381.47	2,064.25	1,858.71	1,716.78	1,614.43	1,538.29	1,480.33
19.00%	7,372.53	4,032.69	2,932.48	2,392.01	2,075.24	1,870.14	1,728.64	1,626.71	1,550.97	1,493.38
19.25%	7,382.07	4,042.41	2,942.60	2,402.58	2,086.26	1,881.61	1,740.55	1,639.03	1,563.69	1,506.47
19.50%	7,391.63	4,052.15	2,952.74	2,413.17	2,097.32	1,893.11	1,752.49	1,651.40	1,576.45	1,519.62
19.75%	7,401.19	4,061.90	2,962.91	2,423.79	2,108.40	1,904.65	1,764.47	1,663.81	1,589.26	1,532.81
20.00%	7,410.76	4,071.66	2,973.09	2,434.43	2,119.51	1,916.23	1,776.50	1,676.26	1,602.12	1,546.05
20.25%	7,420.34	4,081.44	2,983.29	2,445.10	2,130.65	1,927.84	1,788.56	1,688.75	1,615.02	1,559.33
20.50%	7,429.92	4,091.23	2,993.51	2,455.79	2,141.83	1,939.48	1,800.66	1,701.28	1,627.97	1,572.66
20.75%	7,439.51	4,101.04	3,003.75	2,466.51	2,153.03	1,951.16	1,812.80	1,713.86	1,640.96	1,586.03

	1	2	3	4	5	6	7	8	9	10
1.00%	6,912.30	3,473.42	2,327.17	1,754.07	1,410.23	1,181.03	1,017.33	894.57	799.10	722.73
1.25%	6,921.64	3,482.44	2,336.10	1,762.97	1,419.13	1,189.94	1,026.25	903.51	808.06	731.72
1.50%	6,930.99	3,491.47	2,345.05	1,771.90	1,428.07	1,198.88	1,035.22	912.50	817.09	740.78
1.75%	6,940.34	3,500.51	2,354.02	1,780.86	1,437.04	1,207.88	1,044.24	921.56	826.18	749.91
2.00%	6,949.71	3,509.57	2,363.01	1,789.85	1,446.04	1,216.91	1,053.31	930.67	835.33	759.11
2.25%	6,959.08	3,518.64	2,372.03	1,798.86	1,455.08	1,225.99	1,062.43	939.84	844.55	768.38
2.50%	6,968.45	3,527.73	2,381.06	1,807.91	1,464.16	1,235.11	1,071.61	949.07	853.84	777.73
2.75%	6,977.84	3,536.83	2,390.12	1,816.98	1,473.27	1,244.27	1,080.83	958.35	863.19	787.14
3.00%	6,987.23	3,545.95	2,399.20	1,826.08	1,482.42	1,253.48	1,090.10	967.69	872.60	796.63
3.25%	6,996.63	3,555.08	2,408.30	1,835.21	1,491.60	1,262.73	1,099.42	977.09	882.07	806.18
3.50%	7,006.03	3,564.22	2,417.42	1,844.37	1,500.82	1,272.02	1,108.79	986.54	891.61	815.81
3.75%	7,015.45	3,573.38	2,426.56	1,853.56	1,510.07	1,281.35	1,118.21	996.05	901.21	825.51
4.00%	7,024.87	3,582.56	2,435.73	1,862.77	1,519.36	1,290.73	1,127.68	1,005.62	910.88	835.27
4.25%	7,034.29	3,591.74	2,444.91	1,872.02	1,528.69	1,300.15	1,137.20	1,015.24	920.61	845.11
4.50%	7,043.73	3,600.94	2,454.12	1,881.29	1,538.05	1,309.61	1,146.76	1,024.92	930.40	855.02
4.75%	7,053.17	3,610.16	2,463.35	1,890.59	1,547.45	1,319.11	1,156.38	1,034.65	940.26	864.99
5.00%	7,062.62	3,619.39	2,472.60	1,899.92	1,556.88	1,328.66	1,166.05	1,044.44	950.18	875.04
5.25%	7,072.07	3,628.63	2,481.87	1,909.27	1,566.34	1,338.25	1,175.76	1,054.29	960.16	885.16
5.50%	7,081.53	3,637.89	2,491.16	1,918.66	1,575.85	1,347.88	1,185.53	1,064.19	970.20	895.34
5.75%	7,091.00	3,647.16	2,500.48	1,928.07	1,585.38	1,357.55	1,195.34	1,074.15	980.31	905.60
6.00%	7,100.48	3,656.45	2,509.81	1,937.51	1,594.96	1,367.26	1,205.21	1,084.17	990.47	915.92
6.25%	7,109.96	3,665.75	2,519.17	1,946.99	1,604.56	1,377.02	1,215.12	1,094.24	1,000.70	926.31
6.50%	7,119.45	3,675.07	2,528.54	1,956.48	1,614.21	1,386.82	1,225.08	1,104.36	1,011.00	936.77
6.75%	7,128.95	3,684.39	2,537.94	1,966.01	1,623.89	1,396.66	1,235.09	1,114.55	1,021.35	947.30
7.00%	7,138.46	3,693.74	2,547.36	1,975.57	1,633.60	1,406.54	1,245.15	1,124.78	1,031.77	957.89
7.25%	7,147.97	3,703.10	2,556.80	1,985.15	1,643.35	1,416.47	1,255.25	1,135.07	1,042.25	968.56
7.50%	7,157.49	3,712.47	2,566.26	1,994.76	1,653.13	1,426.43	1,265.41	1,145.42	1,052.78	979.29
7.75%	7,167.01	3,721.85	2,575.75	2,004.40	1,662.95	1,436.44	1,275.61	1,155.82	1,063.38	990.09
8.00%	7,176.55	3,731.25	2,585.25	2,014.07	1,672.80	1,446.49	1,285.86	1,166.28	1,074.04	1,000.95
8.25%	7,186.09	3,740.67	2,594.78	2,023.76	1,682.69	1,456.58	1,296.16	1,176.79	1,084.77	1,011.88
8.50%	7,195.63	3,750.09	2,604.32	2,033.49	1,692.61	1,466.72	1,306.51	1,187.35	1,095.55	1,022.88
8.75%	7,205.19	3,759.54	2,613.89	2,043.24	1,702.57	1,476.89	1,316.91	1,197.97	1,106.39	1,033.95
9.00%	7,214.75	3,768.99	2,623.48	2,053.02	1,712.56	1,487.11	1,327.35	1,208.64	1,117.29	1,045.08
9.25%	7,224.31	3,778.46	2,633.09	2,062.82	1,722.59	1,497.36	1,337.84	1,219.37	1,128.25	1,056.27
9.50%	7,233.89	3,787.95	2,642.72	2,072.66	1,732.65	1,507.66	1,348.38	1,230.15	1,139.27	1,067.53
9.75%	7,243.47	3,797.44	2,652.37	2,082.52	1,742.75	1,518.00	1,358.96	1,240.98	1,150.35	1,078.85
10.00%	7,253.06	3,806.96	2,662.04	2,092.41	1,752.88	1,528.38	1,369.60	1,251.87	1,161.49	1,090.24
10.25%	7,262.66	3,816.48	2,671.74	2,102.33	1,763.05	1,538.80	1,380.28	1,262.81	1,172.69	1,101.70
10.50%	7,272.26	3,826.02	2,681.45	2,112.28	1,773.25	1,549.27	1,391.01	1,273.80	1,183.95	1,113.21
10.75%	7,281.87	3,835.58	2,691.19	2,122.25	1,783.48	1,559.77	1,401.78	1,284.85	1,195.26	1,124.79

	1	2	3	4	5	6	7	8	9	10
11.00%	7,291.49	3,845.15	2,700.94	2,132.26	1,793.75	1,570.31	1,412.60	1,295.95	1,206.63	1,136.44
11.25%	7,301.11	3,854.73	2,710.72	2,142.29	1,804.05	1,580.90	1,423.47	1,307.10	1,218.06	1,148.14
11.50%	7,310.74	3,864.33	2,720.52	2,152.34	1,814.39	1,591.52	1,434.38	1,318.30	1,229.55	1,159.91
11.75%	7,320.38	3,873.94	2,730.34	2,162.43	1,824.76	1,602.19	1,445.34	1,329.55	1,241.10	1,171.74
12.00%	7,330.03	3,883.56	2,740.18	2,172.54	1,835.17	1,612.89	1,456.35	1,340.86	1,252.70	1,183.64
12.25%	7,339.68	3,893.20	2,750.04	2,182.68	1,845.61	1,623.64	1,467.40	1,352.22	1,264.36	1,195.59
12.50%	7,349.34	3,902.85	2,759.92	2,192.85	1,856.08	1,634.42	1,478.50	1,363.63	1,276.07	1,207.60
12.75%	7,359.00	3,912.52	2,769.83	2,203.05	1,866.59	1,645.25	1,489.65	1,375.09	1,287.84	1,219.68
13.00%	7,368.68	3,922.20	2,779.75	2,213.27	1,877.13	1,656.11	1,500.84	1,386.60	1,299.67	1,231.81
13.25%	7,378.36	3,931.90	2,789.70	2,223.52	1,887.70	1,667.02	1,512.07	1,398.16	1,311.55	1,244.01
13.50%	7,388.04	3,941.60	2,799.66	2,233.80	1,898.31	1,677.96	1,523.35	1,409.77	1,323.49	1,256.26
13.75%	7,397.74	3,951.33	2,809.65	2,244.10	1,908.95	1,688.95	1,534.68	1,421.44	1,335.48	1,268.58
14.00%	7,407.44	3,961.06	2,819.65	2,254.43	1,919.63	1,699.97	1,546.05	1,433.15	1,347.53	1,280.95
14.25%	7,417.15	3,970.81	2,829.68	2,264.79	1,930.34	1,711.04	1,557.47	1,444.91	1,359.63	1,293.38
14.50%	7,426.86	3,980.58	2,839.73	2,275.18	1,941.08	1,722.14	1,568.93	1,456.72	1,371.79	1,305.87
14.75%	7,436.58	3,990.36	2,849.80	2,285.60	1,951.86	1,733.28	1,580.43	1,468.59	1,384.00	1,318.41
15.00%	7,446.31	4,000.15	2,859.89	2,296.04	1,962.67	1,744.46	1,591.98	1,480.50	1,396.26	1,331.01
15.25%	7,456.05	4,009.95	2,870.00	2,306.51	1,973.51	1,755.68	1,603.58	1,492.46	1,408.57	1,343.67
15.50%	7,465.79	4,019.77	2,880.13	2,317.00	1,984.39	1,766.94	1,615.21	1,504.46	1,420.94	1,356.39
15.75%	7,475.54	4,029.61	2,890.28	2,327.52	1,995.30	1,778.24	1,626.90	1,516.52	1,433.36	1,369.16
16.00%	7,485.30	4,039.46	2,900.46	2,338.07	2,006.24	1,789.58	1,638.62	1,528.62	1,445.83	1,381.98
16.25%	7,495.06	4,049.32	2,910.65	2,348.65	2,017.21	1,800.95	1,650.39	1,540.78	1,458.36	1,394.86
16.50%	7,504.83	4,059.19	2,920.86	2,359.25	2,028.22	1,812.36	1,662.20	1,552.98	1,470.93	1,407.80
16.75%	7,514.61	4,069.08	2,931.10	2,369.88	2,039.26	1,823.82	1,674.06	1,565.23	1,483.56	1,420.79
17.00%	7,524.39	4,078.99	2,941.35	2,380.54	2,050.34	1,835.31	1,685.95	1,577.52	1,496.24	1,433.83
17.25%	7,534.18	4,088.90	2,951.62	2,391.23	2,061.44	1,846.83	1,697.89	1,589.86	1,508.96	1,446.93
17.50%	7,543.98	4,098.83	2,961.92	2,401.94	2,072.58	1,858.40	1,709.88	1,602.25	1,521.74	1,460.07
17.75%	7,553.79	4,108.78	2,972.24	2,412.67	2,083.75	1,870.00	1,721.90	1,614.68	1,534.57	1,473.28
18.00%	7,563.60	4,118.74	2,982.57	2,423.44	2,094.96	1,881.64	1,733.97	1,627.17	1,547.44	1,486.53
18.25%	7,573.42	4,128.71	2,992.93	2,434.23	2,106.19	1,893.32	1,746.08	1,639.69	1,560.37	1,499.83
18.50%	7,583.24	4,138.70	3,003.31	2,445.05	2,117.46	1,905.04	1,758.23	1,652.26	1,573.34	1,513.19
18.75%	7,593.08	4,148.70	3,013.70	2,455.89	2,128.76	1,916.79	1,770.43	1,664.88	1,586.36	1,526.59
19.00%	7,602.92	4,158.71	3,024.12	2,466.76	2,140.10	1,928.58	1,782.66	1,677.54	1,599.43	1,540.05
19.25%	7,612.76	4,168.74	3,034.56	2,477.66	2,151.46	1,940.41	1,794.94	1,690.25	1,612.55	1,553.55
19.50%	7,622.62	4,178.78	3,045.02	2,488.58	2,162.86	1,952.27	1,807.25	1,703.00	1,625.72	1,567.11
19.75%	7,632.48	4,188.83	3,055.50	2,499.53	2,174.29	1,964.17	1,819.61	1,715.80	1,638.93	1,580.71
20.00%	7,642.35	4,198.90	3,066.00	2,510.50	2,185.75	1,976.11	1,832.01	1,728.64	1,652.19	1,594.36
20.25%	7,652.22	4,208.99	3,076.51	2,521.51	2,197.24	1,988.08	1,844.45	1,741.52	1,665.49	1,608.06
20.50%	7,662.10	4,219.08	3,087.05	2,532.54	2,208.76	2,000.09	1,856.93	1,754.45	1,678.84	1,621.80
20.75%	7,671.99	4,229.19	3,097.61	2,543.59	2,220.32	2,012.14	1,869.45	1,767.42	1,692.24	1,635.60

	1	2	3	4	5	6	7	8	9	10
1.00%	7,121.76	3,578.68	2,397.69	1,807.22	1,452.97	1,216.82	1,048.16	921.67	823.31	744.64
1.25%	7,131.38	3,587.97	2,406.89	1,816.40	1,462.14	1,225.99	1,057.35	930.89	832.55	753.89
1.50%	7,141.02	3,597.27	2,416.11	1,825.60	1,471.34	1,235.21	1,066.59	940.16	841.85	763.23
1.75%	7,150.66	3,606.59	2,425.35	1,834.83	1,480.58	1,244.48	1,075.89	949.49	851.22	772.63
2.00%	7,160.30	3,615.92	2,434.62	1,844.09	1,489.86	1,253.79	1,085.23	958.87	860.65	782.11
2.25%	7,169.96	3,625.27	2,443.91	1,853.37	1,499.17	1,263.14	1,094.63	968.32	870.15	791.67
2.50%	7,179.62	3,634.63	2,453.22	1,862.69	1,508.53	1,272.54	1,104.08	977.83	879.71	801.29
2.75%	7,189.29	3,644.01	2,462.55	1,872.04	1,517.91	1,281.98	1,113.58	987.39	889.34	810.99
3.00%	7,198.96	3,653.40	2,471.90	1,881.42	1,527.34	1,291.46	1,123.13	997.01	899.04	820.77
3.25%	7,208.65	3,662.81	2,481.28	1,890.82	1,536.80	1,300.99	1,132.73	1,006.69	908.80	830.61
3.50%	7,218.34	3,672.23	2,490.68	1,900.26	1,546.30	1,310.56	1,142.39	1,016.43	918.63	840.53
3.75%	7,228.04	3,681.67	2,500.10	1,909.73	1,555.83	1,320.18	1,152.09	1,026.23	928.52	850.52
4.00%	7,237.74	3,691.12	2,509.54	1,919.22	1,565.40	1,329.84	1,161.85	1,036.09	938.48	860.58
4.25%	7,247.45	3,700.58	2,519.00	1,928.74	1,575.01	1,339.54	1,171.66	1,046.00	948.51	870.72
4.50%	7,257.17	3,710.06	2,528.49	1,938.30	1,584.66	1,349.29	1,181.51	1,055.97	958.60	880.93
4.75%	7,266.90	3,719.56	2,538.00	1,947.88	1,594.34	1,359.08	1,191.42	1,066.01	968.75	891.21
5.00%	7,276.64	3,729.07	2,547.53	1,957.49	1,604.05	1,368.92	1,201.38	1,076.09	978.97	901.56
5.25%	7,286.38	3,738.59	2,557.08	1,967.13	1,613.81	1,378.80	1,211.39	1,086.24	989.25	911.98
5.50%	7,296.13	3,748.13	2,566.65	1,976.80	1,623.60	1,388.72	1,221.45	1,096.44	999.60	922.47
5.75%	7,305.88	3,757.68	2,576.25	1,986.50	1,633.43	1,398.69	1,231.57	1,106.70	1,010.01	933.04
6.00%	7,315.65	3,767.25	2,585.86	1,996.23	1,643.29	1,408.70	1,241.73	1,117.02	1,020.49	943.67
6.25%	7,325.42	3,776.83	2,595.50	2,005.98	1,653.19	1,418.75	1,251.94	1,127.40	1,031.03	954.38
6.50%	7,335.20	3,786.43	2,605.17	2,015.77	1,663.12	1,428.84	1,262.20	1,137.83	1,041.63	965.16
6.75%	7,344.98	3,796.04	2,614.85	2,025.59	1,673.09	1,438.98	1,272.51	1,148.32	1,052.30	976.00
7.00%	7,354.77	3,805.67	2,624.55	2,035.43	1,683.10	1,449.17	1,282.88	1,158.87	1,063.03	986.92
7.25%	7,364.57	3,815.31	2,634.28	2,045.30	1,693.15	1,459.39	1,293.29	1,169.47	1,073.83	997.91
7.50%	7,374.38	3,824.97	2,644.03	2,055.21	1,703.23	1,469.66	1,303.75	1,180.13	1,084.69	1,008.97
7.75%	7,384.19	3,834.64	2,653.80	2,065.14	1,713.34	1,479.97	1,314.27	1,190.85	1,095.61	1,020.09
8.00%	7,394.02	3,844.32	2,663.59	2,075.10	1,723.49	1,490.33	1,324.83	1,201.62	1,106.59	1,031.28
8.25%	7,403.85	3,854.02	2,673.40	2,085.09	1,733.68	1,500.72	1,335.44	1,212.45	1,117.64	1,042.55
8.50%	7,413.68	3,863.73	2,683.24	2,095.11	1,743.91	1,511.16	1,346.10	1,223.33	1,128.74	1,053.88
8.75%	7,423.52	3,873.46	2,693.10	2,105.15	1,754.16	1,521.65	1,356.81	1,234.27	1,139.92	1,065.28
9.00%	7,433.38	3,883.20	2,702.98	2,115.23	1,764.46	1,532.17	1,367.57	1,245.27	1,151.15	1,076.74
9.25%	7,443.23	3,892.96	2,712.88	2,125.33	1,774.79	1,542.74	1,378.38	1,256.32	1,162.44	1,088.28
9.50%	7,453.10	3,902.73	2,722.80	2,135.47	1,785.16	1,553.35	1,389.24	1,267.43	1,173.80	1,099.88
9.75%	7,462.97	3,912.52	2,732.74	2,145.63	1,795.56	1,564.00	1,400.15	1,278.59	1,185.21	1,111.55
10.00%	7,472.85	3,922.32	2,742.71	2,155.82	1,806.00	1,574.70	1,411.10	1,289.80	1,196.69	1,123.28
10.25%	7,482.74	3,932.13	2,752.70	2,166.04	1,816.47	1,585.43	1,422.10	1,301.08	1,208.23	1,135.08
10.50%	7,492.63	3,941.96	2,762.71	2,176.29	1,826.98	1,596.21	1,433.16	1,312.40	1,219.82	1,146.95
10.75%	7,502.53	3,951.81	2,772.74	2,186.56	1,837.53	1,607.03	1,444.26	1,323.78	1,231.48	1,158.88

$85,000   11.00 - 20.75%   1 - 10 Years

	1	2	3	4	5	6	7	8	9	10
11.00%	7,512.44	3,961.67	2,782.79	2,196.87	1,848.11	1,617.90	1,455.41	1,335.22	1,243.20	1,170.88
11.25%	7,522.36	3,971.54	2,792.86	2,207.20	1,858.72	1,628.80	1,466.60	1,346.70	1,254.98	1,182.94
11.50%	7,532.28	3,981.43	2,802.96	2,217.57	1,869.37	1,639.75	1,477.85	1,358.25	1,266.81	1,195.06
11.75%	7,542.21	3,991.33	2,813.08	2,227.96	1,880.06	1,650.74	1,489.14	1,369.84	1,278.71	1,207.25
12.00%	7,552.15	4,001.25	2,823.22	2,238.38	1,890.78	1,661.77	1,500.48	1,381.49	1,290.66	1,219.50
12.25%	7,562.09	4,011.18	2,833.38	2,248.82	1,901.53	1,672.84	1,511.87	1,393.19	1,302.67	1,231.82
12.50%	7,572.04	4,021.12	2,843.56	2,259.30	1,912.32	1,683.95	1,523.31	1,404.95	1,314.74	1,244.20
12.75%	7,582.00	4,031.08	2,853.76	2,269.80	1,923.15	1,695.10	1,534.79	1,416.76	1,326.87	1,256.64
13.00%	7,591.97	4,041.05	2,863.99	2,280.34	1,934.01	1,706.30	1,546.32	1,428.62	1,339.05	1,269.14
13.25%	7,601.94	4,051.04	2,874.23	2,290.90	1,944.91	1,717.53	1,557.89	1,440.53	1,351.30	1,281.71
13.50%	7,611.92	4,061.05	2,884.50	2,301.49	1,955.84	1,728.81	1,569.52	1,452.49	1,363.60	1,294.33
13.75%	7,621.91	4,071.06	2,894.79	2,312.10	1,966.80	1,740.13	1,581.19	1,464.51	1,375.95	1,307.02
14.00%	7,631.90	4,081.10	2,905.10	2,322.75	1,977.80	1,751.49	1,592.90	1,476.58	1,388.36	1,319.76
14.25%	7,641.91	4,091.14	2,915.43	2,333.42	1,988.84	1,762.89	1,604.66	1,488.70	1,400.83	1,332.57
14.50%	7,651.92	4,101.20	2,925.78	2,344.13	1,999.90	1,774.33	1,616.47	1,500.87	1,413.36	1,345.44
14.75%	7,661.93	4,111.28	2,936.16	2,354.86	2,011.01	1,785.81	1,628.32	1,513.09	1,425.93	1,358.36
15.00%	7,671.96	4,121.37	2,946.55	2,365.61	2,022.14	1,797.33	1,640.22	1,525.36	1,438.57	1,371.35
15.25%	7,681.99	4,131.47	2,956.97	2,376.40	2,033.32	1,808.89	1,652.17	1,537.68	1,451.26	1,384.39
15.50%	7,692.03	4,141.59	2,967.41	2,387.21	2,044.52	1,820.49	1,664.16	1,550.05	1,464.00	1,397.49
15.75%	7,702.07	4,151.72	2,977.87	2,398.05	2,055.76	1,832.13	1,676.19	1,562.48	1,476.80	1,410.65
16.00%	7,712.12	4,161.86	2,988.35	2,408.92	2,067.03	1,843.81	1,688.28	1,574.95	1,489.65	1,423.86
16.25%	7,722.18	4,172.02	2,998.85	2,419.82	2,078.34	1,855.53	1,700.40	1,587.47	1,502.55	1,437.13
16.50%	7,732.25	4,182.20	3,009.37	2,430.75	2,089.68	1,867.28	1,712.57	1,600.04	1,515.51	1,450.46
16.75%	7,742.32	4,192.39	3,019.92	2,441.70	2,101.06	1,879.08	1,724.78	1,612.66	1,528.51	1,463.84
17.00%	7,752.40	4,202.59	3,030.48	2,452.68	2,112.47	1,890.92	1,737.04	1,625.32	1,541.58	1,477.28
17.25%	7,762.49	4,212.81	3,041.07	2,463.69	2,123.91	1,902.80	1,749.35	1,638.04	1,554.69	1,490.77
17.50%	7,772.59	4,223.04	3,051.68	2,474.72	2,135.39	1,914.71	1,761.69	1,650.80	1,567.85	1,504.32
17.75%	7,782.69	4,233.29	3,062.30	2,485.78	2,146.90	1,926.67	1,774.08	1,663.61	1,581.07	1,517.92
18.00%	7,792.80	4,243.55	3,072.95	2,496.87	2,158.44	1,938.66	1,786.52	1,676.47	1,594.34	1,531.57
18.25%	7,802.92	4,253.82	3,083.62	2,507.99	2,170.02	1,950.69	1,798.99	1,689.38	1,607.65	1,545.28
18.50%	7,813.04	4,264.11	3,094.32	2,519.14	2,181.63	1,962.77	1,811.51	1,702.33	1,621.02	1,559.04
18.75%	7,823.17	4,274.42	3,105.03	2,530.31	2,193.27	1,974.87	1,824.08	1,715.33	1,634.44	1,572.85
19.00%	7,833.31	4,284.73	3,115.76	2,541.51	2,204.95	1,987.02	1,836.68	1,728.38	1,647.90	1,586.72
19.25%	7,843.45	4,295.06	3,126.52	2,552.74	2,216.66	1,999.21	1,849.33	1,741.47	1,661.42	1,600.63
19.50%	7,853.61	4,305.41	3,137.29	2,563.99	2,228.40	2,011.43	1,862.02	1,754.61	1,674.98	1,614.59
19.75%	7,863.77	4,315.77	3,148.09	2,575.27	2,240.17	2,023.69	1,874.75	1,767.79	1,688.59	1,628.61
20.00%	7,873.93	4,326.14	3,158.90	2,586.58	2,251.98	2,035.99	1,887.53	1,781.02	1,702.25	1,642.67
20.25%	7,884.11	4,336.53	3,169.74	2,597.92	2,263.82	2,048.33	1,900.34	1,794.30	1,715.96	1,656.79
20.50%	7,894.29	4,346.93	3,180.60	2,609.28	2,275.69	2,060.70	1,913.20	1,807.62	1,729.71	1,670.95
20.75%	7,904.48	4,357.35	3,191.48	2,620.67	2,287.60	2,073.11	1,926.10	1,820.98	1,743.52	1,685.16

	1	2	3	4	5	6	7	8	9	10
1.00%	7,331.22	3,683.93	2,468.21	1,860.38	1,495.70	1,252.61	1,078.98	948.78	847.53	766.54
1.25%	7,341.13	3,693.49	2,477.68	1,869.82	1,505.14	1,262.05	1,088.45	958.26	857.03	776.07
1.50%	7,351.05	3,703.07	2,487.17	1,879.29	1,514.62	1,271.54	1,097.96	967.81	866.61	785.68
1.75%	7,360.97	3,712.67	2,496.69	1,888.79	1,524.13	1,281.08	1,107.53	977.41	876.25	795.36
2.00%	7,370.90	3,722.27	2,506.23	1,898.32	1,533.68	1,290.66	1,117.15	987.08	885.96	805.12
2.25%	7,380.84	3,731.90	2,515.79	1,907.89	1,543.27	1,300.29	1,126.82	996.80	895.74	814.95
2.50%	7,390.78	3,741.53	2,525.37	1,917.48	1,552.89	1,309.96	1,136.55	1,006.59	905.59	824.86
2.75%	7,400.74	3,751.19	2,534.98	1,927.10	1,562.56	1,319.68	1,146.33	1,016.43	915.50	834.85
3.00%	7,410.70	3,760.86	2,544.61	1,936.75	1,572.26	1,329.45	1,156.16	1,026.34	925.48	844.91
3.25%	7,420.67	3,770.54	2,554.26	1,946.44	1,582.00	1,339.26	1,166.05	1,036.30	935.53	855.04
3.50%	7,430.64	3,780.24	2,563.93	1,956.15	1,591.78	1,349.11	1,175.99	1,046.33	945.65	865.25
3.75%	7,440.63	3,789.95	2,573.63	1,965.89	1,601.59	1,359.01	1,185.98	1,056.42	955.83	875.54
4.00%	7,450.62	3,799.68	2,583.35	1,975.67	1,611.45	1,368.95	1,196.02	1,066.56	966.08	885.89
4.25%	7,460.61	3,809.42	2,593.09	1,985.47	1,621.34	1,378.94	1,206.12	1,076.77	976.40	896.33
4.50%	7,470.62	3,819.18	2,602.86	1,995.31	1,631.26	1,388.98	1,216.26	1,087.03	986.79	906.84
4.75%	7,480.63	3,828.96	2,612.64	2,005.17	1,641.23	1,399.06	1,226.46	1,097.36	997.24	917.42
5.00%	7,490.65	3,838.75	2,622.45	2,015.06	1,651.23	1,409.18	1,236.72	1,107.74	1,007.76	928.07
5.25%	7,500.68	3,848.55	2,632.29	2,024.99	1,661.27	1,419.35	1,247.02	1,118.19	1,018.35	938.80
5.50%	7,510.72	3,858.37	2,642.14	2,034.94	1,671.35	1,429.57	1,257.38	1,128.69	1,029.00	949.60
5.75%	7,520.76	3,868.20	2,652.02	2,044.93	1,681.47	1,439.82	1,267.79	1,139.25	1,039.72	960.48
6.00%	7,530.81	3,878.05	2,661.92	2,054.94	1,691.62	1,450.13	1,278.25	1,149.88	1,050.50	971.43
6.25%	7,540.87	3,887.92	2,671.84	2,064.98	1,701.81	1,460.48	1,288.76	1,160.56	1,061.35	982.45
6.50%	7,550.94	3,897.80	2,681.79	2,075.06	1,712.04	1,470.87	1,299.33	1,171.30	1,072.27	993.54
6.75%	7,561.01	3,907.69	2,691.76	2,085.16	1,722.30	1,481.31	1,309.94	1,182.09	1,083.25	1,004.71
7.00%	7,571.09	3,917.60	2,701.75	2,095.30	1,732.60	1,491.79	1,320.61	1,192.95	1,094.30	1,015.95
7.25%	7,581.18	3,927.53	2,711.76	2,105.46	1,742.94	1,502.31	1,331.33	1,203.87	1,105.41	1,027.26
7.50%	7,591.27	3,937.46	2,721.79	2,115.65	1,753.32	1,512.88	1,342.10	1,214.84	1,116.59	1,038.64
7.75%	7,601.38	3,947.42	2,731.85	2,125.88	1,763.73	1,523.50	1,352.92	1,225.87	1,127.83	1,050.09
8.00%	7,611.49	3,957.39	2,741.93	2,136.13	1,774.18	1,534.16	1,363.79	1,236.96	1,139.14	1,061.62
8.25%	7,621.61	3,967.37	2,752.03	2,146.41	1,784.67	1,544.86	1,374.72	1,248.11	1,150.51	1,073.21
8.50%	7,631.73	3,977.37	2,762.16	2,156.73	1,795.20	1,555.61	1,385.69	1,259.31	1,161.94	1,084.87
8.75%	7,641.86	3,987.39	2,772.31	2,167.07	1,805.76	1,566.40	1,396.72	1,270.57	1,173.44	1,096.61
9.00%	7,652.00	3,997.41	2,782.48	2,177.44	1,816.36	1,577.23	1,407.79	1,281.89	1,185.00	1,108.41
9.25%	7,662.15	4,007.46	2,792.67	2,187.84	1,826.99	1,588.11	1,418.92	1,293.27	1,196.63	1,120.29
9.50%	7,672.31	4,017.52	2,802.88	2,198.27	1,837.66	1,599.04	1,430.10	1,304.70	1,208.32	1,132.23
9.75%	7,682.47	4,027.59	2,813.12	2,208.74	1,848.37	1,610.00	1,441.33	1,316.19	1,220.07	1,144.24
10.00%	7,692.64	4,037.68	2,823.38	2,219.23	1,859.12	1,621.01	1,452.60	1,327.74	1,231.89	1,156.32
10.25%	7,702.82	4,047.78	2,833.66	2,229.75	1,869.90	1,632.06	1,463.93	1,339.34	1,243.76	1,168.47
10.50%	7,713.00	4,057.90	2,843.96	2,240.30	1,880.72	1,643.16	1,475.31	1,351.00	1,255.70	1,180.68
10.75%	7,723.20	4,068.04	2,854.29	2,250.87	1,891.57	1,654.30	1,486.74	1,362.72	1,267.70	1,192.96

$87,500   11.00 - 20.75%   1 - 10 Years

	1	2	3	4	5	6	7	8	9	10
11.00%	7,733.40	4,078.19	2,864.64	2,261.48	1,902.46	1,665.48	1,498.21	1,374.49	1,279.76	1,205.31
11.25%	7,743.60	4,088.35	2,875.01	2,272.12	1,913.39	1,676.71	1,509.74	1,386.31	1,291.89	1,217.73
11.50%	7,753.82	4,098.53	2,885.40	2,282.79	1,924.35	1,687.98	1,521.32	1,398.20	1,304.07	1,230.21
11.75%	7,764.04	4,108.72	2,895.82	2,293.48	1,935.35	1,699.29	1,532.94	1,410.13	1,316.32	1,242.76
12.00%	7,774.27	4,118.93	2,906.25	2,304.21	1,946.39	1,710.64	1,544.61	1,422.12	1,328.62	1,255.37
12.25%	7,784.51	4,129.15	2,916.71	2,314.97	1,957.46	1,722.04	1,556.34	1,434.17	1,340.99	1,268.05
12.50%	7,794.75	4,139.39	2,927.19	2,325.75	1,968.57	1,733.48	1,568.11	1,446.27	1,353.41	1,280.79
12.75%	7,805.00	4,149.64	2,937.70	2,336.56	1,979.71	1,744.96	1,579.93	1,458.43	1,365.90	1,293.60
13.00%	7,815.26	4,159.91	2,948.22	2,347.41	1,990.89	1,756.48	1,591.80	1,470.63	1,378.44	1,306.47
13.25%	7,825.53	4,170.19	2,958.77	2,358.28	2,002.11	1,768.05	1,603.71	1,482.90	1,391.04	1,319.40
13.50%	7,835.80	4,180.49	2,969.34	2,369.18	2,013.36	1,779.66	1,615.68	1,495.21	1,403.70	1,332.40
13.75%	7,846.08	4,190.80	2,979.93	2,380.11	2,024.65	1,791.31	1,627.69	1,507.58	1,416.42	1,345.46
14.00%	7,856.37	4,201.13	2,990.54	2,391.07	2,035.97	1,803.00	1,639.75	1,520.01	1,429.20	1,358.58
14.25%	7,866.67	4,211.47	3,001.18	2,402.05	2,047.33	1,814.74	1,651.86	1,532.48	1,442.03	1,371.76
14.50%	7,876.97	4,221.82	3,011.84	2,413.07	2,058.72	1,826.51	1,664.01	1,545.01	1,454.93	1,385.01
14.75%	7,887.28	4,232.20	3,022.51	2,424.12	2,070.15	1,838.33	1,676.22	1,557.59	1,467.87	1,398.31
15.00%	7,897.60	4,242.58	3,033.22	2,435.19	2,081.62	1,850.19	1,688.47	1,570.22	1,480.88	1,411.68
15.25%	7,907.93	4,252.98	3,043.94	2,446.29	2,093.12	1,862.09	1,700.76	1,582.91	1,493.94	1,425.11
15.50%	7,918.26	4,263.40	3,054.68	2,457.43	2,104.65	1,874.03	1,713.11	1,595.64	1,507.06	1,438.59
15.75%	7,928.60	4,273.83	3,065.45	2,468.59	2,116.22	1,886.01	1,725.49	1,608.43	1,520.23	1,452.14
16.00%	7,938.95	4,284.27	3,076.24	2,479.77	2,127.83	1,898.04	1,737.93	1,621.27	1,533.46	1,465.74
16.25%	7,949.31	4,294.73	3,087.05	2,490.99	2,139.47	1,910.10	1,750.41	1,634.16	1,546.74	1,479.40
16.50%	7,959.67	4,305.21	3,097.88	2,502.24	2,151.15	1,922.21	1,762.94	1,647.10	1,560.08	1,493.12
16.75%	7,970.04	4,315.69	3,108.74	2,513.51	2,162.86	1,934.35	1,775.51	1,660.09	1,573.47	1,506.90
17.00%	7,980.42	4,326.20	3,119.61	2,524.82	2,174.60	1,946.54	1,788.13	1,673.13	1,586.92	1,520.73
17.25%	7,990.80	4,336.72	3,130.51	2,536.15	2,186.38	1,958.76	1,800.80	1,686.22	1,600.42	1,534.62
17.50%	8,001.19	4,347.25	3,141.43	2,547.51	2,198.19	1,971.03	1,813.51	1,699.36	1,613.97	1,548.56
17.75%	8,011.59	4,357.80	3,152.37	2,558.90	2,210.04	1,983.34	1,826.26	1,712.54	1,627.57	1,562.56
18.00%	8,022.00	4,368.36	3,163.33	2,570.31	2,221.92	1,995.68	1,839.06	1,725.78	1,641.23	1,576.62
18.25%	8,032.41	4,378.94	3,174.32	2,581.76	2,233.84	2,008.07	1,851.90	1,739.07	1,654.94	1,590.73
18.50%	8,042.84	4,389.53	3,185.33	2,593.23	2,245.79	2,020.49	1,864.79	1,752.40	1,668.70	1,604.89
18.75%	8,053.26	4,400.13	3,196.35	2,604.73	2,257.78	2,032.96	1,877.73	1,765.78	1,682.51	1,619.11
19.00%	8,063.70	4,410.75	3,207.40	2,616.26	2,269.80	2,045.46	1,890.70	1,779.21	1,696.37	1,633.38
19.25%	8,074.14	4,421.39	3,218.47	2,627.82	2,281.85	2,058.01	1,903.72	1,792.69	1,710.28	1,647.71
19.50%	8,084.60	4,432.04	3,229.56	2,639.40	2,293.94	2,070.59	1,916.79	1,806.22	1,724.24	1,662.08
19.75%	8,095.05	4,442.70	3,240.68	2,651.02	2,306.06	2,083.21	1,929.89	1,819.79	1,738.26	1,676.51
20.00%	8,105.52	4,453.38	3,251.81	2,662.66	2,318.21	2,095.87	1,943.04	1,833.41	1,752.32	1,690.99
20.25%	8,115.99	4,464.08	3,262.97	2,674.33	2,330.40	2,108.57	1,956.24	1,847.07	1,766.43	1,705.52
20.50%	8,126.47	4,474.78	3,274.15	2,686.02	2,342.63	2,121.31	1,969.47	1,860.78	1,780.59	1,720.10
20.75%	8,136.96	4,485.51	3,285.35	2,697.75	2,354.88	2,134.09	1,982.75	1,874.54	1,794.80	1,734.72

	1	2	3	4	5	6	7	8	9	10
1.00%	7,540.69	3,789.19	2,538.73	1,913.53	1,538.44	1,288.40	1,109.81	975.89	871.74	788.44
1.25%	7,550.88	3,799.02	2,548.47	1,923.24	1,548.14	1,298.11	1,119.54	985.64	881.52	798.24
1.50%	7,561.08	3,808.87	2,558.23	1,932.98	1,557.89	1,307.87	1,129.33	995.46	891.37	808.12
1.75%	7,571.28	3,818.74	2,568.02	1,942.76	1,567.67	1,317.68	1,139.17	1,005.34	901.29	818.08
2.00%	7,581.50	3,828.62	2,577.83	1,952.56	1,577.50	1,327.54	1,149.07	1,015.28	911.27	828.12
2.25%	7,591.72	3,838.52	2,587.67	1,962.40	1,587.36	1,337.44	1,159.02	1,025.28	921.33	838.24
2.50%	7,601.95	3,848.44	2,597.52	1,972.26	1,597.26	1,347.39	1,169.02	1,035.35	931.46	848.43
2.75%	7,612.19	3,858.36	2,607.40	1,982.16	1,607.20	1,357.39	1,179.08	1,045.47	941.66	858.70
3.00%	7,622.43	3,868.31	2,617.31	1,992.09	1,617.18	1,367.43	1,189.20	1,055.66	951.92	869.05
3.25%	7,632.69	3,878.27	2,627.24	2,002.05	1,627.20	1,377.52	1,199.36	1,065.91	962.26	879.47
3.50%	7,642.95	3,888.24	2,637.19	2,012.04	1,637.26	1,387.66	1,209.59	1,076.22	972.67	889.97
3.75%	7,653.22	3,898.24	2,647.16	2,022.06	1,647.35	1,397.84	1,219.86	1,086.60	983.14	900.55
4.00%	7,663.49	3,908.24	2,657.16	2,032.11	1,657.49	1,408.07	1,230.19	1,097.03	993.69	911.21
4.25%	7,673.78	3,918.27	2,667.18	2,042.20	1,667.66	1,418.34	1,240.58	1,107.53	1,004.30	921.94
4.50%	7,684.07	3,928.30	2,677.22	2,052.31	1,677.87	1,428.66	1,251.01	1,118.09	1,014.98	932.75
4.75%	7,694.37	3,938.36	2,687.29	2,062.46	1,688.12	1,439.03	1,261.51	1,128.71	1,025.73	943.63
5.00%	7,704.67	3,948.43	2,697.38	2,072.64	1,698.41	1,449.44	1,272.05	1,139.39	1,036.55	954.59
5.25%	7,714.99	3,958.51	2,707.49	2,082.84	1,708.74	1,459.90	1,282.65	1,150.14	1,047.44	965.63
5.50%	7,725.31	3,968.61	2,717.63	2,093.08	1,719.10	1,470.41	1,293.30	1,160.94	1,058.40	976.74
5.75%	7,735.64	3,978.72	2,727.79	2,103.35	1,729.51	1,480.96	1,304.01	1,171.80	1,069.42	987.92
6.00%	7,745.98	3,988.85	2,737.97	2,113.65	1,739.95	1,491.56	1,314.77	1,182.73	1,080.52	999.18
6.25%	7,756.32	3,999.00	2,748.18	2,123.98	1,750.43	1,502.20	1,325.58	1,193.71	1,091.68	1,010.52
6.50%	7,766.68	4,009.16	2,758.41	2,134.35	1,760.95	1,512.89	1,336.45	1,204.76	1,102.91	1,021.93
6.75%	7,777.04	4,019.34	2,768.66	2,144.74	1,771.51	1,523.63	1,347.37	1,215.87	1,114.20	1,033.42
7.00%	7,787.41	4,029.53	2,778.94	2,155.16	1,782.11	1,534.41	1,358.34	1,227.03	1,125.56	1,044.98
7.25%	7,797.78	4,039.74	2,789.24	2,165.62	1,792.74	1,545.24	1,369.37	1,238.26	1,136.99	1,056.61
7.50%	7,808.17	4,049.96	2,799.56	2,176.10	1,803.42	1,556.11	1,380.44	1,249.55	1,148.49	1,068.32
7.75%	7,818.56	4,060.20	2,809.90	2,186.62	1,814.13	1,567.03	1,391.58	1,260.89	1,160.05	1,080.10
8.00%	7,828.96	4,070.46	2,820.27	2,197.16	1,824.88	1,577.99	1,402.76	1,272.30	1,171.68	1,091.95
8.25%	7,839.37	4,080.73	2,830.66	2,207.74	1,835.66	1,589.00	1,414.00	1,283.77	1,183.38	1,103.87
8.50%	7,849.78	4,091.01	2,841.08	2,218.35	1,846.49	1,600.05	1,425.28	1,295.29	1,195.14	1,115.87
8.75%	7,860.20	4,101.31	2,851.52	2,228.99	1,857.35	1,611.15	1,436.62	1,306.88	1,206.97	1,127.94
9.00%	7,870.63	4,111.63	2,861.98	2,239.65	1,868.25	1,622.30	1,448.02	1,318.52	1,218.86	1,140.08
9.25%	7,881.07	4,121.96	2,872.46	2,250.35	1,879.19	1,633.49	1,459.46	1,330.22	1,230.82	1,152.29
9.50%	7,891.52	4,132.30	2,882.97	2,261.08	1,890.17	1,644.72	1,470.96	1,341.98	1,242.84	1,164.58
9.75%	7,901.97	4,142.67	2,893.49	2,271.84	1,901.18	1,656.00	1,482.51	1,353.80	1,254.93	1,176.93
10.00%	7,912.43	4,153.04	2,904.05	2,282.63	1,912.23	1,667.33	1,494.11	1,365.67	1,267.08	1,189.36
10.25%	7,922.90	4,163.44	2,914.62	2,293.45	1,923.32	1,678.69	1,505.76	1,377.61	1,279.30	1,201.85
10.50%	7,933.37	4,173.84	2,925.22	2,304.30	1,934.45	1,690.11	1,517.46	1,389.60	1,291.58	1,214.41
10.75%	7,943.86	4,184.27	2,935.84	2,315.19	1,945.62	1,701.57	1,529.21	1,401.65	1,303.92	1,227.05

	1	2	3	4	5	6	7	8	9	10
11.00%	7,954.35	4,194.71	2,946.48	2,326.10	1,956.82	1,713.07	1,541.02	1,413.76	1,316.33	1,239.75
11.25%	7,964.85	4,205.16	2,957.15	2,337.04	1,968.06	1,724.61	1,552.88	1,425.92	1,328.80	1,252.52
11.50%	7,975.35	4,215.63	2,967.84	2,348.01	1,979.33	1,736.20	1,564.78	1,438.14	1,341.33	1,265.36
11.75%	7,985.87	4,226.11	2,978.55	2,359.01	1,990.65	1,747.84	1,576.74	1,450.42	1,353.92	1,278.27
12.00%	7,996.39	4,236.61	2,989.29	2,370.05	2,002.00	1,759.52	1,588.75	1,462.76	1,366.58	1,291.24
12.25%	8,006.92	4,247.13	3,000.05	2,381.11	2,013.39	1,771.24	1,600.80	1,475.15	1,379.30	1,304.28
12.50%	8,017.46	4,257.66	3,010.83	2,392.20	2,024.81	1,783.01	1,612.91	1,487.59	1,392.08	1,317.39
12.75%	8,028.00	4,268.20	3,021.63	2,403.32	2,036.28	1,794.82	1,625.07	1,500.10	1,404.92	1,330.56
13.00%	8,038.55	4,278.76	3,032.46	2,414.47	2,047.78	1,806.67	1,637.28	1,512.65	1,417.82	1,343.80
13.25%	8,049.11	4,289.34	3,043.30	2,425.66	2,059.31	1,818.57	1,649.53	1,525.27	1,430.79	1,357.10
13.50%	8,059.68	4,299.93	3,054.18	2,436.87	2,070.89	1,830.51	1,661.84	1,537.93	1,443.81	1,370.47
13.75%	8,070.26	4,310.54	3,065.07	2,448.11	2,082.50	1,842.49	1,674.20	1,550.66	1,456.89	1,383.90
14.00%	8,080.84	4,321.16	3,075.99	2,459.38	2,094.14	1,854.52	1,686.60	1,563.44	1,470.03	1,397.40
14.25%	8,091.43	4,331.80	3,086.93	2,470.68	2,105.83	1,866.59	1,699.05	1,576.27	1,483.23	1,410.96
14.50%	8,102.03	4,342.45	3,097.89	2,482.02	2,117.55	1,878.70	1,711.56	1,589.15	1,496.49	1,424.58
14.75%	8,112.63	4,353.12	3,108.87	2,493.38	2,129.30	1,890.85	1,724.11	1,602.09	1,509.81	1,438.27
15.00%	8,123.25	4,363.80	3,119.88	2,504.77	2,141.09	1,903.05	1,736.71	1,615.09	1,523.19	1,452.01
15.25%	8,133.87	4,374.50	3,130.91	2,516.19	2,152.92	1,915.29	1,749.36	1,628.13	1,536.63	1,465.82
15.50%	8,144.50	4,385.21	3,141.96	2,527.64	2,164.79	1,927.57	1,762.05	1,641.23	1,550.12	1,479.69
15.75%	8,155.13	4,395.94	3,153.04	2,539.12	2,176.69	1,939.90	1,774.79	1,654.39	1,563.67	1,493.63
16.00%	8,165.78	4,406.68	3,164.13	2,550.63	2,188.63	1,952.27	1,787.59	1,667.59	1,577.27	1,507.62
16.25%	8,176.43	4,417.44	3,175.25	2,562.16	2,200.60	1,964.67	1,800.42	1,680.85	1,590.93	1,521.67
16.50%	8,187.09	4,428.21	3,186.39	2,573.73	2,212.61	1,977.13	1,813.31	1,694.16	1,604.65	1,535.78
16.75%	8,197.75	4,439.00	3,197.56	2,585.33	2,224.65	1,989.62	1,826.24	1,707.52	1,618.43	1,549.95
17.00%	8,208.43	4,449.80	3,208.75	2,596.95	2,236.73	2,002.15	1,839.22	1,720.93	1,632.26	1,564.18
17.25%	8,219.11	4,460.62	3,219.95	2,608.61	2,248.85	2,014.73	1,852.25	1,734.39	1,646.14	1,578.47
17.50%	8,229.80	4,471.46	3,231.19	2,620.29	2,261.00	2,027.34	1,865.32	1,747.91	1,660.08	1,592.81
17.75%	8,240.50	4,482.31	3,242.44	2,632.01	2,273.19	2,040.00	1,878.44	1,761.47	1,674.07	1,607.21
18.00%	8,251.20	4,493.17	3,253.72	2,643.75	2,285.41	2,052.70	1,891.61	1,775.09	1,688.12	1,621.67
18.25%	8,261.91	4,504.05	3,265.01	2,655.52	2,297.67	2,065.44	1,904.82	1,788.75	1,702.22	1,636.18
18.50%	8,272.63	4,514.94	3,276.33	2,667.32	2,309.96	2,078.22	1,918.07	1,802.47	1,716.37	1,650.75
18.75%	8,283.36	4,525.85	3,287.68	2,679.15	2,322.29	2,091.04	1,931.37	1,816.23	1,730.58	1,665.37
19.00%	8,294.09	4,536.78	3,299.04	2,691.01	2,334.65	2,103.91	1,944.72	1,830.05	1,744.84	1,680.05
19.25%	8,304.83	4,547.71	3,310.43	2,702.90	2,347.05	2,116.81	1,958.11	1,843.91	1,759.15	1,694.78
19.50%	8,315.58	4,558.67	3,321.84	2,714.81	2,359.48	2,129.75	1,971.55	1,857.82	1,773.51	1,709.57
19.75%	8,326.34	4,569.64	3,333.27	2,726.76	2,371.95	2,142.73	1,985.03	1,871.78	1,787.92	1,724.41
20.00%	8,337.11	4,580.62	3,344.72	2,738.73	2,384.45	2,155.75	1,998.56	1,885.79	1,802.39	1,739.30
20.25%	8,347.88	4,591.62	3,356.20	2,750.73	2,396.99	2,168.82	2,012.13	1,899.84	1,816.90	1,754.25
20.50%	8,358.66	4,602.64	3,367.70	2,762.77	2,409.56	2,181.92	2,025.74	1,913.95	1,831.46	1,769.24
20.75%	8,369.44	4,613.66	3,379.21	2,774.82	2,422.16	2,195.06	2,039.40	1,928.09	1,846.08	1,784.29

	1	2	3	4	5	6	7	8	9	10
1.00%	7,750.15	3,894.44	2,609.25	1,966.68	1,581.17	1,324.18	1,140.64	1,003.00	895.96	810.34
1.25%	7,760.62	3,904.55	2,619.26	1,976.67	1,591.15	1,334.17	1,150.64	1,013.02	906.01	820.41
1.50%	7,771.11	3,914.68	2,629.30	1,986.68	1,601.16	1,344.20	1,160.70	1,023.11	916.13	830.57
1.75%	7,781.60	3,924.82	2,639.36	1,996.72	1,611.22	1,354.29	1,170.82	1,033.26	926.32	840.81
2.00%	7,792.10	3,934.97	2,649.44	2,006.80	1,621.32	1,364.42	1,180.99	1,043.48	936.59	851.12
2.25%	7,802.60	3,945.15	2,659.55	2,016.91	1,631.45	1,374.59	1,191.21	1,053.76	946.92	861.52
2.50%	7,813.12	3,955.34	2,669.68	2,027.05	1,641.63	1,384.82	1,201.50	1,064.11	957.33	872.00
2.75%	7,823.64	3,965.54	2,679.83	2,037.22	1,651.85	1,395.09	1,211.84	1,074.51	967.81	882.55
3.00%	7,834.17	3,975.76	2,690.01	2,047.43	1,662.10	1,405.42	1,222.23	1,084.99	978.37	893.19
3.25%	7,844.70	3,986.00	2,700.22	2,057.66	1,672.40	1,415.78	1,232.68	1,095.52	988.99	903.90
3.50%	7,855.25	3,996.25	2,710.44	2,067.93	1,682.74	1,426.20	1,243.19	1,106.12	999.69	914.69
3.75%	7,865.80	4,006.52	2,720.69	2,078.23	1,693.11	1,436.67	1,253.75	1,116.78	1,010.45	925.57
4.00%	7,876.37	4,016.81	2,730.97	2,088.56	1,703.53	1,447.18	1,264.36	1,127.51	1,021.29	936.52
4.25%	7,886.94	4,027.11	2,741.27	2,098.93	1,713.98	1,457.74	1,275.04	1,138.30	1,032.20	947.55
4.50%	7,897.51	4,037.42	2,751.59	2,109.32	1,724.48	1,468.35	1,285.76	1,149.15	1,043.18	958.66
4.75%	7,908.10	4,047.76	2,761.94	2,119.75	1,735.01	1,479.00	1,296.55	1,160.06	1,054.23	969.84
5.00%	7,918.69	4,058.10	2,772.31	2,130.21	1,745.59	1,489.71	1,307.39	1,171.04	1,065.35	981.11
5.25%	7,929.29	4,068.47	2,782.70	2,140.70	1,756.20	1,500.46	1,318.28	1,182.08	1,076.54	992.45
5.50%	7,939.90	4,078.85	2,793.12	2,151.22	1,766.86	1,511.25	1,329.23	1,193.19	1,087.80	1,003.87
5.75%	7,950.52	4,089.24	2,803.56	2,161.78	1,777.55	1,522.10	1,340.23	1,204.35	1,099.13	1,015.37
6.00%	7,961.14	4,099.66	2,814.03	2,172.37	1,788.28	1,532.99	1,351.29	1,215.58	1,110.53	1,026.94
6.25%	7,971.78	4,110.08	2,824.52	2,182.98	1,799.06	1,543.93	1,362.40	1,226.87	1,122.00	1,038.59
6.50%	7,982.42	4,120.53	2,835.03	2,193.63	1,809.87	1,554.92	1,373.57	1,238.23	1,133.54	1,050.32
6.75%	7,993.07	4,130.99	2,845.57	2,204.31	1,820.72	1,565.95	1,384.80	1,249.64	1,145.15	1,062.12
7.00%	8,003.72	4,141.46	2,856.13	2,215.03	1,831.61	1,577.03	1,396.07	1,261.12	1,156.83	1,074.00
7.25%	8,014.39	4,151.96	2,866.72	2,225.77	1,842.54	1,588.16	1,407.40	1,272.66	1,168.58	1,085.96
7.50%	8,025.06	4,162.46	2,877.33	2,236.55	1,853.51	1,599.34	1,418.79	1,284.26	1,180.39	1,097.99
7.75%	8,035.74	4,172.99	2,887.96	2,247.36	1,864.52	1,610.56	1,430.23	1,295.92	1,192.28	1,110.10
8.00%	8,046.43	4,183.52	2,898.61	2,258.20	1,875.57	1,621.82	1,441.72	1,307.64	1,204.23	1,122.28
8.25%	8,057.13	4,194.08	2,909.29	2,269.07	1,886.65	1,633.14	1,453.27	1,319.43	1,216.25	1,134.54
8.50%	8,067.83	4,204.65	2,920.00	2,279.97	1,897.78	1,644.50	1,464.87	1,331.27	1,228.34	1,146.87
8.75%	8,078.54	4,215.24	2,930.72	2,290.90	1,908.94	1,655.91	1,476.53	1,343.18	1,240.50	1,159.27
9.00%	8,089.26	4,225.84	2,941.48	2,301.87	1,920.15	1,667.36	1,488.24	1,355.14	1,252.72	1,171.75
9.25%	8,099.99	4,236.46	2,952.25	2,312.86	1,931.39	1,678.86	1,500.00	1,367.17	1,265.01	1,184.30
9.50%	8,110.72	4,247.09	2,963.05	2,323.89	1,942.67	1,690.41	1,511.82	1,379.26	1,277.37	1,196.93
9.75%	8,121.47	4,257.74	2,973.87	2,334.95	1,953.99	1,702.00	1,523.69	1,391.40	1,289.79	1,209.62
10.00%	8,132.22	4,268.41	2,984.71	2,346.04	1,965.35	1,713.64	1,535.61	1,403.61	1,302.28	1,222.39
10.25%	8,142.98	4,279.09	2,995.58	2,357.16	1,976.75	1,725.32	1,547.58	1,415.88	1,314.83	1,235.24
10.50%	8,153.75	4,289.78	3,006.48	2,368.31	1,988.19	1,737.05	1,559.61	1,428.20	1,327.45	1,248.15
10.75%	8,164.52	4,300.50	3,017.39	2,379.50	1,999.66	1,748.83	1,571.69	1,440.59	1,340.14	1,261.13

	1	2	3	4	5	6	7	8	9	10
11.00%	8,175.30	4,311.23	3,028.33	2,390.71	2,011.17	1,760.65	1,583.83	1,453.03	1,352.89	1,274.19
11.25%	8,186.09	4,321.97	3,039.29	2,401.96	2,022.73	1,772.52	1,596.01	1,465.53	1,365.71	1,287.31
11.50%	8,196.89	4,332.73	3,050.28	2,413.23	2,034.32	1,784.43	1,608.25	1,478.09	1,378.59	1,300.51
11.75%	8,207.70	4,343.50	3,061.29	2,424.54	2,045.94	1,796.39	1,620.54	1,490.71	1,391.53	1,313.77
12.00%	8,218.51	4,354.30	3,072.32	2,435.88	2,057.61	1,808.39	1,632.88	1,503.39	1,404.54	1,327.11
12.25%	8,229.33	4,365.10	3,083.38	2,447.25	2,069.32	1,820.44	1,645.27	1,516.12	1,417.61	1,340.51
12.50%	8,240.16	4,375.93	3,094.46	2,458.65	2,081.06	1,832.53	1,657.71	1,528.91	1,430.75	1,353.98
12.75%	8,251.00	4,386.76	3,105.56	2,470.08	2,092.84	1,844.67	1,670.21	1,541.76	1,443.95	1,367.52
13.00%	8,261.85	4,397.62	3,116.69	2,481.54	2,104.66	1,856.85	1,682.76	1,554.67	1,457.21	1,381.12
13.25%	8,272.70	4,408.49	3,127.84	2,493.04	2,116.52	1,869.08	1,695.35	1,567.63	1,470.53	1,394.80
13.50%	8,283.56	4,419.37	3,139.01	2,504.56	2,128.41	1,881.35	1,708.00	1,580.65	1,483.91	1,408.54
13.75%	8,294.43	4,430.27	3,150.21	2,516.11	2,140.34	1,893.67	1,720.70	1,593.73	1,497.36	1,422.34
14.00%	8,305.31	4,441.19	3,161.43	2,527.70	2,152.31	1,906.03	1,733.45	1,606.86	1,510.87	1,436.21
14.25%	8,316.19	4,452.12	3,172.67	2,539.31	2,164.32	1,918.44	1,746.25	1,620.05	1,524.44	1,450.15
14.50%	8,327.09	4,463.07	3,183.94	2,550.96	2,176.37	1,930.88	1,759.10	1,633.30	1,538.06	1,464.15
14.75%	8,337.99	4,474.04	3,195.23	2,562.64	2,188.45	1,943.38	1,772.00	1,646.60	1,551.75	1,478.22
15.00%	8,348.89	4,485.01	3,206.54	2,574.34	2,200.57	1,955.91	1,784.95	1,659.95	1,565.50	1,492.35
15.25%	8,359.81	4,496.01	3,217.88	2,586.08	2,212.73	1,968.49	1,797.95	1,673.36	1,579.31	1,506.54
15.50%	8,370.73	4,507.02	3,229.24	2,597.85	2,224.92	1,981.12	1,811.00	1,686.82	1,593.18	1,520.80
15.75%	8,381.67	4,518.05	3,240.62	2,609.65	2,237.15	1,993.78	1,824.09	1,700.34	1,607.10	1,535.12
16.00%	8,392.60	4,529.09	3,252.03	2,621.48	2,249.42	2,006.50	1,837.24	1,713.91	1,621.09	1,549.50
16.25%	8,403.55	4,540.14	3,263.45	2,633.33	2,261.73	2,019.25	1,850.44	1,727.54	1,635.13	1,563.94
16.50%	8,414.51	4,551.22	3,274.91	2,645.22	2,274.07	2,032.05	1,863.68	1,741.22	1,649.23	1,578.44
16.75%	8,425.47	4,562.31	3,286.38	2,657.14	2,286.45	2,044.88	1,876.97	1,754.95	1,663.38	1,593.00
17.00%	8,436.44	4,573.41	3,297.88	2,669.09	2,298.86	2,057.77	1,890.31	1,768.73	1,677.60	1,607.63
17.25%	8,447.42	4,584.53	3,309.40	2,681.07	2,311.32	2,070.69	1,903.70	1,782.57	1,691.87	1,622.31
17.50%	8,458.40	4,595.66	3,320.94	2,693.08	2,323.80	2,083.66	1,917.14	1,796.46	1,706.19	1,637.05
17.75%	8,469.40	4,606.81	3,332.51	2,705.12	2,336.33	2,096.67	1,930.62	1,810.40	1,720.58	1,651.85
18.00%	8,480.40	4,617.98	3,344.10	2,717.19	2,348.89	2,109.72	1,944.15	1,824.40	1,735.01	1,666.71
18.25%	8,491.41	4,629.16	3,355.71	2,729.29	2,361.49	2,122.81	1,957.73	1,838.44	1,749.50	1,681.63
18.50%	8,502.43	4,640.36	3,367.34	2,741.41	2,374.12	2,135.95	1,971.35	1,852.54	1,764.05	1,696.60
18.75%	8,513.45	4,651.57	3,379.00	2,753.57	2,386.79	2,149.13	1,985.02	1,866.69	1,778.65	1,711.63
19.00%	8,524.48	4,662.80	3,390.68	2,765.76	2,399.50	2,162.35	1,998.74	1,880.88	1,793.31	1,726.72
19.25%	8,535.52	4,674.04	3,402.39	2,777.98	2,412.24	2,175.61	2,012.51	1,895.13	1,808.01	1,741.86
19.50%	8,546.57	4,685.30	3,414.11	2,790.23	2,425.02	2,188.91	2,026.32	1,909.43	1,822.77	1,757.06
19.75%	8,557.63	4,696.57	3,425.86	2,802.50	2,437.83	2,202.25	2,040.17	1,923.77	1,837.59	1,772.31
20.00%	8,568.69	4,707.86	3,437.63	2,814.81	2,450.68	2,215.64	2,054.07	1,938.17	1,852.45	1,787.61
20.25%	8,579.76	4,719.17	3,449.43	2,827.14	2,463.57	2,229.06	2,068.02	1,952.62	1,867.37	1,802.97
20.50%	8,590.84	4,730.49	3,461.24	2,839.51	2,476.49	2,242.53	2,082.01	1,967.11	1,882.34	1,818.39
20.75%	8,601.93	4,741.82	3,473.08	2,851.90	2,489.44	2,256.03	2,096.05	1,981.65	1,897.36	1,833.85

	1	2	3	4	5	6	7	8	9	10
1.00%	7,959.61	3,999.70	2,679.77	2,019.84	1,623.91	1,359.97	1,171.47	1,030.11	920.17	832.24
1.25%	7,970.37	4,010.08	2,690.05	2,030.09	1,634.15	1,370.23	1,181.74	1,040.40	930.49	842.59
1.50%	7,981.14	4,020.48	2,700.36	2,040.37	1,644.44	1,380.53	1,192.07	1,050.76	940.89	853.02
1.75%	7,991.91	4,030.89	2,710.69	2,050.69	1,654.77	1,390.89	1,202.46	1,061.19	951.36	863.53
2.00%	8,002.69	4,041.33	2,721.04	2,061.04	1,665.14	1,401.29	1,212.91	1,071.68	961.90	874.13
2.25%	8,013.48	4,051.77	2,731.43	2,071.42	1,675.55	1,411.74	1,223.41	1,082.24	972.52	884.81
2.50%	8,024.28	4,062.24	2,741.83	2,081.83	1,686.00	1,422.25	1,233.97	1,092.87	983.21	895.56
2.75%	8,035.09	4,072.72	2,752.26	2,092.28	1,696.49	1,432.80	1,244.59	1,103.55	993.97	906.40
3.00%	8,045.90	4,083.22	2,762.71	2,102.76	1,707.03	1,443.40	1,255.26	1,114.31	1,004.81	917.33
3.25%	8,056.72	4,093.73	2,773.19	2,113.27	1,717.60	1,454.05	1,266.00	1,125.13	1,015.72	928.33
3.50%	8,067.55	4,104.26	2,783.70	2,123.82	1,728.22	1,464.75	1,276.79	1,136.01	1,026.70	939.42
3.75%	8,078.39	4,114.80	2,794.23	2,134.40	1,738.87	1,475.50	1,287.63	1,146.97	1,037.76	950.58
4.00%	8,089.24	4,125.37	2,804.78	2,145.01	1,749.57	1,486.29	1,298.54	1,157.98	1,048.89	961.83
4.25%	8,100.10	4,135.95	2,815.36	2,155.65	1,760.31	1,497.14	1,309.50	1,169.06	1,060.10	973.16
4.50%	8,110.96	4,146.54	2,825.96	2,166.33	1,771.09	1,508.03	1,320.52	1,180.21	1,071.37	984.56
4.75%	8,121.83	4,157.15	2,836.58	2,177.04	1,781.91	1,518.98	1,331.59	1,191.42	1,082.72	996.05
5.00%	8,132.71	4,167.78	2,847.24	2,187.78	1,792.77	1,529.97	1,342.72	1,202.69	1,094.14	1,007.62
5.25%	8,143.60	4,178.43	2,857.91	2,198.56	1,803.67	1,541.01	1,353.91	1,214.03	1,105.63	1,019.27
5.50%	8,154.49	4,189.09	2,868.61	2,209.37	1,814.61	1,552.10	1,365.15	1,225.44	1,117.20	1,031.00
5.75%	8,165.40	4,199.76	2,879.34	2,220.21	1,825.59	1,563.24	1,376.46	1,236.90	1,128.84	1,042.81
6.00%	8,176.31	4,210.46	2,890.08	2,231.08	1,836.62	1,574.42	1,387.81	1,248.44	1,140.55	1,054.69
6.25%	8,187.23	4,221.17	2,900.86	2,241.98	1,847.68	1,585.66	1,399.23	1,260.03	1,152.33	1,066.66
6.50%	8,198.16	4,231.89	2,911.66	2,252.92	1,858.78	1,596.94	1,410.70	1,271.69	1,164.18	1,078.71
6.75%	8,209.10	4,242.64	2,922.48	2,263.89	1,869.93	1,608.28	1,422.22	1,283.42	1,176.10	1,090.83
7.00%	8,220.04	4,253.40	2,933.32	2,274.89	1,881.11	1,619.66	1,433.80	1,295.20	1,188.10	1,103.03
7.25%	8,230.99	4,264.17	2,944.20	2,285.93	1,892.34	1,631.08	1,445.44	1,307.05	1,200.16	1,115.31
7.50%	8,241.95	4,274.96	2,955.09	2,297.00	1,903.61	1,642.56	1,457.14	1,318.97	1,212.30	1,127.67
7.75%	8,252.92	4,285.77	2,966.01	2,308.10	1,914.91	1,654.09	1,468.89	1,330.94	1,224.50	1,140.10
8.00%	8,263.90	4,296.59	2,976.95	2,319.23	1,926.26	1,665.66	1,480.69	1,342.98	1,236.78	1,152.61
8.25%	8,274.89	4,307.43	2,987.92	2,330.39	1,937.64	1,677.28	1,492.55	1,355.09	1,249.12	1,165.20
8.50%	8,285.88	4,318.29	2,998.92	2,341.59	1,949.07	1,688.95	1,504.47	1,367.25	1,261.54	1,177.86
8.75%	8,296.88	4,329.16	3,009.93	2,352.82	1,960.54	1,700.66	1,516.44	1,379.48	1,274.02	1,190.60
9.00%	8,307.89	4,340.05	3,020.97	2,364.08	1,972.04	1,712.43	1,528.46	1,391.77	1,286.58	1,203.42
9.25%	8,318.91	4,350.96	3,032.04	2,375.37	1,983.59	1,724.24	1,540.54	1,404.12	1,299.20	1,216.31
9.50%	8,329.93	4,361.88	3,043.13	2,386.70	1,995.18	1,736.10	1,552.68	1,416.53	1,311.89	1,229.28
9.75%	8,340.97	4,372.81	3,054.24	2,398.06	2,006.80	1,748.00	1,564.87	1,429.01	1,324.65	1,242.32
10.00%	8,352.01	4,383.77	3,065.38	2,409.45	2,018.47	1,759.95	1,577.11	1,441.55	1,337.48	1,255.43
10.25%	8,363.06	4,394.74	3,076.55	2,420.87	2,030.18	1,771.95	1,589.41	1,454.14	1,350.37	1,268.62
10.50%	8,374.12	4,405.72	3,087.73	2,432.32	2,041.92	1,784.00	1,601.76	1,466.80	1,363.33	1,281.88
10.75%	8,385.18	4,416.73	3,098.94	2,443.81	2,053.71	1,796.10	1,614.17	1,479.52	1,376.36	1,295.22

$95,000   11.00 - 20.75%   1 - 10 Years

	1	2	3	4	5	6	7	8	9	10
11.00%	8,396.26	4,427.74	3,110.18	2,455.32	2,065.53	1,808.24	1,626.63	1,492.30	1,389.46	1,308.63
11.25%	8,407.34	4,438.78	3,121.44	2,466.87	2,077.39	1,820.43	1,639.15	1,505.14	1,402.62	1,322.10
11.50%	8,418.43	4,449.83	3,132.72	2,478.46	2,089.30	1,832.66	1,651.71	1,518.04	1,415.85	1,335.66
11.75%	8,429.53	4,460.90	3,144.03	2,490.07	2,101.24	1,844.94	1,664.34	1,531.00	1,429.14	1,349.28
12.00%	8,440.63	4,471.98	3,155.36	2,501.71	2,113.22	1,857.27	1,677.01	1,544.02	1,442.50	1,362.97
12.25%	8,451.75	4,483.08	3,166.71	2,513.39	2,125.24	1,869.64	1,689.74	1,557.10	1,455.93	1,376.74
12.50%	8,462.87	4,494.19	3,178.09	2,525.10	2,137.30	1,882.06	1,702.52	1,570.24	1,469.42	1,390.57
12.75%	8,474.00	4,505.33	3,189.50	2,536.84	2,149.40	1,894.53	1,715.35	1,583.43	1,482.97	1,404.48
13.00%	8,485.14	4,516.47	3,200.93	2,548.61	2,161.54	1,907.04	1,728.24	1,596.69	1,496.59	1,418.45
13.25%	8,496.29	4,527.64	3,212.38	2,560.42	2,173.72	1,919.60	1,741.17	1,610.00	1,510.27	1,432.49
13.50%	8,507.44	4,538.82	3,223.85	2,572.25	2,185.94	1,932.20	1,754.16	1,623.38	1,524.02	1,446.61
13.75%	8,518.61	4,550.01	3,235.35	2,584.12	2,198.19	1,944.85	1,767.21	1,636.81	1,537.83	1,460.78
14.00%	8,529.78	4,561.22	3,246.87	2,596.02	2,210.48	1,957.55	1,780.30	1,650.29	1,551.70	1,475.03
14.25%	8,540.96	4,572.45	3,258.42	2,607.94	2,222.82	1,970.29	1,793.45	1,663.84	1,565.64	1,489.34
14.50%	8,552.14	4,583.70	3,269.99	2,619.91	2,235.19	1,983.07	1,806.64	1,677.44	1,579.63	1,503.72
14.75%	8,563.34	4,594.96	3,281.59	2,631.90	2,247.60	1,995.90	1,819.89	1,691.10	1,593.69	1,518.17
15.00%	8,574.54	4,606.23	3,293.21	2,643.92	2,260.04	2,008.78	1,833.19	1,704.81	1,607.81	1,532.68
15.25%	8,585.75	4,617.52	3,304.85	2,655.98	2,272.53	2,021.70	1,846.54	1,718.59	1,621.99	1,547.26
15.50%	8,596.97	4,628.83	3,316.51	2,668.06	2,285.05	2,034.66	1,859.94	1,732.41	1,636.23	1,561.90
15.75%	8,608.20	4,640.16	3,328.20	2,680.18	2,297.62	2,047.67	1,873.39	1,746.30	1,650.54	1,576.61
16.00%	8,619.43	4,651.50	3,339.92	2,692.33	2,310.22	2,060.72	1,886.90	1,760.23	1,664.90	1,591.37
16.25%	8,630.67	4,662.85	3,351.66	2,704.51	2,322.85	2,073.82	1,900.45	1,774.23	1,679.32	1,606.21
16.50%	8,641.93	4,674.22	3,363.42	2,716.72	2,335.53	2,086.97	1,914.05	1,788.28	1,693.80	1,621.10
16.75%	8,653.18	4,685.61	3,375.20	2,728.96	2,348.24	2,100.15	1,927.70	1,802.38	1,708.34	1,636.06
17.00%	8,664.45	4,697.02	3,387.01	2,741.23	2,360.99	2,113.38	1,941.40	1,816.54	1,722.94	1,651.08
17.25%	8,675.73	4,708.43	3,398.84	2,753.53	2,373.78	2,126.66	1,955.15	1,830.75	1,737.59	1,666.16
17.50%	8,687.01	4,719.87	3,410.70	2,765.87	2,386.61	2,139.97	1,968.95	1,845.01	1,752.31	1,681.30
17.75%	8,698.30	4,731.32	3,422.58	2,778.23	2,399.47	2,153.34	1,982.80	1,859.33	1,767.08	1,696.50
18.00%	8,709.60	4,742.79	3,434.48	2,790.62	2,412.38	2,166.74	1,996.69	1,873.71	1,781.90	1,711.76
18.25%	8,720.91	4,754.27	3,446.40	2,803.05	2,425.31	2,180.19	2,010.64	1,888.13	1,796.79	1,727.08
18.50%	8,732.22	4,765.77	3,458.35	2,815.51	2,438.29	2,193.68	2,024.63	1,902.61	1,811.73	1,742.46
18.75%	8,743.54	4,777.29	3,470.33	2,827.99	2,451.30	2,207.21	2,038.67	1,917.14	1,826.72	1,757.89
19.00%	8,754.87	4,788.82	3,482.32	2,840.51	2,464.35	2,220.79	2,052.76	1,931.72	1,841.77	1,773.39
19.25%	8,766.21	4,800.37	3,494.34	2,853.06	2,477.44	2,234.41	2,066.90	1,946.35	1,856.88	1,788.94
19.50%	8,777.56	4,811.93	3,506.38	2,865.64	2,490.56	2,248.07	2,081.08	1,961.03	1,872.04	1,804.55
19.75%	8,788.92	4,823.51	3,518.45	2,878.25	2,503.72	2,261.77	2,095.31	1,975.77	1,887.25	1,820.21
20.00%	8,800.28	4,835.10	3,530.54	2,890.88	2,516.92	2,275.52	2,109.59	1,990.55	1,902.52	1,835.93
20.25%	8,811.65	4,846.71	3,542.65	2,903.55	2,530.15	2,289.31	2,123.91	2,005.39	1,917.84	1,851.70
20.50%	8,823.03	4,858.34	3,554.79	2,916.25	2,543.42	2,303.14	2,138.28	2,020.28	1,933.21	1,867.53
20.75%	8,834.41	4,869.98	3,566.95	2,928.98	2,556.73	2,317.01	2,152.70	2,035.21	1,948.64	1,883.41

	1	2	3	4	5	6	7	8	9	10
1.00%	8,169.08	4,104.95	2,750.29	2,072.99	1,666.64	1,395.76	1,202.30	1,057.21	944.39	854.14
1.25%	8,180.12	4,115.61	2,760.84	2,083.51	1,677.16	1,406.29	1,212.84	1,067.78	954.98	864.76
1.50%	8,191.17	4,126.28	2,771.42	2,094.07	1,687.71	1,416.86	1,223.44	1,078.41	965.65	875.47
1.75%	8,202.22	4,136.97	2,782.02	2,104.65	1,698.31	1,427.49	1,234.10	1,089.12	976.39	886.26
2.00%	8,213.29	4,147.68	2,792.65	2,115.27	1,708.96	1,438.17	1,244.82	1,099.89	987.21	897.13
2.25%	8,224.36	4,158.40	2,803.31	2,125.93	1,719.64	1,448.90	1,255.60	1,110.72	998.11	908.09
2.50%	8,235.45	4,169.14	2,813.98	2,136.62	1,730.37	1,459.67	1,266.44	1,121.62	1,009.08	919.13
2.75%	8,246.54	4,179.89	2,824.69	2,147.34	1,741.14	1,470.50	1,277.34	1,132.60	1,020.13	930.26
3.00%	8,257.64	4,190.67	2,835.42	2,158.10	1,751.95	1,481.38	1,288.30	1,143.63	1,031.25	941.47
3.25%	8,268.74	4,201.46	2,846.17	2,168.89	1,762.80	1,492.31	1,299.31	1,154.74	1,042.45	952.76
3.50%	8,279.86	4,212.27	2,856.95	2,179.71	1,773.70	1,503.29	1,310.39	1,165.91	1,053.72	964.14
3.75%	8,290.98	4,223.09	2,867.76	2,190.57	1,784.63	1,514.32	1,321.52	1,177.15	1,065.07	975.60
4.00%	8,302.12	4,233.93	2,878.59	2,201.46	1,795.61	1,525.41	1,332.71	1,188.45	1,076.49	987.14
4.25%	8,313.26	4,244.79	2,889.44	2,212.38	1,806.63	1,536.54	1,343.96	1,199.83	1,087.99	998.77
4.50%	8,324.41	4,255.66	2,900.33	2,223.34	1,817.69	1,547.72	1,355.27	1,211.27	1,099.57	1,010.47
4.75%	8,335.56	4,266.55	2,911.23	2,234.33	1,828.80	1,558.95	1,366.63	1,222.77	1,111.21	1,022.27
5.00%	8,346.73	4,277.46	2,922.16	2,245.36	1,839.95	1,570.23	1,378.06	1,234.34	1,122.93	1,034.14
5.25%	8,357.90	4,288.39	2,933.12	2,256.41	1,851.13	1,581.56	1,389.54	1,245.98	1,134.73	1,046.09
5.50%	8,369.09	4,299.33	2,944.10	2,267.51	1,862.36	1,592.94	1,401.08	1,257.68	1,146.60	1,058.13
5.75%	8,380.28	4,310.28	2,955.11	2,278.63	1,873.63	1,604.38	1,412.68	1,269.45	1,158.54	1,070.25
6.00%	8,391.48	4,321.26	2,966.14	2,289.79	1,884.95	1,615.86	1,424.33	1,281.29	1,170.56	1,082.45
6.25%	8,402.68	4,332.25	2,977.20	2,300.98	1,896.30	1,627.39	1,436.05	1,293.19	1,182.65	1,094.73
6.50%	8,413.90	4,343.26	2,988.28	2,312.21	1,907.70	1,638.97	1,447.82	1,305.16	1,194.82	1,107.09
6.75%	8,425.13	4,354.28	2,999.38	2,323.47	1,919.14	1,650.60	1,459.65	1,317.19	1,207.05	1,119.54
7.00%	8,436.36	4,365.33	3,010.52	2,334.76	1,930.62	1,662.28	1,471.54	1,329.29	1,219.36	1,132.06
7.25%	8,447.60	4,376.39	3,021.67	2,346.08	1,942.14	1,674.01	1,483.48	1,341.45	1,231.74	1,144.66
7.50%	8,458.85	4,387.46	3,032.86	2,357.44	1,953.70	1,685.79	1,495.48	1,353.68	1,244.20	1,157.34
7.75%	8,470.11	4,398.55	3,044.06	2,368.83	1,965.30	1,697.61	1,507.54	1,365.97	1,256.73	1,170.10
8.00%	8,481.37	4,409.66	3,055.30	2,380.26	1,976.95	1,709.49	1,519.66	1,378.33	1,269.32	1,182.94
8.25%	8,492.65	4,420.79	3,066.55	2,391.72	1,988.63	1,721.42	1,531.83	1,390.75	1,282.00	1,195.86
8.50%	8,503.93	4,431.93	3,077.83	2,403.21	2,000.36	1,733.39	1,544.06	1,403.23	1,294.74	1,208.86
8.75%	8,515.22	4,443.09	3,089.14	2,414.73	2,012.13	1,745.42	1,556.34	1,415.78	1,307.55	1,221.94
9.00%	8,526.52	4,454.26	3,100.47	2,426.29	2,023.94	1,757.49	1,568.69	1,428.39	1,320.43	1,235.09
9.25%	8,537.83	4,465.45	3,111.83	2,437.88	2,035.79	1,769.61	1,581.08	1,441.07	1,333.39	1,248.32
9.50%	8,549.14	4,476.66	3,123.21	2,449.51	2,047.68	1,781.78	1,593.54	1,453.81	1,346.41	1,261.63
9.75%	8,560.47	4,487.89	3,134.62	2,461.16	2,059.61	1,794.00	1,606.05	1,466.61	1,359.51	1,275.01
10.00%	8,571.80	4,499.13	3,146.05	2,472.85	2,071.59	1,806.27	1,618.62	1,479.48	1,372.67	1,288.47
10.25%	8,583.14	4,510.39	3,157.51	2,484.57	2,083.60	1,818.59	1,631.24	1,492.41	1,385.91	1,302.01
10.50%	8,594.49	4,521.66	3,168.99	2,496.33	2,095.66	1,830.95	1,643.92	1,505.40	1,399.21	1,315.62
10.75%	8,605.85	4,532.96	3,180.49	2,508.12	2,107.75	1,843.36	1,656.65	1,518.46	1,412.58	1,329.30

	1	2	3	4	5	6	7	8	9	10
11.00%	8,617.21	4,544.26	3,192.02	2,519.94	2,119.89	1,855.82	1,669.44	1,531.57	1,426.02	1,343.06
11.25%	8,628.59	4,555.59	3,203.58	2,531.79	2,132.06	1,868.33	1,682.28	1,544.75	1,439.53	1,356.90
11.50%	8,639.97	4,566.93	3,215.16	2,543.68	2,144.28	1,880.89	1,695.18	1,557.99	1,453.11	1,370.81
11.75%	8,651.36	4,578.29	3,226.77	2,555.60	2,156.54	1,893.49	1,708.13	1,571.29	1,466.75	1,384.79
12.00%	8,662.76	4,589.66	3,238.40	2,567.55	2,168.83	1,906.14	1,721.14	1,584.65	1,480.46	1,398.84
12.25%	8,674.16	4,601.05	3,250.05	2,579.53	2,181.17	1,918.84	1,734.20	1,598.08	1,494.24	1,412.97
12.50%	8,685.58	4,612.46	3,261.73	2,591.55	2,193.55	1,931.59	1,747.32	1,611.56	1,508.09	1,427.17
12.75%	8,697.00	4,623.89	3,273.43	2,603.60	2,205.97	1,944.38	1,760.49	1,625.10	1,522.00	1,441.44
13.00%	8,708.43	4,635.33	3,285.16	2,615.68	2,218.42	1,957.23	1,773.72	1,638.71	1,535.97	1,455.78
13.25%	8,719.87	4,646.79	3,296.91	2,627.79	2,230.92	1,970.11	1,786.99	1,652.37	1,550.02	1,470.19
13.50%	8,731.32	4,658.26	3,308.69	2,639.94	2,243.46	1,983.05	1,800.33	1,666.10	1,564.13	1,484.67
13.75%	8,742.78	4,669.75	3,320.49	2,652.12	2,256.04	1,996.03	1,813.71	1,679.88	1,578.30	1,499.23
14.00%	8,754.24	4,681.26	3,332.32	2,664.33	2,268.65	2,009.06	1,827.15	1,693.72	1,592.54	1,513.85
14.25%	8,765.72	4,692.78	3,344.17	2,676.57	2,281.31	2,022.13	1,840.64	1,707.62	1,606.84	1,528.54
14.50%	8,777.20	4,704.32	3,356.05	2,688.85	2,294.01	2,035.26	1,854.19	1,721.58	1,621.20	1,543.30
14.75%	8,788.69	4,715.88	3,367.95	2,701.16	2,306.74	2,048.42	1,867.78	1,735.60	1,635.63	1,558.12
15.00%	8,800.19	4,727.45	3,379.87	2,713.50	2,319.52	2,061.64	1,881.43	1,749.68	1,650.12	1,573.02
15.25%	8,811.69	4,739.04	3,391.82	2,725.87	2,332.33	2,074.90	1,895.14	1,763.81	1,664.68	1,587.98
15.50%	8,823.21	4,750.64	3,403.79	2,738.27	2,345.19	2,088.21	1,908.89	1,778.00	1,679.29	1,603.00
15.75%	8,834.73	4,762.26	3,415.79	2,750.71	2,358.08	2,101.56	1,922.69	1,792.25	1,693.97	1,618.10
16.00%	8,846.26	4,773.90	3,427.81	2,763.18	2,371.01	2,114.95	1,936.55	1,806.56	1,708.71	1,633.25
16.25%	8,857.80	4,785.56	3,439.86	2,775.68	2,383.98	2,128.40	1,950.46	1,820.92	1,723.51	1,648.48
16.50%	8,869.34	4,797.23	3,451.93	2,788.21	2,396.99	2,141.89	1,964.42	1,835.34	1,738.37	1,663.76
16.75%	8,880.90	4,808.92	3,464.02	2,800.77	2,410.04	2,155.42	1,978.43	1,849.81	1,753.30	1,679.11
17.00%	8,892.46	4,820.62	3,476.14	2,813.37	2,423.13	2,169.00	1,992.49	1,864.34	1,768.28	1,694.53
17.25%	8,904.04	4,832.34	3,488.28	2,825.99	2,436.25	2,182.62	2,006.60	1,878.93	1,783.32	1,710.00
17.50%	8,915.61	4,844.08	3,500.45	2,838.65	2,449.42	2,196.29	2,020.76	1,893.57	1,798.42	1,725.54
17.75%	8,927.20	4,855.83	3,512.64	2,851.34	2,462.62	2,210.00	2,034.98	1,908.26	1,813.58	1,741.14
18.00%	8,938.80	4,867.60	3,524.86	2,864.06	2,475.86	2,223.76	2,049.24	1,923.01	1,828.80	1,756.81
18.25%	8,950.40	4,879.39	3,537.10	2,876.82	2,489.14	2,237.56	2,063.55	1,937.82	1,844.07	1,772.53
18.50%	8,962.02	4,891.19	3,549.36	2,889.60	2,502.46	2,251.41	2,077.91	1,952.68	1,859.40	1,788.31
18.75%	8,973.64	4,903.01	3,561.65	2,902.41	2,515.81	2,265.30	2,092.32	1,967.59	1,874.79	1,804.15
19.00%	8,985.27	4,914.84	3,573.96	2,915.26	2,529.20	2,279.23	2,106.78	1,982.55	1,890.24	1,820.06
19.25%	8,996.90	4,926.69	3,586.30	2,928.14	2,542.63	2,293.21	2,121.29	1,997.57	1,905.74	1,836.02
19.50%	9,008.55	4,938.56	3,598.66	2,941.05	2,556.10	2,307.23	2,135.85	2,012.64	1,921.30	1,852.03
19.75%	9,020.20	4,950.44	3,611.04	2,953.99	2,569.61	2,321.29	2,150.45	2,027.76	1,936.92	1,868.11
20.00%	9,031.86	4,962.34	3,623.45	2,966.96	2,583.15	2,335.40	2,165.10	2,042.94	1,952.58	1,884.24
20.25%	9,043.53	4,974.26	3,635.88	2,979.96	2,596.73	2,349.55	2,179.81	2,058.16	1,968.31	1,900.43
20.50%	9,055.21	4,986.19	3,648.34	2,993.00	2,610.35	2,363.74	2,194.55	2,073.44	1,984.08	1,916.68
20.75%	9,066.90	4,998.14	3,660.82	3,006.06	2,624.01	2,377.98	2,209.35	2,088.77	1,999.92	1,932.98

$100,000   1.00 - 10.75%   1 - 10 Years

	1	2	3	4	5	6	7	8	9	10
1.00%	8,378.54	4,210.21	2,820.81	2,126.15	1,709.37	1,431.55	1,233.12	1,084.32	968.60	876.04
1.25%	8,389.86	4,221.14	2,831.63	2,136.94	1,720.16	1,442.35	1,243.94	1,095.16	979.47	886.93
1.50%	8,401.20	4,232.08	2,842.48	2,147.76	1,730.99	1,453.19	1,254.81	1,106.07	990.41	897.91
1.75%	8,412.54	4,243.05	2,853.36	2,158.62	1,741.86	1,464.09	1,265.75	1,117.04	1,001.43	908.98
2.00%	8,423.89	4,254.03	2,864.26	2,169.51	1,752.78	1,475.04	1,276.74	1,128.09	1,012.53	920.13
2.25%	8,435.24	4,265.02	2,875.18	2,180.44	1,763.73	1,486.05	1,287.80	1,139.20	1,023.70	931.37
2.50%	8,446.61	4,276.04	2,886.14	2,191.40	1,774.74	1,497.10	1,298.92	1,150.38	1,034.96	942.70
2.75%	8,457.99	4,287.07	2,897.12	2,202.40	1,785.78	1,508.21	1,310.09	1,161.64	1,046.29	954.11
3.00%	8,469.37	4,298.12	2,908.12	2,213.43	1,796.87	1,519.37	1,321.33	1,172.96	1,057.69	965.61
3.25%	8,480.76	4,309.19	2,919.15	2,224.50	1,808.00	1,530.58	1,332.63	1,184.35	1,069.18	977.19
3.50%	8,492.16	4,320.27	2,930.21	2,235.60	1,819.17	1,541.84	1,343.99	1,195.81	1,080.74	988.86
3.75%	8,503.57	4,331.37	2,941.29	2,246.74	1,830.39	1,553.15	1,355.40	1,207.33	1,092.38	1,000.61
4.00%	8,514.99	4,342.49	2,952.40	2,257.91	1,841.65	1,564.52	1,366.88	1,218.93	1,104.10	1,012.45
4.25%	8,526.42	4,353.63	2,963.53	2,269.11	1,852.96	1,575.93	1,378.42	1,230.59	1,115.89	1,024.38
4.50%	8,537.85	4,364.78	2,974.69	2,280.35	1,864.30	1,587.40	1,390.02	1,242.32	1,127.76	1,036.38
4.75%	8,549.30	4,375.95	2,985.88	2,291.62	1,875.69	1,598.92	1,401.67	1,254.12	1,139.71	1,048.48
5.00%	8,560.75	4,387.14	2,997.09	2,302.93	1,887.12	1,610.49	1,413.39	1,265.99	1,151.73	1,060.66
5.25%	8,572.21	4,398.34	3,008.33	2,314.27	1,898.60	1,622.12	1,425.17	1,277.93	1,163.83	1,072.92
5.50%	8,583.68	4,409.57	3,019.59	2,325.65	1,910.12	1,633.79	1,437.00	1,289.93	1,176.00	1,085.26
5.75%	8,595.16	4,420.80	3,030.88	2,337.06	1,921.68	1,645.51	1,448.90	1,302.00	1,188.25	1,097.69
6.00%	8,606.64	4,432.06	3,042.19	2,348.50	1,933.28	1,657.29	1,460.86	1,314.14	1,200.57	1,110.21
6.25%	8,618.14	4,443.33	3,053.53	2,359.98	1,944.93	1,669.12	1,472.87	1,326.35	1,212.98	1,122.80
6.50%	8,629.64	4,454.63	3,064.90	2,371.50	1,956.61	1,680.99	1,484.94	1,338.62	1,225.45	1,135.48
6.75%	8,641.15	4,465.93	3,076.29	2,383.04	1,968.35	1,692.92	1,497.08	1,350.96	1,238.00	1,148.24
7.00%	8,652.67	4,477.26	3,087.71	2,394.62	1,980.12	1,704.90	1,509.27	1,363.37	1,250.63	1,161.08
7.25%	8,664.20	4,488.60	3,099.15	2,406.24	1,991.94	1,716.93	1,521.52	1,375.85	1,263.33	1,174.01
7.50%	8,675.74	4,499.96	3,110.62	2,417.89	2,003.79	1,729.01	1,533.83	1,388.39	1,276.10	1,187.02
7.75%	8,687.29	4,511.34	3,122.12	2,429.57	2,015.70	1,741.14	1,546.20	1,400.99	1,288.95	1,200.11
8.00%	8,698.84	4,522.73	3,133.64	2,441.29	2,027.64	1,753.32	1,558.62	1,413.67	1,301.87	1,213.28
8.25%	8,710.41	4,534.14	3,145.18	2,453.04	2,039.63	1,765.56	1,571.11	1,426.41	1,314.87	1,226.53
8.50%	8,721.98	4,545.57	3,156.75	2,464.83	2,051.65	1,777.84	1,583.65	1,439.21	1,327.94	1,239.86
8.75%	8,733.56	4,557.01	3,168.35	2,476.65	2,063.72	1,790.17	1,596.25	1,452.08	1,341.08	1,253.27
9.00%	8,745.15	4,568.47	3,179.97	2,488.50	2,075.84	1,802.55	1,608.91	1,465.02	1,354.29	1,266.76
9.25%	8,756.75	4,579.95	3,191.62	2,500.39	2,087.99	1,814.99	1,621.62	1,478.02	1,367.58	1,280.33
9.50%	8,768.35	4,591.45	3,203.29	2,512.31	2,100.19	1,827.47	1,634.40	1,491.09	1,380.94	1,293.98
9.75%	8,779.97	4,602.96	3,214.99	2,524.27	2,112.42	1,840.00	1,647.23	1,504.22	1,394.37	1,307.70
10.00%	8,791.59	4,614.49	3,226.72	2,536.26	2,124.70	1,852.58	1,660.12	1,517.42	1,407.87	1,321.51
10.25%	8,803.22	4,626.04	3,238.47	2,548.28	2,137.03	1,865.22	1,673.06	1,530.68	1,421.44	1,335.39
10.50%	8,814.86	4,637.60	3,250.24	2,560.34	2,149.39	1,877.90	1,686.07	1,544.00	1,435.09	1,349.35
10.75%	8,826.51	4,649.19	3,262.05	2,572.43	2,161.80	1,890.63	1,699.13	1,557.39	1,448.80	1,363.39

	1	2	3	4	5	6	7	8	9	10
11.00%	8,838.17	4,660.78	3,273.87	2,584.55	2,174.24	1,903.41	1,712.24	1,570.84	1,462.59	1,377.50
11.25%	8,849.83	4,672.40	3,285.72	2,596.71	2,186.73	1,916.24	1,725.42	1,584.36	1,476.44	1,391.69
11.50%	8,861.51	4,684.03	3,297.60	2,608.90	2,199.26	1,929.12	1,738.65	1,597.94	1,490.37	1,405.95
11.75%	8,873.19	4,695.68	3,309.50	2,621.13	2,211.83	1,942.04	1,751.93	1,611.58	1,504.36	1,420.29
12.00%	8,884.88	4,707.35	3,321.43	2,633.38	2,224.44	1,955.02	1,765.27	1,625.28	1,518.42	1,434.71
12.25%	8,896.58	4,719.03	3,333.38	2,645.68	2,237.10	1,968.04	1,778.67	1,639.05	1,532.56	1,449.20
12.50%	8,908.29	4,730.73	3,345.36	2,658.00	2,249.79	1,981.12	1,792.12	1,652.88	1,546.76	1,463.76
12.75%	8,920.00	4,742.45	3,357.37	2,670.36	2,262.53	1,994.24	1,805.63	1,666.77	1,561.02	1,478.40
13.00%	8,931.73	4,754.18	3,369.40	2,682.75	2,275.31	2,007.41	1,819.20	1,680.73	1,575.36	1,493.11
13.25%	8,943.46	4,765.93	3,381.45	2,695.17	2,288.13	2,020.63	1,832.82	1,694.74	1,589.76	1,507.89
13.50%	8,955.20	4,777.70	3,393.53	2,707.63	2,300.98	2,033.90	1,846.49	1,708.82	1,604.23	1,522.74
13.75%	8,966.95	4,789.49	3,405.63	2,720.12	2,313.88	2,047.21	1,860.22	1,722.95	1,618.77	1,537.67
14.00%	8,978.71	4,801.29	3,417.76	2,732.65	2,326.83	2,060.57	1,874.00	1,737.15	1,633.37	1,552.66
14.25%	8,990.48	4,813.11	3,429.92	2,745.20	2,339.81	2,073.98	1,887.84	1,751.41	1,648.04	1,567.73
14.50%	9,002.25	4,824.94	3,442.10	2,757.80	2,352.83	2,087.44	1,901.73	1,765.73	1,662.77	1,582.87
14.75%	9,014.04	4,836.80	3,454.30	2,770.42	2,365.89	2,100.95	1,915.68	1,780.10	1,677.57	1,598.07
15.00%	9,025.83	4,848.66	3,466.53	2,783.07	2,378.99	2,114.50	1,929.68	1,794.54	1,692.43	1,613.35
15.25%	9,037.63	4,860.55	3,478.79	2,795.76	2,392.14	2,128.10	1,943.73	1,809.04	1,707.36	1,628.69
15.50%	9,049.44	4,872.45	3,491.07	2,808.49	2,405.32	2,141.75	1,957.83	1,823.59	1,722.35	1,644.11
15.75%	9,061.26	4,884.37	3,503.37	2,821.24	2,418.54	2,155.44	1,971.99	1,838.21	1,737.41	1,659.58
16.00%	9,073.09	4,896.31	3,515.70	2,834.03	2,431.81	2,169.18	1,986.21	1,852.88	1,752.53	1,675.13
16.25%	9,084.92	4,908.26	3,528.06	2,846.85	2,445.11	2,182.97	2,000.47	1,867.61	1,767.71	1,690.74
16.50%	9,096.76	4,920.24	3,540.44	2,859.70	2,458.45	2,196.81	2,014.79	1,882.40	1,782.95	1,706.42
16.75%	9,108.62	4,932.22	3,552.84	2,872.59	2,471.84	2,210.69	2,029.16	1,897.24	1,798.25	1,722.17
17.00%	9,120.48	4,944.23	3,565.27	2,885.50	2,485.26	2,224.61	2,043.58	1,912.15	1,813.62	1,737.98
17.25%	9,132.34	4,956.25	3,577.73	2,898.45	2,498.72	2,238.59	2,058.05	1,927.10	1,829.05	1,753.85
17.50%	9,144.22	4,968.28	3,590.21	2,911.44	2,512.22	2,252.60	2,072.58	1,942.12	1,844.53	1,769.79
17.75%	9,156.11	4,980.34	3,602.71	2,924.45	2,525.76	2,266.67	2,087.16	1,957.19	1,860.08	1,785.79
18.00%	9,168.00	4,992.41	3,615.24	2,937.50	2,539.34	2,280.78	2,101.78	1,972.32	1,875.69	1,801.85
18.25%	9,179.90	5,004.50	3,627.79	2,950.58	2,552.96	2,294.93	2,116.46	1,987.51	1,891.36	1,817.98
18.50%	9,191.81	5,016.60	3,640.37	2,963.69	2,566.62	2,309.14	2,131.19	2,002.74	1,907.08	1,834.17
18.75%	9,203.73	5,028.72	3,652.97	2,976.84	2,580.32	2,323.38	2,145.97	2,018.04	1,922.87	1,850.41
19.00%	9,215.66	5,040.86	3,665.60	2,990.01	2,594.06	2,337.67	2,160.80	2,033.39	1,938.71	1,866.72
19.25%	9,227.59	5,053.02	3,678.25	3,003.22	2,607.83	2,352.01	2,175.68	2,048.79	1,954.61	1,883.09
19.50%	9,239.54	5,065.19	3,690.93	3,016.46	2,621.64	2,366.39	2,190.61	2,064.25	1,970.57	1,899.52
19.75%	9,251.49	5,077.38	3,703.63	3,029.73	2,635.50	2,380.81	2,205.59	2,079.76	1,986.58	1,916.01
20.00%	9,263.45	5,089.58	3,716.36	3,043.04	2,649.39	2,395.28	2,220.62	2,095.32	2,002.65	1,932.56
20.25%	9,275.42	5,101.80	3,729.11	3,056.37	2,663.32	2,409.80	2,235.70	2,110.94	2,018.78	1,949.16
20.50%	9,287.40	5,114.04	3,741.88	3,069.74	2,677.29	2,424.35	2,250.82	2,126.61	2,034.96	1,965.82
20.75%	9,299.38	5,126.29	3,754.68	3,083.14	2,691.29	2,438.95	2,266.00	2,142.33	2,051.20	1,982.54

Notes

Made in the USA
Middletown, DE
19 March 2025

72972560R00069